Golden Ages and Barbarous Nations

CRITICAL CONDITIONS: FIELD DAY ESSAYS AND MONOGRAPHS

Edited by Seamus Deane

Golden Ages and Barbarous Nations

Antiquarian Debate and Cultural Politics in Ireland, c. 1750–1800

Clare O'Halloran

UNIVERSITY OF NOTRE DAME PRESS
in association with
FIELD DAY

For my father, Jimmy, and
in memory of my mother,
Gay O'Halloran (née Duggan), 1922–94

Published in the United States in 2005 by
University of Notre Dame Press
310 Flanner Hall
Notre Dame, Indiana 46556
www.undpress.nd.edu

And in Ireland by
Cork University Press
University College Cork, Ireland

© Clare O'Halloran 2004

ISBN 0-268-03721-3

Cataloging-in-Publication Data is available from the Library of Congress

CONTENTS

ACKNOWLEDGEMENTS

This book originated in a doctoral thesis for the University of Cambridge. I am grateful to the Master and Fellows of Sidney Sussex College for a research studentship which enabled me to study at Cambridge, to the President and Fellows of Clare Hall for electing me to a research fellowship, and to the British Academy for a post-doctoral fellowship which allowed me to complete further research in the general area. While at Cambridge I relied on the following for assistance and wish to record my gratitude: Prof. Peter Burke who was my research supervisor, Dr Brendan Bradshaw who oversaw my doctoral work for one year, Dr Mark Goldie, Prof. Norman Zacour, Prof. Ruth Morse, Prof. Stefan Collini, Anna Chaudhri, Rachel McMullan, and David Titterington.

I would also like to thank a number of people for advice, encouragement and in some cases, books, articles and their unpublished research materials: Prof. Tom Bartlett, Dr Damien Bracken, Bernadette Cunningham, Dr Leith Davis, Prof. R.F. Foster, Prof. Vincent Geoghegan, Prof. Máire Herbert, Prof. Jacqueline Hill, Prof. Colin Kidd, Prof. Mícheál Mac Craith, the late Prof. Oliver MacDonagh, Dr Eoin Magennis, Marianne Moore, Diarmuid Ó Catháin, Dr William O'Reilly, Dr Carmel Quinlan, Prof. Norman Vance.

I am grateful to the two anonymous readers for Cork University Press, and to Prof. Seamus Deane, for helpful comments and suggestions. Sara Wilbourne, as publisher at Cork University Press, showed crucial interest in the project from its earliest stages and never failed to be enthusiastic. I am grateful to the Publications Fund of the Faculty of Arts in University College Cork, and to the National University of Ireland for subventions towards the publication of this book. The painting on the front cover, *The Baptism of the King of Cashel by St Patrick* by James Barry, is reproduced by kind permission of the National Gallery of Ireland.

My thanks are due to the staff and owners of the various libraries and archives where I have worked, and particularly to the staff of the Rare Books Room in Cambridge University Library, of the Royal Irish Academy Library, and of Special Collections in the Boole Library in UCC.

Tom Dunne has shared in this project since its inception and has helped immeasurably in the process of bringing it to print. Finally, our sons, Oisín and Fergus, must be mentioned, in recognition of the many times they did not come to visit me in my study.

ABBREVIATIONS

Clonalis	Clonalis House, Castlerea, Co. Roscommon, O'Conor Don Collection
Collectanea	Charles Vallancey (ed.), *Collectanea de Rebus Hibernicis,* vols I–[VII] (Dublin, 1780–1807)
D.C.L.A.	Dublin City Library and Archive, Gilbert Collection
J.R.S.A.I.	*Journal of the Royal Society of Antiquaries of Ireland*
N.L.I.	National Library of Ireland, Dublin
Nichols, *Lit. Illus.*	John Nichols, *Illustrations of the Literary History of the Eighteenth Century.* 8 vols (London, 1817–58)
O'Conor Letters	*The Letters of Charles O'Conor of Belanagare,* eds Robert E. Ward and Catherine Coogan Ward, 2 vols (Ann Arbor, Michigan, 1980)
R.I.A.	Royal Irish Academy, Dublin
T.C.D.	Trinity College Dublin

INTRODUCTION

In 1774 Sylvester O'Halloran lamented the neglect of Irish history and antiquities, which had

> taught people, born in the same climate, breathing in the same air, and con-
> nected to each other by blood, by affinity, and by interest, (*for at this day, we are
> assuredly but one people*) to form distinctions as unnatural in themselves, as they
> have been subversive of the general good of our country![1]

O'Halloran's optimistic belief that Irish history and antiquities could unite the inhabitants of the island, regardless of religion or ancestry, encapsulated the hopes of many antiquaries in the late eighteenth century. In part, this book charts the attempts they made to supply an agreed and authoritative version of Ireland's early history, attempts which ceased in the late 1790s owing to the increasingly fraught political and military situation. The failure to produce 'a general survey of any substantial period of Irish history that could rank with the work of Robertson, for Scotland, or of Hume, for Great Britain', largely determined views of eighteenth-century historiography among historians of an earlier generation. The type of material examined in this study was dis-counted as of little interest, other than to those plotting the halting develop-ment of historical scholarship in Ireland.[2] Dismissals of this kind had their origins in long-standing derogatory views of the antiquary and his endeavours, which can be found as early as the seventeenth century in English satires such as those of Richard Burton and John Earle. Mocked as a 'credulous collector of absurd bogus antiquities' in dramas like Shackerley Marmion's *The Anti-quary* (1641), this image remained so powerful that, despite the significant contribution made by antiquaries to eighteenth-century scholarship and debate (and their stimulation of a public appetite for historical romance), Sir Walter Scott re-used the stock character, as well as Marmion's title, in his novel *The Antiquary* (1816).[3] This was constructed around a comically obsessive bachelor, Jonathan Oldbuck, who surrounded himself with the minutiae of the remote past and was passionately involved in controversies over obscure details and theories. Like all stereotypes it contained a grain of truth, but was a limiting and outmoded description. More importantly, it underestimated the importance of antiquarian writings, which are crucial to understanding the political and literary culture of the early modern and modern periods.

Definitions of the term 'antiquarianism' are numerous, but notoriously dif-ficult and generally unsatisfactory. They centre around two basic premises: that it involved the study of the *remote* past, mainly the pre-Christian and early

Christian eras; and that it was primarily concerned with collection and cataloguing rather than interpretation, which was usually considered to be the historian's art.[4] This general outline is derived from the development of antiquarianism in its earliest form in the fifteenth century, as a by-product of the revival of interest in classical antiquity, the driving force of Renaissance humanism. The recovery and study of the manuscripts and monuments of ancient Greece and Rome, and their careful recording and cataloguing, was the domain of the humanist antiquary, such as Flavio Biondo, whose *Roma Instaurata* (1453) was the first systematic survey of the monuments of Rome, while his *Italia Restaurata* (1457–9) extended the enterprise to the whole of Italy.[5]

Thus, Renaissance interest in classical antiquity determined the focus of antiquarian study. This can be seen clearly in British antiquarianism which, although concerned with the indigenous past, was initially focused on Roman Britain, regarded as the necessary starting point for all studies. It was only after the Reformation, when religious disputes caused a new interest in the early church, that English Protestant scholars began to examine the Anglo-Saxon era.[6] Thus, over time, antiquarianism changed and broadened its definition of 'antiquity', so that by the eighteenth century it ranged from the pre-classical era, concerning the origins of the people of Britain, right up to the high Middle Ages, with a focus on the Gothic style of ecclesiastical architecture. Similarly, the early impulse to amass large miscellaneous collections of the material remains of 'antiquity', however defined, was less in evidence, and collecting for its own sake was no longer the necessary hallmark of the antiquary by the time that Scott lampooned it. In a famous episode in the book, he described Oldbuck's study as filled to overflowing with Roman and 'ancient British' pottery, antique spurs and buckles, thumbscrews, and a library which bore the imprint of a true 'bibliomaniac'.[7] Some antiquarian writing in the eighteenth century belonged to this traditional mind-set, such as, for example, John Horsley's three-volume *Britannia Romana* (1732), which attempted to bring together everything that had thus far been discovered about Roman Britain: its transactions and monuments, coins and inscriptions, place names and ancient geography.[8] But Horsley also included the results of his own archaeological fieldwork, and from the late seventeenth century it is possible to detect the beginnings of the new discipline of archaeology in British antiquarianism.[9]

However, not all eighteenth-century antiquaries were proto-archaeologists; many were uninterested in monuments, and instead based their work on documentary evidence, as the historian mainly does today. The primary distinction made between the antiquary and the historian at the time centred around the concept of causation: historians were often deemed philosophers, concerned largely with the dissection of underlying historical causes, antiquaries with the critical establishment of fact. Contemporary writers defined the relationship between the two disciplines variously. In 1770, in its first volume, the journal of the London-based Society of Antiquaries, *Archaeologia*, published an introduction which set up a simple model: the antiquary, by making collections, supplied the material for the writing of history, which was described as the 'arrangement and proper use of fact'.[10] However, Thomas Burgess, an English antiquary, believed the study of antiquities made a more important contribution to history-writing than that of merely providing materials. It 'supplied the defects of history' by making clear the 'great secret influence' which 'minuter actions' (often dismissed by the historian as 'trifling') had on the most important events.[11] These 'minuter actions', which related to the 'ancient manners and customs of a people', were also highlighted by Thomas Pownall in his *Treatise on the Study of Antiquities as a Commentary to Historical Learning* (1782). This advocated an approach which was close to social and economic history as now understood, in which the antiquary would describe 'the community, whose acts are the subject of history' and investigate its sources of wealth and the nature of its society.[12]

Pownall also attacked the idea that antiquarianism was merely a collecting endeavour, and in his characterisation of the 'false antiquary', deplored the 'error' of 'making endless and useless collections of relics and fragments without scope or view to any one point'. Another criticism which he levelled was the tendency of 'forming too hastily visionary systems'.[13] The notion of 'visionary systems' as the province of the 'false antiquary' points to the existence of a strand of antiquarianism dealing with myths of origin, which is normally omitted from studies of the development of historiography and archaeology, or dismissed, in J.C. Beckett's phrase, as the work of 'cranks'.[14] This is particularly clear in Stuart Piggott's histories of archaeology, notably *Ancient Britons and the Antiquarian Imagination* (1989), which discounted the eighteenth century as a period of 'stagnation' in the development of prehistoric archaeology, because of the prominence of such 'visionary' thought, and devoted more space to the seventeenth century where fantastic accounts were tolerable, as coming from a less sophisticated and therefore understandably credulous age.[15] My approach to antiquarianism is not to limit it to writing on the remote past (though this was its main focus) and to consider its sometimes wild theorising about origins and the nature of early society as having a basis in contemporary concerns. No sharp distinctions are made between antiquaries and historians. Thomas Leland, for example, normally numbered among the latter, joined in antiquarian debates, even in his history of the colonial period.[16] Thus, he moved from antiquarian affairs in the preface to those of a historian in the main text. Antiquaries were, for the most part, the historians of *early* Ireland, and the remoteness of that period, combined with the difficulties of its sources, do much to explain their weakness for grandiose theorising. Throughout this study antiquarian writing has been discussed in terms of religious affiliation which was the governing factor in all interpretations and controversies. 'Protestant' in this study means the established Church of Ireland; there was little Presbyterian antiquarian writing in Ireland in the eighteenth century.[17] However, accounts of the origins of the Church of Ireland contained echoes, at least, of the disputes among Anglicans and Presbyterians over English and

Scottish church history, particularly concerning the episcopal status of the early church.[18]

By and large, these writers were comfortably off; a few were wealthy, but almost all had resources enough to build up libraries, and leisure time in which to write and research. Their occupations differed according to their religion. A number of Catholic historians in the eighteenth century were in the medical profession, one of the few that were open to them. John Fergus, the collector of manuscripts, was a doctor in Dublin around the mid-century. John Curry, one of the main Catholic propagandists on the seventeenth century, was also a Dublin doctor, and Sylvester O'Halloran, the first of the romantic historians, was a surgeon in Limerick.[19] Charles O'Conor was unusual in being a Catholic landowner – his father had managed to consolidate the holding salvaged by his family after the Williamite confiscations – and he divided his time between Roscommon and Dublin.[20] Among Protestants, Church of Ireland clergymen from all levels were prominent. Edward Ledwich, Vicar of Aghaboe in Queen's County, and Thomas Campbell, the incumbent in Clogher, Co. Tyrone, were active and productive writers, conscious of their position in the established church and upholders of its claim to be the true successor to the early Christian foundation in Ireland.[21] Also in this category was Thomas Leland, Fellow of Trinity College Dublin and later rector of a Dublin parish, who is remembered for his three volume *History of Ireland from the Invasion of Henry II* (1773). As well as a number of the aristocracy, such as Lord Charlemont and the Earl and Countess of Moira, who were patrons if not producers of the new history, there was an important group of MPs and government office holders, all operating out of the Exchequer, where the wealthy and influential William Burton Conyngham presided as Teller. Joseph Cooper Walker, author of *Historical Memoirs of the Irish Bards* (1786), worked under Burton Conyngham, as did his cousin, Austin Cooper, who made sketches of the buildings and monuments of the Irish countryside.[22]

The need for some kind of institutional promotion of the study of the past had been recognised as early as the 1740s, when the Physico-Historical Society had foundered almost at once, through lack of financial support.[23] The Select Commitee on Antiquities of the Dublin Society of the early 1770s was equally short-lived.[24] We know from the correspondence of Charles O'Conor, Edward Ledwich, and indeed Richard Lovell Edgeworth (whose interests were more scientific than antiquarian) that they felt particularly isolated in their rural locale; their gentry neighbours had neither time for, nor understanding of, antiquities.[25] It was not until 1785 and the foundation of the Royal Irish Academy that antiquarianism found a supportive, if not altogether stable, environment. The fact that the Academy established antiquities as one of its three foundation committees reflected the importance, even respectability, finally achieved by such writing.[26]

Eighteenth-century antiquaries made a greater contribution to the development of scholarship than Piggott allowed, and their influence was also felt in other ways.[27] In Ireland, antiquaries collected Gaelic manuscripts, most of which they could not understand, but which survived through their care until later generations had acquired the necessary linguistic skills. It has been argued that they had a critical influence on the development of the nineteenth-century romantic Irish novel and on the Literary Revival of the 1890s.[28] This study seeks to demonstrate their importance in other key areas, and in particular to highlight their close relationship to Irish political culture in the eighteenth century. The Catholic question, in particular, was a critical sub-text for almost all Irish antiquarian writing. Works which supported the claim of a great pre-colonial golden age were understood as signalling a pro-Catholic stance, whereas sceptics of the claim were taken as opponents of the relaxation of the penal laws. However, as this study shows, the writings of figures such as Charles Vallancey and Thomas Campbell reflected more complex views than contemporary or modern scholars have acknowledged. A second major aim is to examine Irish antiquarianism in a comparative context, highlighting its relationship to European antiquarianism in the seventeenth and eighteenth centuries. This has to a large extent determined the structure of the study, which is centred around European antiquarian debates about the origins and nature of society, such as orientalism and primitivism. Scotland has been chosen as a more specific comparative framework, largely because it shared a Gaelic culture with Ireland and therefore was closely enmeshed with the Irish past. Indeed, Hiberno-Scottish disputes about that shared past were a major stimulus to antiquarian endeavour in both countries. Also, while they had differing relationships to the British state system, they nevertheless shared certain cultural and political problems.

The secondary literature on Irish antiquarianism is not large but is growing, and is mainly in article form. Prior to my doctoral thesis (1991), the only full-scale work which focused directly on the topic was a 1978 Master's dissertation by Ann de Valera. This did valuable service by establishing the corpus of antiquarian literature and by describing most of the writing in outline, but it lacked an analytical framework.[29] A series of articles by Walter Love, published in the early 1960s, are, regrettably, all that remains of a major project on eighteenth-century Irish historiography which was left unfinished by his early death. These are skilful reconstructions from the manuscript sources of the relations between Protestant and Catholic antiquaries and historians from the 1760s, using especially the large and invaluable correspondence of the main Catholic writer, Charles O'Conor, to illuminate the political difficulties of Catholics involved in antiquarian endeavour in the penal age.[30] This study builds on Love's work, but extends it significantly by looking at the broader antiquarian network, emphasising, for example, the relations between Protestant antiquaries and Gaelic scribes who translated manuscripts on their behalf. Love sketched the unsuccessful attempts by O'Conor and Edmund Burke to encourage, first Thomas Leland, and then Thomas Campbell to write a general historical narrative on the colonial period that would command the support of liberal, enlightened Catholics and Protestants.[31] The failure to produce such a history is also the focus of an article by Jacqueline Hill which is a very useful, if over-schematised, survey of the major writers of the period. Hill's conclusion, endorsing Love's earlier analysis, attributed that failure to the lack of an inter-denominational consensus on the more recent past, and particularly on the vexed question of Catholic rebellion in the 1640s. As long as the political system continued to be based on the exclusion of Catholics from any share of power and justified by reference to Catholic disloyalty in earlier centuries, there was little hope of any agreed history.[32] Hill's argument is persuasive in its main outlines, but, by focusing mainly on the failed attempts at major consensual projects on the colonial era, it minimises the significance of the cooperation that occurred in the late eighteenth century between Protestant and Catholic antiquaries on the pre-colonial period.

Other scholars have chosen to highlight this and to link it to the influential liberal Protestantism of the late 1770s, which urged the dismantling of the penal laws against Catholics. In a seminal article published in 1981, Norman Vance drew attention to a specifically Protestant interest in the Gaelic or pre-colonial heritage, which he linked to the establishment of the Volunteers and to the growing stature of the 'patriot' parliamentary opposition led by Henry Grattan which 'helped to restore to Ireland a self-respect and a patriotic interest in its own past'.[33] According to F.G. James, this new Protestant interest in 'Catholic heritage' and their co-operation with Catholics 'prepared the way for the creation of [a] non-sectarian community of Irish writers and historians'.[34] This 'intellectual interchange among Irishmen from different and conflicting traditions' was explored by Vance over a much wider range of writers and centuries in his *Irish Literature: a Social History* (1990).[35] Like Vance and others, James highlighted the foundation of the Royal Irish Academy in 1785 (which was established by the Protestant élite but was open to Catholics), just three years after the attainment of legislative independence, arguing that it reflected 'the beginnings of a new concept of Irish nationality'.[36] This study proposes a more complex relationship between Protestant patriotism and antiquarianism.

In a major work of comparative literature, Joep Leerssen examined antiquarianism in the context of a developing sense of nationality in Ireland, and he too highlighted the 1780s as a key phase. *Mere Irish and Fíor-Ghael* (1986) is a *tour de force* of sustained analysis of Irish and English literature on Ireland from the twelfth century which charts the growth of an Irish national idea. The final chapter on the eighteenth century analyses what he sees as the last phase in this process: the broadening of the concept of Irish nationality to include the Anglo-Irish. He focuses in particular on patriot politics and Protestant antiquarianism, and argues that through the latter, a significant number of intellectuals and politicians came to share a notion of Irishness that was based on difference from, rather than links with England.[37] In support of this claim, he provides an admirably lucid account of antiquarian and linguistic researches from 1600, and situates them in the broader context of European interest in this sphere. Leerssen's study is indispensable for anyone working in this field, and has been supplemented by his more recent *Remembrance and Imagination* (1996) which extended his work on the development of a national self-image in literature and historical scholarship into the late nineteenth century.

No attempt has been made in this study to adjudicate between the contrasting findings of these two 'schools' – one emphasising the inhibiting, if not crippling, effect of sectarian tension on antiquarian and historical endeavour in the late eighteenth century, the other focusing on its role in creating a shared identity among Protestants and Catholics in the same period – since both perspectives are valid, if partial.[38] Rather, the aim has been to analyse the operation and interaction of both tendencies in Irish antiquarian culture. On the one hand, European cultural fashions, such as Celticism, Gothicism, orientalism and primitivism were refracted through the twin lenses of sectarianism and colonialism, producing texts which were often radically dissimilar in terms of central argument. On the other, Protestant and Catholic antiquaries were driven by similar needs to produce works which would validate the rights of their respective religious communities, whether in terms of religious toleration for Catholics, or of a growing sense of identity with the land of their birth among Protestant descendants of earlier colonists. Some antiquaries optimistically believed these desired validations to be compatible and even mutually enhancing, and an indication that Ireland had moved beyond a past riven by sectarian tensions.

Antiquarian debate has also featured in the work of some historians who have argued that eighteenth-century Ireland was an *ancien régime* society, conforming to the pattern established firstly for pre-revolutionary France and then adopted for many other European countries in the eighteenth century.[39] Ireland, according to this line, was not a colonial society; all major developments, political and social, are explicable purely in terms of contemporary European norms. In an important and suggestive book which came out in 1994, Cadoc Leighton harnessed historical and antiquarian works to support his thesis that the Irish Protestant élite was analogous to *ancien régime* nobilities throughout Europe, in part because its defence of its privileged position was based on 'conquest narratives' or myths (the implications of this for a colonial model are not discussed) that showed how 'the ancestors of the noble élite triumphed over the ancestors of the relatively unprivileged'.[40] However, as Leighton himself admits, no mainland European nobility justified its position, as the Irish Protestant élite did, on the basis of a series of conquests which were partly within living memory.[41] Furthermore, the Irish conquest and associated policies of colonisation and land expropriation, because they were still contested, were not fully in the past, and therefore did not have the status of myth in the eighteenth century. In fact, as this study argues, the Williamite land settlement provided one of the sub-texts to much writing on the past, whether recent or remote, with Catholic writers such as O'Conor, and Protestants like Ledwich, acutely sensitive to the implications of all writing, Catholic or Protestant, which criticised colonial policy in any period.

Moreover, the evidence adduced by Leighton for the centrality of such conquest myths among the élite is thin: just one pamphlet by William Henry published in 1749.[42] If conquest narratives were so crucial to Protestant identity, one would expect a number of histories of the colonial period to have been written in the eighteenth century. In fact, Thomas Leland's narrative history of 1773 was the only one to have been published.[43] The ambivalence of Protestants to the idea of conquest, because of its negative implications for the status of their parliament, has been emphasised by historians of Irish political thought of the seventeenth and eighteenth centuries.[44] Consideration of writings on the pre-colonial period in this study offers a different perspective on such ambivalence. The Protestant works under analysis here did not emphasise the various English conquests, but rather displayed an obsession with the contested Gaelic myth of origins, and also with the early Irish church, appropriating both in different ways as a means of rooting their community historically in Ireland. More recently, Jacqueline Hill has pointed out that while the issue of conquest had loomed large in historical works of the 1690s, a century later the theme of Anglo-Norman and English conquest in Irish history was downplayed, with even the Protestant ultra Richard Musgrave making considerable efforts to avoid using the term, referring instead to the 'arrival' of the English in the twelfth century.[45] That unease had much to do with the fact that Henry II had justified the Anglo-Norman incursion into Ireland by reference to a papal bull, *Laudibiliter*, which gave the sanction of the papacy to the conquest.[46] Thus, the twelfth-century conquest had embarrassing, even 'popish', connotations, while later conquests were too recent to be mythologised. Hill only looks at a small number of works published in the aftermath of the Union, whereas this study examines Protestant ambivalence towards their colonist heritage in greater detail across a range of antiquarian texts.

Those, like myself, who have argued that, in eulogising an ancient Gaelic civilisation, Charles O'Conor was lamenting *inter alia* the conquest and subsequent English colonial policy, are chided by Leighton for our 'simple interpretation' and our attempts to 'find a place for O'Conor in the history of Irish nationalism'.[47] I have never argued that O'Conor was a nationalist of any kind, but rather that he was a traditional Gaelic aristocrat, as much as a sophisticated Enlightenment gentleman, in many of his attitudes.[48] The dismissal of any colonial dimension to eighteenth-century Ireland, and the implication that to argue for such a dimension is to promote a nationalist interpretation of the period, indicate that the *ancien régime* thesis can tend towards a narrow ideological perspective, suspecting nationalist interpretations where there is none.

In spite of such blind spots, the Irish *ancien régime* school of historians has contributed much to our understanding of the eighteenth century, particularly by highlighting and analysing important aspects of Irish ideology and debate which show the influence of Enlightenment forms of thought in Britain and elsewhere.[49] In this context, the work of Colin Kidd, who is not of that school but rather a very fine historian of Scottish political thought, has been invaluable to this study in placing Irish as well as Scottish antiquarian writing squarely in what he has termed 'the eastern periphery of the European Enlightenment'.[50] In *Subverting Scotland's Past: Scottish Whig Historians and the Creation of an Anglo-British Identity, 1689–c.1830* (1993), Kidd examined the impact of changes in the British polity on Scottish historiography, explaining its obsession with the parliamentary ideal in terms of the traumatic loss of the Scottish parliament in 1707, and intermittently looking at Irish antiquarian writing from that parliamentary perspective. In an article published in 1994 comparing the treatment of Gaelic antiquity in Ireland and Scotland, Kidd demonstrated that a similar concern with representative institutions, as one marker of the civility of the early Irish, was present in Irish antiquarian writing.[51] His latest book, a study of ethnic identity within the early modern British world, situates Scottish, Irish, Welsh and English antiquarian thought within the framework of early modern European ideas about the origins of nations and peoples. Kidd's basic argument concurs with my own, that the new settlers in Ireland and their descendants constantly appropriated native pasts, ecclesiastical as well as secular, to justify their position of dominance.[52]

The structure of this study is, above all, determined by a number of European antiquarian debates which had a significant impact on Ireland. Part One concerns the origins debate. Theories of origins were ubiquitous and international, but in Ireland were complicated by having their source in Gaelic mythology, contentious and difficult for Protestant and Catholic writers alike, and complicated by the interventions of Scottish antiquaries. Chapter One treats of the origins debate from the perspective of the Gaelic tradition and its reworking mainly by Catholic antiquaries, who sought to adapt the tradition to the demands of Enlightenment scholarship and politics. Chapter Two continues the discussion of origins in terms of the rival theories of orientalism and Gothicism which were fundamental to Protestant efforts to subvert Gaelic tradition in support of more inclusive myths of origin. Part Two focuses on the two golden age myths which were current in the eighteenth century, one religious, the other secular. The sectarian basis of antiquarian debate was particularly evident in writings on the early Irish church, dealt with in Chapter Three. This commences with the major European vogue for druidism, for which there were unique but contentious Irish sources, creating cultural and political problems for Irish antiquaries who, in the main, were more concerned to promote the myth of early Ireland as a haven of Christian learning, 'the island of saints and scholars'. Chapter Four examines the promotion of a Gaelic golden age of civility which was destroyed by the twelfth-century conquest. In the late eighteenth century, this myth was invigorated by the arrival of the fashionable doctrine of primitivism which was basic to the development of European romanticism. The particular Irish manifestation of primitivism,

focusing on the nature of early Gaelic society, is discussed in detail. Like Gothicism, primitivist ideas came to Ireland principally via Scotland, and the influence of Scottish writers such as James Macpherson and John Pinkerton in
particular is explored. The hostile response to claims of a Gaelic golden age
emphasised the barbarism of native Irish society, which forms Part Three of the
study. Chapter Five examines eighteenth-century writings on native Irish law,
showing that these were still heavily influenced by the key colonial works of
Edmund Spenser and Sir John Davies published in the seventeenth century,
which had argued that Gaelic law lay at the root of Irish barbarism and revolt
and that the common law should have been extended to Ireland far earlier.
Chapter Six examines other seventeenth-century influences on the barbarism
debate, showing that the 1641 Rising and alleged massacres by Catholics cast
a deep shadow which affected antiquarian writings on even the remotest periods. The study concludes with an examination of the antiquarian endeavours
of the Royal Irish Academy, which was established in 1785. Among the ambitious aims of its Protestant Ascendancy founders was the recovery and celebration of Ireland's remote past and its literature, but this project was
overwhelmed by political and sectarian polarisation and conflict in the late
1780s and 1790s. A brief Epilogue points to the long-term political and literary impact of antiquarianism down to the twentieth century.

PART ONE

ORIGINS

GAELS, *SCOTI* AND MILESIANS:
Ethnic Origins and Gaelic Tradition in Ireland and Scotland, 1630–1770

In his famous 1782 speech on 'the Rights of Ireland', in which he put forward the claim for legislative independence, Henry Grattan made a striking reference to the ancestry of two members of the House of Commons whose families had been provincial kings and high kings of Ireland in the pre-colonial period:

> Some of the gentlemen whom I now see in their places, are the descendants of kings; the illustrious gentleman on the far bench [Mr O'Hara]; my illustrious friend near me [Mr O'Neill] – will they derogate from the royalty of their forefathers, bow their honoured heads, or acknowledge the crown of their ancestors . . . ? Are the American enemies to be free, and these royal subjects slaves?[1]

While this emphasis on origins may have been little more than a rhetorical flourish, it indicates an awareness of the background of those Protestant converts who came from the remnants of the native Irish aristocracy. Questions of communal origins and individual ancestry had a particular importance in a recently colonised society such as eighteenth-century Ireland, but there were also lively origins debates among Scottish, Welsh and English antiquaries.[2] The development of communal identity in the eighteenth century was surprisingly dependent on many of the same elements which had been prominent in the medieval period; among these were myths of origin or descent, which Anthony Smith has characterised as the *sine qua non* of identity formation.[3]

In response to the question, 'Where did we come from?', most European peoples had created stories around eponymous heroes, usually derived from classical Greece: for example, Brutus of Troy for the Britons, Francus for the Franks and Romulus for the Romans. These were gradually discarded by historians under the influence of Renaissance ideas about sources, and more complex theories of social and political development.[4] Irish and Scottish writers, however, continued to be heavily dependent on the medieval origin myth which, owing to a shared Gaelic culture, was common to both countries, although, for political reasons, articulated in contrasting ways. In the seventeenth and eighteenth centuries its authority came increasingly to be questioned, and in Scotland it was adapted to take account of developments in historical scholarship.[5] In Ireland, however, writers from across the political and religious spectrum adhered more closely to the traditional account for much longer, leading to tensions between Irish and Scottish scholars over the often conflicting adaptations and interpretations of the tradition during the seventeenth and eighteenth centuries.

The experience of recent as well as earlier colonisation informed all Irish historical writing, and had stimulated major developments in the native tradition. In particular, new compilations, including influential re-tellings of the origin myth, were undertaken in or around times of large-scale colonisation enterprises. Conquest and colonisation, therefore, were key motifs in Irish historical consciousness, as summed up in the title of the first great annalistic compilation, the late eleventh-century *Leabhar Gabhála Éirin*, popularly known in English as 'the book of invasions'. This perspective was reinforced by a central concept in European thought, which regarded invasion and conquest as the main dynamics of historical change. The 'invasion hypothesis' was the model for all pre-history, and involved the projection backwards of the classical and medieval experience of conquest as a means of explaining how western Europe came to be inhabited. This ancient movement of peoples was often put in anachronistic and emotive terms as the violation of historical boundaries, before these had actually existed.[6] In Ireland, the confiscation of most native Irish or Catholic estates in the seventeenth century and their transfer to new English or Scottish Protestant settlers meant that questions of settlement in remote periods had contemporary political resonances. In addition, Catholic theories, developed from the medieval Gaelic myth and its later reworkings, rejected a common origin for the Irish and Britons, and emphasised the independence of Ireland from Britain at all periods prior to the twelfth century when the first phase of English colonisation took place.

Of crucial importance in the seventeenth and eighteenth centuries was the treatment of the medieval annalistic tradition that had put the Irish origin myth into written form. The accuracy or otherwise of the annals was increasingly assessed in terms of the historicity of this myth, and antiquaries struggled with the problem of distinguishing fact from legend and story. Such analysis focused especially on the work of Geoffrey Keating who, in the 1630s, wrote the first narrative history based on medieval sources. Keating was an exponent of traditional Gaelic history, but updated it by a combination of post-Renaissance and Counter-Reformation scholarship and a keen awareness of the new political realities of seventeenth-century Ireland.[7] He also wrote in the contemporary rather than classical Gaelic style. In spite of this, Keating came to be regarded, in the eighteenth century, as *the* exemplar and repository of the medieval historiographical tradition. For this reason, the response to Keating's work often reflected attitudes to that tradition, as well as to the Gaelic world and its culture in general.

The most influential Irish origin legends are to be found in the *Leabhar Gabhála*, 'the foundation and canon of early Irish historiography'.[8] As late as the 1940s when R.A.S. Macalister produced the first published edition, with a translation, it was regarded as an actual source for ancient history and pagan religion, but now it is studied mainly for the light it sheds on the political and cultural mythology of its monastic authors.[9] Their primary purpose was not to collect native traditions as such, but to find a place for Ireland in the biblical history of the world, using the standard medieval authorities on chronology, geography, history, ethnography and language.[10] The *Leabhar Gabhála* is a complex text, consisting of five separate tracts, which were combined in the late eleventh century.[11] Some of it at least was in a written form as early as the eighth century, when Nennius drew on it for his *Historia Brittonum*, but extant versions date from the fourteenth century.[12]

The literal translation of *Leabhar Gabhála* is 'The Book of the Taking of Ireland', and its main theme is the coming of the Gael or Milesians to Ireland, from Egypt via Spain, in around 1000 BC. The arrival of earlier colonies, such as the Partholans, Firbolg and Tuath de Dannan, was narrated separately, and clearly belonged to a different tract, but in spite of its reference to an earlier period, it was included *after* the section on the Milesians. By thus foregrounding them, the compilers of the *Leabhar Gabhála* were clearly intent on giving this latter tribe the strongest title to political and dynastic power. This was probably a response to the process of church reform which, among other things, transformed the monasteries by opening them up to new ideas, and then after the Anglo-Norman conquest, to new people.[13] Just as the two great works of the seventeenth century, Geoffrey Keating's *Foras Feasa ar Éirinn* ('compendium of wisdom about Ireland', *c.*1634), and Ó Cléirigh's *Annála Ríoghachta Éireann* ('annals of the kingdom of Ireland', 1636), were completed at a time of new settlement and written in part to commemorate a passing world, the *Leabhar Gabhála* staked the claim of the putative heirs of the Milesians to be the rightful rulers of the country, whether in the face of competing tribal dynasties,[14] or of the Anglo-Norman adventurers.

The history of the Gael or Milesians in the *Leabhar Gabhála* was based on the journeys of the Children of Israel in the Old Testament, probably owing to a misreading of a passage in Orosius as meaning that Ireland was first seen from Brigantia in Spain, where there was a high watch-tower. As Macalister explained, 'This suggested a reminiscence of Moses, overlooking the Land of Promise from Mount Pisgah: and the author set himself to work out the parallel, forward and backward.'[15] Hence, while the Children of Israel were descended from one of the sons of Noah, Shem, the Gael were said to have been descended from his brother, Japhet. Their wanderings involved a sojourn in Egypt, where their eponymous ancestor, Scota, married the pharaoh, and produced Gaedheal Glas, which gave them two of their names. Having spent some time in Scythia, they moved to Spain, where Míl ruled (whence Milesians). The three sons of Míl set out from Spain to Ireland, subdued the inhabitants, and set up a polity which, it was asserted, lasted without any breaks until that time (i.e., the late eleventh century).

While the extant manuscripts of the *Leabhar Gabhála* date from the fourteenth century, it retained its present shape from the eleventh century; changes after this period were largely an accidental product of poor scribal skills.[16] The next period of major activity in relation to the text was in the seventeenth century. Once again this was a time of political upheaval, resulting in the completion of the partial conquest, begun in the twelfth century, with the Ulster and subsequent plantations establishing the dominance of a new group. These were referred to as the New English, to distinguish them from the older colonial community (now called 'Old English'), descendants of the first waves of colonists in the twelfth century. The main difference between them was religion, the Old English having remained Catholic. Thus, the range of inhabitants (and their allegiances) became immeasurably more complicated in this century, the native Irish having religion in common with the Old English (although still with important differences between them), and Old and New English having origins in England as a common factor. While religion proved, ultimately, a more enduring basis of identity, the issue of ethnic origins came clearly to the fore in this period. It seems significant that new versions of the *Leabhar Gabhála* were made in the first third of the seventeenth century and that its substance also began to appear in new historical narratives. Earlier historians, even of the period immediately preceding this, did not have a detailed knowledge of the myths contained in the *Leabhar Gabhála*. Richard Stanihurst, for example, writing in 1584, had got his information about the origin legends of the *Scoti* (or Milesians) from the Scottish historian, Hector Boece.[17]

Other factors led to the spread of medieval historiography. The dissolution of the monasteries in the previous century had released Gaelic manuscripts, previously available only in monastic libraries.[18] Two of the most important historians of the century were able to take advantage of this: Geoffrey Keating who was a Gaelic speaker, and Sir James Ware who was not, but who employed a native Irish amanuensis to translate for him. Another historian of perhaps even greater importance, in terms of manuscript sources (but having little impact in the following century), was the Franciscan Mícheál Ó Cléirigh, operating from the Irish college at Louvain, a major centre of the Irish Counter-Reformation.[19] He had been sent to Ireland in 1626 to gather together materials for history, and especially hagiography. Among the works of which he and his helpers made corrected copies was the *Leabhar Gabhála*, which Ó Cléirigh incorporated within his Counter-Reformation project, on the basis that it was 'the original fountain of the history of the saints and Kings of Erin, of her nobles and her people'.[20] Having completed their recension of the *Leabhar Gabhála*, Ó Cléirigh, together with his three associates, embarked on their most famous project, *Annála Ríoghachta Éireann*, commonly known as 'The Annals of the Four Masters', which used materials from existing compilations (including their *Leabhar Gabhála*[21]), as well as recording events down to 1616, becoming an important source in its own right for the later period. Neither Ó Cléirigh's version of the *Leabhar Gabhála* nor *Annála Ríoghachta Éireann* were put into print; instead they were circulated in manuscript form. The latter was finally published, with an English translation, only in the nineteenth century.[22]

It was Geoffrey Keating who was most responsible for bringing the origin legends of the Gaelic Irish into common currency. Although his history was not published in the original until the twentieth century, it circulated widely in manuscript.[23] *Foras Feasa ar Éirinn* departed from the annalistic structure that was traditional in Irish historiography, and this may well account for its greater and more immediate impact than the work of the Four Masters. Keating used as a framework the list of kings of Ireland found in manuscripts such as the Book of Leinster, and wove materials from disparate sources, such as stories, semi-historical tracts and historical poems, to produce a readable narrative on Ireland down to the twelfth century.[24] The narrative format also allowed Keating to add to, and to draw new lessons from, these materials. An equally important innovation which ensured the popularity of the work was Keating's choice of an accessible and modern style of language, whereas Ó Cléirigh had retained the archaic and highly stylised Gaelic of the bardic schools.

In recent years, historians have focused on Keating's innovations and have done much to explain how his work departed from traditional historiography. Bernadette Cunningham has situated Keating within his seventeenth-century political and religious contexts, arguing that *Foras Feasa* was 'one man's response to the age in which he lived'.[25] Like Stanihurst before him, Keating was Old English and Catholic, but unlike Stanihurst who lived in the English-speaking Pale, he was born in Munster and spoke Irish. Little is known of his background, except that he was born about 1570 in Co. Waterford and died probably between 1644 and 1650. He studied for the priesthood on the continent, and had links with the Universities of Rheims and Bordeaux.[26] This gave him a thorough grounding in Counter-Reformation theology, and, aside from *Foras Feasa*, his other major works were treatises on the Mass and on death.[27]

Keating's *Foras Feasa* was crucial in making the origin myths and lore of the *Leabhar Gabhála* and other compilations available to new audiences. In addition to his role as populariser, he also contributed to the organic growth of these myths, which had been virtually untouched for five hundred years, by incorporating the colonisers of the twelfth century, namely his own ancestors, into the medieval scheme, in order to provide what Brendan Bradshaw has called 'an origin-legend for Counter-Reformation Catholic Ireland'.[28] In his version, the Anglo-Normans, upon their arrival in Ireland, co-operated with the Gaelic nobility in their efforts to reform and consolidate the Irish church. Conflict between coloniser and colonised was blamed on five Anglo-Norman adventurers who died without issue, thus allowing the main Anglo-Norman settlement to be represented in unambiguously positive terms as 'the culminating episode in the history of the origins of the Irish nation'.[29]

Joep Leerssen has argued that the continuance of the manuscript tradition in Gaelic Ireland long after the printing press had been introduced elsewhere meant that the 'pre-Gutenberg Middle Ages' lasted well into the early modern period and that Gaelic learning remained unchanged. In this context, Keating's *Foras Feasa* illustrates 'the sleeping beauty medievalism of Gaelic antiquarianism', in that he 'wholly disregards any "modern" distinctions between mythical and historical, saga and record; his book is a compendium of legends which it presents as literal truth.'[30] The inverted commas around the term 'modern' hints at a certain uneasiness at the judgement being made, as indeed there ought to be, for this is to measure Keating's history by standards which did not appertain at the time of writing.

Rather than being in the mould of medieval historiography, *Foras Feasa* reflected the post-Renaissance scholarship which Keating had experienced in the course of his continental education. This can be seen in his emphasis on the use of primary sources and his attack on English writers on Ireland who could not read the Gaelic manuscripts.[31] The key to Keating's overall approach lies in his chosen title, 'Compendium of wisdom about Ireland', and stemmed from his belief that the political and social upheavals of his time jeopardised the survival of the manuscript tradition. His response was to list the compilations which he had consulted and to provide a narrative which interwove as much material as possible in an easily comprehensible form.[32] Thus, *Foras Feasa* was devised as a resource for later generations, to provide them with a kind of abstract of Gaelic historiographical tradition taken from manuscripts that, it was feared, would soon be lost or unintelligible.

Indeed, Keating often distinguished between the sources he used, on the basis of their reliability. This is particularly clear in his treatment of the *Leabhar Gabhála* origin legends, where he made plain his belief that at least some of them were fictional. For example, he included the tradition of successive occupations of Ireland before the Flood[33], but added a disclaimer:

> Know, O reader, that it is not as genuine history I set down this occupation, nor any occupation of which we have treated up to this; but because I have found them written in old books. And, moreover, I do not understand how the antiquaries obtained tidings of the people whom they assert to have come into Ireland before the deluge, except it by aerial demons gave them to them, who were their fairy lovers during the time of them being pagans; or unless it be on flags of stones they found them graven after the sub-siding of the deluge, if the story be true . . .[34]

The references here to 'aerial demons' and 'fairy lovers' clearly owed more to irony than to credulity. It is true that, where possible, Keating attempted to resolve the contradictions inherent in material that had come from disparate sources, but in the case of the antediluvian elements of the origin myth, his approach was to record these as part of tradition only.

By contrast, Roderic O'Flaherty, the other major seventeenth-century native Irish antiquary whose work continued to have an influence, adopted a far less sceptical approach. For example, in his *Ogygia: seu, Rerum Hibernicorum Chronologia* (1685), he rehearsed the legend of Ceasara, the granddaughter of

Noah, as fact, on the basis that he 'voluntarily' accepted the veracity of the man-uscript tradition. He also gave the exact date, day of the week and place in Kerry of the landing of the Partholan colony, in the year after the Flood.[35] Although like Keating, O'Flaherty was trained in the bardic tradition, he wrote in Latin for a wider English-speaking and classically educated readership. Para-doxically, the less sophisticated *Ogygia*, by virtue of its being the first book by a Gaelic scholar to be published in London,[36] seemingly marked a departure from the apparently self-enclosed world of Gaelic literature which Keating's unpublished narrative history symbolised. O'Flaherty's main aim was to outline a chronology of Irish history which would establish the antiquity of an Irish kingship, beginning with Milesius, and listing his successors down to the last high king, Ruaidhrí O Conchobhair, in the twelfth century. On the basis of the establishment of the first Scottish kingship by a colony of Irish origin in 500 AD, he hailed the accession to the throne of the Stuarts in 1603 as the restora-tion of the Milesian kingship in Ireland. He hoped for better treatment of the Catholic Irish from their co-religionist and allegedly fellow-Milesian, James II, to whom, as Prince of Wales, *Ogygia* was dedicated.[37] Perhaps because of this political aim behind his chronology, O'Flaherty did not raise questions as to the authority of the material which he employed.

Keating's delicate probing of these questions resembled more the approach of a contemporary Protestant writer, Sir James Ware, who made similar dis-tinctions between legend and fact, and also incorporated these different strands into his narrative.[38] Ware was born in Dublin in 1594, the son of an English officer who was secretary to the Lord Deputy and eventually Auditor-General. Ware also held this latter post, although his tenure was interrupted when his royalist sentiments forced him to spend the period from 1649 to 1660 in France. In his researches, Ware put himself at the meeting point of native and colonist viewpoints, though understandably his sympathies lay more with the latter. He edited and published works by Giraldus Cambrensis, Edmund Campion and Edmund Spenser, making them available to a wide audience for the first time. For his own works he employed the services of Dubhaltach Mac Fhirbhisigh, the last member of a family of hereditary poets, scholars and scribes, who copied and translated Gaelic manuscripts for him.[39]

The results of Ware's access to Gaelic lore and tradition, as well as to clas-sical and contemporary learning, can be seen in his *De Hibernia et Antiquitat-ibus eius Disquisitiones*, published in 1654. The first chapter was devoted to names of the island, 'Scotia' and 'Hibernia', for which he gave many possible explanations, including that of the eponymous heroine, Scota, although point-ing out that it had been 'exploded by men of Learning'. He also listed all the reputed colonies, from that of Ceasara, the niece of Noah, through the Partholans, Fomorii and Milesians, but maintained a distance from such accounts by using the phrase 'it is said', as Keating did also.[40] While not reject-ing the existence of such colonies, Ware agreed with Camden that the dates of settlement were exaggerated, and cautioned that 'the candid Reader cannot but observe, that in those Accounts which are taken out of the Histories of Ireland, concerning the Origin of that Nation, there is a great deal of Fable intermixed with some Truth'.[41]

In addition to providing an outline of Gaelic tradition on origins for a non-Gaelic-speaking readership, Ware was instrumental in introducing contemporary European thought about the origins of language into Irish intellectual debate, which hitherto had given little consideration to the place of Gaelic among European languages. In the early seventeenth century Gaelic and Kymric (or Welsh) were regarded for the most part as unrelated, linked neither to each other nor to any other European languages. As the century progressed, first Welsh and then Gaelic were assimilated within a paradigm positing one original language for the northern European non-classical world, which was given the name 'Scytho-Celtic'. This had not yet happened at the time that Ware was writing, but during his years of exile in France he made the acquaintance of one of the foremost participants in the European debate about Scytho-Celtic, Samuel Bochart, and on his return to Ireland, donated a copy of one of the latter's books, *Hierozicon* (1663), to the Library of Trinity College Dublin.[42]

Within this paradigm there were two alternative models of the descent of the original European language, both of which were to have increasing relevance in Ireland. The first, as put forward by Bochart, brought Scytho-Celticism from its Japhetan roots (the Bible still forming the structure of all models of origin, linguistic and racial), through the Mediterranean, via the Phoenician cities Carthage and Celtiberia, and thence into Celtic Gaul. The alternative route, favoured by scholars such as Marcus Boxhorn of Leyden University, proposed a northern rather than Mediterranean line of migration for the language, in a westerly direction across the continent of Europe. This 'Nordic' route, as the most straightforward, was the dominant model in most countries.[43]

Both the 'Phoenician' and 'Nordic' models had their adherents in Ireland. The medieval Gaelic myth of origin, as shown above, traced a line of migration which was consonant with the 'Phoenician' school of thought, while the 'Nordic' thesis found favour among colonist writers, and later, those of colonist ancestry.[44] However, in the seventeenth century and up to the middle of the eighteenth, it was possible to combine elements of the two, as Ware did. He alluded to both Bochart and Boxhorn in his writing on the origins question. Referring to the various names that Ireland had been given, he included Bochart's suggestion in *Geographia Sacra* 'that Ireland was not unknown to the Phoenicians'.[45] But in his consideration of the Gaelic language, Ware seemed to lean more towards the 'Nordic' model in positing a spread of Welsh into Ireland, whereupon a separate dialect developed.[46]

Gaelic was tied more closely to the Scytho-Celtic paradigm by the pioneering researches of Edward Lhuyd, keeper of the Ashmolean Museum at Oxford, whose comparative philological work, *Archaeologia Britannica*, was published in 1707. Lhuyd established beyond all doubt the relations between

Welsh and Irish, and thus the membership of the latter in the family of European languages.[47] At the same time, the concept of a Celtic race or people
embracing both the ancient Gauls and ancient Britons was being developed,
principally in the work of the French antiquary Paul-Yves Pezron, whose influential *Antiquité de la Nation, et de la Langue des Celtes, autrement appelez Gaulois*
(1703) was translated into English in 1706 as *Antiquities of Nations, more particularly of the Celtae or Gauls, taken to be originally the same People as our ancient
Britains*.[48] The result was the raising of the profile of the Gaelic language,
which had an impact on English-speaking Irish scholars and kept alive an
interest in pre-colonial history and culture.

The works of both Keating and Ware were translated into English in the
eighteenth century, thus promoting interest in the origin myth. The publication
of Keating's *Foras Feasa* in English in 1723 was particularly significant, but even
prior to this a number of translations in both Latin and English were circulat-
ing in manuscript form, indicating the remarkable reputation it had gained.[49]
(Its influence on Irish poetry was also evident from the mid-seventeenth century.[50]) Dermod O'Connor's translation, under the title *A General History of Ireland*, was a sumptuous folio volume, handsomely bound and containing plates
of Brian Boru and the pedigrees of many 'Milesian' gentry families, such as the
O'Carrolls. Most of these families were also subscribers and the book was dedicated to the Earl of Inchiquin, of the O'Brien family, which had converted to
Protestantism but retained a pride in their native Irish ancestry.[51]

O'Connor's translation was careless and defective, even by the relaxed standards of the time, and his mistakes were then attributed to Keating and used
in the attack against him that came later in the century.[52] As a Catholic priest
of the Counter-Reformation from an Old English background, Keating's concerns were markedly different from those of his commercially minded (and
somewhat disreputable) translator,[53] who was aware that the subscribers to
the 1723 volume were predominantly Protestant and unlikely to appreciate
Keating's stance. Thus, the translation changed the tone of the original, simply by replacing 'Catholic' with 'Christian' or by omitting it altogether.[54] Other
changes stemmed partly from the fact that by the 1720s the Old English had
long ceased to be a separate and recognisable group in Ireland. Religion was
now the bedrock of identity, but there was also a move to make birth in Ireland a transcending basis for a common patriotism, as can be seen in O'Connor's preface. Not only did he change Keating's 'old English nobility' to the
'Irish nobility', but he made ancestry and Irish birth alternative but equal motivations for subscribing to the volume:

> [the Irish of noble birth] valued it as the choicest Collection of ancient Records
> that possibly can be recovered from the Ruins of Time, to support the Honour
> of their Ancestors, and to give the World a just Idea of the Dignity of the Coun-
> try where they were born.[55]

O'Connor maintained that Keating's work contained much that was of value in spite of the fables which marred it, and this was to be the general view until the second half of the eighteenth century.[56]

The importance of Keating for both Protestant and Catholic views of the past in the second quarter of the eighteenth century can also be seen in the writings of two lesser known historians, Thomas Comerford and John K'eogh [sic]. The fact that neither writer adverted more than fleetingly to Keating underlines one of the central features of the treatment of the Gaelic tradition in the eighteenth century, which was that Keating's *Foras Feasa* in its English form was viewed less as an important and quite recent narration of that medieval tradition, than as representative of it. Thus, Thomas Comerford's *History of Ireland* (1742) made no mention of Keating either in the text or footnotes, yet it was based largely on *The General History of Ireland*, and the references to Irish manuscripts included in it were part of the common authorial practice of the time of bolstering claims to accuracy and scholarship, rather than a sign of direct familiarity with such sources.[57]

Comerford's modestly produced octavo contrasted with the expensive folio volume of O'Connor's Keating which was designed for a gentleman's library. Dedicating his book to 'The People of Ireland', rather than the usual titled patron, Comerford's aim was 'to cause the Knowledge of Irish History to be as general as possible, since it may be purchased at so small an expense, as here set forth'.[58] His reason for wanting to spread this knowledge was the long-established one: 'to free the Antient People of Ireland from the vile and scandalous aspersions cast upon them by prejudiced and mercenary writers'. Like Dermod O'Connor, Comerford attributed the same 'antient character, of being a worthy, brave and generous people' to 'the old and new race of Irish', and this may provide a clue to the religion of this shadowy author, about whom nothing is known.[59] It has been suggested that he might have been a member of the Catholic merchant family, the Comerfords of Dublin, and that the emphasis on religious piety in the account of the early Middle Ages could indicate that he was a clergyman.[60] The inclusiveness of his defence of the 'Irish' is more likely to indicate that he was a Protestant, but the book is unusual in giving away so little on this basic question.

John K'eogh, by contrast, made his religious and political allegiances very clear. His *Vindication of the Antiquities of Ireland* (1748) was dedicated to Robert Callaghan, a governor of Co. Tipperary, in praise of his support of the 'Protestant Interest . . . against Popery and arbitrary Power'.[61] At the same time, K'eogh stressed the native Irish ancestry of this defender of Protestant rights, and in an appendix traced his pedigree back through generations of Milesian kings to Adam. K'eogh also included an account of his own family, of which his father, the minor divine also named John K'eogh, was the first to be raised as a Protestant. He ended the account with the proud boast that there had been fourteen Milesian monarchs 'of my Name, that swayed the sceptre at the Hill of Tarah'.[62]

While K'eogh based his own identity on the twin poles of religion and Irish origins, he attempted, like Dermod O'Connor before him, to make birth in Ireland an equally valid attachment. He addressed a second dedication to Alicia Callaghan, Robert's wife, who was of planter stock: 'though no Milesian you cannot but have a Value for the Kingdom wherein you drew your first Breath, had your Education, and possess a fine Fortune.'[63] K'eogh viewed with some alarm the growing Anglicisation of native Irish families, who, like the Callaghans, 'were originally noble Milesians', but who, 'in order to make themselves more agreeable to the English' had 'englified [sic] their Names'. His aim was to bring such families 'back to their primitive stock' and, in defending the 'venerable Antiquity of the Irish Nation', to honour them.[64]

From the mid-eighteenth century, antiquarian works seldom emphasised the validity of Irish birth as well as ancestry in any consideration of interest in the past. The passage of time had much to do with this: by this stage all those of colonist descent had Irish-born ancestors. However, the question of origins remained central, partly because from the mid-century Irish antiquarianism became more overtly political. Catholic agitation for the abolition of the penal laws entered a new phase in 1760 when the Catholic Committee was set up. For Protestants, the penal laws were the bulwark of the colonial settlement; abolition raised fears as to their entitlement to land acquired from Catholics by confiscation in the previous century.

The nature of the changes in both politics and the writing of history are encapsulated in the career of Charles O'Conor, long recognised as a key figure in the intersection of the two discourses. His unique dual role as scholarly antiquary and political pamphleteer on behalf of the Catholic Committee ensured that his historical writings had a new sophistication, and included only such traditional elements of Gaelic historiography as suited his political perspective. Yet paradoxically, O'Conor can be seen as an equally important link with seventeenth-century modes of thought, and particularly with the Gaelic world of bardic learning which had gone into sharp decline.

The O'Conor family fortunes had also undergone severe reversals in the Williamite period, much of their land being confiscated because of their Jacobite loyalty. Charles's father had managed to consolidate their remaining small estate, which as Catholics they could only hold under the legal fiction of a Protestant nominal landlord, the Frenches of Roscommon. In the eighteenth century they were a prime example of the relic of the native Irish landowning nobility, particularly since they were descended from the last nominal high king of Ireland, Ruaidhrí Ó Conchobhair (Rory O'Conor), who was defeated by the Anglo-Normans.[65] They continued the Gaelic tradition of artistic and scholarly patronage, and hence in the 1720s the young Charles received instruction from Dominic Ó Duigenan, one of a family of hereditary historians, under whose direction he first began to copy Gaelic manuscripts. While his uncle, Thaddeus O'Rourke, Bishop of Killala, defied the ban on Catholic bishops entering Ireland, he was unable to move freely about the country, and devoted time to the education of his nephew. Charles thus attained proficiency in standard classical subjects, for which purpose he was also sent to school in Dublin for a period.[66]

While making his living as a gentleman farmer, O'Conor began to collect Gaelic manuscripts and to make copies and extracts of others. Among his collection was an original manuscript of the first part of the *Annála Ríoghachta Éireann* by Mícheál Ó Cléirigh and others. The earliest letter in the printed edition of his correspondence, dating from 1731, is a request to a fellow collector, John Fergus, to purchase a manuscript located in France.[67] Increasingly, he was asked by non-Gaelic-speaking historians to make extracts and translations from manuscripts in his possession. In this sense, as Leerssen argues, O'Conor was an important link in a tradition of scribal activity stretching back to medieval times.[68]

In his first antiquarian publication, *Dissertations on the Antient History of Ireland*, published in 1753, it was clear that his project was similar to that of earlier writers – to counter the image of the Irish as uncivilised – but his focus was somewhat different. For instance, Keating had emphasised the religious piety of the early Irish in his repudiation of the stereotype; O'Conor's perspective was altogether more secular, as befitting a writer of the enlightened mid-eighteenth century. His version of civility was of a literate culture in pre-Christian Ireland, which developed without reference to classical Greece or Rome, and, by implication, flourished at a time when Britain was a site of benighted ignorance, before the arrival of the Romans. Although such a picture in essence can also be found in Keating, O'Conor, drawing on the *Ogygia* of O'Flaherty (who may in turn have been influenced by Sir James Ware), made a specific claim of literacy among the pre-Christian Irish:

> Descended from the most humane and knowing Nation of all the old Celts, they imported, very early, the Elements of Letters and Arts into Ireland: Here they improved those Elements into Systems of Government and Philosophy, which their undisturbed State from foreign ambition left them at full Liberty to cultivate, thorough [sic] a long Succession of Ages . . .[69]

This went against the widely accepted view that literacy had accompanied the spread of Christianity throughout Europe.[70]

In this context, O'Conor was content to adopt the *Leabhar Gabhála* version of Irish origins which linked the Gael with the Phoenicians, who were considered to have had one of the earliest written cultures and whose alphabet was known to have formed the basis of the Greek.[71] According to Gaelic tradition, the earlier inhabitants, the tribes of Partholonians, Danans and Belgians, had passed into Ireland from Britain. O'Conor amplified this by characterising these early colonies of Britons as northern Celts of a primitive disposition, living by hunting and not in sedentary communities. The Milesians, Gaels, or Scots (the latter being O'Conor's preferred term), by contrast, were cultured southern Celts and described in opposition to those of Britain and Gaul, whose crude manners were recorded in Caesar and Tacitus.[72] Thus, O'Conor's version of the Gaelic origin myth allowed for colonisation from Britain, as Keating's also had done, but emphasised the cultural superiority of the southern Celtic early Irish over their northern Celtic British neighbours.

While O'Conor included some detail on the invasion of the Milesians, giving, for example, a precise landing date of 1013 BC and the number of ships in the expedition as one hundred and twenty,[73] he omitted much that was in the tradition, such as the eponymous heroine, Scota, and even the figure of Milesius. The latter name, he explained, simply came from 'Milea Espaine' or an anonymous 'Hero of Spain', from whom the colony took the honorary title 'Clan Milea'.[74] He also reassessed the authenticity of other elements of the Gaelic tradition, adopting a more cautious attitude than earlier writers. Keating had been sceptical as to the authority of accounts of the very first pre- or post-Flood invasions, but O'Conor held that on the colony of 'antient Scots' from Spain, the Gaelic annals were also embellished with fantasy and 'not to be taken for strict Truth'.[75] *Dissertations* focused instead on the heroic virtues of indigenous Irish princes of later times, such as Amergin, Achy-Edgathach and Ollam-Fodla, who, 'like Stars in a clouded Night, appear visibly, and some of first Magnitude, casting a Glitter on the shade surrounding them'.[76] Most of these figures have since been shown to be as fictive as Míl Easpaine.

In line with his more secular stance, O'Conor also moved away from the overtly biblical scheme of his predecessors. He declared it 'of no great Consequence' whether the ancient inhabitants of Ireland were descendants of Gomer, the eldest son of Japheth, or of Magog, the younger son.[77] At this stage, his only interest was in arguing the case for an early civilised and literate society on the island through Spanish influence. Gaelic tradition, based solely on indigenous sources (as he believed), no matter how accurate, was no longer enough, in his eyes, to support his claims. He therefore cast around for other authorities which might restore the scholarly standing of the fundamental Gaelic tradition relating to a Spanish colony, and found one in Isaac Newton's *Chronology of Ancient Kingdoms Amended* (1728). This was a late work, published posthumously, and was part of Newton's abiding interest in primitive religion and the prophecies of the Book of Revelation.

In this work, Newton aimed to construct a world chronology using astronomy in conjunction with the established materials, chiefly the historical books of the Old Testament and Herodotus. By calculating the equinoxes, he worked out the date for the (purely mythical) Argonauts' expedition in search of the Golden Fleece as 936 BC, but as a starting point he euhemerised (i.e. made into a historical figure) a king from ancient Greek mythology, Chiron, thus illustrating the mixture of new science and medieval thinking which characterised his approach. He then turned to the conventional tool of chronologists, the estimated length of the reigns of successive kings, and shortened the average from thirty to roughly twenty years, thereby reducing conventional chronologies considerably, and arriving by this method, for example, at a date of 936 BC for the Argonauts. But his purpose in thus shortening the accepted chronologies of the ancient world was to fit them into the pattern of the multiplying offspring of Noah which he had sought to establish in an earlier work, the 'Origines'.[78] Thus, while his results were duly novel in terms of dates, the raw material which Newton utilised was in essence no different from that used by the medieval chronologists, and which had been incorporated into the *Leabhar Gabhála* and other Gaelic compilations.

In comparing Irish accounts with Newton's version, O'Conor used the *Leabhar Gabhála*, Keating's *Foras Feasa* and O'Flaherty's *Ogygia*, giving them the collective name, 'The Native *Fileas*', as if Keating and O'Flaherty were not narrative historians of the previous century, but rather, bardic annalists of a medieval cast. He placed episodes involving heroes from the Irish tradition derived from these, side by side with extracts from Newton's chronology which seemed similar, and by this method he found many parallels including, for example, between the classical hero Hercules and the Irish hero Milesius, who appeared to have similarly named fathers.[79] This coincidence of names can now be explained by the common sources used, namely, earlier medieval chronicles, but, understandably, O'Conor claimed that Newton's amended chronology provided independent corroboration for the Irish tradition of a Spanish invasion:

> Who can behold in the foregoing parallel Relations (so long buried in the Rubbish of Fable) the true Original of this ancient Spanish Nation . . . without owning, at the same Time, that no other antient People of Europe have delivered any Accounts *more important*, or *more authentic*?[80]

O'Conor clearly held great hopes that his discovery of these connections between the work of the great scientist of the previous century and Gaelic sources 'must bring our more recent Accounts into Repute, and command that Attention which had been hitherto denied them by the Learned of this eighteenth century'.[81] However, the only subsequent writer to make use of this argument was the English ecclesiastical historian Ferdinando Warner, who had relied almost exclusively on O'Conor for help in researching his *History of Ireland* (1763).[82] In a survey of the art of chronological writing, James Johnson has argued that the eighteenth century saw the demise of chronology as a conventional historical form.[83] Certainly O'Conor, who spanned most of the century in Ireland, seems to represent the end of this traditional mode of thinking, which in the seventeenth century had absorbed such diverse Irish figures as Archbishop Ussher and Roderic O'Flaherty.

O'Conor's relative expertise in Gaelic sources meant that Keating's *Foras Feasa* was only one of the texts to which he referred. Later, he was to reject it as unreliable, but in this first edition of the *Dissertations* he cited *Foras Feasa* in his footnotes, along with the *Leabhar Gabhála* and other medieval annals, as if it too was a primary source. This, he explained, was because Keating 'has undoubtedly given us several curious Particulars of our ancient History, and to the Want of Access to many of our more valuable Manuscripts, we ought to attribute many of his Faults and his several Omissions'.[84] This relaxed approach to Keating disappeared from the second edition of the *Dissertations* which came out in 1766. Heavily rewritten, to the extent that it should be treated as a separate work, this edition is the work of O'Conor's middle years (he was 56), and has much of the youthful enthusiasm trimmed or replaced by a note of caution. For the first time, he warned against the English translation by Dermod O'Connor: 'The History given in English, under Keating's Name, is the grossest Imposition that has been ever yet obtruded on a learned Age'. However, he also criticised the original in very strong terms: 'Keating's work is a most injudicious Collection; the historical Part is degraded by the fabulous, with which it abounds . . . and such works . . . ought never to be published.'[85]

Foras Feasa and its English translation were also rejected by the Protestant antiquary Walter Harris, who brought out a three-volume edition of Sir James Ware's works in translation between 1739 and 1745. However, Harris made it clear that he objected to the implausible detail of Keating's account of the Milesian migration, and not to the occurrence of a colonisation from Spain.[86] The doubts which Harris felt about Keating's narrative were more cogently expressed in his 'Essay on the Defects in the Histories of Ireland, and Remedies proposed for the Improvement thereof', published in 1750, which was an impressive attempt to set forth the pitfalls of accepting all elements of the Gaelic tradition as historically authentic. In this respect, Harris dubbed Keating 'the Irish Geoffrey of Monmouth' for retailing as truth what Harris argued was poetic invention. Again, Harris, like Ware before him, singled out the eponymous heroine Scota as fictional, but not the claim of a colony from Spain.[87] Harris showed a more sophisticated understanding of the development of origin myths than many later writers, who viewed them merely as the vestiges of medieval credulity to be repudiated in the century of Enlightenment. According to Harris, such myths stemmed from the need to have a 'certain original' and were inevitably embellished: 'Historians, therefore, who talk variously on such subjects, are not justly to be taxed with ignorance and folly; since it is antiquity and the unfaithfulness of oral tradition, that have created the error, and left nothing clear for posterity to depend upon.' This oral tradition, he maintained, had been passed on by bards, whose 'raptures and flights' had been taken by earlier writers, such as Keating, for 'genuine truths'. Instead, he proposed that they should be 'mythologically considered . . . as obvious moral sense may be drawn from most of them'.[88] As an example of this alternative treatment he cited the case of the king named *Síorlaimh*, meaning the long-handed, whom Keating had represented literally as having abnormally long arms, but which Harris read as an allegory of the power of kings reaching out to every part of their domain.[89]

Harris's approach to the Gaelic historiographical tradition up to and including Keating thus had a depth and sensitivity which was lacking in later writers, Catholic and Protestant, who, by and large, either embraced it fully as truly historical or rejected it *in toto* as absurd fantasy. His advice to historians dealing with the records on the early period was 'to separate the sound corn from the chaff and retain only what carries the appearance of probability and truth' and to make 'a due adjustment to the chronology' which would, he claimed, together with a 'plain narrative style' and 'short pertinent reflections', serve 'to set the ancient history of Ireland upon an equal footing with that of any other country'.[90] Arguably, just one person, Charles O'Conor, can be said to have attempted this method.

O'Conor's task was made more difficult by the growth of historical scepticism from the mid-century, which was evident in David Hume's *History of England*, published between 1754 and 1761. This quickly became the standard work on British history and had a profound impact on attitudes to the distant as well as more recent past in all parts of Britain and Ireland. Hume's stress on the barbarity of former ages and on the very recent development of civil society had particular implications for the claims for an ancient civilisation in pre-colonial Ireland.[91] Additionally, his references both to the general question of origins and to the specific case of the peopling of Ireland held little comfort for O'Conor and others. In the opening remarks of his first chapter, Hume characterised research into origins as mere useless dabbling which 'could afford little or no entertainment to those born in a more cultivated age'. He deplored especially the practice of using traditional tales, in the absence of authoritative documentary evidence, only making an exception for 'the antient Greek fictions, which are so celebrated and so agreeable, that they will ever be the objects of the attention of mankind'. The only 'certain means' of investigating the question of origins, was 'to consider the language, manners and customs of their ancestors, and to compare them with those of neighbouring nations'.[92]

This approach presupposed close links between adjacent areas, based on the apparently logical idea that countries were populated by their nearest neighbours. It did not leave much room for the movement of an Iberian colony northwards through the dangerous seas of Biscay to Ireland. Though not particularly interested in the question, in later editions of the *History of England*, Hume added a note to his brief reference to the origins of the Scots and Picts, to take account of the renewed controversy between Irish and Scottish writers over the origins issue. As before, he asserted that the island of Britain had been peopled by Celts from Gaul, who moved into southern Britain and then northwards into Scotland as the Romans advanced. From the north-west of Scotland some of them migrated into Ireland, from where they operated as 'robbers or pyrates' harassing the Romans and North Britons. Eventually some of these 'freebooters' re-settled in Scotland, their 'barbarous manner of life' rendering them more fit than the Romans for subduing the Highlanders.[93] None of this was in keeping with Irish accounts and, in its depiction of the Irish as even less civilised than the Highlanders, was more damaging than earlier stereotyping.

Hume displayed here the typical prejudice of a Lowlander against both Highlanders and the Irish, most succinctly expressed in frequent references to Highlanders as 'Irish', to emphasise their exclusion from the real Scottish nation.[94] Tensions between Scottish and Irish writers about their shared ancient history had occurred regularly since the seventeenth century. The dispute had its roots in the different ways in which the Gaelic origin myth had evolved in the two countries in response to the prospect of English domination. Just as the Irish were stimulated by outside threat to produce a more elaborate version of their oral and written myths in the eleventh-century *Leabhar Gabhála*, the Scots were forced into a similar exercise two centuries later, when Edward II of England claimed their vacant throne. In 1299, the Anglo-Scottish dispute was brought to the court of Rome for adjudication, with English and Scottish lawyers putting forward competing accounts of the history of Scotland and of the origins of its people. Two claims were central to the English case – a common Trojan ancestry for all early inhabitants of the island, and the subjugation of Scotland by King Arthur of the Britons, who had made its king a vassal. The Scots, in response, argued that they were a more ancient people than the Britons, being descended from Scota and Gathelus, who had sailed from Egypt long before Brutus arrived in Britain, and that they had always been free and independent.[95]

It was at this point that the Scottish version diverged from the last phase of the Irish myth. Under the leadership of Simon Breck, it was recounted, a group of Scots migrated from Ireland to north Britain in the fourth century BC, subdued the inhabitants, and established a dynasty, beginning in 330 BC with Fergus I, which had ruled without interruption ever since.[96] In reality, the historical Fergus Mac Erc, from whom this mythic Fergus I was cloned, established the Dalriadic dynasty nearly eight hundred years later, in 500 AD.[97] This revised version of the myth interposed forty-five kings between these two Ferguses, giving the Scots a far more ancient royal dynasty than the English lawyers could produce. The existence of an independent kingship became the central core of the myth, and gradually the other more extraneous and eponymous elements were discarded. In George Buchanan's *Rerum Scoticarum Historia* published in 1582, the kingship myth was given its most authoritative statement and the Egyptian origins of the Scottish race were dropped.[98]

This happened at a time when the independence of the Scottish monarchy was under threat, and subsequently, when James VI became king of Scotland and England in 1603, it became even more important to assert the title of the Scottish monarchy to the oldest lineage in Britain. Scottish perceptions of the past had a British focus, in that a major concern was the definition of Scotland as one of the two sovereign states of the island. Roger Mason has examined this perspective in the sixteenth century, when it first came to the fore, and has characterised it as an attempt by the Scots to assert their right to a relationship based on equality in any projected union of the two crowns. Unsuccessful in this respect, by the seventeenth century it became all the more necessary to continue its assertion for the purposes of national pride and identity.[99]

The Irish historiographical tradition was also put under strain by the evolution of the Scottish myth. In the first place, the renewed claim to an independent Scottish kingdom from 330 BC contradicted one of the factual elements of the Irish tradition, that the Scottish monarchy had been established much later by the Dalriadan colony from Ireland in 500 AD. When, in 1603, the Stuarts assumed the English throne and therefore became kings of Ireland, Irish writers and poets traced the 'Milesian' ancestry of the Stuarts to this event, and hence created an Irish genealogical stake in the new British monarchy.[100] This was energetically refuted by Scottish antiquaries, notably Sir George Mackenzie, who held the position of King's Advocate, in his *A Defence of the Antiquity of the Royal Line of Scotland* (1685).[101] The Hiberno-Scottish dispute over their shared past was further complicated by the Scottish priest Thomas Dempster, who exploited the resemblance between the Latin name for Ireland, *Scotia*, meaning the motherland of the Scoti or Gaels, and Scotland. In three works which appeared in the 1620s, Dempster inverted the historically accurate and hitherto widely accepted model of colonisation from Antrim into Argyll, and claimed Scotland as *Scotia* and Ireland as *its* colony. Dempster's motive for this sleight of hand was to gain for the glory of Scotland any saint or scholar who had the medieval Latin label of *Scotus*. In the process, he annexed the Irish patron saints Patrick and Brigid, and the scholastic philosopher, John Scotus Eriugena, among many others.[102]

While Dempster's claims were immediately refuted by both Irish and English scholars, it was not until 1729, with the appearance of Thomas Innes's *A Critical Essay on the Ancient Inhabitants of the Northern Parts of Britain, or Scotland*, that the Scottish origin myth and its more recent accretions were convincingly challenged by a Scottish writer. Innes was a Catholic priest and Stuart loyalist, educated and based for the most part in France. His work shows the influence of contemporary French historiography, particularly of Henri Bayle and Jean Mabillon, in its concern for documentary evidence.[103] Innes subjected the earlier histories of Hector Boece[104] and George Buchanan to severe scrutiny, and also went back to the primary sources, mainly the lists of Scottish kings. He carefully and effectively demolished the case for the forty-odd kings before Fergus, son of Erc in the sixth century AD. Here, his main target was Buchanan, who had justified the usurpation of Mary, Queen of Scots, by claiming that these forty kings had been chosen by elective rather than hereditary succession, thus providing historical sanction for the removal of a monarch by the aristocracy.[105]

Thomas Rae has extolled Innes as a 'forward-looking historian' who used techniques of documentary criticism in a relatively modern way.[106] However, there were interesting tensions between Innes's methodology and his desire not to undermine either the Stuart Pretender or the honour of Scotland, which at times led to the abandonment of his enlightened historiographical approach. He was particularly conscious that his demolition of the pre-sixth-century Scottish kings might have adverse implications for the Pretender's cause.[107] In consequence, he went to considerable pains to substitute a Pictish hereditary dynasty, into which the Dalriadan Kenneth MacAlpine married in the ninth century to unite the two peoples. Innes calculated that MacAlpine had thus become the seventieth monarch in this line, and that it contained thirty-seven pre-Christian kings, not far short of the fictional Scottish line.[108] In this mathematical way, honour was restored at the same time to the Stuarts and to the reputation of Scottish history by removing the dependence on Irish accounts of the Scottish past. Innes was quite open about his attempt to forge a wholly independent Scottish history. He aimed to establish 'that the royal family, and present inhabitants of Scotland, are in general as well the descendants and progeny of the ancient Caledonians, or Picts, as they are of those Scots who came in from Ireland', so that there would be no need 'to have recourse to the Scots who came from Ireland, for maintaining . . . the antiquity of the royal line of our kings . . . or the ancient settlement of the inhabitants in Britain'.[109] This emphasis on the Picts and Caledonians was later taken up and extended by James Macpherson and John Pinkerton.[110]

Such a major change in the Scottish narrative of their past had a serious knock-on effect on Irish historiography. Innes's demolition of the Milesian genealogy of the Stuarts, so important in the seventeenth century, was not in itself a great blow, and indeed could be regarded as a blessing, now that loyalty to the Hanoverian monarchy was a central issue in Irish politics. However, the arguments used by Innes to discredit Scottish tradition had serious implications for the credibility of Irish origin claims and particularly for the recently published English translation of Keating's *Foras Feasa* which had popularised them. Innes argued that Irish writers could not dismiss Scottish tradition and yet maintain their own as authentic. He rejected the use of Irish annals as a source until they were published and thus exposed to scrutiny.[111] In particular, Innes cast doubt on Irish accounts of the Milesians as 'destitute of all those grounds and historical proofs proper to gain them credit with impartial competent judges of ancient and remote transactions of this nature'.[112] Thus, even though his real aim was to discredit Scottish tradition, he could not ignore its Irish counterpart. Such close interdependence of Irish and Scottish history was a feature of antiquarian writing in both countries even before the emergence of James Macpherson's controversial work.

Macpherson is best known as the creator of *The Poems of Ossian* (1762–3), which he presented as the work of a third-century Highland bard, Ossian, passed down orally in western Scotland until rescued and translated by him. Macpherson's Ossianic output will be considered more fully in Chapter Four, in the context of contrasting Irish and Scottish golden age myths. However, his desire to situate a Gaelic-speaking culture in third-century Scotland contradicted the by now widely accepted view that Gaelic settlement in Scotland did not happen until the fifth century. He therefore attempted to re-establish two of the discredited elements of Scottish tradition: the early inhabitation of north-ern Britain by the Scots, and Thomas Dempster's seventeenth-century claim that Scotland was the motherland of the Scots, and Ireland merely a later colony.[113] Behind this lay another attempt to forge a truly British identity for the Scots, Macpherson claiming the Highland Celt as the authentic British aborigine.

In 1771 Macpherson published a full-length work which put forward this thesis, *An Introduction to the History of Great Britain and Ireland*. Its historical scheme can be best described as British-Celtic, the early inhabitants of Britain being three successive waves of Celts, 'Gaël', 'Cimbri' and 'Belgae'. As each new group arrived, the earlier colonists were pushed northwards, so that the pos-terity of the Gael settled eventually in the most northerly part of the island.[114] This very simple model of colonisation gave the Highlanders the claim to the oldest lineage in the island and the title 'old Britons', which Macpherson occa-sionally employed, together with 'Caledonian Britons'.[115] No dates were given for any of these migrations, but the Caledonian Britons were in possession of the northern reaches before the Romans landed, and of course centuries before the Anglo-Saxons made their appearance on the island. Despite his professed scorn for Thomas Innes, the influence of the latter on Macpherson's argument is very evident, both in his emphasis on a Caledonian Scotland, and in his treatment of Irish accounts. In order to discredit one of the most authoritative elements of Irish tradition – that a colony from Ireland had settled in Scotland in the fifth century AD – Macpherson used the improbability of the tradition of the Milesian colony to cast doubt on the reliability of any part of the Irish narrative.[116] The Irish, according to his scheme, were descendants of Celtic Britons who made their way from Scotland to Ireland, although he clearly had little interest in exploring this Scottish colonisation, beyond asserting its occurrence.[117]

Macpherson's emphasis on the British derivation of the Irish and on the unreliabilty of their traditional history had a considerable impact. The Irish Protestant writers Edward Ledwich and Thomas Campbell, were later to draw on these arguments, although with minimal reference to Macpherson, who by the 1780s was suspected of having forged *The Poems of Ossian*.[118] However, the immediate consequence of his theories, from their first appearance in the dis-sertations and prefaces accompanying *Fingal* (1762) and *Temora* (1763), was to put Irish antiquaries on the defensive. Restatements of the Irish historiograph-ical tradition came from the Catholics, Charles O'Conor and Sylvester O'Hal-loran, but such was the vigour of Macpherson's attack that Protestant writers were also drawn into this new phase of the Hiberno-Scottish controversy.

O'Conor's response was to write a pamphlet, published in 1766, entitled *A Dissertation on the First Migrations and Final Settlement of the Scots in North-Britain; with Occasional Observations on the Poems of 'Fingal' and 'Temora'*. This was then bound with the second edition of his *Dissertations*, which appeared in the same year. O'Conor fitted Macpherson's historical scheme into the traditional Scottish pattern, both of claiming an early monarchy in Scotland – in this case, by creating a novel 'Fingalian' dynasty – and of doing so by purloining heroes from Irish history.[119] In order to defend his historical scheme, Macpherson was forced 'to falsify all antient History, to cover some of his Paradoxes'.[120] O'Conor's reply to Macpherson's claim of a Scottish colonisation of Ireland was to stress that the Dalriadan settlement of the fifth century AD had been the result of a superior Irish force overcoming the Picts. He gave the episode a resounding title: 'the Conquest of the Highlands and Hebrides, by the Dalriada Race'.[121] Macpherson's derogatory comments about the Irish manuscript tradition were of perhaps even more concern to O'Conor. He characterised them as an attempt 'to discredit all the Writings of our earlier Bards, to make room for Ossian, whom he represents as an illiterate Bard of an illiterate Age'. Recognising that Macpherson, despite his protests to the contrary, was heavily influenced by Thomas Innes, O'Conor pointed out that the dissertations prefixed to *Fingal* and *Temora* abounded 'with negative Arguments, drawn chiefly from Mr. Innes, a Priest of the Scotish College in Paris'.[122] This emphasis on Innes's Catholicism and Jacobite loyalty was an attempt to discredit Macpherson by imputing the same politics to him.

While professing to deplore Macpherson's 'illiberal Abuse, and aggressing [*sic*] Insolence', in private O'Conor welcomed the dispute as a means of 'whetting the weapons of research'.[123] Certainly the abrasiveness of Macpherson's style, as much as the nature of his argument, was responsible for drawing ripostes from two Irish Protestant writers who hitherto had not concerned themselves with antiquarian issues. The first of these into print was Thomas Leland, Fellow and Librarian of Trinity College Dublin, and the person responsible for opening that library to Catholic scholars. His major work, *The History of Ireland from the Invasion of Henry II*, appeared in three volumes in 1773. O'Conor had encouraged Leland to undertake the project, thinking him the ideal person to write a 'philosophical' history of the colonial period which, by taking an impartial stance, would do justice to Catholics.[124] O'Conor's disappointment with the work, which he felt to be partisan and therefore unphilosophical, will be dealt with in a later chapter. However, Leland's approach was clearly in the 'philosophical' mode in its professed lack of interest in the origins question or indeed the period prior to the Christian era. Like his role model, Hume, he deemed this to be the business of the antiquary rather than the historian.[125] Yet in an anonymous short book which came out the previous year, Leland himself had entered the controversy over origins which Macpherson's *Introduction to the History of Great Britain and Ireland* (1771) had reawakened. Though in contact with O'Conor at the time, and in one letter mentioning an essay by Thomas Barnard, Dean of Derry, on the same subject, Leland did not tell O'Conor that he was writing his own reply to Macpherson.[126] Leland professed not to think much of Barnard's essay, but it may in part have stimulated him to produce his *Examination of the Arguments contained in a late Introduction to the History of the Antient Irish and Scots* (1772).[127] The

Examination was written in the guise of a 'disinterested observer of this angry debate; not having the honour to be a native of either of the contending nations', although he declared himself 'an ally' of the Irish in the dispute. Leland also stated that his target was Macpherson's theory of colonisation, but his aim was to restore only the authority of the 'old Tradition' of the fifth-century Dalriadan settlement in Scotland and not to rehabilitate the Irish annals as a historical source.[128] Recognising that Macpherson was undermining the historicity of the Dalriadan colony by tying it in with the more doubtful Milesian origin legend, Leland tried to separate the two elements, and argued that doubts about the latter should have no bearing on the former.[129]

Broadening his attack, and using his knowledge of the classics throughout, Leland argued that different standards were being applied to Irish annals and historians than to the Latin and Greek classical writers. While it was well known that 'the credulous Herodotus' derived some of his information from priests 'perhaps not more respectable' than Irish bards, 'the world is not so uncandid as to refuse all credit to the main outlines of a history, because many particulars may be justly exceptionable'. Replying to one of the main charges against the Irish annalists, that they could not have known of the happenings of the more remote period, Leland asked, 'What credit is due to the history of Livy, who took his materials from records then said to be subsisting, but now no longer to be seen?'[130] In the same way, 'the old writers of Ireland . . . refer to the more antient records of the country, still extant . . . in their times: and why they are not to be judged by the same laws as other writers, I profess I cannot discover.' Leland put forward 'general rules for determining the credit due to all historians and annalists, whether ancient or modern'. Those basing their accounts on tradition and hearsay should be treated with caution; those using 'records of the country' should be 'generally admitted as authentick' and preferred over a foreign author's testimony. As in the case of the Greek and Roman histories, 'the date of the oldest manuscript, now supposed to remain in Ireland, or the age of its author, has nothing to do with the credibility of his testimony'.[131]

Leland's repudiation of Macpherson's origins theory had a breadth and a cogency that was lacking in O'Conor's attack. In contrast to O'Conor's emphasis on the detail of the theory, Leland focused more on the weaknesses of Macpherson's method of argument and his scholarship, indicating, for example, where he had misread a passage from Diodorus Siculus, and had completely reversed the meaning of a passage from Sir James Ware.[132] His objective, he declared in the conclusion, was to show 'how far a national prejudice may carry a learned and ingenious writer into false deductions, misapplied quotations . . . evasions of the clearest evidence, when they are found necessary to support a favourite system'. His disinterestedness came from the fact that he did not wish to establish 'any system of my own'; implying that adherents of the rival systems were by definition equally biased.[133] Leland's undoubted sense of perspective about the controversy was only possible because he was not directly threatened in his own work, as O'Conor was, by

Macpherson's assault. His aim, as he stressed a number of times, was not to argue for the authority of the Irish annals but merely to leave their 'credibility . . . exactly upon the same footing with those of other countries, whose histories reach much farther back than their remaining records'.[134] For Leland, most of the Irish tradition might, or might not, be based on real events in the very remote past. O'Conor, by contrast, had to maintain that it was; a harder proposition to defend successfully.

While Leland presented himself as an anonymous outsider to the dispute, neither Irish nor Scottish, Thomas Barnard, Dean of Derry, did not feel the need to disguise his personal or national identity in his essay, 'An Enquiry concerning the Original of the Scots in Britain', published in the *Transactions of the Royal Irish Academy* in 1787. Like Leland, Barnard adopted the position of disinterested adjudicator of the rival systems, '[h]aving read with some degree of attention what has been produced in this controversy on both sides of the question; and compared it as well with the antient histories of the Scots and Irish, as with the evidence of such foreign writers as make mention of them'. Unlike Leland, his response was to attempt a synthesis of the theories put forward by Macpherson and O'Conor, 'to reconcile [rather] than to subvert the arguments of both parties'.[135] He did so by allowing as 'highly probable' that Ireland was peopled in remotest times from Britain, north and south, and that therefore 'the Irish might have been the children, rather than the parents of the antient Caledonians'. But, he argued, this 'concession' did not 'invalidate the history of a certain Milesian Dynasty having in process of time invaded and obtained the dominion of the country without extirpating antient natives'. In support, he used the analogy of the later invasions of Britain by the Romans, Saxons, Danes and Normans, and of Ireland by the Anglo-Normans: 'no one I believe has been so absurd as to infer that either of these kingdoms was peopled as well as subdued by the invaders'. Employing this line of reasoning, he incorporated the Dalriadan colony into his scheme, by presenting it as 'the return to their original country' of the 'antient posterity of the Caledonians, under a Milesian leader'.[136] On the vexed question of the authority of the Irish manuscript tradition, Barnard could not continue in his self-appointed role as conciliator, since there was no mediatory position between Macpherson's vehement rejection and O'Conor's passionate advocacy of it. Instead, Barnard plumped for strong support of their authority as 'true transcripts from antient records then extant, but since destroyed'. The problem, as he saw it, was the same one confronting all historians of remote periods: 'the history of the transactions of those times is mixed with the fictions of later ages, and less to be depended upon'. Added to that, he remarked, perspicaciously, 'we have at this day no fixed criterion to distinguish falsehood from truth'. All that could be done was to treat the accounts found in the older histories 'with a sceptical caution' and to admit 'only [what] is consistent with probability, with the testimony of contemporary historians, and with itself'.[137]

Barnard's synthesising scheme, which tied Ireland more closely to British history, must have been unwelcome to Charles O'Conor. He would also have objected strongly to Barnard's presentation of the Anglo-Norman colonisation as a conquest, as would all those, Protestant as well as Catholic, who took William Molyneux's line that the Irish chieftains had submitted voluntarily to Henry II in 1172.[138] But Barnard's stance of 'sceptical caution' on the historicity of the Gaelic manuscript tradition was close to O'Conor's developing approach from the 1760s. The second edition of the *Dissertations* (1766) shows the impact of the general criticisms levelled by Innes, Hume and Macpherson. The text was tightened up considerably, and many of the more controversial references to politics were removed or toned down.[139] The literacy and civilisation of the early Irish was more clearly defined as the overarching theme of the book. In relation to the origins question and the Milesian tradition, O'Conor retained the section which illustrated parallels between Newton's *Chronology* and Irish tradition and laid more emphasis on it, but he omitted the parallel linking of the eponymous hero of Irish tradition, 'Milea Easpaine' or Milesius, with Newton's 'Hercules or Hero of Spain'.[140] Also dropped was the optimistic forecast that this similarity between Newton's *Chronology* and Irish tradition 'must bring our more recent Accounts into Repute, and command that attention which had been hitherto denied them by the Learned of this eighteenth Century'.[141]

The second edition of the *Dissertations* also reveals O'Conor's growing awareness of the importance of using only the most creditworthy materials. For example, in the Preface he listed his main sources, emphasising his reliance on Ó Cléirigh's *Annála Ríoghachta Éireann* for the Christian period; information not given in the first edition. He also stated that he had used Ó Cléirigh's version of the *Leabhar Gabhála*, which he deemed more accurate than older recensions.[142] Conscious that the absence of printed translations of these sources undermined their credibility and, by extension, his own work, O'Conor had already turned his attention to remedying the situation. In 1763 he approached Francis Stoughton Sullivan, the first Professor of Feudal and English Law in Trinity College Dublin. Sullivan, of the O'Sullivan More family of Kerry, was another example of a Protestant from Gaelic stock who had an interest in early Irish history and manuscripts. In the 1740s and 1750s he had done some work to prepare a critical edition of the *Leabhar Gabhála* and had employed scribes to copy several recensions, among them Ó Cléirigh's.[143] O'Conor proposed that they should collaborate on the translation and editing of the *Annála Ríoghachta Éireann*, and seek the financial backing of the Dublin Society (of which Sullivan was a member) for the project. O'Conor's aim was primarily to preserve bardic language and lore: 'Hereby the classical language of the antient Scots would be preserved; many curious historical facts relative to the politics and manners of the nation would be preserved also; all would be lost if these Manuscripts were burned or otherwise destroyed.'[144] Sullivan readily agreed to the plan and began a Latin translation, using manuscripts lent by O'Conor.[145] O'Conor's correspondence does not reveal why Latin rather than English was the chosen medium, but presumably it was believed to confer greater prestige.

Despite Sullivan's evident enthusiasm, O'Conor was soon pessimistic about the project and particularly about financing its publication: 'After all I am thinking on good Grounds, that the Dublin Society will not meddle with the Matter, tho[ough] certainly such a Publication would do honor to the patrons of literature in Ireland, if any such we have.'[146] The project does not appear to have advanced any further and is not mentioned after this time in O'Conor's correspondence. However, from letters written later we can infer that the main stumbling block was the competence of Sullivan as translator. In 1781, writing to the genealogist Thomas O'Gorman, O'Conor remarked: 'I know well that the late Dr Sullivan was unable to translate many parts (and those the best) of our ancient Annals. None but men trained in our old Classic Phraseology can undertake such a work'.[147] At the same time, it should be noted that Sullivan's translation was still being consulted by antiquaries in 1781, in the absence of any alternative.[148] The problem was that *Annála Ríoghachta Éireann* had been written in the classical language of the learned élite of medieval Ireland, which continued to be the language of high culture until the mid-seventeenth century. It was only when the bardic culture collapsed that the simpler vernacular Irish of Keating became the dominant literary form.

O'Conor continued to be pessimistic about the prospect of organising good translations. In 1783, when O'Gorman approached him with a new plan to have certain annals translated by a Revd McCarthy of Paris, he was only mildly encouraging and implied that the task would be too great. Sending O'Gorman the Annals of Connaught, he wrote that he knew of none but himself in Connaught 'who can read or explain them, and this difficulty being likely to increase every day, it will be more necessary for your copyist to transcribe them exactly as he finds them'.[149] An obvious question to ask is why, if this was the case, O'Conor himself did not undertake the translation? Given that manuscripts were lent freely between individuals and even to some extent by the Library in Trinity College, O'Conor's distance from Dublin was only a minor drawback. It seems even more surprising when he was clearly so exercised by the fear that Gaelic learning was dying out and would soon be irretrievable.[150] The most likely explanation is that O'Conor had enough classical Irish to recognise the enormity of the task but not enough to undertake it.[151] His letters to Thomas O'Gorman were an acknowledgement of this. Yet in his relations with Protestant scholars and antiquaries from Sullivan to Charles Vallancey, O'Conor adopted a more enthusiastic posture on the translation question. He not only assisted them in their projects, but also encouraged them with outrageous flattery to take on work for which he was better suited. This was particularly the case with Vallancey whose grasp of the Irish language was much poorer than he himself liked to claim.[152] O'Conor worked hard to avoid alienating Protestant support for all his causes, whether antiquarian or in the field of contemporary politics.

O'Conor's diplomatic successes in this regard can be seen in his dealings with the Select Committee of the Dublin Society. This committee was set up in 1772 after lobbying by Vallancey; its principal brief being to purchase Gaelic manuscripts and publish them in translation.[153] The President of the Select Committee, Sir Lucius O'Brien, invited O'Conor and his friend John Carpenter, Catholic Archbishop of Dublin, to become corresponding members of the committee, hitherto entirely Protestant.[154] Such an invitation to a Catholic ecclesiastic was unprecedented, and to O'Conor, writing to his son after he and Carpenter had attended their first meeting of the Committee, it represented 'a revolution in our moral and civil affairs the more extraordinary, as in my own days such a man would only be spoken to through the medium of a warrant and a constable'.[155] If, on the level of social interaction between Protestant and Catholic antiquaries, the Select Committee seemed to indicate a new departure, it was a severe disappointment in scholarly terms. Three thousand copies of an appeal for information about Gaelic manuscripts elicited forty replies and information about one manuscript, a copy of the 'Seancas Mór' which was held in the British Museum.[156] The only manuscript purchased with Dublin Society funds was not medieval in provenance, but much more recent and written either in Latin or English rather than Irish. This was Roderic O'Flaherty's unpublished response to Sir George MacKenzie's attack on *Ogygia*, which had been offered for sale to O'Conor but at too high a price.[157] He feared he would not recoup his money in subscriptions if he published it, 'the public [having] no Taste for our historical Controversies'.[158] Vallancey and Leland got the agreement of the Committee to purchase the manuscript and to invite O'Conor to edit it for publication. For O'Conor the attractions of the project were twofold. Firstly, it would allow him to respond to Macpherson's *Introduction to the History of Great Britain and Ireland* (1771), and to do so by appending an essay to O'Flaherty's earlier vindication of the Irish historiographical tradition against Scottish calumnies: 'Thus we should have the latter as well as the former Historical Hypotheses of the North British Writers demolished in one book.'[159] Secondly, O'Conor was deeply conscious of the political significance of the invitation from the Committee: 'Their recommendation [of the publication of the work] would, I own, be an inducement to me to undertake it.'[160] Thus, the publication of O'Conor's edition of O'Flaherty's *Ogygia Vindicated* (1775) represented his success in achieving not only institutional backing for his antiquarian work, but the patronage of some of the most influential Protestant politicians and churchmen. However, not even the backing of the Dublin Society could advance the more general project of making the Irish manuscript tradition available in English translation. It would take another two generations of scholars and the intervention of the Ordnance Survey to achieve this in the 1840s.[161]

O'Conor's growing unease with at least some aspects of the Gaelic historiographical tradition is clearly visible in his dealings with another Catholic antiquary, Sylvester O'Halloran. O'Halloran, a medical doctor and surgeon in

Limerick, was drawn into antiquarianism by Macpherson and the Ossian poems, and by the general scepticism about Irish tradition expressed by David Hume and others. His first excursion into print was in 1763 with an essay and an open letter to Macpherson published in Wilson's *Dublin Magazine*.[162] Next came *Insula Sacra* (1770), in which he decried the 'reproachful passiveness and silence' of 'the Irish nation' in the face of attacks 'on our History and Annals' by Hume and Macpherson.[163] He proposed a revival of 'our antient History', and two years later published his own contribution, *An Introduction to the Study of the History and Antiquities of Ireland* (1772).

This was a defiant restatement of much of the traditional lore (including the eponymous heroes, Scota, Gathelus and Milesius and his sons), more in keeping with the style of the younger O'Conor of the first edition of the *Dissertations*:

> By these [annals] it appears that from the most remote antiquity, the Irish were a LEARNED, a PIOUS, and WARLIKE nation; that they were originally a Scythian colony, who . . . first settled in Egypt; . . . that Niul . . . married Scota, daughter to the king of Egypt, and resided near the Red sea, and had an only son called Gathalus . . ., the Egyptians becoming jealous of these people, expelled them . . . they sailed to Spain and from thence invaded Ireland in thirty ships . . . [164]

The story of the migration of the Milesian Irish was to be believed, maintained O'Halloran, by virtue of its very status as tradition: 'We see the same unvarnished tale transmitted from age to age, from the remotest antiquity, without the least alteration'.[165] He also claimed that the island of Britain was named, not after Brutus of Troy as the British origin myth retailed, but after an Irish hero, Breotan, who at some unspecified but early time led a colony into northern Britain. For this he alleged support from 'the *Gabhalcha Eirion* [i.e. *Leabhar Gabhála*], or *Conquests of Ireland*, the *Psalter of Cashel*, and many other most respectable pieces of Irish antiquity'.[166] The tale of 'Briotan son of Fearghus Leithdhearg, son of Neimhidh', who went to dwell in the neighbouring island, was to be found in Keating's *Foras Feasa*, who gave as his source for it the very compilations listed by O'Halloran.[167] O'Halloran's work appears to have been heavily dependent on Keating, in spite of assurances to his readers that he possessed a copy of every manuscript that he cited.[168]

However, the collateral evidence which O'Halloran advanced in support of the Irish origin legend owed something to contemporary ideas of the study of the remote past. In claiming that a similarity of manners and customs existed between the early Irish, and the Egyptians, Greeks and Spanish, O'Halloran was following, albeit loosely, Hume's recommendation that research into remote origins should be confined to comparing the language, customs and manners of contiguous nations.[169] Adherence to the tradition meant that the element of proximity had to be ignored by O'Halloran, and the comparison of customs was very sketchy. The imprecision of the exercise can be demonstrated by one example: 'the very dress of the Spaniards is found exactly to agree with the old Irish one, . . . their customs are pretty much the same, and even their passion and inclinations.'[170]

While O'Conor limited his use of the claim of Spanish origins to argue for the early literacy of the Irish, O'Halloran employed it more freely over a range of topics. Thus for example, on the question of whether the Irish were building in stone before the Anglo-Norman conquest (often used in arguments over the benefits of colonisation), he argued that their knowledge of architecture had come from their Spanish and Egyptian ancestors.[171] These exaggerated claims made by O'Halloran for Gaelic tradition put increasing strains on his relationship with O'Conor, on whom he relied almost from the outset for help and approval.[172] Having had success in persuading O'Halloran that the Ossian poems were largely forgeries, O'Conor was less influential in shaping the *Introduction* (1772) and *The General History of Ireland* (1778). Their correspondence reveals O'Conor constantly urging caution to O'Halloran, in regard to his translations from the Irish, his etymologies and particularly his reliance on the accuracy of the annals for the earliest periods.[173] O'Conor was unenthusiastic about O'Halloran's *Introduction* when it was passed to him, being more impressed by the 'magnificent' production than the content.[174]

By the time of O'Halloran's second major work, *The General History of Ireland*, published in 1778, there was a complete rift between them, and O'Conor did not appear among the list of subscribers. O'Halloran's last known letter to O'Conor rehearsed the main point of disagreement between them:

> You kindly communicate to me, your opinion of our Antient History; and the very little Certainty to be Expected from our Early Annals. I own it has not Appeared to me, in quite so Unfavourable a light. I have Considered it in Every point of view, with Critical Severity; and do think, it claims a greater degree of Credit, than the remote Annals of any other Nation . . .[175]

The dispute between O'Conor and O'Halloran indicates the extent to which writing the ancient history of Ireland had become fraught for all those engaged in it by the late eighteenth century. While the origin question remained of central importance, attracting, if anything, more interest than before, it had become inextricably linked to the disputed status of the medieval historiographical tradition. Sceptics of, and believers in, that tradition waged bitter battles from the late 1770s onwards. New origin theories were propounded and fought over, but ultimately the same pattern predominated, in that the still recent history of colonisation was the shadowy backdrop against which they were seen and judged.

PHOENICIANS AND GOTHS:
the Milesian Origin Myth Undermined, 1770–1810

The new phase of Protestant interest in Irish antiquities in the third quarter of the eighteenth century was stimulated in part by two currents in general European cultural debate – orientalism and Gothicism. Great strides were being made in oriental studies as French and English scholars, such as Abraham Anquetil-Duperron and Sir William Jones, worked to recover and understand the Persian and Sanskrit languages from ancient manuscripts. These scholarly developments created a European vogue for the Orient (even greater than the Ossian-inspired vogue for the Scottish Highlands) which shaped nineteenth-century romanticism.[1] Gothicism was far less based on scholarship and was a wider current of thought that had been in existence for many centuries. It was centred around the heritage of the historic Germanic or Teutonic barbarian tribes, and thus was strongest in northern Europe, including England where the Anglo-Saxon past was increasingly emphasised.[2] Protestant writers, notably Charles Vallancey and Edward Ledwich, were quick to adapt ideas from orientalism and Gothicism to the question of Irish origins, with major consequences for the status of Gaelic tradition. Rather than disappearing from the antiquarian agenda, as was happening to foundation myths elsewhere, the Irish myth of a Milesian colonisation from Spain was transformed by Vallancey using orientalist theories, and subverted by Ledwich with the help of Scottish writers. This renewed emphasis on the origins question is an indication of the continued, and even growing, importance of the linked issues of ancestry and identity for Protestants in the late eighteenth century. Catholic antiquaries, such as Charles O'Conor, had hopes that Protestant interest in the origins question would help to defend the status of Gaelic tradition against the Enlightenment scepticism of David Hume, and more especially the direct challenge of James Macpherson. Ultimately, however, these later Protestant contributions to the origins debate reflected their own specific political and cultural needs and proved counter-productive in defending tradition.

Charles Vallancey was born in Flanders in 1726 to French Huguenot parents who moved to England when he was a child. Educated at Eton and the Royal Military Academy, Woolwich, he began his army career in 1747 in the Tenth Regiment, and was appointed to an engineers' corps when the regiment came to Ireland in 1750. He spent the rest of his long life in Ireland, attaining the rank of general, and combining his military work of fortification design and cartography with antiquarian pursuits.[3] In 1772, Vallancey wrote in great excitement to Charles O'Conor of an 'extraordinary discovery' involving the allegedly Carthaginian speech in Plautus' comedy *Poenulus*, which Vallancey claimed 'was as good Irish as can possibly be written in my humble opinion, spoken by an illiterate Carthaginian, transcribed by an ignorant soldier (such is the Interpreter Plautus introduces) and on Classic Ground'.[4] The Carthaginian or Punic speech in this play had fascinated scholars and philologists on the continent since the time of Joseph Scaliger (1540–1609). In *Geographiae Sacrae* (1646), the French scholar and friend of Sir James Ware Samuel Bochart, had argued that the speech was closely related to Hebrew.[5] Vallancey called Bochart a 'great orientalist' but believed that, through his ignorance of Irish, he had missed a vital link in the development of primitive languages.[6] Vallancey was not the first to see parallels between Gaelic and the Punic speech in *Plautus*. The Gaelic scholar and scribe Tadhg Ó Neachtain had made an Irish rendition, known to the late eighteenth-century scribe Theophilus O'Flanagan, who wrote a description on the inside cover of Ó Neachtain's manuscript, giving the Punic translation special mention and dating it to 1739.[7] It is probable that Vallancey had this manuscript in his possession, and announced Ó Neachtain's work as his own discovery.

However, there is some evidence that Vallancey's initial scholarly interest in the Irish language was stimulated by a recent work by James Parsons, and was only deflected towards 'Phoenicianism' by the Punic speech.[8] Parsons' *Remains of Japhet* (1767) was an investigation into the origin of European languages, which claimed that the Irish and Welsh were the 'original nations' of Europe and that their languages were dialects of 'Japhetan', which, together with Hebrew, were the tongues spoken before Babel.[9] As the 'only unmixed remains of the children of Japhet, upon the globe', he argued, they deserved 'more liberal treatment' by English writers.[10] Parsons was born in Devonshire, but educated in Ireland when his father took up a post as a barrack-master there.[11] He claimed to have studied Irish and to have read manuscripts such as the *Leabhar Gabhála*, but he drew primarily on Keating's *Foras Feasa* in translation and on O'Conor's *Dissertations*.[12] Parsons was an unusual figure in London society: a physician trained in Paris who became Foreign Secretary to the Royal Society, he dabbled in many fields other than language origins, and had a particular interest in deformities of the human body.[13] *Remains of Japhet* seems to have been merely a brief excursion into Celtic antiquities by Parsons, but it had a lasting impact on Vallancey.[14]

Much of the existing analysis of Vallancey concentrates on his first two publications, the *Essay on the Irish Language* (1772) and the *Grammar of the Iberno-Celtic Language* (1773). The *Essay* argues for both the 'strongest Affinity, (nay a perfect Identity in very many Words)' between Gaelic and 'the Celtic, Punic, Phoenician and Hebrew Languages' and declares it to be 'a Punic-Celtic Compound'. The implications of this for the status of Irish were great, making it 'a Language of the utmost Importance, and most desirable to be acquired

by all Antiquarians and Etymologists'.[15] Vallancey's claims for the eastern origin of Gaelic placed him with native Irish historians, such as O'Conor and
O'Halloran, who sought to uphold the traditional account of origins contained
in the *Leabhar Gabhála* and in Keating's *Foras Feasa*. At this early stage, Vallancey seemed to encourage this by citing Keating and other antiquaries in
support of the tradition of the 'Fomhoraicc's or African Pirates in Ireland' and
by including a reference to Edmund Spenser's acceptance of such a colony of
Phoenicians or Africans.[16] Native Irish writers always cited the positive
remarks of English commentators such as Spenser, and before him Giraldus
Cambrensis, as authoritative, by virtue of these writers' generally hostile perceptions of the country and its people. Vallancey also actively sought to identify with the native Irish perspective by denying his English origins in the
preface to the *Essay*, referring to himself in an offhand way as 'an Irish man
but little skilled in Hebrew'.[17] Although the *Essay* came out anonymously, he
signed the preface with his initials, which hardly indicated a serious desire to
hide his true identity.

The result of Vallancey's self-presentation was that he was perceived to be
not only an adherent of the native Irish or Catholic viewpoint, but also to share
in the political programme of the 'patriot' grouping in the Irish parliament.
The English antiquary Michael Lort, writing in 1784 to Thomas Percy, then
Bishop of Dromore in Co. Down, linked Vallancey's antiquarian and philological work with hopes for greater political freedom, which he had heard
expressed by 'many Irish officers, ecclesiastics and others' whom he had
encountered in his travels on the continent, and who seemed 'big with expectation of their island recovering that independence and pre-eminence which
it once had, as they supposed, over its sister island'. He finished by asking
rhetorically, 'To what do Vallancey's researches tend, but to prove she is the
elder sister?'[18] More recent commentators, Norman Vance and Joep Leerssen,
have also seen a political agenda behind Vallancey's eccentric theories. In a
valuable article on what he termed the 'Gaelo-Phoenicianism' of which Vallancey was the leading proponent, Leerssen pointed to its 'undeniable political dimension' and focused on a striking short passage in Vallancey's *Essay* for
proof. Writing of the scarcity of manuscript materials for Irish history, Vallancey made an explicit parallel between the Irish and Carthaginians, in terms
of their subjugation to imperial power. The great library of the Carthaginians
had been burned in the sack of the city by the Romans and, like the Irish, their
history had been written 'by their most bitter Enemies'.[19] Leerssen rightly
pointed to what he termed the 'explosiveness of an equation between
Irish–English and Carthaginian–Roman relations [which] could be lost on no
one', and he placed Vallancey and his theories squarely on the 'patriot' side of
the Irish political spectrum.[20] For Norman Vance, however, Vallancey had 'an
oddly touching romantic patriotism for a country not his own', and was spell-
bound by the Celtic past. Vallancey, according to this characterisation, was
'quite unconscious of any tension between his official position with the army

which supported the English domination of Ireland and his imaginative sympathy with the old Ireland before the coming of the invader'.[21] Both of these contradictory positions echo the contemporary perceptions of Vallancey as champion of the Catholic Irish and as Celtomaniac or dreamer, but an examination of his politics and of his voluminous writings over his long career reveal him to be a more complex figure than the Carthage–Rome parallel quoted above seems to indicate.

Vallancey's surviving correspondence concentrates mainly on his antiquarian interests and reveals little of his political opinions, beyond a limited support for Catholic relief, chiefly in relation to property law.[22] However, a close study of his writings show that he made further references to Carthage and Carthaginians in a number of his later works, but not all of these support the notion of a parallel with Ireland's situation. In an essay published in 1783 in *Collectanea de Rebus Hibernicis*, his own journal, he made brief reference to the Nemedians, one of older tribes on the island, suffering 'the yoke of the Carthaginians'.[23] In the following year in his *Vindication of the Ancient History of Ireland*, he was more explicitly negative about the Carthaginian impact on Ireland, referring to the inhabitants of Ireland in ancient times applying for relief from 'the Carthaginian yoke of slavery'.[24] Thus, some twelve to fourteen years after he first made the Carthage–Rome analogy, Vallancey was reversing or, at least, subverting it. His 'patriot' sympathies remained, in some respects, as a bizarre reference in an essay on the Brehon law tracts written in the same period shows. Collating terms from these manuscripts with Arabic (a language in which he had no training), he linked 'Gratan' with an Arabic word allegedly meaning 'a lord, a chief of a people, master of a family, most excellent'.[25] Given that this appeared in 1782, the year of 'legislative independence', and that these law tracts were notoriously difficult to decipher, this seems to be an imaginative piece of flattery directed at the leader of the 'patriot' group, Henry Grattan, and in that sense an example of the early beginnings of what has been termed 'the Grattan mystique'.[26] Twenty years later, he again used the Carthaginian–Irish trope, in the *Prospectus of a Dictionary of the Language of the Aire Coti, or, ancient Irish, compared with the Language of the Cuti, or ancient Persians* (1802), giving it a similar political meaning as the first time he had used it.[27] The reason why Vallancey temporarily abandoned the Carthaginian analogy in the 1780s may lie precisely in its explosive nature and his consequent unease at its use. Given his career ambitions in the army, it would have been politic to move back from the 'patriot' position.

However, a close examination of his early writings indicates that his politics were far less liberal than either contemporaries or later commentators have imagined. His second book, *A Grammar of the Iberno-Celtic, or Irish Language*, which came out in 1773, is important in this respect. Although Vallancey himself had but an imperfect grasp of Irish, he was helped in this project by two Irish speakers, Charles O'Conor and the scribe Maurice O'Gorman, who was later employed by the Royal Irish Academy. Their influence and the technical nature of the task meant that Vallancey had less space to indulge in his theories, and the result is that it is seen as the most useful of his books.[28] However, commentators thus far have failed to note that Vallancey envisaged the *Grammar* as a tool for Anglican proselytisation in Ireland, thus putting it in an established tradition.[29] In the 'Preface', he censured the Protestant clergy for 'their neglect of learning of the Irish tongue, which is the only language understood by one half of their parishioners, and the only language in which they will receive instruction'. Alluding to the efforts of Ussher, Bedell and Robert Boyle in the previous century to provide Irish language versions of the Old and New Testaments, which might 'induce the Irish, to consider a little better of the old and true way, from whence they have hitherto been misled', Vallancey launched an impassioned and pious appeal for unity 'under one shepherd': 'Shall one million inhabitants of this unhappy country be deprived of reading the scriptures, and judging for themselves? Is there no bishop Bedell, no Robert Boyle left among us?'[30]

This call for a renewed campaign of proselytisation through Irish can be interpreted as a cynical attempt to ensure the sale of the *Grammar* to the widest possible market. However, there is some evidence that Vallancey did actually support such a campaign, and did not hold to the idea of even limited religious toleration for Catholics.[31] Among the papers of Thomas Orde, Chief Secretary in Dublin Castle from 1784 to 1787, who formulated a proposal for a national education scheme, there is an unsigned note by Vallancey on the education of Irish Catholics, advocating a strategy to deny them access, ultimately, to any. Catholics should be included in such a scheme, in the expectation that 'foreign powers' who at present indulged them 'in an education gratis . . . will certainly take away these privileges if they consent to, or accept of a domestick education'. Having thus caused the closure of the Irish colleges abroad, 'we may pass an act of Parliament taking from them, the principle of domestick education now held out to them: – it has been done in former ages and may again be repeated'.[32] Thus, Vallancey's sentimental attachment to a country not his own evidently did not extend to its majority religious community. He clearly supported the more conservative wing of the patriot movement, represented by Henry Flood and Lord Charlemont, who opposed the further relaxation of the popery laws. Moreover, his contempt for poor Catholics comes across in the plentiful, dismissive and sometimes hostile references to them, including calling spoken Gaelic the 'jargon yet spoke by the unlettered vulgar'.[33]

Vallancey's sincere identification with Anglicanism marks him definitively apart from Catholic antiquaries who made similar claims for the antiquity of the Irish language. He himself strove to make apparent the distance separating him from their project, writing in 1783, 'I am of no party, have no system to support, but write for information.'[34] However, this public disclaimer was at least partly belied by his explanation to the English antiquary Thomas Burgess that while he was indeed a defender of 'the ancient Irish History', his aim was to 'bring forth a new System of the History of the continent and of the Britannic Isles'.[35] Irish history and the Irish language were not the primary focus, but rather a tool to explicate wider philology and history, and in particular to further understanding of the close links between oriental and western European languages. The dual nature of his self-perceived role, as vindicator of Irish history and as orientalising philologist, was apparent as early as 1773 in the *Grammar.* On the one hand, he claimed that this work had been 'involuntarily drawn' from him because of the 'repeated indignities . . . cast on the history and antiquities of this once famed and learned island, by many writers of Great Britain'. On the other, however, he explained that it had been prematurely published, owing to the urgings 'of many learned men, not only of Great Britain and Ireland, but of many other states of Europe', who held the view that 'the primitive Iberno-Celtic, or Irish Language, which by being preserved in all its purity in this sequestered island, is the only key to the ancient history of these great European nations'.[36]

Vallancey's project was far more novel than his contemporaries allowed, and indeed than most cultural historians and literary scholars of Ireland have understood until recently. Thomas Trautmann's *Aryans and British India* (1997) is particularly important in situating Vallancey in an imperial rather than purely Irish context.[37] This is a survey of the impact in Britain of the Indo-European or Aryan concept, a new theory of language formulated in the late eighteenth century and derived from acquaintance with Sanskrit, the ancient language of India. Trautmann argues that Sir William Jones, the foremost English philologist and jurisprudence expert employed by the British East India Company, who first posited the idea of an Indo-European language family, did so as part of an ethnological rather than philological project. Jones aimed to investigate the origins of the three peoples of Asia, namely, Indians, Arabs and Tartars, using not only language and letters, but also religion and philosophy, architecture and sculpture, and arts and manufactures. In his annual Anniversary Discourses to the Asiatick Society of Bengal between 1784 and 1794, Jones revealed his findings, which in essence amounted to an attempt to reconcile the history of Asia with that put forward in the Bible. Thus, according to Jones, these three original peoples were the offspring of the three sons of Noah, namely, Ham, Shem and Japhet. In Trautmann's view, the entire project was one of 'forming a rational defense of the Bible out of the materials collected by Orientalist scholarship, more specifically a defense of the Mosaic account of human history in its earliest times'.[38] Jones's work, therefore, can be placed in a tradition that also encompassed Isaac Newton's chronological work, which had been influential on Charles O'Conor, and the Greek mythological studies by Jacob Bryant, which, as will later appear, were formative for Vallancey. The central aim of this tradition was to provide independent corroboration of the Bible's version of history after the Flood.[39] Additionally, Jones aimed to safeguard this new phase of orientalist scholarship of which he was steward, by ensuring that its largely positive appraisal of the

Hindu religion and culture could not be presented as undermining of Christianity. According to Trautmann, it was a project 'to make the new Orientalism safe for Anglicans'.[40]

This theory, however, ignores the extent to which Jones's Sanskrit scholarship was predicated on his judicial role, as Hans Aarsleff pointed out in *The Study of Language in England, 1780–1860* (1967). Jones embarked on the study of Sanskrit in 1785, two years after his arrival in Calcutta as a judge of the Supreme Court of Judicature. Realising that he needed to know native law at first hand and that he could place 'no reliance . . . on the opinions or interpretations of the professors of the Hindu law, unless he were qualified to examine their authorities and quotations, and detect their errors and misrepresentations', he began to study the ancient language in which native Indian law had been written. Within a year, he was expressing satisfaction that he had made sufficient progress in it to make it 'an impossibility for the Mohammedan or Hindu lawyers to impose upon us with erroneous opinions'.[41] Aarsleff comments that 'an ancient language once more became the object of learned attention because it contained the law that still governed the present', making an analogy with the Elizabethan study of Anglo-Saxon, but a far more exact parallel can be made with the Elizabethan and Stuart colonisation projects in Ireland, in which considerable attention was paid to native Irish or Brehon law by English administrators, in a bid to extend their control.[42]

By the 1780s Vallancey was visibly aligning himself with both the scholarly and political concerns of the major figures of what Raymond Schwab called 'the Oriental Renaissance'.[43] His awareness of the political liabilities associated with work on Irish antiquities, which were increasing in this decade of agrarian unrest in Munster, may have been an additional reason for Vallancey to relocate his topic. As an army officer and military engineer in charge of fortification, Vallancey was closely involved with Dublin Castle in their efforts to quell the Rightboy disturbances.[44] At the same time, he was pushing the ostensible roots of Gaelic culture and pre-Christian religion further into the Orient, until his work bore virtually no relation to that of O'Conor or earlier Irish writers, and was thus distanced from their political agenda. While his researches were still ostensibly based on Gaelic manuscript sources, and he considered himself a defender of Irish tradition, publishing *A Vindication of the Ancient History of Ireland* in 1786 and *A Further Vindication* in 1804, it was a tradition largely of his own creation. In the second edition of the *Grammar*, which came out in 1781, Jacob Bryant supplanted Sir Lucius O'Brien (who had been president of the by-now defunct Select Committee on Antiquities of the Dublin Society) as dedicatee, and an essay was added 'shewing the Importance of the Iberno-Celtic or Irish Dialect, to Students in History, Antiquity, and the Greek and Roman Classics'.[45] Bryant's monumental analysis of Greek mythology, *A New System, or, an Analysis of Ancient Mythology*, which appeared between 1774 and 1776, compared biblical history with certain Greek classical histories, in order to prove that the former was 'most assuredly true' in

every particular. Sir William Jones disapproved of Bryant's etymological methods, but embraced his conclusions.[46] Vallancey was particularly taken with
Bryant's relatively sophisticated view of mythology, which did not assess it
wholly on the basis of either truth or fable, as Enlightenment thinking tended
to do, but saw it as growing organically from tribal memory. Bryant set out 'to
shew, that all the rites and mysteries of the Gentiles were only so many memorials of their principal ancestors; and of the great occurrences, to which they
had been witnesses'.[47] This approach was adopted wholeheartedly by Vallancey in *A Vindication of the History of Ireland* (1786).

Without stating so directly, Vallancey's *Vindication* was predicated on Keating's *Foras Feasa*, underlining again how this work, in its English translation,
stood for the whole corpus of Irish medieval historiography, rather than being
regarded as a relatively recent narrative account based on it.[48] However, Vallancey's defence of Keating's work was not based around the argument that it
was an accurate record of the remote Irish past, but rather the opposite. Under
Bryant's influence, Vallancey claimed that the early Irish, like all migrating peoples, had retained memories of their ancestors' travels and had incorporated
them into their history in an adapted form. Irish manuscript histories recorded
their epic journey from Asia through eastern Europe to the outer reaches of
western Europe, and thus contained the key to all the great civilisations of the
world, east and west: 'the fabulous history of the Greeks is borrowed of the
ancient Persians and is to be discovered in what is improperly called the
ancient history of Ireland'.[49] He blamed this confusion of mythology with history, which had led to a 'general disgust' with traditional Irish accounts, on
'the ignorance of the Translators, who, zealous for the antiquity of their Country, did not, or would not see, that the early periods of this History, related not
to Ireland, but to those parts of Asia their Ancestors came from'. These 'translators' had misunderstood the term 'Eirin', taking it to mean Ireland, when it
really referred to Iran or Persia.[50] By this sleight of hand, Vallancey wholly ori-
entalised his project and at the same time actively identified himself with the
British and French scholars of the Oriental Renaissance. He clearly saw himself doing for Ireland's ancient law tracts, the Brehon laws, what Anquetil-
Duperron and Sir William Jones were in the process of doing in their
commentaries on Hindu law.[51] In one of his essays on the Brehon laws, Vallancey praised their work and 'the pains they have taken to free the eastern
nations from *barbarism* and *despotism*, by proving these people to have had a
written law, time immemorial, [which] reflects honour on their humanity'.[52]
Shorn of the term 'despotism', an indispensable element of the western stereotype of the Orient, this was an apt description of Vallancey's concept of his
own role in Ireland. His aim in publishing translations of the Brehon laws was
'to demonstrate that so far from being savage and barbarous, the [Irish] were
refined, polished and learned'.[53]

There were obvious parallels between Vallancey's career as a soldier,
engineer and cartographer in Ireland, and the orientalists of the East India

Company, all of whom, whether soldiers or not, were engaged directly in the colonial enterprise.[54] Indeed, the fact that Sir William Jones compiled a Persian grammar in 1771 specially for the use of the East India Company, may well have encouraged Vallancey to publish his grammar two years later.[55] Trautmann, however, minimises Jones's formative influence on Vallancey, alleging that the latter's adoption of the Mosaic account of the peopling of the world, which was prominent in the preface to his *Grammar of Iberno-Celtic*, predated his enthusiastic immersion in the findings of the new orientalism.[56] This makes little sense, since in that same book Vallancey mentioned favourably 'the laborious works of the learned Jones', presumably referring to Jones's *Grammar*.[57] Trautmann's confusion stems from his failure to recognise that there were two separate and distinct phases to Jones's scholarship, one Persian in the late 1760s and early 1770s, and one focused on Sanskrit, a full ten years later following his legal studies.[58] Vallancey was equally influenced by both.

Late in his career, Jones offered important, if indirect, encouragement for the theory of a common Celtic and Indian origin, through his speculations about the relationship between Celtic and the Persian and Sanskrit languages; in one instance, he noted a resemblance between Celtic ogham script and Persian runes.[59] Vallancey took Jones's musings several stages further, as was his wont, and extrapolated from them definite racial and cultural links between Ireland and India, claiming that 'the Brahmins deriv[ed] their origin from the Tuatha Dadann of Irish history, being a mixture of the Southern Scythians with the Dedanites of Chaldaea'.[60] When Vallancey sent Jones a copy of the *Vindication*, he responded in a diplomatic vein, deeming it a 'learned work' which he had read with pleasure, but added: 'We shall soon I hope see faithful translations of Irish histories and poems. I shall be happy in comparing them with the Sanskrit, with which the ancient language of Ireland had certainly had an affinity.'[61] As Garland Cannon has pointed out, the phrase 'faithful translations' was a coded critique of Vallancey's project,[62] but the letter was quoted in Dublin as evidence of the renowned orientalist's support for his work.[63] Jones gave his honest estimation to a more intimate correspondent: 'Have you met with a book lately published with the title of a *Vindication of the Ancient History of Ireland*? It was written by a friend of mine, Colonel Vallancey; but a word in your ear – it is very stupid.' He dismissed the claim that the Irish were descended from the Persians as 'visionary' and was 'certain, that [Vallancey's] derivations from the Persian, Arabick and Sanscrit languages, are erroneous'.[64]

However, if the renowned 'Oriental' Jones was only distantly polite to Vallancey about his work, some others offered him encouragement and a measure of co-operation. Significantly, these were scholars who, like Vallancey, pursued visionary schemes unfettered by scholarly caution or scepticism. The Anglican cleric Thomas Maurice was among the first to write histories of ancient India without the benefit of knowing Sanskrit. Relying heavily on Jones's work, Maurice produced an impressive looking list of publications, including *Indian Antiquities* in seven volumes (1794–1800). According to Trautmann, 'T[t]he whole structure and much of the substance of these works is from Jones, but without his genius'.[65] Maurice's primary object was to counteract the attraction of the Hindu religion as a possibly older, and an alternative system of belief to Christianity, and he enlisted Vallancey in his campaign to prove, *pace* Jones, that Hinduism was derived from Mosaical theology and could be used, therefore, to affirm the truth of Christian scripture.[66] In *Sanscreet Fragments, or Interesting Extracts from the Sacred Books of the Brahmins, on Subjects Important to the British Isles* (1798) Maurice adopted Vallancey's thesis about an Indo-Scythic migration to Ireland, and, using information that could only have been supplied by him, claimed that Lough Derg had been a place of pagan pilgrimage where 'bloody Mithraic rites were once celebrated'.[67] He also included a translation by Vallancey of an 'ancient Irish manuscript', a hymn to the sun, in which the latter asserted that 'T[t]he ancient heathen deities of the pagan Irish[,] Criosan, Biosena, and Seeva, or Sheeva, are doubtless the Creeshna, Veeshnu, Brahma, and Seeva, of the Hindoos'.[68] All of this was held by Maurice to corroborate his claim in the sixth volume of *Indian Antiquities* that an ancient Brahmin colony had visited the British Isles.[69]

Both Maurice and Vallancey were drawing on the work of Francis Wilford, an officer in the army of the East India Company, who was one of the first Europeans to study India's legendary history and geography, contained in manuscripts known as the Purānas.[70] Like Jones and Maurice, Wilford was also aiming to prove that there had originally been but one natural religion: 'the greatest part of the legends, which formerly obtained all over the Western parts of the world, from India to the British Isles, were originally the same with those found in the mythology of the Hindus.'[71] He also detected Christian symbols, such as the cross of Calvary, in Hinduism, in support of his overall argument that it had evolved from Old Testament religion.[72] But Wilford introduced a new and more overtly imperial dimension to British orientalism in his work on ancient Indian geography. He claimed to have found evidence in the Purānas that 'the White Island' referred to in Hindu mythology was England and that the British Isles were the 'Sacred Isles of the Hindus'.[73] Wilford sent this passage from the Purānas to Vallancey via a mutual acquaintance, Gore Ouseley, and Vallancey, not surprisingly, enthusiastically endorsed this interpretation.[74] In his own reading of the passage, Vallancey found references to Ireland, notably the Giant's Causeway, which Wilford incorporated into his findings, later published in *Asiatick Researches*, the journal of the Asiatic Society of Bengal.[75] His 'Essay on the Sacred Isles in the West' concluded that the British Isles were not only sacred in Hindu mythology, but also among the Greeks, and were renowned as such in all mythologies, including 'by the followers both of Brahma and Budd'ha, by the Chinese, and even by the wild inhabitants of the Philippine Islands'.[76] Thus, the great gains which the British empire had made in Asia in the Seven Years War were pre-ordained in the mythologies of Asia. Wilford's exploitation of Indian culture sanctioned not only the paramount status of the Christian religion of the coloniser (as others such as Jones had done) but, more specifically, it justified the British colonial enterprise in India as natural and beneficent. Moreover, in the introduction to this essay, Wilford made a confession which, in its outlines, encapsulated the colonial essence of this scholarship. He had studied Sanskrit with a 'pandit', the term for a Hindu learned in ancient Indian languages, philosophy, religion and jurisprudence. When Wilford had embarked on his study of the Purānas, he had enlisted this pandit as his research assistant to read through the manuscripts and make extracts, having briefed him about the information sought. Unfortunately, the pandit had obligingly forged lengthy passages which Wilford had used in some of his articles published earlier in *Asiatick Researches*, and much admired by Sir William Jones. The discovery of this fraud caused Wilford some embarrassment but not enough to abandon his 'White Island' thesis to which he was ideologically committed.[77]

The colonial relationship of pandit and Captain Wilford in Bengal mirrors that of Colonel Vallancey and his scribe and Irish teacher, Maurice O'Gorman, in Dublin. Although there are no known instances of similar fraudulence on the part of Vallancey's scribes, the circumstances were the same: the scribe was poor, his only capital being his knowledge of the colonised culture. The army officer had ultimate power, yet was completely dependent on the scribe's help to cement his reputation as an authority on this culture. It is almost impossible to document the relationship between Vallancey and O'Gorman (all that remains are casual references in the correspondence of Vallancey and O'Conor).[78] But it was almost certainly even more unequal and ambiguous, more clearly a relationship between coloniser and colonised subject, than that revealed in the letters exchanged between Vallancey and Charles O'Conor, who was, in many respects, his social equal. It was to O'Conor that Vallancey first turned for help when he began to study the Irish language in 1771. O'Conor, writing to his close friend John Curry, referred to a 'very kind letter from Mr Vallancey, requiring some satisfaction about the antiquity of our Irish literature', but basically dismissed him as one of the 'mere holiday readers and writers who have much curiosity to gratify, and *perhaps a name to establish by new discoveries in the wilds of antient times*' [my italics].[79] By the following year, O'Conor was taking Vallancey more seriously, and Vallancey in turn was making more demands on him, at one stage looking for Irish proverbs and for Gaelic poems with translations 'to dress up this Embryo infant', meaning his *Essay on the Antiquity of the Irish Language*.[80] This was before Vallancey had come upon the Ó Neachtain manuscript which diverted him into Phoenicianism. O'Conor was enthusiastic about the *Essay*, which he saw as providing much needed support for the tradition of a Spanish colony and the early use of letters in Ireland, then under attack from James Macpherson.[81] In order to alert the British reading public (always his aim), he wrote to the *London Chronicle* in 1772, welcoming Vallancey as a follower of the principles of comparativist linguistic study laid down by Lhuyd and Leibniz, and as an opponent of those like Macpherson who dismissed the study of ancient manuscripts as worthless, and relied instead on etymologies.[82] Given Vallancey's subsequent departure into the wilds of etymology and Hindu mythology, O'Conor's hopes were misplaced. He continued to extol the virtues of the *Essay*,[83] but in his correspondence with Vallancey he adopted a cautionary tone about the later projects, mitigated by a pronounced deference to Vallancey's position. The latter was well known for taking umbrage at the mildest criticism, and O'Conor soon learned to hold back accordingly. As Vallancey's designs became more ambitious he became even more dependent on O'Conor. He planned an Irish dictionary with corresponding oriental words, and made clear that he would be calling on O'Conor for considerable assistance: 'as you would recollect the Corresponding Word in the Irish as soon as I read the Hebrew Word, whereas I have to seek it under all the various modes of Orthography – a laborious [undertaking] you must acknowledge.'[84]

Vallancey soon made it plain that he found it hard to accept O'Conor having divergent views from his own, and greeted what appears to have been the latter's change of opinion to conform with his own thus: 'I never received a letter which gave me so much pleasure than your last – we now start from the same goal [sic].'[85] By 1773, O'Conor was deferring in a sycophantic manner to Vallancey, who had proved that his interest in the Irish language and antiquities was of a longer duration and immeasurably more effective than most 'holiday readers'. In the same year he was instrumental in the establishment of the Dublin Society's Committee of Antiquities and in procuring for O'Conor an invitation to become a corresponding member of it. O'Conor was drawing up an essay which he hoped the Committee would sponsor, and wrote to Vallancey, 'I purpose to make use of your *Discoveries* in notes to strengthen what I have advanced in the *Memoir*, so that the Committee of Antiquarians think it worthy of publication.'[86] While this may have been a matter of calculated flattery, it also indicated O'Conor's awareness of the exalted reputation and influence which Vallancey had achieved following the publication of his *Essay*. He now needed Vallancey as much, if not more, than Vallancey needed him. O'Conor's fawning reached new depths in 1774:

> You have been destined to restore our Irish Celtic to its primitive vigor, as well as trace it to its true roots . . . Your publications will become more and more important, more and more called for in France and England, as you proceed . . . In any service you assign me, you will find me most ready; for in some departments I think I may be useful to you.[87]

By the 1780s he was reluctant to point out any errors made by Vallancey for fear of how his criticism would be received. Writing in 1781 to his friend Thomas O'Gorman about the most recent volume of Vallancey's *Collectanea de Rebus Hibernicis*, he commented: 'I found some capital mistakes . . . as well as some good observations, but I thought it not polite to point out those mistakes to the Colonel except in one or two instances, which I trust gave him no offense.'[88] He did venture to correct one of Vallancey's etymologies, in a letter of 1784 which was deferential in the extreme (perhaps in compensation), but was forced to withdraw this humbly in his next: 'I thank you for shewing me my mistake.' Nevertheless, he stubbornly repeated his warning that Vallancey should only publish 'such [etymologies] . . . as will be thoroughly satisfactory, Such I mean as no Supercilliousness [sic] of Criticism can lay hold on.'[89] Vallancey's vanity and growing defensiveness was such that O'Conor no longer felt his advice was heeded. In 1786, when Vallancey sent him a draft of what was probably the introduction to his *Vindication*, O'Conor observed resignedly to Thomas O'Gorman that he had 'ventured to mark out one [mistake] . . . and probably he [Vallancey] is satisfied still that the mistake is on my side, not on his'.[90]

In Vallancey we see the conjunction of two parallel cultural phenomena of the late eighteenth century that Trautmann has termed Indomania and Celtomania. He sees them as running together 'at a rather profound level', in that 'an openness to the one tends to go with an openness toward the other, and that, contrarily, anti-Irish feeling on the part of the English and the Scots tends to go with hostility towards the Indians and, as well, toward the claims of language to show a relationship among them'.[91] This benign description of the two enthusiasms is correct on one level, but more fundamentally, the political values informing both could be, and often were, profoundly colonial and therefore exploitative. If Vallancey's frequently hostile references to the popular culture of the Irish poor are taken as representative of his views of the majority Irish population, then he can hardly be said to be 'open' in Trautmann's terms.[92] Instead, in both cases, we see the manipulation of the subject culture and heritage by officers of the imperial power for purely domestic purposes.

Vallancey built his considerable reputation on the back of the *Essay* and the *Grammar*.[93] On its appearance, the *Essay* had sparked off an immediate interest in Gaelic in Trinity College Dublin, which had long ceased to offer teaching in the language.[94] Vallancey reported that two Fellows, one a biblical scholar, had begun lessons, having been 'convinced' by him 'of the strong Affinity between Irish and Hebrew'.[95] He also received private praise from Edmund Burke, and an offer from Thomas Barnard to translate the *Essay* into Latin to ensure a wider audience.[96] Yet the only antiquary to embrace his ideas to the extent of adopting them in his work was Sylvester O'Halloran. His *General History of Ireland*, published in 1778, opened with a reference to the Babylonian, Chaldaean, Egyptian and Chinese chronologies and their application to Irish history, which allowed him to give an exact date for the arrival of the Milesian colony.[97] He also adopted the Carthaginian–Irish parallel as first put forward by Vallancey, by writing about the Carthaginians in the same terms as he wrote about the early Irish. Thus, the Carthaginians had been 'a learned as well as a most powerful people' who 'were a much more polished people than the Romans themselves'. They had suffered from the 'wretched policy' which the Romans had adopted from the Greeks, of 'representing all their enemies as barbarous'.[98] Characteristically, O'Halloran went even further than Vallancey with this Irish–Carthaginian link, arguing for continuous contact between Carthage and Ireland after the settlement there of the Carthaginian Milesians, and surmising that they had sent troops to fight alongside their kin in the second Punic war against the Romans. He defended the 'rashness' of this 'conjecture' by reference to the 'days of distress and persecution, which followed the Reformation' when the Irish fought in the service of France and Spain: 'why doubt [then] the probability and possibility of their lending their troops to the Carthaginians in days of splendour, especially when the country was so full of inhabitants.'[99]

But within a few years Vallancey's ideas came under attack from Edward Ledwich, whose 'Scandian' theory of Irish origins was derived from Boxhorn's Nordic model, and thus posited a northern or Scandinavian route of colonisation, which ran directly contrary to Vallancey and to the tradition of a Spanish colony.[100] The debate between them was played out in the pages of Vallancey's own journal, *Collectanea de Rebus Hibernicis*, which he had put at the disposal of the Hibernian Antiquarian Society. This short-lived successor to the Select Committee on Antiquities of the Dublin Society was set up in 1779 with the backing of William Burton Conyngham, a prominent and wealthy politician and official in Dublin Castle. The aim of the new society was to publish drawings and descriptions of Ireland's antiquities. Vallancey and Ledwich were among the seven members (O'Conor was another), but the heat of their quarrel over Vallancey's orientalist speculations was such that the society was disbanded in 1783.[101]

Vallancey's later works were not as well received, quite understandably, since they became ever more eccentric, rambling and incoherent. In the *Vindication of the Ancient History of Ireland* (1786), his longest and most ambitious book, the structure of the text collapsed, as he failed to control either his material or his thoughts, and information spilled over into vast notes, with annotations even to items in the index.[102] It was after this that a letter-writing campaign ridiculing Vallancey got under way in the *Dublin Chronicle*, with contributions by Ledwich, Thomas Campbell and William Beauford.[103] Yet there were many who, while recognising the tendentiousness of much of his later work, were loath to condemn him, because of their continued support for the Celto-Phoenicianism of his *Essay* and *Grammar.* This emerges very clearly from the correspondence of Daniel Beaufort, a Protestant clergyman with antiquarian interests who drew up a map of the island, which was published with a commentary.[104] In January 1790 he wrote to a Danish acquaintance with some reluctant praise for Ledwich's theories: 'you will see that he rejects entirely the antient Milesian or Phenician history of the colonisation of Ireland . . . I believe there is much more of the truth, certainly less fable, in his hypothesis, if I may call it so, than in O'Flaherty's and his followers.'[105] But two months later, in a letter to Joseph Cooper Walker, author of *Historical Memoirs of the Irish Bards* (1786), he confessed that he could not regard 'the Milesian story' as entirely apochryphal, 'tho[ough] it be covered over with fabulous wonders', and ultimately put his trust in Vallancey's *Essay* rather than in Ledwich: 'The punick scene of Plautus has great weight in that scale, and an able orientalist, to whom I lately lent [it] was highly pleased with it.'[106] Walker himself continued to accept an oriental link, and in a commentary on some of the poems translated by Charlotte Brooke in *Reliques of Irish Poetry* (1789), compared one named 'Conloch' to the Persian epic *Shah Namah*, and said of another that it 'bears evident marks of an oriental origin'.[107] Other writers felt caught between the two hypotheses and their supporters, and had to seek advice. For instance, William Hamilton, who published an account of Co. Antrim which covered the geology and antiquities of the area, wrote to Lord Charlemont in the mid 1780s, wondering how to 'conduct' himself in relation to 'the Milesian Irish, whom I am neither competent to defend, nor willing to desert'. The dangers of the situation were clear to him: 'The Scandinavians will certainly souse me in the Baltic, for any word which I may chance giddily to say: and the Milesians will as surely hang me up, for what I may omit to say.'[108] His way out of this dilemma was to avoid mention of the subject of origins in his book.[109]

Vallancey's reputation may have remained high in 'patriot' circles, however, through the 1780s, to judge by the will of Henry Flood, drawn up in 1790. Flood stipulated that a considerable portion of his estate should be left to Trinity College Dublin to promote the study of Irish, by the purchase of Gaelic manuscripts and by the establishment of a Chair of Irish philology, the first holder of which should be Vallancey, 'seeing that by his eminent and successful labours in the study and recovery of that language he well deserves to be so first appointed'.[110] The bequest was controversial and was immediately challenged by Flood's family, causing his close friend Lawrence Parsons to produce a pamphlet defending it.[111] Flood had never appeared to have any interest in antiquarian or philological matters, but Parsons avowed that this was far from the case. Flood, he maintained, 'was wont to combine the most distant things; to bring the East and West into a juxta-position' and had seen the parallels between the East India Company scholars and Vallancey:

> Often did Mr Flood remark to me, that while in the East ingenious men were collecting and translating, with such laudable industry, the antient writings of the inhabitants of that region between [the] Indus and the Ganges, the valuable memorials of our own island were neglected and perishing.

Thus, for a 'patriot' like Flood, Vallancey's orientalist phase was not alienating or seen as an aberration. According to Parsons at least, Flood fully subscribed to the notion that 'many of the truths of antient history were to be found at these two extremities of the lettered world' and that from 'the comparison of these extremes' would emerge 'the immutable coincidences of truth'.[112] Like in his earlier Celto-Phoenicianist work, the later Vallancey could still be perceived as promoting the self-image of Ireland, and more particularly of Irish Protestants in their struggle for parity of rights with Englishmen.[113]

However, the Scandian thesis continued to grow in influence throughout the 1780s, partly in response to the renewed interest in the Saxon or Gothic[114] heritage of Britain, and particularly to the work of the Scottish antiquary and Goths enthusiast John Pinkerton. Research into the Saxon past in England had been stimulated in the first instance by the Reformation. Protestant antiquaries such as John Bale and Matthew Parker traced the roots of the reformed church to the Anglo-Saxon period, in which the church was said to have been independent of Rome.[115] Religious needs gave way to political argument in the seventeenth century when, in their conflict with the Stuart kings, parliamentarians derived their liberties from the Anglo-Saxons, and antiquaries searched records for proof that the English parliament had its origins in an earlier Anglo-Saxon institution.[116] Allied to this Saxonist theory of political origins was the corollary concept of the 'Norman Yoke', which identified monarchical absolutism as an alien import of William the Conqueror.[117] These theories, together with developments in historiography, were responsible for the decline in status of Geoffrey of Monmouth's twelfth-century history which had put forward a British origin myth designed to unite the various peoples of England and Wales.[118] What had begun as a theory in religious and political controversy quickly took shape as a new Saxonist foundation myth of the English nation. However, as Colin Kidd has recently established, elements of the British myth, in particular the idea of an ancient British parliament antedating any Saxonist foundation, continued to have a place in the political lexicon right up into the nineteenth century.[119]

Significant re-formulations of 'the Norman yoke' and Saxonist political theories began to appear in the second half of the eighteenth century, as part of a renewed interest in parliamentary reform stimulated by the Wilkesite agitation and the American revolution.[120] In Scotland, the radical 'Friends of the People' adapted the ideas of the English radical and Saxonist John Cartwright, and, claiming that the Saxon or Gothic inheritance belonged to the whole of Britain, declared that the free constitution of Scotland was as ancient as that of England.[121] This kind of adaptation of English political ideas, part of the pattern of Scottish response to their subordinate position in the British state, was not always possible in the Irish context. For example, the political implications of the 'Norman Yoke' thesis were different in Ireland. For native Irish writers, the idea of a 'Norman Yoke' had obvious political value, but not in the context of Saxon freedoms, since by their own accounts the Irish were Celts or Scytho-Celts, Egyptian and Spanish in origin, who developed their own individual constitution and society without reference to the rest of Europe. According to this formulation, the Anglo-Normans undermined a specifically *Irish* polity which had developed independently of British models, whether Saxon or not.

Irish Protestant historians, by contrast, seeing colonisation as the progenitor of modern Irish institutions, identified the Normans in Ireland as a progressive force, although mitigated by a belief that they had also been responsible for Romanising the independent Irish church.[122] In William Molyneux's *The Case of Ireland, Stated* (1698), the classic text of Protestant 'patriot' sentiment, which defended the right of the Irish parliament to be the sole legislative body for Ireland, virtually the entire argument turned on the medieval parliamentary rights and privileges of the Anglo-Normans and their Old English descendants. Arguing that the Irish parliament had been established by Henry II on the same principles as that of England, Molyneux tried to show that laws had been enacted in Ireland 'by the *Peoples* [sic] *consent in Parliament*, to which we have had a very *antient Right*, and as full a Right as our next Neighbours can pretend to or challenge'. Thus, the Irish parliament had enjoyed, and should enjoy once more, the full Gothic liberties of its sister parliament in the mother country. Together, they were the chief survivors of 'this noble Gothick Constitution' and should be preserved as such.[123] Molyneux was aware of the flaw in this logic; given that the Old English had remained Catholic and pro-Stuart and had had their lands confiscated, claims of institutional or settler continuity with the Anglo-Norman past seemed not only forced, but also potentially compromising. Once again, ethnic origins proved to be an awkward question for Irish Protestants of recent settler ancestry. While they could lay claim to a Gothic identity via that ancestry, the rights of their parliament and indeed of their church were predicated on native Irish and Old English heritages. It is not surprising therefore that Protestant antiquaries tried to appropriate these as their own.

The 'Scandian' theory can be seen in this light, as an attempt by its proponents to establish the Gothic racial origins of all of the inhabitants of Ireland. Thus, they were particularly influenced by the Scottish antiquary John Pinkerton, whose theory of the Gothic origins of the Scots was also limited to the racial issue. Gothicism in Ireland was sectarian in its basis in a way that Celticism had not been. In Scotland, however, the division between Celticists and Gothicists was not religious, but was based on geo-political perspectives. The major Celticists were from the Highlands, notably James Macpherson and his distant cousin John Macpherson (1710–65).[124] Pinkerton was a Lowlander, born in Lanarkshire, and strongly hostile towards Highlanders and Gaelic culture. According to Leah Leneman, Lowland perceptions of the Highlanders underwent considerable change in the second half of the eighteenth century, following the eclipse of clan society after Culloden. Earlier views of the Highlanders as barbaric softened as the Jacobite threat receded after the '45, and a process of romanticisation began. This was intensified by Macpherson's Ossian poems, and led to the adoption of Highland accoutrements such as bagpipes, tartans and kilts as national dress.[125] Scotland was also affected by the conjunction of Celtomania and Indomania, partially mediated through Vallancey's writings. In his address to the Society of Antiquaries in Scotland in

1787, the Earl of Buchan, who was an acquaintance of Vallancey's, referred to Sir William Jones's recent discovery of the Asiatic origin of the European peoples, and suggested that a comparison of 'the religious ceremonies and customs of the ancient Highlanders . . . with those described by the Asiatic Society of antiquaries' would produce 'much important reflection'.[126] In a similar vein, a Scottish follower of Vallancey tried, without success, to convince John Pinkerton that Highland customs such as the practice of singing while grinding the corn 'shows our Celts to have been of Eastern origin'.[127] Jones's affirmation of the kinship between Celtic and Persian and Sanskrit gave a boost to Scots Gallic enthusiasts, as can be seen in Alexander Stewart's *Elements of Gaelic Grammar* (1801), which boasted that 'the Gaelic bears a much closer affinity to the parent stock than any other living European language'.[128]

But this amelioration of the image of the Highlander was by no means universal.[129] Pinkerton was part of the reaction against this process and against the widespread vogue for the Celts throughout Europe. His *Dissertation on the Origin of the Scythians or Goths* (1787) complained that 'this may be called the Celtic century, for all Europe has been inundated with nonsense about the Celts'.[130] His earlier books were collections of Scottish verse, in the style of Thomas Percy's *Reliques of English Poetry* (1765), indicating his interest in the preservation of Scottish non-Gaelic literature.[131] But his formulation of an alternative theory of origins marked a departure from the task of merely recovering Lowlands culture to one of asserting its supremacy over the Gaelic, by virtue of its alleged German or Gothic roots.[132]

Pinkerton's Goths were Scythians from Asia who swept across Europe and displaced the previously established Celts, pushing them out to the western reaches of the continent until they were left only in Ireland and the Scottish Highlands.[133] The rest of Scotland was peopled by a Gothic tribe from Scandinavia whom he denominated *Piks*, a Scandinavian-looking orthography in place of the more familiar 'Picts'. These Piks settled in Scotland long before the *Cumri* or Celts from northern Europe and the Scots from Ireland arrived, and were therefore 'the real ancestors of the people'.[134] They settled in north Britain, he claimed, around 300 BC, at the same time as another Gothic tribe, the Belgae, colonised the southern part of the island. Since these Belgae were 'the real ancestors of three quarters of the present English', Pinkerton was making a claim for an equality of status between Scots and English on the basis of their common Gothic ancestry centuries before the Anglo-Saxon presence.[135] Thus, he was not attempting to forge a new Lowland Scot identity, but rather, like the Macphersons before him, to argue for a British insular identity which would give parity of status to Scotland within the United Kingdom.

Much of Pinkerton's argument was tendentious and lacking in any corroborating evidence. He used techniques of declamation and aggressive counter-attack in an attempt to disguise the conjectural nature of his theory, denouncing in particular the work of the two Macphersons and of Irish writers, chiefly O'Conor, as products of the 'Celtic mind', confused and inaccurate like the earlier Gaelic manuscript tradition.[136] His overtly racist attacks on Highlanders, which included advocating the plantation of colonies of industrious Lowlanders among them, were exceeded only by his grotesque characterisation of Irish Celts or 'Wild Irish' as 'some of the veriest savages in the globe; [who] seem by nature intended as a medial race between beasts and men'. In an aside calculated to please Irish Gothicists, he asserted that the 'chief families in Ireland and the industrious and civilized part of the people' were all of Gothic descent, being, 'Scots, Danes, Norwegians, and latterly [sic] English and modern Scots'.[137] In a second edition, published in 1814, Pinkerton virtually admitted that this abuse had been a diversionary tactic and altered some of the worst passages, in one instance substituting 'rude people' for 'natural savages'.[138] Even those Protestant writers in Ireland who enthusiastically endorsed the Gothicist theory of origins, and who shared the traditionally negative colonist perspective on the native Irish, were uncomfortable with Pinkerton's tone and style. Edward Ledwich thought him 'rude and ill-bred in the extreme and of most violent and untutored passions', but added '[y]et I will keep him'.[139] William Beauford, Ledwich's assistant, also liked Pinkerton's work, in spite of what he saw as dogmatism and abuse.[140] Even Thomas Campbell who, unlike Ledwich and Beauford, clearly felt affected personally by Pinkerton's characterisation of the Celtic Irish, was attracted to his basic Gothicist theory. Writing to Thomas Percy, he confessed, 'were it not for those prejudices which overpower him, he would be much to my taste, for his learning is solid, and he is, what few bookish men are, very communicative.'[141]

Despite their reservations about Pinkerton, both Ledwich and Campbell were polemical writers of the same stamp as the Scottish antiquary, seeking controversy rather than avoiding it. Their onslaught on Vallancey and adoption of Pinkerton's overtly racialist brand of Gothicism was a reflection of the increasingly polarised political situation of the late 1780s and 1790s, which greatly affected Irish antiquarianism. In his correspondence with Joseph Cooper Walker, Ledwich was explicit in linking traditional antiquarian writing on origins with a Catholic political programme of religious toleration. In 1786 he boasted that a 'literary history' upon which he was engaged (probably *Antiquities of Ireland*) 'mauls Vallancey, O'Conor and O'Halloran most confoundedly', and with characteristic arrogance predicted that it was 'too polemic, and I fear *erudite* to be generally pleasing'.[142] He dismissed O'Halloran as a 'galled papist' and O'Conor as being wedded to 'his old Firbolgs and apologies for his Rom. [sic] Catholics', although he did admit to having some respect for the latter's command of Gaelic and his 'good share of taste'.[143] However, he reserved his most serious criticism for John Curry, whose work was a defence of Catholic conduct in the 1640s and who therefore posed the greatest challenge to the Protestant monopoly on power, which was justified in part by reference to the alleged massacre of Protestants by Catholics in 1641.[144] He linked Curry's writing with that of Arthur O'Leary, a prominent Catholic cleric and controversialist: 'Get me Curry['s book] when finished. I have my doubt about the fate of Protestantism in the hands of the latter and O'Leary.'[145] Curry's books demonstrated 'what is uppermost in the minds of papists – their lost estates and the want of success in their numerous rebellions to recover them'.[146] As James Kelly has shown, the liberal Protestant reform impetus of the 1780s came increasingly under attack by conservatives who feared for the colonial Act of Settlement if Protestant power was eroded by any further Catholic relief measures.[147] For Ledwich in particular, the remote past was a battleground on which such political concerns were to be fought, and the liberal view challenged; Gothic origins theories seemed an ideal weapon.

In his early writings, Ledwich had espoused a more moderate position on the origins question, in part reflecting the dominant position of Vallancey in Irish antiquarianism at that stage. Letters by Ledwich written in 1779 show how conscious he was of Vallancey's power in comparison to his own humble role as a country parson, '[b]uried in an obscure corner and incumbered with a small family'.[148] He was also aware that the theory of a Phoenician colonisation of Ireland 'hath received the countenance of very eminent men, and therefore is to be treated with delicacy'.[149] Added to that, his early work appeared in the journal edited and published by Vallancey, the *Collectanea de Rebus Hibernicis*. His 'Essay on the Study of Irish Antiquities', published in 1781, shows that at this stage Ledwich hoped to maintain good relations. He praised the 'excellent productions' of Vallancey and suggested a way of reconciling a Gothicist theory of origin with the latter's orientalism. While the Irish druidic religion was eastern in origin, it was not brought by Carthaginians, but rather by 'Asiatic Goths' who arrived with their leader Odin, 'the great legislator and deity of the northern nations', in 24 BC, bringing with them such practices as 'the adoration of the sun, the burning of their children and their dead'.[150]

Thus, in this period Ledwich, like a number of Protestants before and after him, attempted a synthesis of 'systems' on this question of origins.[151] But on a related issue, the mystery of the round towers, he maintained an openly Gothicist stance in defiance of Vallancey, who believed the towers to have been built for the purposes of fire worship, the central tenet of the religion imported into the island from the Orient.[152] In 'A Dissertation on the Round Towers in Ireland', also published in Vallancey's *Collectanea* in 1781, Ledwich argued 'with the utmost diffidence' that the towers were built by the Danes, and (still with an eye to the Phoenicianists) were belfries modelled on Saracen minarets which the Danes had encountered on their voyages to southern Spain. In a revealing sentence, he admitted the attraction of such mysteries for him. The numerous round towers and their unknown origin, he stated, 'have opened to men of leisure and erudition, a spacious field for hypothesis and conjecture'.[153] The evident satisfaction with which he beheld this 'spacious field' is just one of many indications that Ledwich's reputation as a sceptic (still surprisingly strong) is based largely on his own claims.[154] While he derided the unsubstantiated theories of Vallancey, his own most controversial ideas often had equally little evidence to support them, as he admitted privately to Joseph Cooper Walker.[155]

Ledwich repudiated Vallancey's theories unambiguously later in that same year and still in the *Collectanea*, indicating his growing confidence. He expressed disgust 'with the incredible round of fictions' and 'eccentric wanderings of Keating, O'Flaherty and their followers', and posited successive waves of colonisation from Britain as the most 'rational' origins theory.[156] Finally, in *The Antiquities of Ireland*, most of which came out first in serial form in 1788 and 1789 and was then published as a book in 1790, he propounded his full Gothicist approach, combining elements from three non-Irish historians, which included Macpherson as well as Pinkerton from Scotland, and also the English antiquary John Whitaker. Interestingly, these three writers were not in agreement – both Pinkerton and Whitaker rejected Macpherson's *Introduction to the History of Great Britain and Ireland* (1771), for example – and Ledwich picked and chose from their arguments to suit his own, wholly Irish concerns. Whitaker's *Genuine History of the Britons Asserted* (1773) was a response to Macpherson's claim that the Highland Scots were the descendants of the ancient Britons, and therefore the holders of the title 'aboriginal inhabitants' of the island. He injected an Anglocentric, colonial and gendered note into this debate, accusing both Irish and Scottish historians of lacking 'the enlarged and masculine turn of thinking, which commenced near two centuries ago in England' and therefore of continuing to give credence to the 'misshapen brood of . . . former fictions', of which Macpherson's origins theory was a case in point.[157] In *The History of Manchester* (1771–5), the first volume of which was published just weeks before the appearance of Macpherson's *Introduction*, he had put forward his own theory. This made southern Britain the source of all colonies in Ireland, which then sent offshoots to Scotland. These colonists were 'native Britons' who were dislodged by the invasion of the Belgae in two waves, the first in 350 BC and the second in 100 BC, and were called 'Scuites' (Scots), that is, 'Wanderers or the Refugees of Britain'. As evidence, Whitaker cited Macpherson's Ossian, probably meaning *Temora*, since he was an enthusiast for these poems and used them extensively as a source in the *History of Manchester*.[158]

Ledwich combined elements of Macpherson with an amalgam of Whitaker and Pinkerton. Thus, he accepted Macpherson's theory of Celts from Scotland moving into Ireland, but argued that further colonies of Goths, made up of Belgae and Picts, later settled in large numbers over the island.[159] He also made the Fianna and Fionn Mac Cumhaill, heroes from the Fionn cycle of tales on which Macpherson had drawn for the Ossian poems, pirates from Finland who seized land and settled in Ireland.[160] This audacious attempt to 'Gothicise' almost the whole of early Irish history extended to arguing that the Scots and Picts of Ireland were offshoots of 'the Saxon Nation'.[161] Such arguments eliminated all ethnic distinctions between Irish and British, and made the colonisations of the twelfth century (and later) part of an ancient and continuous process of British settlement in Ireland.[162] They also undermined the tradition of an independent and culturally superior Milesian civilisation prior to the twelfth century.

Thomas Campbell's Gothicism was of a more moderate kind than that of Ledwich. Unlike the latter, he had begun as a genuine admirer of Vallancey in his first book, *A Philosophical Survey of the South of Ireland*, published in 1777. This was an unusual work, written in epistolary form, ostensibly by an English visitor reporting on a tour around Leinster and Munster to a friend at home. Campbell's aim was to provide information about Ireland, 'the least known about country in England', and to make the 'value of Ireland' better appreciated. It thus fitted into an established form of colonial literature, which sought to explain Ireland to an English audience. Indeed, Campbell's two primary authorities were Edmund Spenser's *A View of the Present State of Ireland* (1596), and Sir John Davies' *A Discovery of the True Causes why Ireland was never Subdued until his Majesties Raigne* (1612), classics of the colonialist perspective.[163] Looking for support for Vallancey's collation of Gaelic with the Punic passage in Plautus, Campbell found it in Spenser's acceptance that the Irish had indeed their origins in Spain.[164] But the *Philosophical Survey* was more than an endorsement of current ideas and enthusiasms in antiquarianism. As Campbell later explained, 'The book was undertaken merely to recommend toleration in Ireland, and a more liberal communication of commercial and political privileges in England'.[165] As the choice of 'philosophical' in the title indicated, it purported to give a considered view, in the rational spirit of the century, of the country and its problems. Thus, while endorsing Spenser's view that the Irish were 'at least among the most ancient people in this end of the world', he also doubted the importance of these antiquity claims.[166] He wished to get away from such questions, arguing that the concentration on the 'migrations . . . from Scythia' actually took from the credit of Irish historiography, and that the events of 'subsequent periods' were more important.[167]

In his next project, Campbell tried to put this prescription into practice. This was to be a proper narrative history of the colonial period, to be entitled 'The History of the Revolutions of Ireland'. It was never published, largely because Campbell became obsessed with overturning the dominance of orientalist origin theories and the claim of a great pre-colonial Gaelic civilisation.[168] Instead, his second and final book was on the early Christian period, but as its title, *Strictures on the Ecclesiastical and Literary History of Ireland* (1789), indicated, it was primarily a critique of contemporary writings; its main target being, unsurprisingly, Vallancey. In effect, it constituted a public repudiation by Campbell of his earlier support for Vallancey's theories. That support had called his judgement into question, and he had come to feel a great deal of embarrassment about *A Philosophical Survey*, which was still attracting attention in the late 1780s. *Strictures* began as a series of essays, entitled 'Sketch or Summary View of the Ecclesiastical and Literary History of

Ireland', which Campbell wrote under the Spenserian pseudonym 'Ierneus', for a newspaper, the *Dublin Chronicle*, between December 1787 and March 1788.[169] In these essays Campbell adopted the Gothicist thesis, arguing that all the later colonising peoples were Scythians, or northern Europeans, and that one of the legendary tribes of Ireland, the Tuath de Danann was Danish, thus pointing to a Danish colonisation in the first century AD. He also cited the Fionn cycle as evidence of Scythian settlement, which may have given Ledwich the idea of making the Fianna of Finnish origin in his *Antiquities of Ireland*, published later in 1788.[170]

Campbell's 'Sketch' appeared in the *Dublin Chronicle* at the same time as letters by Ledwich and William Beauford that mocked at Vallancey and his theories. Campbell later included these letters in *Strictures*, thus giving the impression of a concerted effort by all three of them to overturn the dominant orthodoxy and to supplant it with their own theories. While they shared a common concern to undermine what Ledwich dismissively called 'your orientalisms and your Oghams'[171], they differed somewhat in their perspective. Ledwich was genuinely interested in pursuing the Gothic in Ireland. He wrote to Joseph Cooper Walker asking for further information regarding an anecdote he had heard that Irish was still spoken in Iceland, sounding uncannily like Vallancey when he referred to the 'Iberno-Icelandic dialect, which to me is a real curiosity, tho' I have had occasion to collate many words common to both tongues'.[172] Similarly, he had hopes of finding that the people living in the Mourne Mountains of Counties Antrim and Down were Picts rather than Celts, and that their language might be found to be Pictish, long considered extinct.[173]

By contrast, both Beauford and Campbell took a synthesising approach that attempted to incorporate the Milesians into Gothicist origin theory. This point of view was also expressed by Daniel Beaufort, when he surmised that it did not appear to him 'at all inconsistent with the Scandinavian hypothesis, that a colony from Spain should have settled in the South and West'.[174] Of these, William Beauford was the more marginal figure, mainly remembered for his part in the attack on Vallancey. A schoolmaster in Athy, Co. Kilkenny, he lacked the status and influence which, as clergymen, Ledwich and Campbell enjoyed.[175] He stood in the shadow of Ledwich for the most part, and had little success in his antiquarian endeavours. Ledwich frequently accused him of plagiarism but, despite this, acted to some extent as his patron, employing him as draughtsman for some of the architectural drawings in *Antiquities of Ireland*.[176] His independent projects, a history of Ireland up to the twelfth century and an essay on Macpherson's Ossian, did not appear in print, and may well have been held back by Ledwich who had limited respect for his talents.[177] All his published work appeared in compendium volumes or journals – the *Collectanea de Rebus Hibernicis*, *Transactions of the Royal Irish Academy*, and in Joseph Cooper Walker's *Historical Memoirs of the Irish Bards*, which had articles on Irish music and the harp by Beauford and Ledwich. Beauford's range of interests was large, encompassing most of the antiquarian concerns of the day: Irish music, popular customs, topography and place names, Macpherson's Ossian, and the Brehon laws. He claimed to speak Irish and to have made a study of law tract manuscripts in his possession, but such claims appear dubious, and were treated as such by his contemporaries.[178] He clearly had more enthusiasm and industry than learning and, by dint of submitting numerous essays to the Royal Irish Academy, succeeded in having two published. However, he was never made a member, even when Ledwich joined and could have put him up for election.[179]

In his early phase, when he published some essays in the *Collectanea*, Beauford's two main influences were Ledwich and Vallancey. Thus, he admitted Phoenician influence and detected Egyptian symbolism among the carvings at Newgrange, but maintained that the source of contact with the Orient were Celts from Britain who had received this knowledge from Phoenician traders.[180] These Celts moved in waves from northern Britain over the course of nearly a millennium, 'whence we may infer, the intire population of this country from Britain was completed in the space of eight hundred years'.[181] Unlike Ledwich, he did not simply dismiss the Milesian tradition as worthless fable, but tried to assimilate it to his theory of a wholly British peopling of Ireland. In 1783 he alleged that antiquaries had misinterpreted the annals, and that the Milesians were in fact 'British colonists, who under the conduct of their druids and chiefs, fled from the terror of the Roman arms, at the commencement of the first century'.[182]

Campbell also attempted to explain the tradition of a Spanish colony in the light of his own Gothicist origins theory. He suggested first of all that the tradition of a Phoenician colony might have arisen from the desire of later writers to associate their ancestors with such a famous race, but he also hypothesised that 'a very considerable intercourse did formerly subsist between Spain and Ireland', owing to the common Scythian origin of the Goths of Spain and the Scots of Ireland.[183] That Beauford and Campbell should thus attempt, however half-heartedly, to make their origins theories compatible with the native Irish tradition is worthy of note. It indicated the power of that tradition, as well as the need of the descendants of colonists, who lacked an established myth of origins of their own, to assimilate themselves into the mythology of the colonised. Their ambiguous relationship to the Gaelic or pre-colonial past was also connected to the crisis in the Protestant sense of identity in the late eighteenth century. Letters by Ledwich and Campbell show that they were acutely conscious that Protestants of settler ancestry were now perceived in Britain as fully Irish and therefore as open to similar stereotyping as the majority Catholic population.[184] This is particularly clear in the correspondence relating to Richard Gough's edition of Camden's *Britannia* (1789), for the Irish part of which they acted as consultants.[185]

Gough, a prominent and abrasive English antiquary, editor of *Archaeologia*, the journal of the Royal Society of Antiquaries, brought out all their unease in relation to metropolitan culture and to the poor reputation of Irish antiquarianism in England. Campbell, for example, was at pains to persuade Gough that the 'Sketch' in the *Dublin Chronicle* reflected his mature opinions and that the *Philosophical Survey* was to be ignored as the work of an inexperienced young man. When Gough sent Campbell part of his manuscript to read in February 1788, the latter was dismayed to find his own views cited from this earlier work, that round towers were of Phoenician origin, with Gough's comment that this argument seemed 'unfortunate'. Campbell replied that it was indeed unfortunate but that he had 'long abandoned those Eastern ideas, which he rashly conceived, from his personal respect of a certain writer, whose adherence to them, and Celtic nonsense (as Pinkerton truly calls it), has brought him into as much contempt on this side of the Channel as on yours'. He enclosed a copy of one of the essays from the *Dublin Chronicle*, and begged Gough to delay publication of the *Britannia* until his 'Sketch' had appeared in full and could replace the *Philosophical Survey* as a representation of his views.[186]

Campbell clearly felt uncomfortable in writing for an English editor. He suspected that Gough would not approve of his habit of making frequent references to contemporary Irish politics in his antiquarian work, and rehearsed this fear in a letter to Lord Dacre, a neighbour of his, who had recommended him for the task. Dacre reported this to Gough, and reassured him of Campbell's 'candour and dispassionateness in regard to political matters' and of 'his goodwill to England, though, in the right sense of the word, a good patriot as to his own country'.[187] Campbell's letters to Gough were peppered with allusions to his nationality and to the unfavourable English stereotype of the Irish. For instance, in his explanation of the genesis of the *Philosophical Survey*, which was supposed to have been written by an Englishman, he commented: 'for what could be more absurd than for an Irishman, professedly, to write his travels in his own country; though perhaps some may think that absurdity congenial with the Irish character'.[188] Later, a misunderstanding arose between them over postage arrangements. Apparently, Gough had an agreement with Joseph Cooper Walker who worked in the Treasury in Dublin, whereby the proof sheets of the *Britannia*, which he sent over for comment, could be returned to him post-free. However, Campbell, who held a living in Clogher, Co. Tyrone, at some distance from Dublin, was unacquainted with Walker and therefore unaware of this arrangement, sent Gough his 'Historical Sketch of the Constitution and Government of Ireland' by ordinary post. Gough objected to paying the charge on this and in a letter no longer extant, berated Campbell for not directing it via Walker. Campbell's wounded reply says much about the inferiority complex of many Irish Protestants: 'I was not acquainted with your correspondents in Ireland; but Ireland, at your distance, subtends but a small angle in the eye of an Englishman.'[189]

The next phase of this spikey correspondence continued in the same vein. Campbell believed that Gough, or some 'little politician' at the printing press, had 'intentionally mutilated' a paragraph of his writing. He protested that he had expressly asked that 'all or none should be suppressed' and defended himself as a responsible writer: 'You must observe how dispassionately I have treated this subject. I have reprobated our idle systems of antiquity, and combated [sic] Mr Molyneux where I found him wrong.' It is clear that Campbell linked Celticist antiquarianism with 'patriot' ideology, and that his disparaging of both was connected. He believed that Gough, as an Englishman, could not interpret this political code, and would read Campbell's sometimes trenchant criticisms of English colonial policy in Ireland as 'patriot', whereas in fact Campbell had called for a commercial union of the two kingdoms in his *Philosophical Survey*.[190] In a highly defensive letter, he acknowledged that 'Ireland is not an enlightened country, and I wish that we are all as the English are', but in turn asked Gough to accept 'that some individuals of this poor country may know as much of the real facts of the story as those who despise us so much that they will not be at the trouble to know the truth'.[191]

Campbell's sensitivity in this correspondence to the negative British image of the Irish was echoed in his discomfort at Pinkerton's hostile characterisation of the Celts and particularly the Irish.[192] This sensitivity may have been increased by Campbell's occasional sojourns in London, including one in 1775, where he was for a time a member of Samuel Johnson's circle.[193] The memoir of Campbell, which precedes his letters in John Nichols's *Illustrations of the Literary History of the Eighteenth Century* (1817–58), emphasised his perceived exoticism in this group, and included a portrait of Campbell in a letter to Johnson by Mrs Thrale, describing him as 'very handsome, very hot-headed, loud and lively, and sure to be a favourite with you . . . it diverts me to think what you will do when he professes that he would clean shoes for you; that he would shed his blood for you; with twenty extravagant flights'. Also recounted is Campbell's Irish Bull about Johnson, that 'having seen such a man was a thing to talk of a century hence'.[194] His reception in London as an obtrusive and 'flashy' Irishman contrasted with his experience in Paris in 1787, where, speaking no French, he was taken for English. In his account he was obviously delighted to be addressed as 'Signor Anglois' and basked in all the praise of England and its culture which came his way.[195] The pleasure which he took from this assumption puts his adoption of an English persona for his *Philosophical Survey* into a different perspective, suggesting more than purely political reasons for choosing to do so.

Edward Ledwich had also spent time out of Ireland, first in America in the 1760s as chaplain to the 55th Foot Regiment, and then in England as curate in the parishes of Coombe and Harnham, near Salisbury in Wiltshire.[196] His first publication was an account of local antiquities, *Antiquitates Sarisburienses*, which came out anonymously, but is unmistakably of his oeuvre in terms of style and sceptical seeming approach.[197] But once established in Ireland, from 1772, he remained in his rural parish until his move to Dublin in 1790 or 1791, and he does not appear to have visited England again.[198] There are several varied instances of Ledwich's unhappiness with the English stereotype of the Irish. He clearly thought of the Hibernian Antiquarian Society project as a patriotic one that would have a positive effect on English attitudes.[199] The dissolution of the society, occasioned as it was by his quarrel with Vallancey, may have served to cool somewhat his patriotic ardour, but he continued to be exercised in private by the problem. Even in 1788, at the same time that he was conducting the anti-Vallancey letter campaign in the *Dublin Chronicle*, he was also composing, for the same newspaper, an attack on the anonymous writers for the *Monthly Review* and other critical journals in England, some of whom had written unfavourably about Walker's *Historical Memoirs of the Irish Bards* (1786). Ledwich had contributed two essays to the volume and also much advice and encouragement to the young Walker, as their correspondence testifies. The extent of his involvement is indicated by his referring to this counter-attack as 'a Vindication of ourselves', rather than of Walker alone.[200] Claiming to espouse 'the cause of Irish literature', the 'Vindication' began by denouncing the reviewers, not as English, but as Irish and Scottish 'renegades': 'There is no Irishman but must view with indignation and contempt the efforts of those London scribblers, called *Reviewers*, to damp the Genius and impede the rising prosperity of this nation'. Instead of forming a 'just estimate' of the work, the reviewers had merely attempted 'to raise a laugh at the expense of the Irish'.[201] He quoted from one particularly sarcastic reviewer in the *Monthly Review* (now identified as the well-known English musicologist Charles Burney), who slyly linked the claims made for an early Irish civilisation with the Rightboy disturbances then in progress in Munster, referring to 'the uncommon politeness and urbanity with which the natives of Ireland hough their neighbour's cattle, nay ham-string, and even massacre their neighbours themselves'.[202] Ledwich deplored this 'malicious pleasure at any unfortunate circumstance, which can depreciate this kingdom and its natives in the eyes of foreigners'.[203]

It is worth considering why Ledwich chose to reply in an Irish periodical rather than in the *Monthly Review*, or indeed in any of the English newspapers, where these kind of views could be more effectively challenged. In addition, while Burney directed his most severe criticism at Walker, he also implied that Ledwich's essay was ignorant, and mockingly called him and Beauford 'the two great musical critics and antiquaries'.[204] One might have expected Ledwich to respond directly, in order to defend his own reputation, if not Walker's. Although we can but speculate as to Ledwich's failure to do so – was it a reluctance to move out of his own relatively unthreatening Irish literary sphere? – it contrasts interestingly with Charles O'Conor's policy of *always* seeking a London publisher for his open letters, for maximum effect.[205] Part of Ledwich's defence of *Historical Memoirs of the Irish Bards* revealed an interesting strain of insecurity about Irish antiquarian writing and its critical reception:

> Clouded as the early antiquities of this country are by fiction, it was impossible

for any writer, how guarded soever, not to be open to the shafts of petulance and
illiberality, when the difficulty and obscurity of the subject were not properly
estimated.[206]

Privately, he advised Walker that he should make major revisions for a second
edition: 'I would wish you to enter deeper, and totally reject Keating's legends,
and his followers.'[207] Perhaps Ledwich's posture of extreme scepticism in
Antiquities of Ireland arose out of a fear of experiencing a similar drubbing in
the English press.

Like Campbell, Ledwich was uneasy in his dealings with Richard Gough,
which began in March 1787. He regularly assured Gough that his views on Irish
antiquities were not 'orientalized'.[208] This desire to distance himself from the
dominant orientalist theories of Irish origins extended to downplaying his Irishness, as when he assured Gough that he could expect the fullest assistance from
Beauford and himself: 'I have no doubt, but, as originally a Briton, and by
engraftment an Anglo-Hibernian, as I am, he will further your plan to the
utmost of his abilities.' Later in the same letter, when describing the break-up
of the Hibernian Antiquarian Society, he referred to his expulsion by Vallancey
as an expatriation.[209] Despite these efforts to impress on Gough his English
ancestry and his alienation from Irish antiquarianism, and particularly from its
recent and most significant institutional manifestation, the Royal Irish Academy (which he refused to join for some years), Ledwich felt ill-used by the Englishman. He particularly resented Gough's revising an essay on church
architecture which he had submitted to *Archaeologia*.[210] Gough apparently took
exception to part of Ledwich's critique of Thomas Warton, poet and author of
The History of English Poetry (1774–81), and warned him that 'the Society of
Antiquaries will [not] admit laughable jocularity into their *Archaeologia*'.[211]

Ledwich's feelings of resentment were compounded when, on publication of the three-volume edition of Camden, Gough sent him a complimentary copy of the third volume only, relating to Ireland. He wrote a sour little
note on its frontispiece: 'I assisted Mr Gough in this Edition, and he spon-
taneously promised a Copy of the Work in three Volumes folio, but put me
off with this paltry Volume.'[212] His annotations contain a striking admission
by Ledwich both of his Old English descent and his family's previous Jacobite loyalties, information omitted from the biographical sketch which he
supplied for Warburton's *History of the City of Dublin* (1818).[213] Beside a section appended by Gough, entitled 'The Annals of Ireland', in which mention
was made, in the entry for 1329, of John, Roger and Thomas Ledewich, Ledwich wrote the following:

> These were the Ancestors of the Reverend Edward Ledwich, so often quoted in
> this work. They were originally seated in the hundred of Mundsley in Shrop-
> shire, from thence they removed (a branch of them) to Cheshire, and from
> thence emigrated to Ireland with de Burgo, AD [left blank]. He bestowed large
> possessions on them in Longford, Westmeath and other parts of Connaught,

and made them Palatinate Barons as they appear here in 1339. Ledwithtown in the Co. Longford, preserves the memory of one of their antient seats. They suffered in the perpetual convulsions and revolutions in Ireland, and Col. James Ledwich, my great great Grandfather lost his life and fortune by adhering to King James at the battle of the Boyne.[214]

This confession provides an important key to Ledwich's antiquarian writing and politics. The extremely conservative Protestantism which inform them may well reflect his family's recent political and perhaps even religious conversion.[215] His extreme Gothicism is also more understandable when seen in the context of his own Anglo-Norman ancestry. He was always particularly harsh about the Old English, deploring their gradual loss of 'the manliness of sentiment and propriety of conduct which they brought with them into the island'.[216] If the Anglo-Normans were not the proper conduit for a desired Gothic heritage, then Ledwich could bypass them and provide deeper and less compromising Teutonic roots. In addition, his absolute support for the English conquest and rule (unlike Campbell, who admitted some flaws in English policy towards Ireland[217]) may have amounted to over-compensation for his Jacobite connections.[218]

In the extremism of his views Ledwich resembled one of the leading Irish politicians of the day, John Fitzgibbon, who was also from an Old English family and whose father was among the first generation of Catholics to convert to Protestantism following the penal laws.[219] Fitzgibbon held the offices of attorney general and lord chancellor, and came to represent the most intransigent conservative views within the Ascendancy, giving his paramount allegiance to the British connection, rather than to his class. He was an early and passionate advocate of Union, and equally vehement in his opposition to relaxation of the penal laws. His speeches at the time of the Union contained harsh invectives against the Irish, and particularly the Irish Catholic, character.[220] He also attacked the English colonists of previous centuries, although, unlike Ledwich, his denunciations included more recent settlers, particularly the Cromwellians, depicting them all as rapacious freebooters.[221] Like Ledwich in the sphere of cultural debate, Fitzgibbon represented the extreme of mainstream Protestant reaction against the liberal pluralism of the previous decades. His recent biographer surmises that his attitude toward his own people and culture 'originated in a contempt born of self-hatred'.[222]

Individual concerns about origins and ancestry, therefore, were often influential in shaping the many shades of Irish response to the political crises of the late eighteenth century. Personal histories and affinities also played a role in determining attitudes to the past. The growing sense of an Irish Protestant identity in this period led antiquaries from that community to endeavour to root themselves more securely in Irish history either by the creation of new origin legends or the manipulation of the Milesian myth. Catholic antiquaries, on the other hand, fared less well. They relied largely on another Protestant,

Vallancey, to defend and invigorate Gaelic tradition, but found that their hopes were misplaced, as his theories came to be viewed as increasingly arcane and ultimately ridiculous.[223] In Ireland, as elsewhere, it was fashionable to deride such visionary schemes as unworthy of an enlightened age. However, the enthusiastic, even passionate, espousal of Gothicist and orientalist theories in Ireland and their adaptation to suit the cultural and political needs of both religious communities was a testament to the continued importance of the origins question, and of the disputed scholarly status of native tradition, in a society still conscious of recent colonisation.

PART TWO

GOLDEN AGES

ISLAND OF DRUIDS,
SAINTS AND SCHOLARS:
Religious Roots

The role of religion in the colonial period in Ireland, and its continued use as the basis of the political system in the eighteenth century, inevitably created problems for the historical treatment of religious topics. This intensified rather than diminished in the last two decades of the eighteenth century, with the growth and ultimate dominance of a reactionary Protestant Ascendancy ethos in response to a more assertive Catholicism. Antiquaries have been considered throughout this study largely in terms of their religious affiliation, which shaped their views even of purely secular matters like the origins and nature of Gaelic society. This emerged even more clearly in debates on the history of Irish religion, yet Protestant and Catholic scholars began from the same starting point, that of an Irish religious golden age, 'the island of saints and scholars', which was central to the sense of identity of both communities. Beyond that, there was little agreement and much heated controversy, particularly on the linked questions of the relationship of the early Irish church with Rome and on the role of the papacy in the coming of the Anglo-Normans to Ireland. Even the religious element in pre-Christian times was difficult for Irish scholars to deal with, to the extent that unique Gaelic sources on the druids, a subject that was of widespread European interest, could not be properly exploited.

The Renaissance rediscovery of the classical writers of Greece and Rome also made available a new source for the history of the barbarian peoples of pre-Christian Europe. These texts revealed something of the religion of the Celtic tribes, and brought the figure of the druid into the literature of the early modern period. However, it remained a shadowy outline; one modern authority on Celtic religion has written that 'even the combined evidence from all available sources leaves our knowledge of pagan Celtic religion in a state of the most rudimentary vagueness'.[1] Since the iconographic and archaeological evidence is still inconclusive, the principal source remains the testimony of the Greek and Roman writers which Renaissance scholars used. But these texts present major problems, stemming from the fact that their authors were observers of an alien way of life and religion, and thus the picture drawn by them reflected their own experiences and interests.[2] This pattern continued until very recently, so that '[n]early everyone who has written of them at any length has written of Druids of his own making'.[3] A good example of this tendency can be found in the work of the sixteenth-century Scottish historian

Hector Boece, whose *Scotorum Historiae a Prima Gentis Origine* was published in 1526. Boece was intent on giving his native country a long tradition of piety and learning, and presented the British druids as early moral philosophers on the model of Renaissance scholars of his own time.[4]

Writers in Britain were particularly free to conceive of their druids in whatever way they chose, since all the classical testimony related to the mainland of Europe, and mainly to Gaul. The entire tradition of a British druidism rests on one sentence in Julius Caesar's *Conquest of Gaul*: 'The Druidic doctrine is believed to have been found existing in Britain and thence imported into Gaul; even today those who want to make a profound study of it generally go to Britain for the purpose.'[5] This allowed British writers to apply Caesar's description of the Gaulish Druids as theologians, philosophers, teachers and magistrates to their own country, and to cite selectively from other classical texts by, for example, Pliny, Diodorus Siculus and Pomponius Mela.[6] The late sixteenth-century English antiquary William Camden led the way in promoting the image of an indigenous British druid. He searched the classics for all possible references to British history and to the druids, often, in his enthusiasm, misinterpreting the texts. In the first edition of *Britannia* (1586), he referred to them as 'our Druids', but his ideas about them were not at all fixed and changed quite radically over time. For example, in the second edition published in 1587, he claimed that they had prepared the Britons for Christianity, but by the fourth edition of 1594 their religion had become 'a dismal and confused heap of superstition'.[7] Nevertheless, the *Britannia* was responsible for making the druids into a British institution, while leaving it open to later writers to imagine them in different ways and contexts.

Irish antiquaries also looked to the classics as the main source for druidism, although early Irish manuscripts contained much information on the subject. These texts were early medieval written versions of fragments of an older, orally transmitted tradition, already remote and archaic to the scribes and scholars who first brought them into manuscript form.[8] The accounts of the druids presented in the Irish texts differed significantly from those of the classical writers, and may explain the relative neglect and lack of impact of the Irish accounts on the European literature on the subject. In contrast to the classical sources which offered general descriptions of Celtic druids as a learned, official caste, Irish sources presented individual druids, whose actions were most often associated with magic; the Irish word *draoi*, which is the equivalent of the Gallic *druidae*, means magician or diviner. It has been suggested that eighteenth-century writers on the druids in general were not comfortable with the early medieval Irish version and preferred the anonymous and more 'modern' figures of the classical accounts.[9]

Most eighteenth-century Irish antiquaries were also reluctant to make use of this unique source, which was available to them primarily through Geoffrey Keating's compendium, *Foras Feasa ar Éirinn*, written in the 1630s. One notable exception was John Toland, the notorious deist and whig polemicist of the late seventeenth and early eighteenth centuries. Toland was the author of the only Irish work on pagan religion, 'Specimen of the Critical History of the Celtic Religion', written in 1719 and published in a collection of his writings in 1726, four years after his death.[10] He was born in Co. Donegal in 1670 and was raised as an Irish speaker and a Catholic, but at the age of sixteen he rejected that religion and enrolled at Glasgow University. There he developed the free-thinking, anti-authoritarian and republican principles which motivated all his writing, nowhere more clearly than in his notorious *Christianity not Mysterious* (1696).[11] The subtitle of this book outlined its main argument: 'a Treatise shewing, That there is nothing in the Gospel contrary to Reason, nor above it: and that no Christian Doctrine can properly be call'd a Mystery'. Toland claimed that the churches had set out to render rational Christianity unintelligible to ordinary people: 'The uncorrupted Doctrines of *Christianity* are not above their Reach or Comprehension, but the Gibberish of your *Divinity Schools* they understand not.'[12] The outcry against Toland was immediate and extreme; in 1697 the book was burned publicly in Dublin by the hangman, and Toland was denounced as 'an inveterate enemy to revealed religion' by Peter Browne, Fellow of Trinity College Dublin and later Bishop of Cork.[13] The Irish Anglican opposition to free-thinking has been analysed by David Berman, who argues that Toland's attack on Christian mysteries represented a fundamental challenge to the constitution of church and state: 'For if there were no Christian mysteries, then there could be nothing to separate the rival Christian religions or sects . . . and no basis for the Penal Laws.'[14] Berman places such opposition to natural religion at the centre of Irish philosophy in the first half of the eighteenth century, and points out that the first extensive, critical history of deism to be published in England was written by another Irishman, John Leland.[15] Jonathan Swift, George Berkeley and Philip Skelton believed that free-thinkers were really disguised Catholic missionaries whose aim was to destroy Protestant Ascendancy in Ireland.[16] As a Catholic turned dissenter, John Toland was especially feared by this group. Adverting to the widespread suspicions about Toland's background, Swift called him 'the great Oracle of the Anti-Christians . . . an Irish Priest, [and], the son of an Irish Priest'.[17]

Toland's 'Specimen of the Critical History of the Celtic Religion' was conceived as an introduction to a planned major history of the druids, which would have developed further his challenge to the Christian churches.[18] For Toland, the druids epitomised all the dangers of organised religion; a 'Heathen Priesthood' who fostered ignorance among the people in order to 'procure power and profit' for themselves. A history of the druids would, therefore, represent a '*complete History of Priestcraft*, with all its reasons and ressorts [sic]'.[19] But there were other strands interwoven with this straightforward polemical attack on the Christian clergy, which reveal interesting aspects of Toland and his relationship to Irish antiquarianism. As an Irishman, a former Catholic and, for a brief time, Anglican, an ardent British whig and republican, yet also a cosmopolitan free-thinker, Toland's sense of identity was expressed in multiple ways.[20] Recently however, Toland's Irish roots and in particular his Gaelic-speaking background have received considerable attention. The 'Specimen' was the most overtly Irish and personal of his works, in which he cited his own observations of the customs of the Irish peasantry, as well as landmarks from his childhood in Donegal which were associated with the druids.[21] He also highlighted the value of ancient Irish manuscripts in furnishing materials for such a history, referring specifically to the Book of Ballymote, which was in the library of Trinity College Dublin, and to the collections of the Earl of Clanricarde and the Duke of Chandos, although there is no evidence that he actually consulted these.[22] While he got the title of the Book of Ballymote wrong (referring to it as 'Ballimore'), the rendition of all the Gaelic names is usually correct, indicating that Toland's Irish was of a high standard.[23] He was also able to decipher, and correctly identify, the name of the author of a copy of the Gospels dating from 1138, which, although written in Latin, used Gaelic orthography and material. He cited this manuscript as evidence of the Protestant nature of early Irish Christianity.[24] Alan Harrison, who has made a special study of Toland's Gaelic scholarship, argues that his level of expertise in reading old Irish could only have been achieved through his association either with one of the schools of traditional learning in Donegal or with a local scholar in the vicinity who had himself been trained in one of those schools.[25]

For Toland, the wealth of early Irish manuscripts was a matter of pride, given the vagaries of Ireland's past: 'notwithstanding the long state of barbarity in which that nation hath lain, and after all the rebellions and wars with which the kingdom has been harrass'd; they have incomparably more antient materials . . . for their history [than] any other European nation'.[26] He claimed that the Irish had been 'strangely sollicitious [sic], if not to some degree superstitious, about preserving their books and parchments; even those of them which are so old, as to be now partly or wholly unintelligible'. The oldest of these were pre-Christian and written by druids, who had set down their 'rites and formularies', together with their 'Divinity and Philosophy'.[27] It followed, therefore, that 'the use of Letters had been very antient in Ireland' and that 'there florish'd [sic] a great number of Druids, Bards, Vaids, and other authors in Ireland long before Patric's [sic] arrival; whose Learning was not only more extensive, but also much more useful than that of their Christian Posterity'.[28] Toland's advocacy of 'primevous Irish learning' antecedent to the arrival of Christianity owed much to Roderic O'Flaherty's *Ogygia*, which he cited frequently and with approval in his 'Specimen'. He also used Mathew Kennedy's *A Chronological, Genealogical and Historical Dissertation of the Royal Family of the Stuarts* (1705), which, like *Ogygia*, reasserted the Milesian genealogy of the Stuarts, but also restated the claim of James the Pretender to be rightful king. Thus, Toland had no qualms about relying on the support of Jacobite antiquaries in his efforts to vindicate the civility of the early Irish.

Toland's druids were central to his version of the pre-Christian golden age, but they were drawn in ways which often seemed contradictory. They were 'sacred in their function, illustrious in their alliances, eminent for their learning, and honour'd for their valor', but also 'dreaded for their power and influence'.[29] In Toland's account, the tradition that Christianity had been embraced more eagerly in Ireland than elsewhere was explicable only in terms of the exaggerated respect which the Irish had for priests of any kind, and which arose because the druids had charge of the education of the children of the nobility, 'whereby they had an opportunity (contrary to all good politics) of molding [sic] and framing them to their own private interests and purposes'.[30] Like Keating in *Foras Feasa*, Toland emphasised their magical powers, but indicated his own scepticism by calling them 'pretenders to magic' and their activities 'pretences to work miracles, to fortel [sic] events by Augury and otherwise, to have a familiar intercourse with the Gods . . . and a thousand impostures of the same nature'.[31] Thus, Toland condemned the druids for developing all the corruptions he associated with 'priestcraft', but still lauded them as purveyors of ancient wisdom and of a rational religion which he clearly approved of, emphasising 'their two grand doctrines of the Eternity and Incorruptibility of the Universe, and the incessant Revolution of all beings and forms'.[32] However, this pure druidic religion could be dissociated from priestly corruptions, as in Toland's depiction of the 'philosopher king', Cormac Ulfhada, who fostered learning and military prowess, 'made light of the Superstitions of the Druids in his youth', and in old age 'led a contemplative life: rejecting all the Druidical fables and idolatry, and acknowledging only one Supreme Being, or first Cause'.[33] For a recent biographer of Toland, this represents an attempt in later life to find congenial roots for himself; to fashion a 'seamless genealogy that made all the wise ancients, including the druids, his philosophical ancestors'.[34] In view of Toland's multiple identities, it can also be regarded as one variation on the pattern of Protestant need to find a past located in Ireland. In Toland's case, this created past was more free-thinking than Anglican, but it was nevertheless Protestant in its essentials, and never indicated any sympathy for Catholicism.[35] The corruptions displayed by Toland's druids were those that Protestants assigned to 'popery'; chiefly the use of superstition by a powerful clerisy to enslave a people.

Toland's argument that the remaining literature of early Ireland constituted an important and authentic resource for the history of the druids owed much to Keating's *Foras Feasa*, as did his brief account of famous Irish druids, although Toland did not acknowledge this.[36] This omission is curious, given the theory put forward by Harrison and Berman that Toland gave assistance to Dermod O'Connor in his translation of *Foras Feasa*, published as the *General History of Ireland* (1723).[37] Claims to this effect were made at the time of publication by O'Connor's disgruntled former patron, Anthony Raymond, and others, in an attempt to discredit O'Connor by linking him to the notorious free-thinker. They alleged that Toland's advice was responsible for changes made in the translation to Keating's original in regard to paganism.[38] While there is no hard evidence for this, Harrison and Berman have suggested one example of a change made in the 1723 translation which may indicate the hand of Toland. This is where an instance of the magical powers of the druids in *Foras Feasa*, in which they drove out demons by thrusting 'a stake of quicken tree through the trunk of every dead person who would be rising up against them', was reproduced in *The General History*, but was made more Christian by the addition that this might have been 'the Hand of Heaven' at work.[39] On the other hand, *The General History* also accentuated the role of magic, adding such terms as 'inchanters [sic]', 'necromancy' and 'charms and incantations', where in the original, Keating had simply used the Gaelic words for magic (*draoigheacht*) and magician/druid (*draoi*).[40] This emphasis on the supernatural in the 1723 edition was part of a confused tendency to stress the religious role of the druids, also dubbed 'priests' and 'soothsayers' by O'Connor.[41] Keating, for example, included the pagan rituals of the druids and recounted their assembly on 'the eve of Samhain to offer sacrifice to all the gods' and their burning of 'victims' in a fire.[42] In his version, O'Connor mingled Christian and pagan elements anachronistically: 'The sense of this sacred fire was to summon the Priests, the Augers and Druids of Ireland, to repair thither and assemble upon the Eve of *All Saints*, in order to consume the sacrifices that were offered to their *Pagan* Gods.'[43] While this ambivalent attitude towards the religious role of the druids may have reflected the influence of Toland, equally it may have stemmed from a widely shared uncertainty about the nature of pre-Christian religion, already noticed in William Camden, and which remained a constant feature in both Irish and Scottish antiquarian writing in the eighteenth century.

The difficulties which the druids posed for the eighteenth-century writer can be seen most clearly in the Ossian poems of James Macpherson, which avoided any reference to Celtic religion. The only spirits to be featured are the ghosts of dead heroes which occasionally appeared before the bard Ossian, and the epic machinery of the poetry is human rather than divine.[44] The reviewer in the *Annual Register* pointed out that the heroic atmosphere of the poems was untouched by pagan sacrifice and superstitions: 'the total silence of the poem with regard to the grosser parts of the druidical religion, and the retaining what was more pure and poetic . . . induce a suspicion of more art than simplicity in the poem.'[45] Macpherson had anticipated this charge in his introductory essay to *Fingal*, in which he made the absence of religion an aspect of the poetry he was translating, rather than of the society from which it came:

> That race of men carried their notions of martial honour to an extravagant pitch. Any aid given their heroes in battle, was thought to derogate from their fame; and the bards immediately transferred the glory of the action to him who had given that aid. Had Ossian brought down gods, as often as Homer hath done, to assist his heroes, this poem had not consisted of eulogiums on his friends, but of hymns to these superior beings.[46]

In a strikingly similar vein to Toland, he included an attack on the Celtic druids as 'a cunning and ambitious tribe of men', who used their 'mighty reputation among the people' to take over 'the management of civil, as well as religious, matters'.[47] This essentially secular explanation of druidic power, and his exclusion of the magical as well as the religious from his romantic view of Scotland's heroic age, is proof of Macpherson's sensitivity to contemporary English views of the backward Celt.

Charles O'Conor was also increasingly unsympathetic to druidism in his work, although he began as an admirer of their theology, if not of the druids themselves. The first edition of the *Dissertations* (1753) had a chapter on the religion of the ancient Irish, in which he repeated the widely held belief that Celtic paganism was based on Old Testament forms of worship and doctrine, 'grafted upon the Religion of Nature, and, partly, deduced from the clearest Fountains of the old Patriarchal Worship'.[48] He made their religion a cornerstone of the civility of the early Irish, 'rendering them a benevolent, whilst their Researches in Philosophy rendered them a wise, People'. But the growing corruption of the druids, which he termed 'Druid Craft', was only held in check by wise government and 'the Genius of the Nation'.[49] In the second edition of the *Dissertations* (1766), O'Conor omitted the section on the religion of the early Irish, and indirectly repudiated the idea that druidism was close to Old Testament religion, by removing the reference to 'Patriarchal Worship'. The sole allusion to druids and druidism was made in relation to the coming of Christianity: 'The obscure Taper of heathen Theism, was extinguished in the Light of the Christian, and druidic Superstition, once separated from the civil Establishment, disappeared by Degrees.'[50] Accusations of human sacrifice and abuse of power made the druid an embarrassing and unwelcome figure in the Celtic golden ages created by O'Conor and Macpherson, and may partly account for their de-emphasising of the religious element. In O'Conor's case, an increased sensitivity to English opinion may also be related to his involvement in the Catholic Committee, founded between the publication of the two editions of the *Dissertations*. The Committee's denial of any clerical dictation of Catholic political attitudes would hardly be helped by continued emphasis on a powerful ancient clerisy. In addition, the insistence in the Irish tradition on the druid use of magic served to discredit the authority of Irish manuscript sources on issues of greater importance to O'Conor.

Other Scottish and Irish writers were less inhibited by such concerns, and put druids at the centre of their depictions of pre-Christian Gaelic society. John Smith and Sylvester O'Halloran shared a similar view of Celtic druidism which expressly denied its negative aspects. Smith was a Presbyterian minister in Campbeltown, Kintyre, a Gaelic speaker and upholder of the authenticity of Macpherson's *Poems of Ossian*. Responding to the criticism of the latter made in the *Annual Register*, he fabricated a series of Ossianic poems which abounded in references to druidism and were published in his *Galic Antiquities* (1780).[51] They were prefaced by a history of the druids, with special emphasis on those of 'Caledonia', consisting of a paean of praise to 'the moderation of the Druids . . . and the mildness with which they exercised their sway'. Smith's druids were priests, magistrates, philosophers and physicians, whose skills had nothing to do with magic or artifice. On the question of human sacrifice, he did not absolutely deny that it took place, but sought to minimise it: 'If the Druids ever offered any human sacrifices, it is no more than most other ancient nations, and even the Greeks and Romans, are known to have been often guilty of.'[52] He also used an argument put forward earlier by O'Halloran in his *Introduction to the Study of the History and Antiquities of Ireland* (1772), that the charge of human sacrifice had been made by the Romans in an attempt to discredit the druids who stirred the people into revolt against them.[53]

O'Halloran was unique among Irish antiquaries in foregrounding druidism, which was almost the first issue dealt with in the *Introduction*.[54] Just as all beneficial social and cultural developments in Europe had their origins, according to O'Halloran, in pre-colonial Ireland, so too, it was 'the prime seat of Druidism'. His rationale for this was an unacknowledged borrowing from Keating, making 'the smallest alteration' of Caesar's statement in *The Conquest of Gaul*, to read that druidism had originated in the British Isles rather than Britain.[55] This allowed him to use, and to quote at length from, Caesar and other Roman and Greek writers on the druids, and to present these as a learned class of 'divines, legislators, philosophers and poets', rather than the crafty magicians of Keating's *Foras Feasa* and of Gaelic tradition.[56] He also sought to connect his druids to the Christian priesthood by claiming that the many 'schools and colleges' that they had founded were later turned into 'Christian seminaries'.[57] In a similar vein, although with somewhat more subtlety, John Smith had his Caledonian druids retreat from the Romans to the fastness of Iona, a centre of monasticism, 'where [druidism], though weak and effete with years, . . . lived till the gospel, *that glorious day spring from on high, visited the multitude of the Gentile isles*, and banished with its light this spectre of darkness'.[58]

In the case of O'Halloran, this attempt to make the druids Christian priests *avant la lettre* was part of the Irish Catholic interpretation of the pre-colonial period, in which the advent of Christianity, rather than bringing a revolution in manners, served only to accentuate the innate civility, piety and learning of the early Irish. Geoffrey Keating had put forward this line in *Foras Feasa*, by stressing the ease with which Patrick had founded churches and ordained clergy,[59] and by extolling the proto-Christian piety of certain Irish kings who ruled long before the arrival of St Patrick in 431 AD. Conor Mac Neasa, king of Ulster in the first century BC, for example, was told by his druid that 'the Jewish people would put Christ to death by torment', and, in his great distress at the news, had a fatal accident. Cormac Mac Airt, high king in the third century, was granted the Christian faith directly by God, because of 'the excellence of [his] deeds, and judgments, and laws'.[60]

Keating had emphasised the continuities between pagan and Christian Gaelic Ireland by making St Patrick an agent of reconciliation between the old and the new. In Keating's account of the pagan period, the *seanchus*, or antiquarian records of Ireland, were examined and confirmed every three years at the *feis* of Tara, described as 'a great general assembly like a parliament, in which the nobles and the *ollamhs* [professors or learned men] used to meet . . . to lay down and to renew rules and laws, and to approve the annals and records of Ireland.' Although the high king, Laoghaire, refused to accept the Christian faith from Patrick, he nevertheless included the missionary in this vital activity. A group consisting of Patrick and two other bishops, three kings (including the pagan Laoghaire) and three *ollamhs* 'purified and arranged and established the Seanchus'. Following this, 'the nobles of Ireland decreed that the charge of it should be entrusted to the prelates of Ireland, and these prelates ordered that it should be copied in their own chief churches'.[61] This story was used by most Catholic writers in support of the authenticity of Gaelic historical tradition. For example, in the *Dissertations*, O'Conor was relatively uninformative on the religious activities of St Patrick, but made much of this more secular episode, in which as a member of 'the great Senate of the Nation, called the FES of TEAMOR', he was 'appointed one of the famous Committee of Nine, to whom was intrusted the Reform of the Civil History of the Nation; so as to render it instructive to Posterity', making it 'the most authentic Body of History then extant'.[62] In the less guarded Introduction to the first edition of the *Dissertations*, O'Conor made St Patrick an almost wholly secular figure who was accepted 'in Quality of a *Statesman*, as well as *Apostle*', and whose 'Business as a Politician, consisted in correcting the *Intemperance* of Liberty'. However, an uncomfortable awareness that this might well be taken in a hostile manner to support claims that the Catholic clergy had long interfered in the political domain led O'Conor to stress that Patrick only assisted in the reform of government 'to the furthest Limit that the Genius of the Nation would permit: He went *no farther*'. The result of his intervention was that government, as much as religion, flourished from then on.

O'Conor's St Patrick bore all the hallmarks of a progressive eighteenth-century whig politician, whose rational religion was eminently suited to the maintenance of liberty and of social order, and was, therefore, the antithesis of popery.[63] However, Patrick could equally feature as the antithesis of enlightenment; to be deplored rather than emulated. For Toland, Patrick prefigured the Church of Ireland clergy of his own time who had supported the burning of his *Christianity not Mysterious*. The alleged burning of the books of druid learning at Patrick's instigation gave Toland the opportunity to indulge in a rhetorical condemnation of such unenlightened behaviour:

> What an irreparable destruction of History, what a deplorable extinction of arts and inventions, what an unspeakable detriment to Learning, what a dishonor upon human understanding, has the cowardly proceeding of the ignorant, or rather of the interested, against unarm'd monuments at all times occasion'd![64]

O'Halloran, who was alone in citing Toland favourably, also blamed St Patrick for the burning of the philosophical and theological writings of the druids.[65] In his *Historical Memoirs of the Irish Bards* (1786), Joseph Cooper Walker blamed 'the wide chasm in our annals' on Patrick's 'excess of . . . zeal' in destroying 'several hundred volumes relating to the affairs of our druids in particular'.[66]

Negative depictions of St Patrick, at least, could therefore command cross-denominational support, but in the main, manipulations of the patron saint usually served sectarian purposes. For example, Protestant writers, such as Walter Harris and Thomas Campbell, made much of Patrick's parentage, alleging that he was the son or grandson of a priest, which helped their claims that the established church, with its married clergy, was the real heir of the early Christian church.[67] Overall, however, it is remarkable how little Patrick featured in antiquarian writing, given his centrality as patron saint of the Irish. His feast day on 17 March had been the occasion of popular celebration and the wearing of crosses and shamrock since at least the seventeenth century.[68] Indeed, in 1739 Walter Harris complained that 'our deluded countrymen' spent St Patrick's Day 'in Riot and Excess; as if they looked upon him, only in the light of a jolly Companion'.[69] However, by that stage, the feast day was also celebrated officially by the viceroy and administration in Dublin Castle. The development of Patrick as a national symbol was extended when a new and exclusively Irish order of knighthood, the Order of the Most Illustrious Knights of St Patrick, was instituted by George III in 1783.[70] It appears as if his function in antiquarian writing was also mainly symbolic, of use only to reinforce arguments about the authority of Gaelic tradition or the nature of the early Irish church and society.

Accounts of the early church in the eighteenth century were characterised by confusion and inconsistency, arising mainly from conflicting political needs. Protestant concern to establish descent from an early Irish church independent from Rome, for example, conflicted with their support for the twelfth-century Anglo-Norman invasion which had papal approval. Similarly, in their low-key campaign for the repeal of the popery laws, Catholic historians were anxious to avoid over-identification with Rome (a major justification for the anti-Catholic laws) and had problems in reconciling the coming of Christianity with their tradition of a glorious pagan past. Church history in Ireland, as elsewhere, was largely a product of the Reformation and of the various disputes over Protestant claims to be the authentic Christian church rather than a mere breakaway faction, as Catholic polemicists maintained. From the late sixteenth century numerous works in Latin by Irish apologists on both sides were published.[71] By the mid-eighteenth century, however, one book from this era of doctrinal dispute still exerted a dominant influence: Archbishop James Ussher's *Discourse of the Religion Anciently Professed by the Irish and British*, first published in 1622. This contended that on key points of doctrine, 'the Religion professed by the ancient Bishops, Priests, Monks and other Christians in this land, was for substance the very same with that which now by public Authority is maintained therein'.[72]

By assuming a direct lineage between the early Christian church and the established Church of Ireland, Ussher gave his co-religionists an important means of circumventing at least part of the allegation that they were colonial usurpers, alien in religion as well as blood. According to one recent view, Ussher was intent on giving the Church of Ireland its own origin legend to buttress its constitutional status as the national church; and reinforced this at every available opportunity by using the first person plural: 'our ancient church', 'our ancestors', 'our Patrick'. However, while Ussher's *Discourse* can be seen as a 'brilliant attempt to forge a new identity' for Irish Protestants, it was a project fraught with difficulties and contradictions.[73] For example, this attempt to 'anchor the reformed protestant church firmly to a Gaelic past' took place at a time when renewed colonisation ensured that the Church of Ireland was fast becoming an Anglicised church staffed by New English clergy, who were unlikely to welcome being linked, however tenuously, to a Gaelic culture which they regarded as irredeemably barbaric.[74] In the Irish context, therefore, the Reformation dispute had colonial dimensions which were still of relevance in the late eighteenth century, given that the Church of Ireland had not succeeded in converting the majority population from Catholicism. In view of this failure, it was, if anything, more reliant on history to justify its establishment.

Keating's *Foras Feasa* was also influential in regard to ideas about the early church. This history of Ireland from pagan times to the coming of the Anglo-Normans was, on one level, an Old English Catholic history (written in Irish), involving a complex mixture of two seemingly conflicting themes. A romantic account of native Irish pagan and Christian endeavour was coupled with support for the twelfth-century conquest which signalled the beginning of the end of native Irish government. Such complexity ensured that its English translation, published in 1723, had much to offer both Catholic/native Irish and Protestant/colonist perspectives. Elements of these two very different texts by Ussher and Keating informed the writings of both Catholic and Protestant historians in the following century and to a large extent determined the main debates on the history of the early Christian church, which revolved around three interlinking issues. The first concerned the view that early Christian Ireland had been a golden age of outstanding monastic learning, the 'island of saints and scholars', which was common to both religious traditions. Contrasting perceptions of pagan Irish society and of the impact of Christianity on it, however, belied apparently shared perspectives in this area. The idea of the independence of the early church from Rome also commanded broad Catholic and Protestant support, but in this case the contemporary debate over the popery laws was a complicating factor for both sides. A third theme concerned the role of the papacy in the Anglo-Norman invasion of the twelfth century, and here conflicting contemporary concerns within, as well as between, traditions came most sharply into focus and resulted in tortuous special plead-ings on both sides.

Central to both Protestant and Catholic accounts of the early church was the notion that Christianity had been generally and immediately accepted by the pagan Irish in the fifth century and that the island had become a scholarly haven for those fleeing the turmoil of continental Europe. In the words of Charles O'Conor, 'When Europe groaned under the Servitude of Gothic Igno-rance, Ireland became a prime Seat of Learning to all Christendom.'[75] Behind this apparent unity, however, lay fundamentally different historical and polit-ical perspectives which determined the way in which the 'saints and scholars' image was used. For the Protestant community, who were mainly the descen-dants of English and Scottish colonists of the sixteenth and seventeenth cen-turies, the coming of Christianity was an important landmark, signalling the beginning of an Irish past with which they could identify. In their view, Chris-tianity brought civilisation to a barbaric native Irish people and was, therefore, the precursor of the colonisation process which had brought, not alone their ancestors to Ireland, but also the benefits of the English language and law.

Catholic narratives of the native Irish past were built around the premise that pagan Ireland had developed a sophisticated and literate society while the rest of Europe was in a state of unregenerative barbarism, and it was into this pattern that they attempted to fit the advent of Christianity. In *Foras Feasa*, Keating had formulated the classic argument. Pagan Ireland had had a quasi-Christian morality which, he maintained, had ensured the widespread accep-tance of the Christian message.[76] Eighteenth-century writers expanded on this effort to subsume the experience of conversion by foreign missionaries within their picture of Ireland's unique pagan civilisation, but in doing so they often drifted far from Keating's seventeenth-century Counter-Reformation stance. For example, O'Conor adhered to Keating's basic line, but was more secular in emphasis, highlighting the sophistication of pagan society rather than its proto-Christianity. Citing as a maxim that 'Christianity got its least Opposition from the learned and civilised Nations', he maintained that its rapid progress in Ireland was unsurprising.[77]

But in his more flamboyant version of a pagan high culture, Sylvester O'Halloran claimed that the title 'Insula Sanctorum et Doctorum' had been acquired long before the arrival of St Patrick. Ireland had been 'the great school of Europe' from pre-Christian times; the influence of its druidic religion had extended not just to Britain but even to Rome where gods of Irish origin were worshipped, and the Greeks, he claimed, had called the pagan Irish 'the sacred generation'.[78] In line with his enthusiasm for the druids, O'Halloran was ambivalent, and sometimes hostile, in his treatment of the 'new religion' and argued that it was not responsible for Ireland's reputation as a centre of learn-ing and sanctity. The Christian missionaries were 'extremely ignorant' and 'rather the enemies, than the friends of literateurs [sic]' and played no part in the establishment of centres of learning which had existed in Ireland 'from the most profound antiquity'. He likened pagan Irish society to that of China, the location of a recent Christian mission: 'Like the modern Chinese, they suffered [the missionaries] peaceably to preach their doctrine, and instruct their pupils.' He was particularly critical of the effect of the new religion on the martial spirit of the Irish, a recurring theme in his work. Employing a similar analysis to that which Edward Gibbon used four years later in the *Decline and Fall of the Roman Empire*, O'Halloran argued that Christianity was 'a mortal blow to the greatness of Ireland', sapping the strength of the warrior class: 'Instead of those elevated notions of military glory, of intrepidity, and independence, so much cherished by their ancestors, they were now taught patience, humility and meekness.'[79]

On the other hand, O'Halloran did posit one favourable view of early Christian Ireland – as a place of religious toleration. Alleging that the old and new religions coexisted peacefully for over three centuries (and attributing this to the pagan element), he made a direct contrast with the contemporary situation in Ireland and elsewhere:

> What a lesson of instruction to modern nations! Had such wise and conciliatory measures animated the councils of European states in these later times, happy had it been for the public. Spain would not have been debilitated by the expulsion of the Moors . . . France would not have regretted the revocation of the edict of Nantz; and after a profound peace for eighty years, the effects of the *Popery Laws* would not have been felt in Ireland.[80]

Like all Catholic writers, O'Halloran's view of the past was strongly coloured by his dissatisfaction with the contemporary position of Catholics. His representation of pagan and early Christian Ireland as the epitome of a well-governed society was an indirect appeal for the restoration of religious liberty.

This oblique approach, playing down the importance of religion as a governing force and instead stressing the natural virtue and morality of the native Irish, was characteristic of Catholic historians living and writing in Ireland, who were directly concerned with the pragmatic politics of surviving and repealing the penal laws. It is instructive to compare them with the Abbé James MacGeoghegan, whose three-volume *Histoire de l'Irlande* was published in Paris between 1758 and 1762. MacGeoghegan was born in Ireland in 1702, but received his education in France where he was ordained a priest. He was attached to the Irish College in Paris and for a time was chaplain to the Irish Brigade in France, to whom the *Histoire* was dedicated.[81] As an emigré priest in France, MacGeoghegan's views were at odds with those of O'Conor and O'Halloran in fundamental ways. In contrast to their acceptance of the 'Glorious Revolution' and the Hanoverian monarchy, MacGeoghegan was a Jacobite and upholder of the Stuarts' claims. He espoused a forthright Catholic position in his work, which had as its principal theme the heroism and devoutness of Irish Catholicism throughout history, and was an undisguised attack on the popery laws. MacGeoghegan made Christian Ireland the outstanding golden age; the first four centuries of Christianity were 'the most brilliant in the entire history, ancient and modern, of this people'.[82]

In emphasising the arrival of Christianity as a major turning point, Mac-Geoghegan echoed the arguments of Protestant writers, for whom it was also a crucial landmark, signalling the beginning of an Irish past with which they could identify. While Thomas Leland politely but firmly ruled out the pretensions to a pagan high culture in his *History of Ireland* (1773), he cited O'Conor with approval when discussing the validity of early Christian Ireland's reputation for learning, and accepted that the title 'Island of Saints' had a factual basis.[83] Among the most enthusiastic Protestant proponents of this view was Thomas Campbell, whose *Strictures on the Ecclesiastical and Literary History of Ireland* (1789) partly aimed to prove that Ireland 'was the School of the West' in the early Middle Ages.[84] In an appeal that clearly was addressed to Catholic writers such as O'Conor and O'Halloran, he argued that the Christian period could provide more scope for national pride than the pagan, and that the epithet 'Insula sanctorum et doctorum' was 'more honourable to my native country, than to recur to Druidical whimsies and fabulous times'.[85]

A large part of *Strictures* was devoted to short biographies of some Irish scholars from the fifth to the tenth century, emphasising their intellectual strengths and influence in Europe as well as in Ireland. In this, Campbell was following an established Protestant interest, begun by Sir James Ware in the seventeenth century and continued by Walter Harris, who extended, corrected and translated from Latin Ware's work on Irish writers.[86] However, Campbell was unusual in making his account the basis of a direct attack on the Scottish historian John Dalrymple, who had made derogatory comments about Irish national character in *Memoirs of Great Britain and Ireland* (1771). Campbell argued that these figures were 'a sufficient vindication of the insulted genius of Ireland, during the ages in which they existed' and that furthermore 'there is no reason for suspecting that . . . since that time . . . the intellectual powers of our people [have] diminished'.[87] O'Halloran had also attacked Dalrymple in an appendix to his *Introduction to the Study of the History and Antiquities of Ireland* (1772).[88] The crucial difference between the two, however, was that the Protestant Campbell chose the Christian rather than the pagan past as a means of counteracting negative Scottish and English images of Ireland. The Christian period in Irish history, and the claim to sanctity and scholarship had, if anything, a greater importance for Irish Protestants than Catholics, as one means of defence against hostile characterisation by English and Scottish writers.

Protestant eulogies of early Christian Ireland as a haven of learning could, however, have more divisive and sectarian overtones. For example, in his *Antiquities of Ireland* (1790), Edward Ledwich attributed this alleged scholastic eminence, not to native Irish scholarship, but to the influence of British monks and clerics who had fled to Ireland in the sixth and seventh centuries to escape the censure of 'the Roman Pontiffs' and their interdiction of schools and teaching in England 'on account of the heresies constantly springing up there'. Echoing O'Halloran to some extent, he argued that the Roman church was anti-intellectual: 'the Benedictines and other Roman monks despised learning, laying more stress in their rules on abstinence and manual labour than on letters.'[89]

Superficially, Ledwich and O'Halloran appear to have been arguing from a broadly similar standpoint; one which emphasised Ireland's achievement of pre-eminence in scholarship without reference to the Roman church. The independence of the Irish church from Rome had earlier been stressed by both Ussher and Keating. For Protestants, it was vital to their claim that their established Church of Ireland was the heir of the early church rather than being merely of sixteenth-century origin. Keating's corroboration of the lack of Roman influence, though not of the Protestant claim derived from it, accounts partly for the popularity of the 1723 English translation of *Foras Feasa*. The list of subscribers to this handsomely produced volume featured many prominent Protestants, thereby vindicating the decision of the translator to remove the Counter-Reformation perspective of the original, often by the simple device of substituting 'Christian' for 'Catholic'.[90] This Gaelic Old English history by a Catholic priest thus became, paradoxically, a powerful validating element in the development of Protestant historical consciousness.[91]

The Protestant claim made the question of independence from Rome a problematical one for Catholics, especially in the context of late eighteenth-century politics, and they tried to resolve it in a number of different ways. The Abbé James MacGeoghegan rejected the traditional position and asserted that close links had existed between Ireland and Rome throughout almost the entire early Middle Ages.[92] While this stance removed the consensus supporting the Protestant claim, it also laid Catholics in Ireland open to the charge of popery and buttressed Protestant arguments against any relaxation of the penal laws. This dilemma must have been particularly clear to Charles O'Conor whose *Dissertations* appeared in its second edition during the first campaign organised by the recently established Catholic Committee, of which he was both a member and propagandist.[93] It may be one reason why O'Conor does not seem to have recommended MacGeoghegan's work. As on other contentious matters, the first edition of O'Conor's *Dissertations*, which came out in 1753 before the formation of the Catholic Committee, showed a less cautious approach on the early church. Here, citing Bede, he asserted, not its independence, but merely that owing to Ireland's remote situation and 'the distractions [in] Europe', all communication between Rome and Ireland was severed for one hundred and fifty years, until 716. But he maintained that this break did not occasion any divergence in doctrine between Ireland and Rome, and recommended that 'modern Controvertists [sic]' should pay close attention to 'a Fact of this Notoriety'.[94]

This oblique challenge to Protestant claims was further toned down in the second edition, where the early Christian era was dealt with only in a brief and circumspect way.[95] O'Conor now attempted to distance himself from the tradition of a wholly independent church, by outlining a relationship with Rome which did not imply domination. Thus, St Patrick's mission to Ireland had full papal approval, which his successors retained. In addition, his Roman connections were underlined by simple repetition: 'The chief Planter of the Gospel in Ireland was by birth a Briton, but a Roman by Education; and he is known at present by his honorary Roman name, Patritius.' However, having stressed the Roman origins of the Patrician mission, O'Conor then portrayed the Irish church as proceeding on the basis of that authority without the need of regular Roman direction.[96]

It was difficult to deny Patrick's Roman links or the fact that his mission to Ireland had some form of papal approval. Protestants resolved this problem in a variety of ways. Thomas Campbell, for example, argued that Patrick, 'our great reformer', had in fact introduced papal doctrine and practice, but made a distinction between the Roman form of worship in the fifth century and 'the corrupt mass of superstition to which it has since grown'.[97] However, Edward Ledwich was not prepared to accept evidence of any links with the papacy, no matter how early, and in the fifth number of *Antiquities of Ireland*, which came out in early 1789, he simply denied the existence of St Patrick: 'his whole story is a fiction invented long after the time in which he is supposed to live.' The various lives of St Patrick and in particular the *Confession* which Ussher had considered authentic, Ledwich dismissed as 'the juvenile exercise of some Monk of the eleventh or twelfth century'. Significantly he had nothing but praise for the work of the Catholic Bollandists in Antwerp, whose aim was to retrieve what was factual from the hundreds of saints' lives written in the Middle Ages. Perhaps seeing himself as an Irish Protestant equivalent, he recommended these 'liberal, learned and enlightened Roman Catholic writers, who saw the disgrace brought on religion, and the real injury done it, by lying miracles and horrible blasphemies'.[98]

Ledwich was not the first to doubt the historicity of Patrick; in the seventeenth century Jean de Launoy, known as *le dénicheur des saints*, and the Anglican theologian Henry Maurice had raised the question. However, the intervention of an Irish Protestant on the side of the doubters was instrumental in causing a re-examination of the lives of saints. The 'Patrician problem' has continued to attract the attention of scholars, and there have been claims of up to three different Patricks.[99] While Ledwich raised a legitimate scholarly question, his motives for 'unsainting St Patrick', as he privately termed it, were decidedly mixed.[100] Not the least of these was the hope that he might generate more sales by this means.[101] He also seems to have relished sectarian controversy for its own sake, taking advantage of every opportunity to rile 'all the O's and Mac's'.[102] By this 'annihilation' of St Patrick, Ledwich aimed to provoke 'all the Irish literati', and reported with grim satisfaction to Joseph Cooper Walker that he had succeeded to the extent that he had to curtail the campaign, fearing that his 'personal safety might be endangered from the blindness of bigotry and superstition'.[103]

Ledwich introduced another anti-Patrician innovation into his interpretation of early Irish Christianity that was at odds with his general Gothic origins theory. In place of a Roman conversion led by Patrick, he proposed that missionaries from Asia had come to Ireland before the fifth century, bringing with them Eastern doctrine and practice, as well as an unshakeable opposition to 'Romish corruptions [which] lasted in Ireland for more than ten centuries'. His proud boast of 'the orientalism of our rites and ceremonies' sat oddly with his contempt for Vallancey.[104] Once again, it brought him close to Sylvester O'Halloran who, over a decade earlier when under Vallancey's influence, had proposed at first tentatively and then, characteristically, as a fact, that the different tonsure and Easter practice adopted by the early church pointed to an Asiatic conversion of the Irish.[105] It is indicative of Ledwich's total opposition to the idea of a Roman early Irish church that he would put forward an orientalist hypothesis at the same time as he was deriding Vallancey for such opinions.[106] However, he differed radically from O'Halloran in his emphasis on the shared experience of Ireland and Britain in this as in all other respects. Ledwich argued that British clergy coming over to Ireland were also instrumental in the transmission of Eastern dogma and practice,[107] whereas for O'Halloran and all other Catholic writers the main significance of contact with the Orient was that it gave Ireland its own unique link with the ancient world that excluded Britain.

In Ledwich's account the early church actively resisted any extension of Roman authority to Ireland, refusing to obey 'an extra-national jurisdiction'.[108] His friend Mervyn Archdall, also a clergyman and the author of *Monasticon Hibernicum* (1786), a history of Irish monastic foundations, followed this line, stressing the refusal of early monastic orders to adopt a Roman form of rule.[109] These accounts of an independent and anti-Roman church went far beyond Ussher's claim, which had centred on the unique conformity between early Christian teaching and those of the reformed church in Ireland. In Ussher's time, doctrinal issues were of central importance, as Reformation churches clashed with Counter-Reformation Catholicism over the fundamentals of Christianity. Such doctrinal disputes were no longer of primary concern in late eighteenth-century Ireland, where the politics of the religious settlement predominated.[110] Significantly, Ledwich explained in his *Antiquities of Ireland* that his first intention was to produce a new edition of Ussher's *Discourse*, but that his own notes and additions 'unexpectedly became too extended for such a purpose'.[111] The Protestant emphasis on long-standing Irish hostility to Rome, so evident in texts written in the late 1780s, is another reflection of the opposition of these writers to any further relaxation of the popery laws.

Like Ledwich, Thomas Campbell extended his analysis of the early Irish church beyond the confines of the seventeenth-century dispute. His *Strictures on the Ecclesiastical and Literary History of Ireland* was dedicated to Edmund Burke and self-consciously proclaimed its adherence to the rationalist values of the Enlightenment. Thus, his brief biographies of Irish writers in the early

Middle Ages emphasised figures whose work had incurred papal censure as contrary to Roman orthodoxy. For example, he presented 'that great luminary' Virgilius (excommunicated for declaring the earth to be spherical rather than flat) as an eighth-century Irish Galileo who paid the penalty for challenging papal superstition. The ninth-century philosopher John Scotus Eriugena was similarly highlighted as an opponent of the erroneous Roman religion, for his work on the eucharist which rejected the doctrine of transubstantiation.[112] Ledwich took up this theme in his *Antiquities of Ireland*. Eriugena, he claimed, was a rationalist, whose work displayed 'all logical and metaphysical refinements carried to the highest degree'.[113]

However, for Ledwich, the eighth-century monks known as Culdees, long a source of controversy among ecclesiastical historians of Scotland, were the real heroes in the pantheon of anti-Roman Irish churchmen. It is now known that these monks were members of a reform movement which began in Ireland and spread to Britain. This movement advocated the anchorite ideal as a counterbalance to the tendency towards laxity in the older monasteries. The origin of their name has been established as *céle dé*, Gaelic for 'servants of god'.[114] They became a central element in the disputes between the supporters of Anglicanism and Presbyterianism in Scotland, as proof for or against an episcopalian form of church government in Scotland in the early Middle Ages.[115] In the seventeenth century, James Ussher and Henry Spelman challenged the Scottish claim, made originally by Hector Boece in 1526, that the Culdees had been confined to northern Britain, and pointed out the evidence for the existence of Culdee monasteries in Ireland, Wales and England.[116] Ledwich also took up this theme, and argued that the Scots, 'rivals of the Irish in every branch of antiquities', were once again guilty of appropriating the Irish past by claiming 'these Monks as their own . . . nor do they want the aid of forged charters, or the plausible tales of elegant writers to support this fiction'.[117]

While Ledwich was unmoved by the Hiberno-Scottish controversies over Gaelic culture and history which preoccupied Catholic writers, he felt a definite sense of ownership of Ireland's early Christian heritage. In his view, the Culdees were an Irish monastic order founded in the sixth century by Columba, who followed a rule that differed in substantial ways from Roman practice. Ledwich claimed that they had been erased from the Irish historical record by their Romanist opponents; and he aimed to end this conspiracy of neglect and 'to restore them, and the lustre which their actions acquired to their native country'. The virtual absence of a literature on the history of this group in Ireland gave Ledwich considerable scope for imaginative writing. Like a latter-day Reformation martyrologist he portrayed the Culdees as victims of Roman authoritarianism: 'For centuries they preserved their countrymen from the baleful contagion, and at length fell a sacrifice in defence of their ancient faith.'[118] While this symbolic Protestantisation of such figures and movements from the pre-colonial past constituted a significant departure from

Ussher's emphasis on doctrinal issues, it was nonetheless a continuation of his basic project of forging an origin legend for Irish Protestants and for their established church.[119]

That sense of ownership of the Christian era can also be seen in Ledwich's response to Giraldus Cambrensis's criticism of the unreformed state of the Irish church in the twelfth century. While the latter's pejorative comments on the manners of the native Irish were acceptable to Ledwich, he objected strenuously to derogatory remarks made about the independent Irish church. He alleged that as a Romanist, Cambrensis was inspired by hatred of the Culdees, and dismissed his testimony, on this issue only, as expressive of a 'the vindicative spirit of their old persecutors'.[120] There are other signs of a certain defensiveness in Ledwich on this question, especially in his insistence that the Irish church remained 'pure and primitive' in its religion while 'corruptions' were creeping in elsewhere in Europe. Clearly a 'primitive' church, but not a primitive society, was something to be proud of, but he was uneasy that this primitivism in religion could also be construed in the negative sense which he himself usually adopted. In support of its non-Roman nature, he claimed that the Irish church practised the 'Oriental custom of lay-baptism', which involved immersion in milk, and added the comment: 'This was not a barbarous custom as a superficial reader may imagine.'[121] This rooting of Protestant historical consciousness in the early Christian period can also be seen in Ledwich's use of the personal 'I' and 'we' in relation to it. For example, his interest in the publication of a work on Irish ecclesiastical architectural remains stemmed from a belief that 'it would vindicate the honour of this country in remote times, and evince that at no period were we destitute of fine feelings'.[122]

The Catholic response to this encroachment on what was considered a native Irish rather than colonial heritage was muted, owing to a number of factors. In the first place, their version of the past was dominated by the tradition of a great Irish civilisation functioning in isolation from the continent until the twelfth century, unbesmirched by the *mores* of European society. To deny that the early church was independent from Rome would have meant breaking with an integral part of this tradition, and yet their upholding of it allowed Protestant writers a distinct advantage. One means used to undercut the Protestant claim was to distinguish between church doctrine and discipline. Overturning Ussher's thesis (although without any overt reference to it), Catholics argued that any real divergence from Rome that had occurred had been in the area of religious practice rather than dogma, and centred primarily around the continued use in Ireland of a different paschal calendar long after Rome had attempted to impose a uniform one. O'Conor called the dispute schismatic, but still dismissed it as 'trifling' and unconnected with dogma.[123] Similarly, O'Halloran asserted that between the fifth and the twelfth centuries, when Ireland had no 'connection or correspondence' with Rome, in matters of doctrine the Irish church remained in 'a miraculous conformity' with orthodox teaching.[124] MacGeoghegan, however, was not prepared to accept that the Irish church was singularly out of line even on issues of discipline, arguing that diversity in matters such as liturgy, tonsures and the celebration of Easter was widespread throughout the Christian church and furthermore that the extent of Irish heterodoxy had been exaggerated.[125] The Catholic challenge to Ussher's thesis in this period never expanded further than these blanket assertions of essential harmony with Rome. There was no attempt to refute Ussher on the various points of dogma, such as transubstantiation, purgatory or miracles, for example, upon which he had constructed his thesis. The new Catholic historiography had quite other and more political concerns.

While Ussher's authority gave Protestant writers a certain confidence about the historical legitimacy of their church, they were less sure of their ground when considering the role played by the alliance between the papacy and Henry II in the conquest of Ireland in the late twelfth century. This issue was integral to the history of the pre-colonial church and particularly to its condition in the period leading up to the arrival of the Anglo-Normans. The agreement between Henry II and the English pope, Adrian IV, was set out in the bull, *Laudabiliter*, drawn up in 1155, which alleged that the Irish church was in need of reform. In return for the granting of the lordship of Ireland to the English crown, Henry undertook to institute a reform programme, and to ensure that the papal levy, Peter's Pence, was collected and remitted to Rome rather than to the archdiocese of Armagh as had been the Irish practice.[126] This alliance presented problems for both Catholic and Protestant historians. In dealing with this papal collusion in what they saw as *the* disastrous turning point in Irish history, Catholics faced a major dilemma. If they denounced the papal action, they risked giving offence to Rome and its representatives, the Irish Catholic bishops; however, a failure to express some sort of opposition to this intervention by the papacy in an area of temporal jurisdiction would only fuel Protestant fears that Catholics gave their first allegiance to Rome rather than to the English crown, even when it was to their disadvantage to do so. The Protestant position lacked any comparable contemporary risks, but their dilemma was no less real: how to develop a stance encompassing, on the one hand, revulsion at the alliance which allegedly resulted in the Romanisation of the Irish church under the supervision of Anglo-Norman ecclesiastics, and, on the other, support for the coming of the Anglo-Normans to Ireland, as the first step in the colonisation process which had so recently ended.

Both Catholic and Protestant writers sought to explain this upheaval in ways which put the emphasis as far as possible on outside factors and groups. In some cases this involved a significant modification of the 'island of saints and scholars' image, in a way that stressed the vulnerability of the country and its church to events in Europe, instead of its role as a sanctuary from them. The chief culprits, according to this reasoning, were the Vikings, whose incursions into Ireland as well as other parts of western Europe were blamed for the disintegration of civil and ecclesiastical society in the ninth century. Catholic writers often referred to them as 'Normans' rather than 'Danes' or 'Vikings', as if to emphasise their kinship with the equally unwelcome colonists of the twelfth century. According to O'Conor, the 'Golden Days' came to an end when 'the fierce and heathen Nations of the North of Europe pour[ed] in upon Ireland'.[127] In the second edition of the *Dissertations*, he went further, by associating these 'Normans' with the Goths: 'The Normans, who issued forth from the same Gothic Hive with the old Saxons and Franks, infested this Kingdom, first by their Incursions, and then by actual settlements.' Significantly, O'Conor always chose to employ the alternative and conflicting meaning of the terms Goth and Gothic, which related to the Germanic tribe's role in the destruction of the great civilisation of Rome, rather than their putative development of political liberties. From O'Conor's viewpoint, the Goths were simply barbarians, and their appearance in western Europe signalled the beginning of 'that Period which generally concludes in Barbarism'.[128] MacGeoghegan also emphasised the destructive impact of the Vikings as having prepared the way for the Anglo-Norman conquest. They destroyed the government, weakened religion, and their commerce introduced corruption into Ireland. The resultant factionalism among Irish kings and chieftains over the following three hundred years in turn created circumstances 'favourable to the ambition and cupidity of a neighbouring country'.[129]

Among Protestants, Ledwich, once again, came closest to Catholic accounts in the emphasis he gave to the ills brought on the country by these foreigners, but as the harbingers of the Roman church rather than of the Anglo-Normans. Converted to Christianity by the Anglo-Saxons who followed Rome, the Vikings, according to Ledwich, conducted a vendetta against the Irish church and massacred its independent monastic orders. At the same time, 'these bigotted [*sic*] semi-pagans . . . would not suffer their Bishops to be ordained by the Irish, but sent them to Canterbury' and thus 'forced on a reluctant people all the corruptions of Rome'. But the evil done by the Vikings in Romanising the Irish church was to be balanced by the later consequences of this connection with Canterbury, which 'first suggested to the English princes the acquisition of Ireland through the donation of the Pope'. Having been forced by his tortuous historical explanation to this unpalatable conclusion, Ledwich could extricate himself only by the pious assertion that this was part of 'the inscrutable providence of God designed for the final happiness of the Isle'.[130]

The claim in *Laudabiliter* that the intervention of the Anglo-Normans, at the behest of the papacy, was justified by the corrupt nature of the Irish church in the twelfth century also posed problems for those committed to the 'Protestant' nature of that church. Just as Catholic writers had found in the Vikings an external force explaining the destabilisation of Irish secular and religious society, so some Protestant writers focused on the survival of a force in Irish Christianity which was foreign to its inherent 'Protestant' nature, that is, elements of pre-Christian paganism. Thus, Campbell found 'Paganism loitering

in the land, and sometimes maintaining its ascendancy in the highest sta-
tions'.[131] Ledwich also argued that Irish Christianity had been contaminated
by lingering pagan beliefs through a mistaken pragmatic leniency in the conversion process.[132] These definitions of 'paganism' were also post-Reforma-
tion, which meant that orthodox Roman Catholic beliefs, such as the power
of miracles or purgatory, were so described; even though this involved a tar-
nishing of the bright image of 'the island of saints and scholars' subscribed to
by most Protestant writers.

Catholic historians, however, were not prepared to see the golden age thus
modified, and in particular they attacked the assertion contained in *Laudabiliter* and also in the writings of Giraldus Cambrensis, that the Irish church
was unreformed prior to the arrival of the Anglo-Normans. They argued that
an internal reform movement was in train before the end of the eleventh century which, by the time of *Laudabiliter* in 1155, had brought the church
broadly into line with Rome. Keating had made much of the various councils
and synods held in the first half of the twelfth century, focusing in particular
on the Synod of Kells in 1152, when four new archbishoprics had been established by the papal legate sent by Rome.[133] For eighteenth-century Catholic
writers this was, in O'Halloran's words, 'a manifestation of the lasting union
between Rome and Ireland' before the drawing up of the papal bull.[134]

The argument that the papacy had been fully apprised of the measures
being taken to bring the Irish church into conformity with Rome raised the
awkward question why Pope Adrian IV had put his signature to a bull alleging that there had been no such reform. One obvious response was to see
Adrian as the victim of misinformation. O'Halloran alleged that the source was
the author of a life of St Malachy, Bernard of Clairvaux, who, being 'entirely
devoted to Rome', opposed the privileges of the Irish church and denounced
them as corruption.[135] MacGeoghegan, more conventionally, blamed Henry
II, but alone of Catholic writers in this period, pointed out that the pope too
was English, and therefore susceptible to pressure. MacGeoghegan was also
unusual in giving the text of *Laudabiliter* and for his outspoken condemnation
both of it and of the follow-up bull issued by Adrian's successor, Alexander III.
However, the denunciation was accompanied by the allegation that this second bull at least, was not a genuine papal document, but was forged in England. Denying papal responsibility gave MacGeoghegan the only possible
means of attacking the bulls without implying papal culpability. The unease of
which these contradictory explanations were symptomatic came to the fore
particularly when MacGeoghegan touched on the question of whether, if *Laudabiliter* was genuine, Adrian had been entitled to claim papal sovereignty over
Ireland. While he felt that the papacy had no right to *dispose* of crowns or kingdoms, he shied away from an assessment of how far papal power extended
into the temporal as opposed to the spiritual domain, deeming it to be an issue
of theology rather than history.[136]

Prudence dictated that in Ireland this apparently crucial issue was not even raised by Catholic historians. Charles O'Conor, for example, dwelt on the secular aspects of the conquest only and omitted all reference to the state of the Irish church. He did not even mention that the agreement between Henry and the pope took the form of a papal bull, calling it instead an 'Alliance with the Court of Rome'. His brief assessment of the outcome of that agreement was bitterly fatalistic in tone, and unfavourable to both parties, in that he likened Henry to 'another Joshua', commissioned to 'enter Ireland in a hostile Manner, and put the Inhabitants to the Sword, for the Good of Religion, and the Reformation of Manners'.[137] Issues such as the authenticity of the bulls and the respective rights of English king and pope were best avoided, as his friend Thomas Leland was later to point out: 'I hope there is no Roman Catholic of any enlightened mind, who at this day believes that the Pontificate can dispose of Kingdoms, or empower any prince to cut honest men's throats, under the pretence of his being appointed by the See of Rome.'[138] O'Conor needed no such reminders; his role in the Catholic Committee made him unusually sensitive to political implications, and his diplomatic reticence on this crucial historical issue is, therefore, just as revealing as the tortuous explanations of MacGeoghegan.

Ledwich referred with evident glee to the discomfiture of Catholics on the question of papal sanction for the twelfth-century conquest,[139] but it was not entirely straightforward for Protestant writers either. While the Ussherite thesis allowed them to claim that their religion had its roots in Ireland long before the conquest, it also had the effect of making their colonial forbears responsible for its temporary suppression and replacement by a Roman church. It was difficult to deny this embarrassing conclusion, but Ledwich, for one, attempted to deflect some of that responsibility, by reversing MacGeoghegan's argument and alleging a *papal* conspiracy, in which Henry was only an instrument, to eradicate 'the ancient faith and practice of the Irish'.[140] However, since this line of argument led him dangerously close to condemning the conquest, he drew back, changed tack and argued that one benefit of the religious policies of the Anglo-Normans had been to contribute 'the first step towards reconciling the natives of both countries to each other . . . to make them of one religion'. It thus became an acceptable aspect of colonial, if not religious, policy.[141] Thomas Campbell also attempted to make the best of it, by arguing that Catholics should be grateful to the Anglo-Normans and their king, 'for it was Henry II who first brought the Irish nation to an uniformity of worship, and an exact conformity in doctrine and discipline, with the church of Rome'.[142]

William Hamilton was alone among Protestant writers in condemning the conquest as a Romanising crusade, which established 'a religion which has deluged the kingdom with blood, and has been the great source of almost all its calamities'. In his *Letters from the Coast of Co. Antrim* (1786), his hostility towards English rule was similar to that expressed by Joseph Cooper Walker in *Historical Memoirs of the Irish Bards*, published in the same year, but he was

unique among antiquaries in combining this 'patriot' critique of English policy with an overt and virulent opposition to Catholicism as 'the rank superstition of Rome'. He was aware that he was putting forward 'a paradox [almost]
too wild and too novel to gain credit' when he accused 'the Protestant kingdom of England of introducing popery with all its attendant train of miseries,
into Ireland', and applauded the Irish as 'the genuine votaries of the reformed
religion'. His defence of this statement was couched in unreserved terms:

> Yet methinks when we cast our eyes on King Henry the Second, advancing
> toward this devoted nation, bearing in one hand the bloody sword of war, and
> in the other the iniquitous bull of Pope Adrian, granting him unlimited author-
> ity to root out heresy and to extend the empire of Rome – we see an irrefragable
> argument to prove that this was not originally an island of popish saints, and
> that the jurisdiction of Rome was not unquestionably established here . . . [143]

Hamilton's frankness on this issue is striking, given that he was unwilling to
broach the subject of origins in the same book for fear of offending the rival
theorists, Vallancey and Ledwich,[144] but it was in stark contrast to the ambivalence which characterised all other contributions by antiquaries of either religious persuasion to this debate.

The failure of the Reformation in Ireland, the consequent division of society on denominational lines and the continued role of religion in the political
power structures prevented the descendants of colonist and colonised from
achieving an agreed narrative on their only common golden age of 'saints and
scholars'. As Catholic relief measures began to be passed from 1778, sectarian
polarisation increased, thus making it even less likely that this would happen.
At the same time that some common ground was being sought in the literature and laws of Gaelic Ireland for a secular golden age, political forces were
exerting a pull on antiquarianism that ultimately led to the abandonment of
such attempts to create a shared past for the two religious communities.

OSSIAN AND THE IRISH BARDS:
Primitivism and Patriotism

In the summer of 1779, Gabriel Beranger, a Huguenot artist born in Rotterdam who moved to Ireland in about 1750, travelled to the west of the country to make sketches of various antiquities and monuments for William Burton Conyngham, founder of the Hibernian Antiquarian Society. He was accompanied by an Italian artist, Michael-Angelo Bigari, a guide, Lewis Irwin, and an interpreter, Terance McGuire, who was also literate in Gaelic.[1] On the small island of Ennismurray off the coast of Co. Sligo, Beranger recorded that they saw 'Irishmen in the true State of nature, hospitable . . . inocent [sic] and merry'.[2] His reports emphasised their hospitality, cleanliness and spartan living conditions and he observed that they seemed 'blessed with All the necessaries of life' and desired nothing more.[3] Beranger's perspective on this island people was heavily influenced by primitivism, a fashionable doctrine of the second half of the eighteenth century which was grounded in the belief that the best condition of man and human society was the earliest, when the world had a simplicity since lost. Ideal representations of an original 'state of nature' were derived from earlier encounters with the indigenous peoples of the Americas and were closely connected to the concept of the 'noble savage'. These ideas were given renewed currency in the late eighteenth century when new voyages of discovery, principally by Louis de Bougainville and James Cook in the 1760s and 1770s, brought word of the Polynesian peoples of the South Pacific.[4]

European writers presented the islanders of Tahiti in particular as 'exotics' whose simple, natural culture replicated those of Greece and Rome in their earliest phases.[5] As Bernard Smith has noted in *European Vision and the South Pacific* (1985), Cook's expeditions to the South Seas, which included scientists as well as artists, had made the flora, fauna and native peoples of the Pacific better known to Europeans than those of many less distant regions. The plan of operation of these expeditions, involving the meticulous observation and recording of phenomena, became the blueprint for many later journeys of exploration.[6] Judging by his letters and diaries, Beranger had read these reports, and clearly saw his own role in the west of Ireland as akin to that of the artists employed by Cook to record his voyages.[7] Accounts of the Pacific voyages provided the narrative model for his description of the party's first encounter with the islanders:

> The inhabitants Seeing us make towards them were collected on the Shore, and received us with open arms, and being warned by Mr Irwin to imitate him, we

followed his example and embraced the females, who returned the civility with as much cordiality as if we had been their nearest relations . . . 8

He made direct parallels between the native women of Ennismurray and of Tahiti, although with the reassurance that the Irish female peasants displayed none of the notorious sexual promiscuity of the Tahitians:

I fancied to be at Ottaheite [a name for Tahiti], since we found here the same good nature, but accompanied by modesty in the Sex, who grants plenty of inocent [sic] Embraces, Since they could not Enjoy our Conversation . . . 9

After two days, in recompense to the islanders for their hospitality, the visitors gave them beads, ribbons, tobacco and whiskey, embraced the females once more, and bade farewell in a ceremony that was 'so affecting . . . that for a long time we continued in a thoughtful silence'.10

Beranger was not alone in seeing parallels between the distant exoticism of the Pacific and that of Ireland. In 1775 the English naturalist Gilbert White (1720–93) had proposed a Pacific-type expedition to Ireland, 'a new field, and a country little known to the naturalist', which would enlist the services of botanists and draughtsmen. For a 'person of a thinking turn of mind', observation of the inhabitants would be as important as that of the plant-life, since '[t]he manners of the wild natives, their superstitions, their prejudices, their sordid way of life, will extort many useful reflections'.11 The somewhat hostile perspective of White may reflect a hardening of primitivist feeling, which was intensified by the death of Captain Cook in February 1779 (five months before Beranger's expedition), killed in Hawaii in a fracas with a group of natives, although news of his fate did not reach Europe until January 1780.12 Cook's death was commemorated in paintings, in poetry and in a pantomime, La Mort du Capitaine Cook, which was first put on in Paris in 1788, and in London and provincial centres, including Dublin and Limerick, the following year.13 While individual natives continued to be depicted as 'noble savages' in most of these representations of Cook's death, meditations on the general character of the native peoples of the Pacific became more negative. Traits such as their alleged emotional volatility, moving from laughter to gloom or rage in an instant, which had been presented previously as an indication of natural virtue and an absence of artifice, became, following the death of Cook, tokens of natural viciousness.14 The transformation from 'noble' to 'ignoble' savage was often swift.

This may explain why there was little or no writing in full primitivist mode by Irish writers in this period. In Ireland, primitivism, like romanticism of which it was part, was always mediated through the ongoing colonial debate. The earliest of those colonial writings, Giraldus Cambrensis's Topographica Hibernicæ (1188), had stressed the degeneracy and barbarism of Gaelic society.15 This negative image had been invoked in the sixteenth and seventeenth centuries by commentators like Edmund Spenser and Sir John

Davies, to justify both the original conquest and its projected completion.[16] It was rebutted by Irish Catholic writers, such as John Lynch, for example, who published the first full-scale attack on Giraldus in *Cambrensis Eversus* (1662), systematically answering many of his most damaging arguments. Geoffrey Keating's response to such negative stereotyping was to re-vivify the tradition that a great Gaelic golden age of civilisation had existed in the pre-colonial period, which was the central theme of his *Foras Feasa ar Éirinn*.[17] Thus, the myth of barbarism was countered by one of civility, and this dualism was to remain a dominant feature of the colonial debate. In effect, both sides created an *idea* of Gaelic society which existed outside historical time and was shaped to a large degree by contemporary preoccupations. In this fraught political context, primitivist fantasies were hardly sustainable, except perhaps by a relative outsider, such as Beranger. Irish antiquaries' at best ambivalent response to European primitivism is most visible in relation to the Ossian poems of James Macpherson, whose historical work, as we have seen, had a considerable impact on the origins debate. However, in terms of representations of Gaelic society, Macpherson's Ossian poems were even more influential on Irish antiquarian writing in their highlighting of a rich, vanished literary tradition. They were also critical in shaping late eighteenth-century perceptions of that tradition and of the society which produced it.

Macpherson produced three collections of poems between 1760 and 1763 which purported to be translations from Gaelic of the works of a third-century Scottish bard, Ossian the son of Fingal, King of Morven, whose many exploits they celebrated.[18] In old age, beset by blindness, Ossian recalled the battles fought by Fingal and his warriors (of which he was one), their love affairs and their feasting, singing and story-telling. Although greeted with acclaim all over Europe as the authentic voice of primitive poetry, doubts about the poems were expressed almost immediately and with gathering force as time went on. By the beginning of the twentieth century, received wisdom was that the poems were forged by Macpherson, but in recent years this verdict has been challenged both by literary historians, who have rethought the general concept of forgery and the editing of texts, and by Gaelic scholars, notably Derick Thomson, who established the extent to which Macpherson had used original Gaelic sources, collected while touring the Highlands in 1760. He highlighted instances in *Fingal* where Macpherson was remarkably faithful to his sources, not in the sense of translating literally, but in terms of imagery and sometimes language, even though in general his 'refining and bowdlerising pen' had transformed the nature of the Highland oral tradition.[19]

As Fiona Stafford has pointed out, Macpherson had been exposed to primitivist ideas at university in Aberdeen, where many of his teachers had been students of Thomas Blackwell, the author of a classic primitivist text, *An Enquiry into the Life and Writings of Homer* (1735).[20] The world of Ossian, the picture of manners and the glorification of a literature shaped by a turbulent world of constant warfare, reflected existing theories about early society rather than generating new ones. Hence, writers all over Europe recruited Ossian to already established causes; and there is a growing literature on the reception of the poems in Europe, linking the enthusiasm for them to a variety of factors, ranging from a revolt against stifling classicism in Italy and Russia, to a growing primitivism among social theorists and philosophers.[21] Herder, for example, had worked out his ideas of language development and of oral poetry before reading Ossian, and his enthusiasm for the poems can be attributed in part to their apparent support for his thesis.[22] Similarly, Lord Kames, the influential Scottish socio-historian, defended the authenticity of the poems against the sceptics on the basis that they were the perfect illustration of stadialism, a theory of social development which posited a series of stages, from hunting through pastoral to commercial, which all societies were believed to have experienced.[23]

In contrast to this overwhelming European enthusiasm, in Ireland the response was intermittent, fragmented and characterised by ambivalence. An important overview of the significance of Ossian for northern European literature by John Greenway provides a possible framework for understanding the discrepancies between the Irish and general northern European responses. He identified the poems as a type of mythic narrative which legitimised the values of sentimental primitivism and gave authority to several primitivist fantasies of the Nordic past. Ossian was used to counter the slur of Nordic barbarity with the idea of a primitive northern genius or northern Homer.[24] Irish writers were similarly involved in counteracting the barbaric image of Ireland in Britain, which had for many centuries been an integral part of colonial discourse. Those from a native Irish or Catholic, rather than Protestant planter background, did so by depicting a glorious and highly sophisticated pre-colonial golden age which contrasted with their present perceived situation as disadvantaged colonial subjects. Ossian could not be easily used to validate that imagined past, in part because their fantasy did not conform to the primitivist paradigm which the poems represented. The nostalgia of English primitivists for, for example, the lost innocence of a former age, went hand in hand with the belief that late eighteenth-century England was the epitome of a well-ordered, wealthy and progressive society.[25] But in Ireland, the idea of the 'primitive' was too close to the traditional but still prevalent English view of Irish culture and society, and initially neither Catholic nor Protestant writers identified sympathetically with it.

A second factor which affected the Irish response was the shared Gaelic culture of Ireland and Scotland. The historical scheme proposed by Macpherson, in the paratexts of the poetic works and later in the *Introduction to the History of Great Britain and Ireland* (1771), ran contrary to the widely accepted view in positing a Gaelic-speaking colony in third-century Scotland, about two hundred years before the settlement of the Dalriadans from North Antrim in Argyll. As seen in Chapter One, part of the Irish response to Macpherson consisted of a number of refutations of his origins theory. For a long period, charges of anachronism and fraudulence were the only reaction, and there was little scholarly analysis of the texts or discussion of their literary merit. In England the debate on Ossian was centred around two questions which most writers attempted to keep separate: the authenticity of the poems and their literary merit.[26] This kind of separation was impossible in Ireland, where the forgery question tended to obscure all other considerations. A sympathetic overview was finally achieved by an Irish novelist rather than antiquary, in Lady Morgan's *Wild Irish Girl*, published in 1807, some forty years after the first appearance of the Ossian poems.[27] That the forgery question predominated is understandable, since Ireland was the only country which seemed, at the time, to lose from the popular acceptance of Macpherson's creation. The traditional tales that he had exploited were recognisably of Irish origin, and his heroes, Fingal and Ossian, were versions of Fionn Mac Cumhaill and Oisín of the Fionn cycle, part of a pre-Christian Gaelic oral tradition, for which the earliest surviving manuscript versions date from the twelfth century, although the bulk of them are from as late as the seventeenth century.[28]

The notion of 'ownership' of the Fionn cycle and of the corpus of early Gaelic literature and myth which was the basis of so much acrimony between Irish and Scottish historians since the previous century, stemmed from the very limited understanding of medieval sources prior to the nineteenth century. Ideas such as 'truth' and 'myth' (or 'fable') were perceived as mutually exclusive, and there was no understanding of the fact that medieval literature, like any other, constantly developed; or that fragmentation of the Gaelic tradition was exacerbated by the decline of the polity which had supported it. According to this mind-set, if 'truth' was static, then variation was a proof of fiction or corruption; there could only be one version of any narrative that was authoritative. In this context, a dispute over the historical validity of Macpherson's version of the traditional tales was inevitable.

The spread of Gaelic Irish lore to Scotland in the early Middle Ages entailed its adaptation to indigenous circumstances: thus, the heroes of the Fianna and Red Branch tales became Scottish and the scenes of battles were also adapted accordingly. In the eyes of Irish writers, however, eager for their country's honour, Macpherson's depiction of Fingal as a Scottish rather than an Irish chief and Ossian as a Scottish bard was a theft of genuinely Irish heroes. It evoked memories of an earlier phase in the Hiberno-Scottish dispute, when Thomas Dempster had annexed recognised Irish saints and philosophers to the Scottish pantheon.[29] Similar notions of ownership lay behind Macpherson's derogatory references to Irish historical and literary sources. Aware that they could be used to suggest that his translations were a fraudulent concoction, he set out to undermine their credibility. In the preface to *Fingal* (1762) he dismissed the Irish tales of the Fianna attributed to Oisín as 'spurious pieces', full of anachronisms, and written by later Irish bards who had passed off their compositions as Ossian's and had caused the Irish to believe 'that Fingal was of Irish extraction, and not of the ancient Caledonians, as is said in the genuine poems of Ossian'.[30] In the final part of the poetic trilogy, *Temora* (1763), he branded Geoffrey Keating and Roderic O'Flaherty as 'idle fabulists' and their works as 'credulous and puerile to the last degree'.[31] Significantly, *Temora* is now estimated to be the least genuine of the trilogy, in that it contains only one poem which is based on a traditional tale; whereas *Fingal* was made up of several such, and also shows signs that Macpherson had consulted Keating and O'Flaherty.[32] His later audacious assault on these two writers in *Temora*, therefore, was a strategic defence; a tactic which he employed in other ways also against possible Irish discovery.[33]

As the author of the *Dissertations on the Antient History of Ireland* and an acknowledged Gaelic scholar, Charles O'Conor was the most likely candidate to counteract Macpherson's distortions of the Irish past. In view of the widespread enthusiastic reception of the Ossian poems, it is somewhat surprising that his refutation took the muted form of a pamphlet which was then attached to the second edition of his *Dissertations*, published in 1766.[34] One possible explanation is that O'Conor regarded the fraud as so blatant that it would take only one closely argued essay to expose it. His private correspondence seems to indicate a certain complacency at this early stage, as in a letter to John Curry in October 1765: 'Macpherson resembles the cuttle fish, which endeavours to escape by involving itself in a flood of muddy liquor, not unlike ink. It cost me some labour to bring him into open light; I then found it easy to master him.' He also felt that his reply to Macpherson's 'abusive notes and dissertations' belonged with the new edition of the *Dissertations*, as 'it is a vindication of the chief things therein advanced'.[35] The central thesis of O'Conor's 1753 *Dissertations* had been that the early Irish were a highly cultivated people who were literate long before Christianity arrived in Ireland.[36] The case he made, however, was laboured and unconvincing, even to his own eyes, since there were no documents surviving from pre-Christian times to corroborate the theory, and he recognised that such evidence was the only acceptable kind.[37] Macpherson's purported translations from the Gaelic of a third-century Scottish bard, whose works had been composed as well as preserved orally through the ages, may have been a godsend to Herder and the early German romantics who were developing ideas of just such an oral folk poetry, but for O'Conor the notion of an exclusively oral medium of communication undermined his portrayal of early Ireland as a sophisticated, aristocratic and, above all, literate society, and it had thus to be attacked as part of the established British tendency to depict the Irish as barbaric.

In his pamphlet, O'Conor treated Macpherson's Ossian mainly as another move by a Scottish writer to annex part of the Irish past as their own, and as a malicious response to the earlier exposure of the seventeenth-century Scottish claim to be the rightful *Scoti*.[38] Concentrating for the most part on the notes and prefaces to *Fingal* and *Temora*, in which most of Macpherson's offensive historical interpretation was located, O'Conor seldom addressed himself to the actual poems, except to point out, quite shrewdly, that much of their considered poetical merit was based on their 'apparent antique Dress, and an oriental Scriptural Turn in the Expression'. But in spite of 'an affecting Grace in the sentiment, and an Imagery nobly sublime', he found them to be repetitive and to have 'a poor Machinery', and surmised that by being presented as 'Works of a remote Antiquity' rather than 'mere modern Compositions', 'their Inequalities and Blemishes are easily overlooked, in Favor of their Beauties and Wild Ornaments'.[39]

It is clear that O'Conor's animosity was directed at the historical background that Macpherson had sketched and not at his alleged pirating of the original Irish tales, on which O'Conor placed little or no value. In an aside he dismissed these originals as 'Romances, and vulgar Stories',[40] while later in the 1770s he made his attitude more plain: 'the crude tales on Fin Mac Cumhal, and other Irish warriors, were picked up, and cast in a new and pleasing form', but these original tales in reality were 'mere amusements for the vulgar, recited in various shapes to this day, among them' and were 'destitute of taste and elegant invention'.[41] Privately, he admitted a preference for Macpherson's polished versions (as Lady Morgan's Irish heroine, Glorvina, was to do). In 1785, he assisted Joseph Cooper Walker in the task of collecting Gaelic poems and songs which would illustrate Historical Memoirs of the Irish Bards (1786). Writing on the problem of getting sensitive translations, he seemed to propose Macpherson as the model: 'I fear your Translations, if they are not done by able hands, are to be doubted . . . for few enter into the spirit of Irish compositions nowadays. I never knew any that approach near it, but Macpherson, who perverted them.'[42] Thus, O'Conor's unshakeable opposition to The Poems of Ossian was clearly one based on his own cultural and political preoccupations, rather than on any desire to preserve popular Gaelic tradition from the corruption entailed in Macpherson's reshaping of it to suit primitivist tastes. If Macpherson's depiction of Gaelic society had not so violently contradicted his own, he might well have moderated his opposition.

In this connection, it is interesting to look more closely at the backgrounds and motivations of O'Conor and Macpherson for explanations of these contrasting views. Usually presented as implacable opponents of each other's work, they were actually involved in the same process of mediating between two apparently irreconcilable cultures, Gaelic and English. It is worth pointing out that they shared a similar background: both were born into Gaelic-speaking communities which were in the process of transformation and into distinguished families within those communities. O'Conor belonged to a minor branch of the dynasty which had been hereditary provincial kings of Connaught until the twelfth-century conquest, while Macpherson was related to the clan chiefs of his Highland birthplace, Badenoch, the Macphersons of Cluny. Jacobite risings had a profound impact on both their lives, although neither participated. O'Conor was not yet born when his grandfather fought on the side of James II. He was one of the last to surrender and was penalised accordingly in the Williamite confiscations, in which the family lost most of their land.[43] Charles O'Conor's mother retained her Jacobite sympathies until her death, but O'Conor, born in 1710, gave no hint of sharing them.[44] James Macpherson was only ten years old at the time of the 1745 uprising, in which his relative and clan chief, Ewan Macpherson of Cluny, played a prominent part. In the aftermath of Culloden, his home at Badenoch swarmed with troops searching for Ewan who hid out in the surrounding hills until 1755, when he made his escape to France. The Cluny estates and those of thirteen other rebel clan chiefs were forfeited to the crown. Draconian laws were introduced to break up the remains of the distinctive Highland society, including the banning of the use of Gaelic in schools.[45] Thus, O'Conor and Macpherson witnessed the break-up of the Gaelic societies in which they were reared, and this traumatic experience is reflected in the Gaelic worlds which they created in their work.

However, differing adult concerns shaped varying and crucially conflicting portrayals. Whereas Macpherson lamented the disappearance of the customs, language and way of life of Highlanders in general, O'Conor was more exercised by the threatened extinction of the high literary culture of the learned classes of Gaelic society, which had been a part of his education. In his childhood, the family kept up some of the customs of the almost vanished Gaelic aristocracy, acting as patrons to poets and musicians such as Turlough Carolan, the blind composer, who had taught the young Charles to play the harp. While elements of the traditional lore were still common among the increasingly *déclassé* Gaelic poets, O'Conor was virtually the only person in English-speaking society with even a limited competence in the archaic language of bardic literature. As he grew older he came to associate the final disappearance of that world with his own death.[46] His efforts to pass on his knowledge were not successful, and he seemed overwhelmed by the enormity of the task. In 1781 he engaged a local boy, Martin Hughes, as a scribal apprentice, but the difficulties of making a living at this kind of work were such that, much to O'Conor's dismay, within two years the trainee had left to become a servant in Dublin.[47] However, if O'Conor had little hope of single-handedly creating a future for bardic learning, he could at least give it an impressive past. This may partly explain his unwavering commitment to the existence of a literate culture in pre-Christian Ireland. He continued to make use of the Milesian tradition, because it traced the Irish back to Spain and to the Phoenicians, from whom they allegedly learnt their alphabet, and thus were able to develop such an early literacy. He was more interested in proving Phoenician *influence* than descent; what he called, 'the Commerce of [our] Spanish Ancestors with the lettered Nations of Phenicia [sic] and Egypt'. Once they settled in Ireland, however, all such contacts ceased and the Milesians became 'a People sequestered from all the learned Nations, and indebted to their own Industry for any Progress they made in the useful Arts of Life'.[48]

While Macpherson celebrated the orality of his third-century Gaelic society, O'Conor strenuously sought to subvert such a primitivist view. Since he could not produce any actual manuscript remains of this pre-Christian culture, his case rested on ogham writing. This was a type of runic script in which the letters of the Latin alphabet were represented by sets of parallel lines, upright or diagonal, meeting or crossing a straight baseline. It was used for commemorative inscriptions on standing stones, and is now thought to date from the early Christian period.[49] O'Conor, taking an idea from the seventeenth-century antiquary Roderic O'Flaherty, claimed that ogham bore no relation to the Latin or Greek alphabets and therefore pre-dated their adoption in Christian Ireland.[50] He was even incautious enough to claim that ogham was derived directly from the Phoenician.[51] However, the ogham alphabet, no matter what its origins, was hardly convincing evidence of a sophisticated pagan society, although the discovery of the Callan ogham stone in the 1780s raised expectations that it might become such.[52] In the clash with Macpherson, O'Conor's case was undermined both directly and indirectly by the former's insistence on and, indeed, proud boast of, a purely oral Scots Gaelic culture. It is interesting that the sceptical public reaction to O'Conor's claim of an early literate civilisation and to Macpherson's defence of the Ossian poems against forgery charges was the same: that they should produce the manuscript evidence.

In old age, while he never gave up the claim, O'Conor somewhat modified and moderated his views on the nature of this pre-Christian civilisation. The 1780s was a period of great political change in Ireland. The first Catholic Relief Act had been passed in 1778; in 1782, Poynings' Law was amended and the Declaratory Act repealed, thus seeming to give the Irish parliament more powers to regulate domestic affairs. Despite his age and ill-health, O'Conor was buoyed up by these developments. He had written the *Dissertations* as part of his campaign to end the penal laws against Catholics and to counteract the negative image of the barbaric Irish which had long been used as a justification for their subordination. His vision of early Irish society was one in which learning, industry and piety predominated; characteristics which he implied would come to the fore again if religious toleration was introduced.

Political developments seemed to signal that the authorities accepted his arguments that, as he put it in a letter, 'indeed we are all become *good Protestants in politics*' and that Jacobitism was now as remote as 'the principles which animated the hostile parties of York and Lancaster in a former period'.[53] Perhaps this was why his late writings were more open to the possibility that early Ireland was not the wholly polished civil society that he had once envisaged. In 1784 he was prepared to admit that, along with 'the elements of arts and literature', the Milesians had introduced 'the coarse manners of their Scytho-Celtic ancestors' and that 'on their arrival in Ireland they mixed with a still coarser people than themselves'.[54] He also conceded that unspecified 'barbarous customs' had existed among the early Irish[55], but at no point did he come close to accepting the stadialist approach of distinctive stages of social development in Ireland, which Macpherson had adopted for his version of early Celtic society in Scotland.[56] Insofar as he had a coherent view, O'Conor seemed to adhere to the older concept of a cyclical model of historical process, put forward by Machiavelli, among others.[57] According to O'Conor's version of this scheme, barbarism could occur at any time in society's development and was a direct consequence of faction or corrupt government, and not of Irish national character, as English writers such as Spenser and Hume suggested.[58] This model also allowed him to defend the early importation of letters into Ireland, since a later downturn into 'ignorance and barbarism' in which 'Letters were retained, but little applied to the Cultivation of Human Life and Manners' was quite likely and then itself subject to reversal.[59]

Markedly different political motives lay behind Macpherson's portrayal of third-century Scotland as a warrior society. Richard Sher has shown that the project of gathering material in the Highlands which resulted in the Ossian poems, was connected with the campaign for a Scottish militia, and with the desire among the Edinburgh élite for a Scottish literature that was recognised as equal, if not superior, to that of England. A number of the Scottish literati sponsored Macpherson to produce translations of Gallic poetry which would further both ends at once.[60] Macpherson's primitivism also ensured that his version of the Celtic past would differ from that of O'Conor. The Scot regarded the third-century Fingalian society of the poems as a golden age which epitomised the first or savage stage in the progress to civility, when an absence of property and luxury prevented the corruption which accompanied the later phases of barbarity and civilisation. Macpherson's Caledonians 'retained the pure but unimproved language of their ancestors together with their rude simplicity of manners'. He gave them all the characteristics associated with the idealised savage: they were 'fierce, passionate and impetuous', 'in love with slaughter', but also 'plain and upright in their dealings, and far removed from the deceit and duplicity of modern times'.[61] His references to modern civilisation were negative in the extreme, referring to 'the great channel of corruption which pollutes the human mind in an advanced stage of civility'.[62]

This nostalgic strain in Macpherson's work was only partly a yearning for supposedly third-century simplicities; it was also an elegy to the pre-Culloden Highlands of his childhood. He openly sought to connect these two worlds, one imagined, the other experienced, by using anecdotal evidence of allegedly strong traces of pagan superstition still in existence among a people whom he termed 'the ancient Scots'.[63] In the dissertation prefixed to Fingal (1762), Macpherson lamented the transformation which increased communications and commerce had wrought on the Highlands, destroying 'that leisure which was formerly dedicated to hearing and repeating the poems of ancient times'. He went on to refer to those who had left the Highlands to make their careers elsewhere, as he also was in the process of doing. Exposure to 'foreign manners' has caused them to 'despise the customs of their ancestors', with the expected consequences for their culture: 'Bards have been long disused, and the spirit of genealogy has greatly subsided. Men begin to be less devoted to their chiefs, and consanguinity is not so much regarded.'[64] On one level, all of Macpherson's Scottish writings can be read as a symbol of his enduring 'devotion to his chiefs', despite a growing involvement in English politics and commerce; their sentimentalism was as much a product of the experience of self-imposed exile in the metropolis as of the literary taste of the age.[65]

Such nostalgia was entirely absent from the writings of O'Conor, who took a far more pragmatic view of his surroundings. When, for example, in the *Dissertations*, he described the Irish climate, he emphasised, prosaically, the constant cloud and rain, instead of Ossianic-type mists, and deplored the lack of drainage schemes to improve the boggy terrain.[66] Improvement and industry were constant themes in both his books and his correspondence; in particular, the barrier to progress and prosperity in the country as a whole which the penal laws constituted.[67] Had his religion not precluded it, he would no doubt have been an enthusiastic member of the Dublin Society, the principal vehicle of new agricultural techniques in Ireland.[68] These Enlightenment concerns are explicable in terms of O'Conor's principal livelihood as a farmer. While Macpherson had left his birth place at the age of sixteen to go to university, O'Conor stayed on in Roscommon and continued the task of consolidating the family lands which his father had begun.[69] Although he complained of his scholarly isolation and pined for Dublin and his antiquarian and political friends there, his writing was the product of that particular experience even more than of metropolitan culture.[70] But O'Conor also retained an essentially aristocratic attitude to his world. Strongly aware of his illustrious ancestors, he saw his own friendship with the Catholic Archbishop of Dublin, John Carpenter, in terms of the relationship between the last high king, Rory O'Connor, and the then archbishop, Laurence O'Toole, in the twelfth century.[71] In his contempt for popular literature, in his oft-expressed fears for the survival of Gaelic learning, and in his regrets at not having had a patron, O'Conor echoed the earlier complaints of the bardic and post-bardic poets of the previous century.[72] Thus, his perspective on the Gaelic world, and his portrait of the pre-colonial golden age, were shaped by both archaic and Enlightenment attitudes, which were equally derived from aristocratic notions of society and politics.

By contrast, Sylvester O'Halloran strongly identified with the Ossianic world of James Macpherson, and greeted the poems with great enthusiasm. In many ways, O'Halloran was more representative of the changed nature of Irish Catholic society in the mid-eighteenth century than O'Conor. As an eye surgeon in Limerick who had received his training in London and Paris, O'Halloran was a member of the new middle class which came to dominate Catholic politics from the late eighteenth century.[73] He also had a very different background in Gaelic culture, having been taught some Irish language and history by his family connection, the Gaelic poet Seán Clárach Mac-Domhnail, one of the eighteenth-century writers who developed new popular forms of Gaelic poetry in place of the aristocratic bardic tradition with which O'Conor identified.[74]

Macpherson's Ossian caused O'Halloran to take up the writing of history part-time, while continuing his successful medical practice. In 1763 he wrote an article and open letter to Macpherson on the subject for the *Dublin Magazine*, and these constituted the first considered Irish contribution to the Ossian debate. He described himself in the first article as 'a gentleman, who, by inclination or study, had little intention to meddle on disquisitions of this nature; but whom his love for his country, for want of a better pen, induced to undertake, and search into the records of antiquity'. The title of the piece, '*The Poems of Ossine, the Son of Fionne mac Comhal, Reclaimed: By a Milesian*', underlines how different O'Halloran's initial response was from that of O'Conor three years later.[75] While O'Halloran began by calling Macpherson's *Fingal* an instance of 'Caledonian plagiary' in the tradition of early Scots like Dempster, and while, like O'Conor, his main concern was to refute Macpherson's preface and historical notes, he believed at this stage that these were genuine productions of Oisín, though much altered by succeeding generations. Unlike O'Conor, he did not wish to repudiate the actual poems, but to establish their Irish origin. His initial treatment was, consequently, less severe. If Macpherson had not taken liberties with the texts, wrote O'Halloran, 'he would have deserved the same applause with many other modern critics and translators'.[76]

This relatively benign view was absent from the open letter to Macpherson, written after the publication of *Temora*, which attacked the Scot as 'an enemy to antiquity' for his distortions of the historical record, and 'a broacher of fables' for the liberties he took with the Gaelic originals.[77] Despite this harder line, however, O'Halloran's correspondence with O'Conor in 1765 showed a basic disagreement and in particular his persistence in regarding the poetry as a valuable source, if properly presented. Only four of those letters, written in February and March 1765, deal with Macpherson, and O'Conor's replies are no longer extant, but it is possible to infer his opinions from O'Halloran's letters. In his first, O'Halloran made it plain that he had not relinquished his original idea of reclaiming the poems of Ossian as Irish: 'I think the thoughts so noble, that it would be, doing our Country an Injury, to call them, in Question'; rather, the task was to establish their Irish provenance and to refute 'the Scandalous remarks, of their Infamous translator'.[78] O'Conor immediately replied, arguing strongly against O'Halloran's belief, but the latter held out against total repudiation of the poems: 'The reason[s] you advance against the Genuiness [*sic*] of Macpherson's poems are very weighty: I cannot nevertheless healp [*sic*] thinking, that their Bases are real originals.' O'Halloran made it plain that the main attraction for him was Macpherson's primitivist inflections: 'The Customs and manners so different from anything modern; the thoughts and similies [*sic*] drawn from Nature, and the sentiments so noble, and so Correspondent to that of our antient Heroes, make a great Impression.'[79]

This disagreement between O'Halloran and O'Conor over the value of the Ossian poems can best be understood in relation to their contrasting

approaches to Irish history at this time. While both wrote to counteract negative outside images of the Irish by describing the glories of the pre-colonial
past, they used dramatically different frameworks. In the second edition of the
Dissertations, O'Conor emphasised political developments and presented the
history of early Ireland as the unsuccessful struggle to achieve a system of government resembling the contemporary British model. While the monarchy was
elective rather than hereditary, '[the] Commons were admitted into a Share of
the Legislature'. However, the ancient Irish constitution was 'too much under
the controul [sic] of aristocratical Principles', although 'our antient Kings
attempted to set Bounds, by the Convention of the States at Teamor'.[80] He con-
centrated on the political skills and learning of the early Irish, and expressly
excluded their military deeds. In an account of the reign of Hugony in 350 BC,
he played down the force which the king allegedly used to maintain and
extend control over his territory: 'His military Exploits, had we a minute
Account of them, would afford but little Instruction at this Distance of Time.
The Improvements he made in the Constitution are more worthy of Attention.'[81] Later, in 1773, in an essay presented to the Select Committee of Antiquities of the Dublin Society, O'Conor expressed the belief that the annals could
only be relied on for the historic period from the first century AD, adding the
comment that prior to that time, 'most of our other Monarchs or pretended
Monarchs are remarkable for nothing, but killing one another'.[82]

O'Halloran's primary interest was precisely in those military and heroic
aspects of Gaelic society. In many ways, his version of the golden age combined elements of Macpherson's and O'Conor's: martial prowess governed and
refined by a sophisticated and literate culture. In the *Introduction to the Study
of the History and Antiquities of Ireland*, he declared the Irish to have been 'from
the most remote antiquity . . . a LEARNED, a PIOUS, and WARLIKE nation'.
To this end, they had 'standing armies' and a 'naval force', and 'from time to
time, they poured troops into Britain and Gaul, which countries they long kept
under contribution'.[83] According to O'Halloran, the most distinctive and
civilised of the military customs and laws and manners of Europe had originated among the Irish Celts and had been spread by them throughout
Europe.[84] In particular, he tried to prove that the medieval concept of chivalry
and knighthood had its origins in pre-Christian Ireland. One of the Irish
'antient militias' in his account was the Fianna, led by Fionn Mac Cumhaill,
who was also the warrior chief Fingal of Macpherson's poetry and a legendary
hero in the Gaelic tradition.[85] Macpherson's anaemic versions of third-century
manners and sensibilities fitted perfectly into O'Halloran's imaginative creation
of a noble and chivalric Irish past, and may well have had a crucial influence
on him. His depiction of the code of honour of the Irish 'knights' appears to
owe much to this source, and to the medieval romances which also informed
Macpherson's perspective: 'everything was determined by honourable war; no
surprizes, no subterfuges, or superior generalship was known; and to attack
an enemy under any kind of disadvantage, was highly dishonourable.'[86]

The military glories of the native Irish was not a new theme; O'Halloran was simply giving it a medievalist colouring, much as Macpherson was doing with the Scottish tradition of bearing arms. In both cases, defeat in the Jacobite wars and later risings had not only brought charges of endemic disloyalty, but had also called into question the military valour of the Scots and Irish. These recent reversals made it all the more necessary to produce a long pedigree of national bravery.[87] Shortly after the 1745 Jacobite rising during which Ireland was quiet, John K'eogh had made 'the courage and bravery of the martial Irish from ancient time til the present' a central part of his *Vindication of the Antiquities of Ireland* (1748). He gave an account of the 'native Courage and martial Exploits of the Milesians' up to and including the Williamite wars, where only 'the Hand of Providence' gave victory to the Williamite forces. Even more surprisingly, he praised the 'valour' of the Irish Brigade at the Battle of Fontenoy (1745): 'For as I have been informed, we should have obtained a complete Victory there over the French, only for some Irish Battalions, which turned the Scale.' K'eogh's background as a Protestant clergyman of 'Milesian' descent seemed to enable him to move freely between native Irish and Protestant Irish positions with little or no difficulty, and at times to merge the two.[88]

As a Catholic, Charles O'Conor could only feign the freedom of movement of a figure like K'eogh, by adopting the persona of a Protestant in much of his pamphleteering on behalf of the Catholic Committee. However, the younger O'Conor, the anonymous author of the first edition of the *Dissertations*, written at about the same time as K'eogh's *Vindication*, was much less cautious about expressing controversial opinions than he later became when his identity was known. Significantly, while the 1753 *Dissertations* focused on the learning and government of early Ireland, it also highlighted those military heroes who had launched forays against the Romans in Britain. Even his description of the rapid conversion of the Irish to Christianity used a language more suited to warfare: 'The people embrace it by a sort of spiritual Violence.'[89] O'Halloran often resembled the younger O'Conor in his enthusiasm, colourful prose style and openly partisan position on the treatment of Catholics. Indeed, the battles between them over Macpherson's Ossian and later over the reliability of the annals, on one level, serve to underline the often striking disjunctions between O'Conor's early and later antiquarian works.

O'Halloran believed himself to be uniquely radical in his decision to make frequent allusions to the contemporary political situation in his books.[90] In his defence of Gaelic civilisation, he railed against English writers such as Hume who attempted to 'make the public believe that we were barbarians, till such time as by every kind of oppression, they had rendered us truly such'.[91] He used every opportunity to protest against the iniquities of the penal laws, at one point reversing the argument about states of barbarism and civility, making eighteenth-century Ireland 'little better than [in] a state of nature' owing to these laws which, if rescinded, would allow it to reclaim 'those improvements which IT ONCE POSSESSED, and which it is capable of.'[92] In the 1753 *Dissertations*, O'Conor had been similarly indiscreet in contrasting contemporary and pre-colonial Ireland:

> And who can deny, but that, even in the Days of Tacitus, a Country, so rich in Inhabitants and native Commodities, must be infinitely wealthier than it is at present, when we see two thirds of the People living, like the Tartars, upon Roots, without Raiment, and without Habitations? . . . But we are doomed to be singular in Extremes; to be a great and learned People under the smallest Advantages, a miserable and (if we believe our Neighbours) dull Nation amidst the greatest.[93]

This was one of many passages removed from the second edition, in which he tried to make the same argument with more subtlety. While the first edition had been printed in a Catholic printing house, the second was taken on by George Faulkner, the liberal Protestant publisher who was an influential figure in Dublin politics. The need to appeal to the Faulkner circle may well have been another reason for moderating his tone. Also, by the time of the second edition, when Hume's *History of England* had reinforced the stereotype of the barbaric Irish of 1641, O'Conor was beginning to associate military deeds with a state of barbarism, and hence the hostile or dismissive references to them.[94]

Despite the evident attraction of Macpherson's Ossian for O'Halloran, he ultimately deferred to O'Conor's superior scholarship and social position, and repudiated the poems as a source for the manners and customs of third-century Ireland.[95] Subsequently, the Irish response to the Ossian poems was coloured by the renewed dispute about Irish and Scottish origins which Macpherson had provoked, and by the derogatory picture of the Gaelic culture of Ireland which he had painted as part of this. In his *Grammar of the Iberno-Celtic* published in 1773, Charles Vallancey answered Macpherson's claim in *Temora* that Scots Gaelic was the mother tongue and Irish merely a corrupt dialect which, in its written form, 'bristled over with unnecessary quiescent consonants, so disagreeable to the eye, and which embarrass rather than assist the reader'.[96] On the contrary, Vallancey replied, with a characteristically blithe disregard of logic, the original Scots Gaelic version of one of the poems in *Temora* which Macpherson had included, showed its *novelty* by its corrupt language, and was therefore 'a proof of the unlettered ignorance of the *ancient* Gaelic Scots' [my italics].[97]

The confusion here was symptomatic of the general Irish response and of the limited and superficial nature of Gaelic scholarship in this period. In many ways it was unequal to the challenge of the Ossian controversy. The absence of a proper dictionary and grammar of Scots Gaelic made it impossible to refute Macpherson's assertion that the Gaelic originals of his translations had remained unchanged and intelligible after centuries of alleged oral transmission.[98] However, the success of the poems was instrumental in enhancing the status of Gaelic culture and encouraging a new interest in it, both in Scotland and Ireland.[99] From the late 1770s, Irish Protestant writers, such as Joseph

Cooper Walker, Charlotte Brooke and the novelist Lady Morgan, became attracted to the Gaelic world, now seen primarily in terms of its music and poetry.[100] This was a major shift in perspective from earlier colonial casts of mind which had dwelt on the seductive yet destructive nature of Gaelic society and the threat its barbarism posed to good government and the new settlers. Catholic antiquaries were very conscious of this sea-change in attitude. Writing to O'Conor in 1781, Thomas O'Gorman remarked: 'It must indeed be very pleasing to us old Irish to see such a Spirit at present diffused among our late oppressors and it is incumbent on us to give them every Aid in our Power toward forwarding and keeping up such Zeal in them.'[101] This renewed Protestant interest in the Gaelic world, which Seamus Deane has dubbed 'the first Celtic revival', pointed to a growing security among the colonial élite in relation to what was a receding indigenous culture.[102] Paradoxically, the growth of a more Irish-based identity among Protestants made them less secure too, in that they also felt compromised by the traditional negative stereotype.[103] However, in cultural terms it was liberating in that it allowed them to extend the search for a distinctive cultural and political identity by developing Anglo-Irish literary versions of Gaelic originals on the model of Macpherson. Their explorations of the Gaelic world were also part of the general European interest in popular culture at the end of the eighteenth century which resulted in collections of traditional songs, of which Thomas Percy's *Reliques of English Poetry* (1765) and, indeed, Macpherson's Ossian were early instances.[104]

Charles O'Conor was quick to recognise that in the 1760s there might be a new and wider readership for Celtic antiquities, although as evidence of this, he cited the impressive English sales of Ferdinando Warner's *History of Ireland* (1763), rather than the despised Ossian poems.[105] His ill-fated plan in the early 1760s to translate and publish Irish manuscript materials, with the help of Francis Stoughton Sullivan and the backing of the Dublin Society, was a direct response to this.[106] Typically, he envisaged the promotion of the reputation of the Irish annals by this means, rather than the popularisation of Gaelic poetry, which meant little to him in the scholarly sense. It was Thomas Campbell who recognised that, notwithstanding Macpherson's derogatory comments about the Irish language, his 'animated exhibition of the spirit of Ossian' had created a market for Gaelic poetry rather than annals, and he advocated the collection, translation and publication of its literary remains as a matter of urgency.[107] Indeed, the first successfully completed translation project was of literary works from the popular tradition,[108] intended as a contribution to the Ossian controversy, by Mathew Young, a clergyman and Fellow of Trinity College Dublin. He was born in the vicinity of Charles O'Conor's home in Roscommon; his father, Owen Young, is recorded as having leased land from the O'Conor Don in Castlerea, and there were many contacts between the two families. He entered Trinity in 1766 and studied mathematics, but he also learned Irish, probably from Maurice O'Gorman, the scribe employed by the College.[109]

Young had a very different approach to the Ossian controversy than O'Conor or O'Halloran. He focused on the texts produced by Macpherson, instead of the surrounding apparatus of prefaces and footnotes, in an attempt to establish what, if any, Gaelic sources had been used. He even went on a collecting expedition to the Highlands in 1784, and compared the material he had gathered there with Irish tales, either still extant in oral form or contained in manuscript in Trinity College. His findings were published in the first volume of the Royal Irish Academy's *Transactions* (1787), and included the poetry he had collected, together with his English translations. Young's paper has been judged 'one of the most scholarly productions thrown up by the controversy over Macpherson's Ossian', although the translations show only a limited grasp of the language.[110] His verdict on the question of the authenticity of Macpherson's translations was judicious. He believed that Macpherson was not the sole author, but that he had adapted original tales, and that these originals were the very Irish ballads dismissed by him as 'spurious' in *Fingal*.[111] Until Macpherson's originals were produced, it would be impossible to ascertain what was original, adaptation or new creation, and he therefore cautioned against using the Ossian poems as a source for the 'manners, customs, laws, the state of arts and sciences amongst the ancient tribes of these countries'.[112]

Young's Royal Irish Academy paper may well have prompted others, notably Sylvester O'Halloran, to look to Irish literary material as a less compromised source for the nature of Gaelic society than the Ossian poems. In the second volume of the *Transactions* (1788), O'Halloran produced a specimen of poetry and translation, which he titled 'A Martial Ode, sung at the Battle of Cnucha, by Fergus, Son of Finn'.[113] The battle was believed by O'Halloran to have taken place in 155 AD, a century earlier than the setting of Macpherson's Ossian, and O'Halloran was emphatic that the poem was an accurate portrayal of that age: 'It marks the Manners and Customs *of the day*, the Information, Civilization and Politeness of the Ancient Celtic Warriors'; in essence, his standard amalgam of military prowess with a sophisticated civilisation. The shadow of Macpherson loomed large and O'Halloran sought to distance his translating endeavour from the Ossian poems: 'This ode (not like the Impositions of Jas. Macpherson) is to be met with, in numbers of hands, with others equally sublime and animating.'[114]

Joseph Cooper Walker's *Historical Memoirs of the Irish Bards* (1786) and Charlotte Brooke's *Reliques of Irish Poetry* (1789) bore the clearest imprint of Macpherson's Ossian and of the primitivist vogue. *Historical Memoirs*, as its title suggests, owed something to the works on the Welsh bardic tradition by Evan Evans and Edward Jones, which in turn were partly inspired by the popularity of Ossian, while Brooke took as her model Thomas Percy's *Reliques of English Poetry* (1765), which had also capitalised on the interest in traditional ballads and tales from the late 1750s.[115] Yet in spite of these influences, both books revealed an ambivalent primitivism, which turned on the interconnected questions, for Irish writers, of orality versus literacy, and barbarism versus civility. This ambivalence may perhaps be explained by the fact that they were to some extent co-operative projects, involving a number of well-known antiquaries besides the nominal authors, and that most of these were devoid of any primitivist enthusiasm.

As Walker was a literary novice and had no background in Gaelic history or culture, he enlisted the help of all the established antiquaries – among them, O'Conor, O'Halloran, Vallancey and Ledwich – who contributed advice, material, and, in the case of Ledwich, articles on music and the harp. The timing of this co-operative effort is striking, since by 1785 when Walker began his research, these antiquaries had formed into two opposing camps and were berating each other as ignorant and incompetent in the pages of the *Collectanea de Rebus Hibernicis* and privately in their correspondence. Walker was a likeable young man who may have flattered these older men by his eagerness to learn from them. In addition to this combination of enthusiasm and deference, he seems to have had considerable tact and diplomacy, since he managed to remain friends with all of them, in spite of the growing sectarian and political polarisation of the late 1780s and 1790s.[116] The preface to *Historical Memoirs* contains an interesting example of this skill. He acknowledged the help of many people, detailing the particular ways in which they had been of assistance. Thus, for example, Mathew Young had read and commented on his manuscript, while Theophilus O'Flanagan, of Trinity College Dublin, advised him on the Gaelic language. However, his acknowledgement of the contributions of O'Conor, Vallancey and Ledwich was a study in ambiguity: 'The learned can best appreciate my obligations to the Reverend Edward Ledwich, to Charles O'Conor Esq., and to Charles Vallancey.'[117]

The structure of *Historical Memoirs* was loose, as befitting a work made up of disparate contributions, and on a topic for which there was a dearth of historical evidence, particularly if Macpherson's poems were to be ruled out, as Mathew Young had recommended. However, the absence of accessible Irish materials meant that Walker often used the Ossian poems, albeit in an ambiguous way. His method was to quote from *Fingal* and *Temora* in the text, while in his footnotes hinting at the unreliability of Macpherson.[118] Walker had intended to write a rather different book, a biography of Turlough Carolan, the blind harper composer who died in 1738; a memoir of a real and recent 'Irish bard'.[119] In an undated letter among the O'Conor papers, Walker explained his plans: 'I mean to prefix a "Dissertation on the Irish Bards" to my Life of Carolan, in which I shall touch on the Irish Music'.[120] But as its title suggests, *Historical Memoirs* used the reverse of that format, with only a very short account of Carolan appended to a general essay on the Irish bards. In *The Keeper's Recital*, Harry White speculated that Walker's decision to relegate Carolan to an appendix had to do with the latter's undoubted interest in, and use of, contemporary Italianate musical forms and styles. This vitiated Walker's division of musical styles into the natural, embodied in the songs of the traditional bards, and the artificial, to be heard in the drawing rooms and concert halls of Europe. Carolan was not a musically convincing representative of the Irish bardic tradition as Walker conceived it and so was banished to the end of the book.[121]

However, it is very likely that Carolan's demotion had as much to do with his character and life history as his music. Right from the beginning of the project, Walker had very clear ideas about how he would present Carolan. He relied on Charles O'Conor, who in his youth had known the harper, for most of the biographical information, sending him detailed questions as to Carolan's early years, his family, musical education and blindness. He also sought the permission of O'Conor to use the more fashionable term 'bard' rather than the Gaelic *file* which the latter favoured.[122] A final query strongly indicates the main influence on Walker in his conception of Carolan: 'When young was he fond of walking alone thro[ugh] woods, by rivers and among rocks like Beattie's Minstrel?'[123] The Scottish poet James Beattie had written a long and very popular poem, *The Minstrel, or the Progress of Genius*, in 1774, about the early life and training of a medieval poet and musician. Its main appeal lay in its blending of sentimentalism, medievalism and primitivism with echoes of the Bible and a host of other sources, such as Shakespeare, Spenser and Milton. Macpherson's Ossian and Thomas Gray's *The Bard* (1757) were important contemporary influences.[124]

Walker clearly had hopes of making a similarly romantic figure out of Carolan; his blindness and harp playing made him fit to be an Irish Homer, Ossian and Milton all combined. However, it would seem that his researches yielded little of the heroic qualities of Beattie's minstrel, Edwin. Although the 'Life' began in grand style with Walker predicting that Carolan's birthplace of Nobber, Co. Meath, would soon be visited 'by lovers of natural music' as Stratford-upon-Avon was by admirers of Shakespeare, it very quickly became anecdotal with O'Conor supplying most of the reminiscences. In true primitivist style, Walker saw Carolan as 'a fine natural genius'; 'His melodies, though extremely simple, give pleasure even to the most refined taste'.[125] Unfortunately, to Walker's obvious disappointment, many of the well-known stories concerned Carolan's prodigious consumption of alcohol, which ruined the portrait of a *refined* natural genius.[126] While such a recent 'national bard' could be used to challenge the stereotype of barbarism, it was a major drawback that, in addition to creative genius, Carolan did not display the essential qualities of virtue and honour. Walker therefore shifted the focus to the generality of Irish bards in the dim and distant past, where no evidence of distasteful personal habits could undermine the portrayal of Ossianic manners and atmosphere, and where his imagination was allowed free rein. Thus, the bardic schools in pagan times 'were sunk in the bosom of deep woods of oak . . . all was gloomy and peaceful; silent and awful'. Into this scene he introduced his version of Beattie's *Minstrel*, who 'in order to relieve his mind from the severity of academic duties, "essay'd the artless tale", as he wandered through his groves, obeying the dictates of his own feelings, and painting from the rude scenes around him'.[127]

Walker's primitivist leanings were most pronounced in his treatment of Irish music. Arguing from the general premise that music, in its earliest phases of development, was, like language, characterised by 'a natural expression', Walker described ancient Irish music as 'the voice of nature'.[128] It was characterised by a 'wildness' and 'an insinuating sweetness, which forces its way, irresistibly to the heart, and there diffuses an exstatic [sic] delight, that thrills through every fibre of the frame . . . Whatever passion it may be intended to excite, it never fails to effect its purpose.'[129] However, almost at once, Walker qualified this primitivist interpretation, by arguing that Irish music, while sharing many of the universal marks of early music, was nonetheless 'distinguished from the music of every other nation' by virtue of that 'insinuating sweetness'. Significantly, only 'an ear formed in Ireland, would instantly recognise the native music of his country'; Walker thereby staking his claim of ownership of at least one aspect of native Irish culture, despite his planter origins.[130] Thus, Irish music shared in the universality of early music and at the same time was unique. This dualism which undercut Walker's primitivism also characterised his method of argument in *Historical Memoirs*. He attempted to combine his own Macphersonian vision of Irish music as wild and emotional with O'Conor's theory of a golden age of Irish literate civility. Asking rhetorically, 'Can that nation be deemed barbarous, in which learning shared the honours next to royalty?', he went on to claim that '[w]arlike as the Irish were in those days, even arms were less respected amongst them than letters'.[131]

Walker tried to restrict the quality of wildness to Irish music alone, leaving untouched the natives who performed and listened to it. Paradoxically, the cultivation of such music among the early Irish 'evinces a degree of refinement of manners and of soul amongst the Irish'.[132] At the same time, Walker deplored refinement, at least in its eighteenth-century manifestation, which had removed 'the ear so far from the heart, that the essence of the music . . . cannot be reached'. The consequence was the popularisation of Italian music and the wholesale neglect of 'our sweet melodies and native musicians'.[133] Walker's contradictory views on the impact of refinement were symptomatic of his whole approach. While on the one hand upholding the O'Conorite thesis of a learned culture in early Ireland, he also emphasised its orality, claiming that 'musical notation was not known amongst the aborigines of this island' and that therefore 'remains of their music have been handed down to us by tradition, in its original simplicity'.[134] But if simplicity and an oral transmission characterised the music, the bard was presented as embodying the opposite qualities. The training of bards was highly organised and rigorous, involving twelve years of study under the tutelage of druids in 'Seminaries or Colleges . . . in different parts of the kingdom'.[135] Walker attempted to resolve the tension between competing claims of literacy and orality by maintaining that 'it was the policy of the times, to confine the use of letters, so long known in this kingdom, to the professors of learning, the Druids'. Thus, the bards were taught to read and write as part of their general education, but *specialised* bardic knowledge was transmitted orally to them, so that they could perform successfully among the illiterate general population.[136]

Charlotte Brooke faced many of the same problems as Walker in reconciling a fashionably primitive perspective with the traditional approach of O'Conor *et al* in her *Reliques of Irish Poetry*, which is generally regarded as the most significant work of the first Celtic revival.[137] She was the daughter of Henry Brooke, a colourful, even disreputable figure with a varied literary career. Among his most notable works was the play *Gustavus Vasa* (1739), a meditation on patriotism, but widely perceived as an attack on the Walpole administration and therefore banned by the Lord Chancellor before the first performance.[138] He had also written *The Farmer's Letters*, which were anti-Catholic pamphlets warning of the danger of Irish rebellion in 1745; and then in 1760 had a change of heart (perhaps feigned), and wrote *The Tryal of the Roman Catholics of Ireland* (1761) for the Catholic Committee, urging religious toleration.[139] Brooke knew no Irish himself, but it may have been through his influence that Charlotte developed an interest in Gaelic literature. At one point in his life he dabbled in Gaelic antiquities, but his motives for so doing seem to have been at least partly commercial. He attempted, unsuccessfully, to plagiarise materials for an Irish history which Charles O'Conor had gathered in the 1740s for Brooke's cousin.[140] In 1759, he produced an anonymous *Essay on the Antient and Modern State of Ireland*, which drew mainly on O'Conor's *Dissertations*, and extolled the glories of the pre-colonial period.[141] He also wrote an Ossianic-like epic, 'Conrade', subtitled 'The Song of the *Filea* of Ancient Days, Phelin the grey-hair'd son of the son of Kinfadda'.[142]

According to her biographer, Charlotte Brooke studied the Irish language for two years and was responsible for the English translations of Gaelic poetry and song in Walker's *Historical Memoirs*, who then persuaded her to undertake this separate volume.[143] To some extent, it continued the co-operative effort among antiquaries, as she found it hard to obtain a sufficient number of poems to fill the volume, and asked for specimens to be sent to her.[144] Some letters to her indicate that each side in the antiquarian dispute hoped to pressure her into adopting their opposing Gothicist and orientalist theories of origins. William Beauford sent her a copy of a poem *Laoid na Deirg*, and tried to persuade her that the Gaelic word *fion* referred to Scandinavians (Finns) who settled in Ireland in early times.[145] Charles Vallancey took exception to one of her translations, which he felt did not bring out the oriental nature of pagan worship in Ireland:

> I need not Madam inform you that the Pagan Irish, like all the Orientals did believe the moon was devoured once a month by a Monster, was buried and rose again to life by the Art of the priests – be so good as to read the poem again with this idea and I believe you will perceive the subject is as I have explained it.[146]

By and large, despite such persuasion verging on bullying, Brooke, like Walker, held to the more traditional Milesian line of O'Conor and O'Halloran, presenting herself as their follower: 'My comparatively feeble hand aspires only (like the ladies of ancient Rome) to strew flowers in the paths of these lau-relled champions of my country.'[147] Leith Davis has recently argued that Brooke's pose of self-deprecation was conditioned largely by eighteenth-century social attitudes to women writers. A woman risked her reputation by entering into print and therefore into the public sphere.[148] Brooke, like most women before her, justified her action by minimising it; she was merely the translator of the poetry, not the author; a disciple of male antiquaries, rather than an independent voice.[149] In the preface, Brooke explained her purpose in translating Gaelic poetry as a double one. Firstly, 'the productions of our Irish bards' should be made known to 'our countrymen', so that they could witness 'a glow of cultivated genius . . . sentiments of pure honor . . . and man-ners of a degree of refinement, totally astonishing, at a period when the rest of Europe was nearly sunk into barbarism'. But like many writers of the time, Brooke also had an English audience in mind, and couched her purpose in that regard in interestingly gendered terms. Claiming that 'we are too little known to our noble neighbour of Britain', she imagined the British and Irish muses as unacquainted:

> let us then introduce them to each other! together let them walk abroad from their bowers, sweet ambassadresses of cordial union between two countries that seem formed by nature to be joined by every bond of interest, and of amity.[150]

Cathal Ó Háinle has described *Reliques* as an exercise in 'cultural unionism', which aimed to provide 'for a romantic public, romantic interpretations of verse which had little or nothing of romanticism in it'.[151] But Brooke, in fact, resisted the notion of cultural union, by insisting on the difficulties of ade-quately conveying the nuances of Gaelic poetry through the medium of Eng-lish.[152] Since Britain was the younger of the two muses, so English, which she dubbed a 'modern language', could not capture the essence of Gaelic: 'One compound epithet must often be translated by two lines of English verse, and, on such occasions, much of the beauty is necessarily lost.'[153] Thus, Brooke's apology for the inadequacies of her translations rested as much on the alleged inferiority of the English language as on her own talents.

Leith Davis has pointed out that a different voice emerges in Brooke's anno-tations to her translations, one far more self-assertive and politically com-plex.[154] In the notes, Brooke made greater claims for the antiquity of much of the poetry under translation than in the preface. Focusing in particular on what she termed the 'War Odes', she echoed Walker on the wildness of Irish music as a proof of the early dating of the poetry:

> the enthusiastic starts of passion; the broken, unconnected, and irregular wild-ness of those Odes which have escaped the wreck of ancient literature in this

kingdom, sufficiently and incontestably point out their true originality to every *candid* reader.[155]

Brooke argued that evidence for the antiquity of the poems came from 'the structure of the compositions, and the spirit which they breathe', rather than from archaic forms or terminology. Thus, the imprint of antiquity could be seen on poems whose language was relatively modern; they too could 'breathe the true spirit of poetry'.[156]

Brooke did not mention Macpherson or the Ossian poems, despite focusing mainly on poems derived from the Red Branch and Fionn cycles, from which he had drawn his originals. She may not have wished to become involved in the controversy and thus put at risk the image of genteel scholarship which she created for herself in the preface. Equally, her ignorance of the sources may have resulted in her failing to recognise the overlap.[157] However, there are some indications that she decided to produce a volume of poetry which would achieve the same effect as Macpherson had for the image of Scotland, a companion piece rather than a rival to *Fingal* and *Temora*; and this was indeed how the English reviewers perceived it.[158] In *Historical Memoirs*, Walker explained that Brooke had first heard Gaelic poetry and tales as a child on her father's farm where a labourer read 'to a rustic audience' from 'two volumes of Irish manuscript poems':

> The bold imagery, and marvellous air, of these poems, so captivated her youthful fancy, that they remained for some years strongly impressed on her memory. When Mr Macpherson's Ossian's Poems were put into her hands, she was surprized to find in them her favourite Irish tales, decked with meretricious ornaments; and her blustering heroes, Fin, Con, Cuchullin, etc. so polished in their manners.[159]

Yet in spite of this alleged unhappiness with the polish of Macpherson's verse, Brooke's translations suffer from the same gentility, lacking the robustness, even coarseness, which was a characteristic of the material she was handling.[160] Her Cuchullin was as refined and civilised as Macpherson's Cuthullin, and her footnotes often challenged many of the same offensive elements of the Celtic stereotype, for example a lack of cleanliness, as Macpherson had addressed indirectly in the poems, and more openly in his *Introduction* (1771).[161] She argued, with a vehemence that was at odds with the tone of her preface, against the 'anti-Hibernian' critics who represented 'our early ancestors' as '*barbarians, descended from barbarians, and ever continuing the same*'.[162] She admitted that her aim in translating the poetry was primarily antiquarian rather than literary: '[w]ith a view to throw[ing] some light on the antiquities of this country, to vindicate, in part, its history, and prove its claim to scientific and military fame'.[163] Thus, Gaelic poetry, or what she termed the 'productions of Irish Bards' could help to restore the reputation of Ireland, because they exhibited 'a glow of cultivated genius . . . and manners of a degree of refinement, totally astonishing, at a period when the rest of Europe was nearly sunk into barbarism'.[164]

This political note undermined Brooke's insistence that hers was a work of purely cultural explanation for an English-speaking audience. Like Walker, Brooke was intensely aware of the political ramifications of attempting to popularise bardic poetry. As Kate Trumpener has argued in *Bardic Nationalism*, the figure of the bard in works like these operated as a symbol of cultural defiance against 'the arrogant assumption of the English that other cultures are there to be absorbed into their own'.[165] Earlier in the century, Charles O'Conor had openly connected poetry with valid political opposition in the first edition of the *Dissertations* (1753). Stating that the bards had used their poetry to stir their patrons to rebellion, he added the gloss that they themselves had not called it rebellion, but rather 'nothing less than *the Spirit of Liberty*, and the *Assertion of the Rights of their Fathers*'.[166] He gave his own translation of one such poem, of the post-bardic period, which included a line begging God for deliverance from 'the insulting *Saxon* children of Ireland, and her native *Irish Aliens*'.[167] All references to militant bards were omitted from the second edition in 1766, to which he put his name, and which reflected his developing sensitivity to the feelings of influential liberal Irish Protestants and also to the danger of being seen to advocate or support rebellion.

In contrast, Brooke and Walker, by virtue of being Protestant, could afford to be less cautious than their Catholic antiquarian mentor in their treatment of the military role of the bard. Walker, commenting on Spenser's characterisation of the bards in his time as wholly under the control of their unworthy Gaelic patrons to whom they wrote dishonest praise poems, asserted that they 'frequently exercised their talents with zeal, to preserve their country from the chains which were forging for it'. His bards displayed great military courage, flinging themselves 'in the midst of the armies of their much-injured-countrymen, striking their harps . . . til they raised the martial fury of the soldiery to such an elevated pitch, that they often rushed on their enemies with the impetuosity of a mountain torrent'.[168] Similarly, Walker felt free to attack English rule in Ireland in the Middle Ages as 'the iron hand of tyranny' which 'kept the natives in a state of absolute anarchy, refused them the privileges of subjects, and only left them the lands they could not subdue'.[169] He also made English policy central to his explanation for the 'plaintiveness' of the musical style of the colonial period. The bards, he speculated, were driven into hiding by 'the sword of oppression' and spent their time 'in gloomy forests, amongst rugged mountains, and in glens and valleys resounding with the noise of falling water, or filled with portentous echoes'. Their melancholy increased to such a degree that 'their voices, thus weakened by struggling against a heavy mental depression, [rose] rather by minor thirds, which consist but of four semitones, than by major thirds, which consist of five'.[170] This Ossian-inspired and ultimately bathetic account should not distract from the fact that Walker's hostile references to English rule were in line with 'patriot' feeling in Ireland in the 1780s. They are also a measure of the extent to which Irish Protestant identification with Gaelic culture in the late eighteenth century seemed to be attached to that political stance.[171] Writing to the minor English poet William Hayley shortly after the publication of *Historical Memoirs*, Walker explained why he had adopted a Catholic Milesian framework: 'Partial to my country, I could not treat its antiquities with the contempt which your countrymen in general seem to think they deserve.'[172]

Brooke discounted Walker's theory of the origins of the melancholic strain in Gaelic music and poetry; in her view, the latter, at least, had always been pensive or sombre, since its principal inspirations, love and war, 'presented no subject to sport with'. She also elevated the primitivist rationale over the political, by asserting that for the bards 'both art and nature came arrayed in simple dignity'. They lacked 'that variety of circumstances, and appearance, so calculated to call forth fancy, and diversify ideas', and thus their compositions always used two classic styles, 'plaintive tenderness, or epic majesty'.[173] This was in contrast to the French poets who 'abound in works of wit and humour', and, albeit to a lesser extent, even to those of England, 'at least one half of [whom] are merely men of wit and rhyme'.[174] Brooke made no direct allusion to the English colonisations or to English policy in Ireland, probably in order to avoid the charge of stirring up controversy. All her references to such matters were ambiguous. For example, the statement that Ireland had been 'harassed by war and rapine; and her records plundered by foreign invaders, and envious policy' could, in the context in which it was made, be taken to refer to the Viking incursions as well as the later conquests.[175] In her commentaries and notes, Brooke highlighted 'instances of disinterested patriotism' and 'a spirit of elevated heroism' in the poems.[176] Appealing to contemporary Irish patriotism, she called for the preservation 'of these reliques of ancient genius' by 'Irishmen – all of them at least who would be thought to pride themselves in the name, or to reflect back any part of the honor they derive from it'.[177] Fionn emerged from her commentary as 'the greatest [hero] of them all', who united 'the ardour of the warrior [with] the firmness of the patriot, and the calmness of the philosopher'.[178] More significantly, however, she made Oisín, the putative composer of many of the poems, an archetypal figure who expressed the essence of emotion, including patriotic sentiment: 'it is the *Son*, – the *Father*, – the *Hero*, – the *Patriot* who speaks; who breathes his own passions and feelings on our hearts.'[179] Thus, these poems were intended by Brooke to rouse contemporary patriotism and pride in Gaelic culture. However, the military theme of many of them had a dangerous resonance in 1789. For example, in 'Magnus the Great', the warrior and poet Fergus made a speech of defiance to Magnus, chief of the invading Danes, which Brooke glossed thus:

> How exquisitely is the character of Fergus supported! He greets the enemy with courtesy: he is answered with insolence; yet still retains the same equal temper,

for which he is everywhere distinguished. We see his spirit rise, but it is with something more noble than resentment; for his reply to Magnus breathes all the calmness of philosophy, as well as the energy of the patriot, and the dignity of the hero.[180]

Not surprisingly, Brooke's emphasis on patriotism and military heroism struck a chord with United Irishmen in the 1790s, although she was no longer alive to witness this. Indeed, several future United Irishmen were subscribers to the *Reliques*.[181] As Mary Helen Thuente has recently argued, the ancient Irish bards were 'both a model and a popular literary motif for many United Irish writers'. They symbolised the struggle of liberty over tyranny, much as O'Conor, Walker and Brooke had presented them; however, the main literary influence on the United Irish in this context was, in fact, English: Thomas Gray's *The Bard* (1757).[182] Among the many poems on the theme of the heroic bard to be published in the United Irish newspaper, the *Northern Star*, was one by James Glass, which featured an aged bard, similar to Macpherson's Ossian and Brooke's Oisín, who recounted, with his 'HARP OF WOE' how 'Ierne drops the tear of woe' for her 'ravaged' country and 'slain warriors'. His aim, however, was not merely to lament or to commemorate defeat, but rather to evoke further defiance:

> O cou'd I glow with Ossian's living fire,
> I wou'd a thousand warriors yet inspire,
> With all their father's love of deathless fame,
> While tyrants trembled at their awful name,
> Their valiant deeds should fire the Poets song
> Their glories live on his immortal tongue.
> Must you Hibernians ever wear the chain?

To take account of the new Paineite politics and rhetoric, this updated Ossian finished with a flourish: 'Proclaim to ev'ry land, this glorious theme,/ The rights of man alone shall reign supreme.'[183] In 1795, selections from the *Reliques of Irish Poetry* were published in *Bolg an tSolair: or, Gaelic Magazine*, also a United Irish venture and published by the *Northern Star*. This, the first magazine devoted to the study of the Irish language (and of which only the first issue was published), contained an abridged Irish grammar and vocabulary of English and Irish, as well as six of Brooke's translations of modern songs, and a long extract from her version of the poem about the Fianna, 'The Chase'. As Thuente concludes, the aim was to emphasise 'the contemporary as well as the ancient riches of Irish language and culture', but always with a view to making the magazine a vehicle for United Irish propaganda.[184]

A Harp Festival was organised in Belfast in 1792 by a group who had close ties with the United Irishmen. In their circular advertising the event, they explained that their intention was 'to preserve from oblivion the few fragments which have been permitted to remain, as monuments of the refined taste and genius of their ancestors' and they appealed for the support of 'the Irish patriot and politician'.[185] Thus, they were responding to the call made by Brooke to 'the poet, the historian, and the public-spirited' to aid in the patriotic rescue of what she had called 'these little sparks from the ashes of [Ireland's] former glory'.[186] In the advertisement, the harpers were referred to as 'those descendants of our Ancient Bards, who are at present almost exclusively possessed of all that remains of the Music, Poetry and oral traditions of Ireland'.[187] The plan was to tempt the harpers to Belfast with the prospect of a competition with prizes, and then to lay on two experts, one in the Irish language and antiquities, the other in music, 'to transcribe and arrange the most beautiful and interesting parts of their knowledge'.[188] However, as a clear indication of the political dimension now attaching to such endeavours, the festival was held from the tenth to the thirteenth of July to coincide with a celebration of the fall of the Bastille, marked by a procession which included hundreds of Volunteers and United Irishmen.[189] It may well be that the presence of the harpers at such a gathering was intended as an actual rather than symbolic reminder of the role of the bards in rousing the courage of the Irish troops in battles against the invader long ago.

Brooke did not live to see her work used thus to champion the radical cause, but Walker witnessed the political events of the 1790s with growing disquiet. His patriot stand-point had become more extreme in *Historical Essay on the Dress of the Ancient and Modern Irish*, published two years after *Historical Memoirs*, in 1788. The barbarous nature of Irish dress had been one of the themes of colonial writing from Giraldus Cambrensis on. Edmund Spenser, in particular, had recommended its suppression, on the basis that enforcement of English dress (and language) would bring in its train English manners and English civility.[190] Walker used the essay on dress to make a swingeing attack on the English who 'for many centuries after they had invaded this island, used oppressive and unwarrantable measures to bring the natives into subjection'. Compelling the Irish into conformity with English 'dress and manners' was merely a 'specious pretext of civilizing them . . . only the more easily to bow their heads to the yoke'.[191] He also took the opportunity to reply to critics such as Ledwich, who charged 'that I dwell with too much energy on the oppressions of the English; treading, sometimes, with a heavy step, on ashes not yet cold'. His defence was that he was only carrying out his duty by relating 'unexaggerated historic truths'. But, anxious that his work should not be seen as a criticism of *current* English policy in Ireland, he claimed that 'the wrongs of the English only live now in the page of history', and implicitly disavowed any separatist sentiment: 'Mingling their blood with ours, that brave people have conciliated our affections. We have taken them to our arms, and stifled the remembrance of their oppressions in a warm embrace.'[192] The ambiguities of this statement, linking 'affections' with the terms 'stifle' and 'oppressions', are indicative of Walker's uneasy political stance in the late 1780s. However, by the mid-1790s he, like other liberal Protestant Gaelic enthusiasts, had rowed back from the 'patriot' position. The optimistic view that Anglo-Irish conflict was confined, in his own words, to the 'page of history' was finally shattered by the 1798 rebellion. In May 1798, the Scottish antiquary John Pinkerton wrote to him for news of the insurrection, asking, in particular, for a description of the pikeheads used by the rebels. Replying 'amidst all the horrors of an open rebellion', Walker directed Pinkerton to the *Historical Essay* on Irish Dress, which had included 'a memoir on the armour and weapons of the Irish' incorporating illustrations of the traditional pike and other weaponry.[193] What, in 1788, had been unremarkable antiquarian dabblings in the material culture of the past, now assumed a dangerous contemporary dimension. Native Irish rebels and their weapons had re-emerged from the page of history, as the bards had prophesied, but without the romantic gloss which poets and antiquaries had given retrospectively to Fionn, Oisín, and the heroes of the Fianna. Instead, they evoked the spectre of more recent, and more brutal, armed encounters in the seventeenth century. These were ghosts that had never really gone away.

PART THREE

BARBARISM

IRISH CUSTOM, LAW AND LAWLESSNESS

The growing tendency by Protestant writers in the second half of the eighteenth century to depict native Irish society in a positive fashion was balanced by a concurrent reanimation of the older colonial accusation of Irish barbarism. In 1772, Charles O'Conor received a formal invitation from Sir Lucius O'Brien to become a corresponding member of the Select Committee on Antiquities of the Dublin Society. According to O'Brien, the aim of the committee was to show to 'our Neibours [sic]' that 'the Inhabitants of this Island were at all Times Respectable', in order that the present day Irish would not be treated as 'a Barbarous [and] Contemptible People'.[1] This example of Protestant concern at such hostile perceptions can be explained partly in terms of changes in Irish affiliation and identity which were taking place over the course of the seventeenth and eighteenth centuries. The blurring and near disappearance of the sixteenth-century categories of 'native Irish', 'Old English' and 'New English' meant that Irish Protestants also increasingly resented and felt compromised by the stereotype of the barbarous Irish.[2] As a descendant of the Gaelic rulers of Clare, O'Brien may have felt this more keenly than most. However, Walter Harris, from colonist stock, had been equally exercised by this development as early as the 1740s. In 1747, quoting from a tract entitled *The Present State of Ireland* (1738), Harris listed with dismay the description of the Irish as 'uncivilised, rude and barbarous' and holding to customs of incest, divorce, robbery and murder which they 'count no infamy'. He asked rhetorically: 'When such an odious picture is drawn of us, who . . . can refrain from a just indignation?' But, underlining his still strongly Protestant perspective, Harris's main fear was that prospective new settlers would be deterred: 'For a stranger would as soon settle at the Cape of Good Hope among the Hottentots, before the European colonies got footing there, as in a country branded with such infamy.'[3] Whatever the motivation, from around the middle of the eighteenth century there was a growing acceptance among Protestants of the Gaelic past as a shared Irish concern, since contemporary attributions of incivility were grounded in classical and medieval descriptions of Irish society as barbarous.[4]

It was during this period that a new and exciting source for the precolonial period, the Brehon law tracts, came to light, fostering new attempts at understanding the role of native Irish law in Gaelic society. It allowed Protestant antiquaries, such as Thomas Leland, to depict that society in a more favourable light, although such depictions were refracted through seventeenth-century experience, and traditional prejudices against native Irish law always reasserted themselves. Two manuscript volumes of these law tracts were made available to O'Conor and Vallancey in 1769, through the offices of Edmund Burke, who borrowed them from his friend, Sir John Sebright, the MP for Bath, and passed them on to Leland as Librarian of Trinity. These had been part of the collection of Edward Lluyd, the Welsh antiquary and philologist, and author of the pioneering Irish and Welsh dictionary, *Archaeologia Britannica* (1707).[5] One of the volumes contained the *Bechbretha*, or judgments in cases relating to bees, which is the oldest surviving legal tract. This was composed about the middle of the seventh century, but like all the tracts, survives as a fourteenth- to sixteenth-century manuscript.[6] While O'Conor could decipher very little of the texts,[7] Vallancey, with his usual unbounded confidence, claimed that he could read them perfectly, although this was far from the case.[8] In the fourth and tenth numbers of his *Collectanea* (1780 and 1782), he included some specimen translations, but candidly, and naïvely, admitted that these were imperfect because he was 'ignorant' even of 'the law terms in the English language'.[9]

There were, and still are, formidable obstacles to the study and translation of the law tracts. In the first place, the language is technical and often deliberately obscure, and scribes did not always understand what they were copying, resulting in guesswork and corruption. Secondly, a number of the most important tracts have been transmitted only in mutilated and disjointed excerpts scattered through various manuscripts. D.A. Binchy believed that the modern study of Irish law began prematurely. When a commission was set up in 1852 to transcribe and translate the law tracts, Zeuss's *Grammatica Celtica* had not yet appeared, and 'the older Irish language was still an uncharted sea'. The two leading scholars of the time, John O'Donovan and Eugene O'Curry, produced seventeen volumes of transcripts and twenty-five of translation, which were published in six large volumes as the *Ancient Laws of Ireland* (1865–1901). Although this represented a pioneering achievement, their transcription was often inaccurate and their translation also guesswork.[10] Twentieth-century scholars re-edited many of the texts, and in 1978 Binchy collected the surviving legal material in a new six-volume edition, *Corpus Iuris Hibernici*. Thus it took two hundred years, from the time of the arrival of the Sebright manuscripts, for proper translations and analyses to emerge. Modern accounts by Binchy and others of the development of Brehon law scholarship begin with O'Donovan and O'Curry in the mid-nineteenth century. As Walter Love pointed out, the contribution of Vallancey was not to scholarship *per se*, but to the collection and preservation of manuscripts in the late eighteenth century.[11] His translations were conjecture on a scale undreamt of by O'Donovan and O'Curry. Nevertheless, they had an impact, and raised hopes of a new source for the history of early Irish society.

Until this time, the perceived authorities on Gaelic law were colonial commentators from Cambrensis on. The dominant figure was the English-born legal expert and poet Sir John Davies (1569–1626), who, between the years 1603 and 1619, held successively the offices of solicitor-general and attorney-general in Ireland. Davies' *A Discovery of the True Causes why Ireland was never Entirely Subdued* (1612) called for a completion of the conquest of Ireland, and to that end, for the extension of English common law to all people and all parts of the island. In Davies' analysis, law was one of the fundamental marks of sovereignty, and the continued existence of a Gaelic legal system over large areas constituted a major barrier to full English civil government of Ireland.[12] Davies, like Spenser two decades before him, called for the inclusion of the native Irish within the common law; hitherto all but the five royal families of O'Neill, O'Melaghlin, O'Connor, O'Brien and MacMurrough had been denied such access.[13] For Davies, the Brehon law (which was the name traditionally given to Irish customary law) by its nature induced rebellion in the people, made good government impossible, and brought 'Barbarisme and desolation upon the richest and most fruitfull Land of the world'.[14] Echoing Spenser, he singled out the customs of gavelkind and tanistry as particularly iniquitous.[15] Irish gavelkind, or shared inheritance, was a form of land tenure which involved the vesting of ownership in the extended kin group. Individual allotments of land were temporary and subject to periodic redistribution. Tanistry was the scheme of succession, whereby the successor to a chief or king was nominated from within the extended kin group. The successor was the one deemed 'most worthy', which to English observers such as Davies, led to a system of succession by *forte maine*, often plunging rival factions or groups into violent civil strife. They concluded that no stable political order could be built on an elective succession and frequent redistribution of land.[16] In addition, Davies deplored the Irish system of fines (called 'erickes' or 'erics') levied in criminal cases, including those such as murder and robbery which, under English law, were punishable by death.[17]

Davies' characterisation of native Irish law as anarchic became the standard critique. In the first edition of the *Dissertations* (1753), O'Conor only half-heartedly defended elective succession over primogeniture, on the basis that it was a safeguard against inheritance by 'a half-Ideot [sic]'.[18] This was not included in the second edition, so that O'Conor let the particular case for tanistry go by default, and to some extent even followed the Davies line by stressing the weakness of kingship and the factionalism of pre-colonial Irish society.[19] In a new chapter on the Brehon laws, focusing mainly on gavelkind and the system of 'erics' or fines, he cautioned against 'modern Writers' who, like Davies, made general judgements about them, based on 'the evil Effects of those Institutes in latter Times, without considering that they were calculated for distant Periods of Time, for certain Stages of Policy, and for peculiar Manners, under the Control of a national Legislation'.[20] He pointed out that 'Ireland had prospered for several Ages' under native law and had become 'the prime Seat of literary Knowledge to all Christendom'.[21] It was only following the Anglo-Norman conquest that the Brehon laws broke down, rendering 'our

Island a Desart [sic], and our People Savages', but the true cause of this was the conquest itself, which ushered in 'a perpetual State of Hostility, in which the People were exercised, either among themselves, or with the common Enemy, who gave them no Quarter'.22 Thus, while O'Conor explicitly agreed with Sir John Davies that English law should have been extended much earlier,23 he stopped short of accepting that, had this happened, the Anglo-Norman conquest 'might well have been a blessing', as Leighton has recently claimed.24 Underlying O'Conor's analysis was the argument that the Brehon laws had worked well under an independent Irish polity; it was only following its destruction that the native legal system decayed and English law was required to take account of new political realities.

The nature of Gaelic society prior to the conquest was also a significant issue for Thomas Leland in his *History of Ireland from the Invasion of Henry II*, published in 1773. Leland had developed a cordial friendship with Charles O'Conor from the mid-1760s and at the same time a growing interest in, and identification with, the Gaelic past. In a playful letter to O'Conor in 1769, he described himself as *'prisci conscius Avi* [conscious of former times], as much as if I were a Milesian, instead of a Cromwellian'. He also wrote of a sojourn in a valley in Co. Wicklow, which he termed 'classic Ground', where 'the great Sept of the O'Briens once reigned, and milked their cows in State' and where 'that Scoundrel Dermuidh MacMurrough might very likely have come and encamped . . . in some of his Scampering Expeditions over the Mountains of Glendalough'.25 The emphasis, now as then, on Leland's treatment of the 1641 massacre in his narrative of the colonial period has obscured the very real efforts which he made to counter the representation of the pre-colonial Irish as barbarous. This was particularly striking in his first venture into Irish history: the pamphlet refuting James Macpherson's controversial theory of Scottish and Irish origins, which came out in 1772, the year before his *History of Ireland*. His self-presentation as an anonymous and 'disinterested observer' allowed him more freedom to tackle many of the issues surrounding the hostile image of the Gaelic Irish and the Catholic defence against it, subsequent on Hume's *History of England* (1754–62), as well as Macpherson's work.26 On the key question of barbarism, Leland borrowed a line of reasoning from Geoffrey Keating, differentiating between the nobility and the common people, and arguing that the latter had indeed been 'in an ignorant state'. But then, in a significant and strongly-worded comparison with England, he pointed out that national character was generally, although inaccurately, inferred from the manners of the 'lower people', and that on this basis it would be possible to claim that the English were 'a set of brutal ferocious Islanders', devoid of politeness and learning, merely because 'the scum of London are the most brutal people on earth'.27

In his *History of Ireland*, published the following year, Leland took issue with Davies' characterisation of pre-colonial Gaelic society as barbarous, in a preliminary 'Discourse of the Ancient Manners of the Irish', devoted largely to the Brehon laws and using the Sebright manuscript translations by Vallancey. Carefully written and argued, it nonetheless reveals the tension between his liberal political stance and the deep-seated Protestant suspicion of native Irish law and society. He began, in a way no doubt pleasing to Charles O'Conor, by correcting the idea allegedly put forward by Davies that native Irish law had been preserved by oral rather than written transmission;[28] the Sebright manuscripts clearly proved him wrong.[29] He then painted a picture of a well-regulated society, in which the duties and tributes of chieftains were 'accurately ascertained' in law, and in which property was 'guarded by a number of minute institutions, which breathe a spirit of equity and humanity'.[30] He stressed the fact that hospitality, often seen as one of the positive attributes of native Irish character, was enjoined by law, remarking that 'the benevolent spirit of Christianity served to enforce and countenance such manners'.[31] Using the law codes (which he claimed regulated dress), he also tackled directly one of the most negative allegations, habitual Irish nakedness, and pronounced as 'totally incredible' the claim by the English writer Fynes Moryson, in 1617, that even the Gaelic chieftains wore no clothes.[32] Far from being anarchic, Leland suggested, the early Irish were 'the greatest lovers of justice', and (in a side-swipe at the Anglo-Norman adventurers) commented: 'With shame we must confess, that they were not taught this love of justice by the first English settlers.'[33]

But when he came to those aspects of Brehon law which Davies had highlighted as iniquitous, Leland did not deviate from the colonial analysis. Tanistry and gavelkind were the cause of instability and lack of advancement in civilisation. On the system of 'eric', Leland seemed ambivalent, acknowledging that 'the most outrageous offences' were punishable only by fine, but concluding that 'at this day' such arrangements 'will not be regarded as a distinguishing mark of barbarity'; a judgement which appeared to reject the charge of barbarism, while at the same time providing grounds for it.[34] His final summing up strove for an appropriately 'philosophical' balance between the traditional colonial approach and the more favourable perspective which the Sebright manuscripts appeared to support:

> In a word, it appears from all their legal institutions yet discovered, that the Irish, in their state of greatest composure, were indeed by no means barbarous, but far from that perfect civility which their enthusiastic admirers sometimes describe as their peculiar characteristic.[35]

However, once out of this preliminary discourse and into the main narrative on the colonial period, Leland gave up the attempt at impartiality on native law and society, and returned to his 'Cromwellian' roots. The extension of English law in the seventeenth century meant that 'the native Irish were thus invested with all the privileges of subjects', and were 'emancipated from the tyranny of barbarous chieftains'.[36] Leland, like many other Protestants, was unable to escape the straitjacket of traditional modes of thought when dealing with the colonial period, and particularly with the most recent phase of colonisation.

Thus, while the Sebright manuscript collection had offered some defence against the colonial depiction of Gaelic society as anarchic and barbaric, it was not sufficient to transform ideas of native Irish law and society which, since the twelfth century, were fundamental to justifications of colonisation. This was to become particularly clear in the political crises of the 1780s and 1790s, during which Leland's partial re-evaluation of the Brehon laws was rejected in the works of Thomas Campbell and Edward Ledwich, and the classic colonist texts of Cambrensis, Spenser and Davies were reinstated as the sole authorities on Gaelic society. These canonical texts were often mediated through Enlightenment scholarship concerning the process of civilisation, but the message remained the same: the claim of a glorious pre-colonial civilisation could not be reconciled with the fact of recent Irish barbarism.

Davies' *Discovery* was reprinted five times in Ireland in the eighteenth century. By contrast Spenser's *View* was reprinted just once, in 1763 in Dublin. This new edition contained a short life of the author, in which Spenser was considered as a poet only, with no reference being made to the *View*, nor to the political attitudes espoused therein, suggesting perhaps that the 'life' was taken from elsewhere. It was a companion piece to an edition of Davies' *Discovery* produced two years before in the same format, which had also ignored his political role in Ireland.[37] Two of the five editions or reprints of the *Discovery* made explicit reference to the contemporary political situation. In 1733, Thomas Sheridan, friend of Dean Swift, dedicated an edition to the Earl of Barrymore and, reflecting the ongoing controversy over Ireland's constitutional status and Irish Protestant grievances about the patronage system, appealed to him 'to think of some Methods, whereby we may recover a little Life to our Trade, and some Share of the Preferments for the younger Sons of Gentlemen here'.[38] Much later, in 1787, an edition of a number of Davies' Irish political works, including the *Discovery*, was published in Dublin. The unnamed editor justified its publication by reference to 'the acknowledged independence of Ireland' which had 'prompted the inquiries of many gentlemen with regard to its previous history and former constitution'.[39] Surprisingly there was no reference to the Rightboy unrest in Munster which was prompting many to question the changes that had been made in the previous decade, both constitutional and in the realm of the popery laws.[40]

In his earliest antiquarian work, *A Philosophical Survey of the South of Ireland* (1777), Thomas Campbell had Spenser's *View* and Davies' *Discovery* as his 'pocket companions' on the journey.[41] In *Strictures on the Ecclesiastical and Literary History of Ireland* (1789) Campbell reiterated their importance for him: 'who could be better informed than they? men so learned, so sagacious and so inquisitive, and who lived so long in the country'.[42] However, Campbell's use of Spenser, in particular, changed during the course of these two books, mirroring his shifting attitude to the question of a pre-colonial civilisation in Ireland. Thus, in *Philosophical Survey* he cited with approval Spenser's acknowledgment of the Spanish origin of the Irish and also his endorsement of the antiquity of the Irish language.[43] In *Strictures*, however, echoing Spenser and citing the opinion of Swift, he dismissed that language as a barrier to progress and said it would be better for the country if it 'were wholly obliterated and universally abolished'.[44] While in 1777 he was prepared to allow 'that civilisation had made a considerable progress' before the Anglo-Normans, by 1789 such a claim in itself had become a sign of a lack of civility:

> it will be difficult to persuade the rest of the world, that we ourselves are perfectly civilized, till we are able to conceive, and willing to confess, that our ancestors were barbarians: as every other nation in the universe . . . at one time or another, is acknowledged to have been.[45]

Despite his confident tone, Campbell was uneasy about using the term 'barbarous' as a description of 'the Irish nation'. In one of his essays in the *Dublin Chronicle* in 1788, Campbell explained that 'this epithet has never been used as expressive of any particular disposition of mind, but only as relative to manners'.[46] By and large, Campbell adhered to this distinction between native Irish manners and national character, but his examples of uncivilised Irish customs were often taken from the present and used to undercut the claim to past greatness. Thus, for example, in *Strictures*, he pointed to the alleged prevalence of ploughing by the tail, commenting, 'A people whom I have so often seen draw their horses by the tail, in spite of statutes against the barbarous practice, should not thus vainly glory in their ancestors [*sic*] skill in agriculture.'[47]

Campbell's scepticism extended to the claims made for the Brehon laws as evidence of a pre-colonial civilisation. Citing Spenser and Davis, as well as the near-contemporary English jurisprudence expert William Blackstone, Campbell dismissed the argument that the laws were written down early on, but rather 'the jurisdiction of the Brehons was altogether arbitrary and uncertain without any written law or rule'. The Brehon laws in the Sebright manuscripts, he asserted, related to the colonial period and to 'a people in the most rude state that we can conceive capable of writing'; a people who were still 'barbarous'.[48] Conscious that his enthusiastic support for the image of the 'island of saints and scholars' was undermined by such arguments, Campbell resolved the conflict by adopting, as Leland had done before him, the approach favoured by Geoffrey Keating in the 'Introduction' to *Foras Feasa ar Éirinn*, namely, distinguishing between a barbarous common people and a civilised nobility. Campbell asserted that the 'people at large had [not] emerged from their primeval ignorance and rudeness, at the very time their country was dignified with the title of *insula sanctorum et doctorum*, and that in any case, 'those worthies, whose eminent abilities obtained for their country this distinguished character, displayed their talents, chiefly, in foreign countries'.[49]

Campbell quoted, and then attacked, O'Conor's claim that 'the irruption . . . of Henry II proved the utter ruin of the Irish nation'.[50] Prior to the conquest, he asserted, the body of the people were the abject dependents of an uncertain set of barbarous chieftains; who divided and subdivided the nation among themselves, and used their wretched followers as the determined tools of their beggarly yet bloody ambition.[51]

Bearing this in mind, the condition of the native Irish was, at the very least, no worse after the conquest than before.[52] This approach was far from the outright defence of colonisation which might be expected from the enthusiastic proponent of Spenser and Davies. But Campbell was a more complicated figure politically than a cursory look at his writings might suggest. Behind his polemical attacks on Vallancey and, at times, on O'Conor and O'Halloran was an uncomfortable awareness that contemporary politics informed both sides of the antiquarian debate to a large degree. Just as Vallancey tried to escape from the pro-Catholic political connotations of his Celticist antiquarianism, so Thomas Campbell chafed at the pro-government associations of his dissenting position. He tried explicitly to break that connection by declaring: 'As I would support no fabulous farrago of Irish antiquity, neither shall I defend any system of English impolicy. No! not one, from the barbarism of the statute of Kilkenny to the finesse of the Commercial propositions.'[53] It is significant that he chose the term 'barbarous' to describe a law passed in the fourteenth century which traditionally was seen as an attempt to exclude the native Irish from the Pale area and from the benefits of English law.[54]

   Strictures is peppered with allusions, almost all negative in tone, to English strategy in Ireland through the centuries and to government policy in his own time. Campbell was not an enthusiast for the rights of the Irish parliament, but echoed 'patriot' politicians to the extent of being sharply critical of English commercial policy on Ireland. However, he believed that a union between England and Ireland was the best way of addressing such concerns, and at times brought a unionist perspective to bear on his historical analysis. Had Henry II made 'a complete reduction of Ireland' and 'communicated to all the natives the common benefits of the English laws and the English constitution', 'England and Ireland would have been long since, incorporated as one people'. Instead of fostering union, Henry's policy had contrived 'mutual depression and mutual destruction'.[55] Campbell's attack on the commercial restrictions and strong support for the Volunteers and their role in securing a free trade in 1780 were unexceptional and entirely compatible with the growing conservatism of politics in the late 1780s.[56] What was unusual, among Protestant antiquaries at least, was that he blamed the barbarism of the common people on 'the restraints imposed on their commerce', which 'have retarded their progress towards civilisation, and cherished that idleness and sloth, which is not peculiar to the Irish, but which is inseparable from the backward state'.[57] Even more remarkably, he linked this detrimental policy to the penal laws implemented in the reign of Queen Anne, describing them as 'that monstrous addition to Elizabeth's code of penal statutes already existing against the Roman Catholics; at a time when they had not committed any new offence'.[58] Sounding, as he often did in this book, a note of characteristic Enlightenment distaste for earlier religious enthusiasm, he blamed the later phase of penal legislation on 'religious zeal'.[59] On the policy of denying Catholics access to education, he asked rhetorically: 'Should an enlightened Legislature, conspire with an unenlightened Priesthood, in detaining its votaries in primeval ignorance?'[60] The term 'primeval ignorance' had previously been used by him in reference to the pre-colonial Irish, thus reinforcing, consciously or unconsciously, the argument that the centuries since then had done little to improve the native population.[61]

Campbell's views on the popery laws in *Strictures* were unchanged since his *Philosophical Survey* in 1777. In the earlier work, written just prior to the first of the Relief Acts, he had tackled the claim that Irish popery was 'more virulent than elsewhere'. If this was so, it arose from the policy of keeping 'the Irish dark and ignorant', of making them 'poor and unhappy, and then we wonder that they are so prone to tumult and disorder'.[62] In *Strictures*, he pronounced himself satisfied with the relief measures thus far, but made it clear that he advocated toleration, not equal rights: 'Give them every privilege in common with other separatists from the establishment, except a right of carrying arms, and votes in any department of state . . . these are boons which never should be conceded to them.' Instead, these should be held back as an 'allure' to tempt Catholics into conformity 'after a new generation of rich and well-informed Catholics has sprung up'.[63] Thus, Campbell's attribution of barbarism and incivility to the Gaelic Irish had a double political import. On the one hand, it was an example of the Protestant backlash against Catholic claims of a glorious pre-colonial civilisation. On the other, his emphasis on the contemporary residue of this historic barbarism was an integral part of his harshly critical analysis of the impact of the penal laws against Catholics.

Campbell's fellow-clergyman, Edward Ledwich, was equally exercised by the issue of barbarism, which provided the framework for almost all of his antiquarian writings. In 1778 in a letter offering assistance to William Burton Conyngham, he advised him to send Gabriel Béranger's antiquarian drawings to the king, as this 'would tend to rescue this country from the Idea of barbarism, too generally entertained of it'.[64] Ledwich set out to correct the stereotype of the barbarous Irish, which he felt was being unfairly applied to Protestants like himself, by restoring it to those to whom it had earlier exclusively applied, that is, Catholics, whether of native Irish or Anglo-Norman descent. His attempted resuscitation of this traditional Protestant perspective used Cambrensis, Davies and Spenser, but was also supported by a battery of Enlightenment learning, chiefly from the Scottish conjectural historians such as Lord Kames and Adam Ferguson. These were among the founders of a school of socio-history which examined the origins and development of civil society in general, rather than in any particular country.[65] As such, they focused on what Ferguson called 'the General Characteristics of Human

Nature' and on the 'advances . . . of the species itself from rudeness to civilization', using 'conjectures' and 'opinions' of 'what man must have been in the first stage of his being'.[66] Macpherson had applied their theory of the stages of society to the world of *Fingal* and *Temora*, situating it in the first, or savage, stage of development, the period of original simplicity and primordial values. The second stage, barbarism, was a period of transition, between savagery and the final stage of refinement.

In general, barbarism was viewed with revulsion by eighteenth-century writers; there were fears of a return to that stage, even though the historical process was no longer generally seen as circular.[67] Ledwich placed the pre-conquest Irish in that transition stage, awaiting the Anglo-Norman colonisation which would eventually usher in civilisation. That process was not a continuous one, however, as the early colonists were seduced by native Irish custom, and, by the early fourteenth century, had 'insensibly contracted a familiarity with, and a fondness for the dissipated manners of the natives', degenerating so far that they 'adopted their vices' and even mode of dress.[68]

In his earliest and somewhat more emollient writings, especially his contributions to Vallancey's *Collectanea* at the beginning of the 1780s, Ledwich tried to accommodate his conservative views to the prevailing enthusiasm for the pre-colonial period in Ireland. Thus, the Celts were barbarous, but were 'by no means so rude and ignorant as is generally imagined; we have classical authority, that the Celts used earthen dishes at their tables, and pottery seems to have been well understood'.[69] But if this was his concession to the O'Conor and Vallancey school, the craft of pottery hardly approached their conception of a sophisticated early Gaelic Ireland. Even in his later and more cautious phase, O'Conor maintained that the early Irish 'were not Barbarians, in the common acceptation of that word', and that 'they endeavoured to cultivate themselves' and 'built a local civilization of their own'.[70] Although O'Conor and Ledwich differed so fundamentally, the chasm between them had little to do with primitivist theories. Ledwich did not espouse these wholeheartedly as, for example, Macpherson had done; he merely utilised those aspects that suited his colonial perspective. For example, he made no effort to hold up the first stage of society in Ireland as an ideal one, but emphasised its violence and cruelty, characteristics which were normally associated with the barbarous state.[71]

Ledwich made particular use of Cambrensis and defended the highly negative picture of Gaelic society which emerged from this notoriously politically charged source by reference to the writings of the Scottish conjectural school. He quoted a passage in which the twelfth-century Irish were described as 'despising agriculture, inattentive to civil wealth and regardless of law' and argued that it supported the theories of Scottish stadialists:

> The Irish had quitted the hunter, and advanced to the shepherd-state, the second stage in the civilization of mankind; but their manners were little altered;

their food, their domestication and every other circumstance, showed, that the liberty, the ferocity and untamed nature of tenants of the forests, were far from being reclaimed, and still farther from submitting to the salutary restraints of legal institutions.[72]

He was also fascinated by what he saw as the persistence of barbaric custom into the modern period, and likened the seventeenth-century Irish to the nomadic Scythians of Herodotus' *History*, on the universalist basis that 'the manners and customs of rude nations are nearly the same in all parts and all ages of the world'. His somewhat slender evidence in support of this comparison was an order of the Confederate assembly in Kilkenny, made in 1647, which sought to prevent displaced groups from Ulster from roaming with their cattle and destroying the crops of others.[73]

By 1788 when he embarked on his major work *Antiquities of Ireland*, Ledwich had come under the influence of another Scot, John Pinkerton, whose Gothicist racial theory was far distant from the work of the conjectural school. However, he too made use of their theories in his allegations that the Celts were still 'mere radical savages, not yet advanced even to a state of barbarism'.[74] Ledwich and Pinkerton shared a confrontational approach and a mistrust of the contemporary Celticist vogue. Pinkerton may also have lent support to Ledwich's decision to ignore Gaelic sources for the most part in his work. In his *Dissertation on the Origin of the Scythians or Goths* (1787), Pinkerton denounced the reliance on Celtic annalists, for 'falsehood is the natural product of the Celtic mind'. Instead he elevated the classical sources as the only authorities on early Britain and Ireland: 'ancient authorities are facts in history, and incontrovertible'.[75] In a like manner, Ledwich claimed the classical writers to have been impartial on Ireland, and preferred their testimony of the barbarism of the Irish over Irish accounts to the contrary. Also echoing Pinkerton, he maintained that the Belgae (or Firbolgs), an allegedly Gothic tribe which succeeded the Celts in Ireland, were 'a very different and more civilised people'.[76] Ledwich was also influenced by Pinkerton's work on coinage in Scotland, and included a chapter on the 'ancient Irish coins', which concluded that there was no minting carried on in Ireland until after the Anglo-Norman conquest.[77] The pagan Irish, being 'in everything the children of Nature', had no need of money, and those of the Christian era never progressed beyond using their cattle as a sign of wealth and the medium of exchange.[78]

Ledwich thus seems to have gained sufficient confidence from his reading of the Scottish conjecturalists and of Pinkerton to mount a damaging challenge to contemporary notions of a pre-colonial civilisation in Ireland. However, his overriding concern was to counter Vallancey's orientalist theories by Gothicising as much of the remote Irish past as was possible. This can be seen clearly in his treatment of the Brehon laws in *Antiquities of Ireland*. His earlier diplomatic stance, when he asserted that Vallancey's 'view of our legal institutions

. . . frees us from the charge of barbarism, and our Brehons from that of ignorance', had been abandoned by this stage.[79] In 1788 he confessed to Joseph
Cooper Walker that using Vallancey's Brehon law translations entailed the risk
of appearing 'childish and ridiculous' should these be wrong, but even worse,
'This step would for ever blast my credit, and rank me with the most contemptible Irish Antiquary.'[80] Despite his fears, Ledwich made considerable use
of these translations in the absence of any alternative, but he used them for two
seemingly contradictory yet linked purposes.[81] In the first place, he attempted
to undermine the Sebright manuscripts, by attacking the notion that they
demonstrated the existence of an ordered and civilised pre-colonial society:
'In them none of the great lines of jurisdiction are marked: there is no statement of public revenue and expenditure, or of military affairs. Nothing
appears but a picture of rude life and the policy of a barbarous people.'[82] But
he also set out to discredit the manuscripts, which had been so effectively
touted by Vallancey as an authoritative historical source. They were only 'a
miscellaneous jumble', made up, he alleged, from disparate old parchment
rolls belonging to the Maguire clan, and this explained the contradictions in
the material.[83] Thus, his response to the law tracts was shaped more by his
feud with Vallancey than anything else.

It also meant that he departed from the traditional Protestant analysis of
the Brehon laws derived from Spenser and Davies, and adopted by Thomas
Campbell in *Strictures*. That critique always highlighted the iniquities of
tanistry and gavelkind as described by Davies. Ledwich nodded in that direction by calling tanistry 'highly injurious to the public peace by exciting competitions and animating factions', and included a long passage from Davies on
its evils.[84] But he was far more interested in attempting to prove that the Brehon laws were Germanic or northern in character and therefore in origin.
Thus, for example, his main point on tanistry was not in relation to its effects,
but rather that its 'general prevalence' proved that 'our customs were in perfect unison with those of the northern nations'.[85] Having demonstrated that
the Brehon laws 'carry on their face indubitable marks of a northern original',
he was not only prepared to assign to them a greater degree of antiquity than
Spenser and Davies, but also alleged that they had long been a written law. In
doing this, he lapsed into the first person plural, always a sign of personal and
ethnic identification on his part, and asserted '[t]hat we had written laws in the
eighth century, I am able to show', going on to adduce examples of eighth-
century Irish canon law as proof. These canons, together with the Brehon laws,
when compared with Germanic law, provided 'the most decisive evidence of
the derivation of the Irish from northerns and . . . the most incontestable proof
of the idea advanced and pursued in this work'.[86]

If Ledwich had little interest in pursuing the effects of the Brehon laws,
he nevertheless placed great emphasis on the judicial abolition of gavelkind
(in 1606) and of tanistry (in 1608) as a combined landmark in Irish history.
Once the 'pernicious and fatal system of Brehon laws' was abolished, 'a dawn

of happiness first appeared on this isle'. The process of 'reclaiming the Irish from barbarism and evil morals' had already begun in the previous century under the auspices of the Reformation and of renewed colonisation, but it was the abolition of the Brehon laws which 'completely emancipated' them from 'the oppression of temporal and spiritual tyranny'.[87] For Ledwich, the ending of native Irish law had marked the beginning of civilisation and therefore of the modern period. It ushered in a new era of government intervention that had 'brought us from the vilest obscurity and misery to opulence and refinement, and to a respectable rank among the nations of the earth'.[88] In one of his few references to contemporary politics in *Antiquities of Ireland*, he warned that only 'the firm support of . . . government can . . . perpetuate such signal blessings'.[89]

While often rightly bracketed together for their dissenting approach to Irish antiquities, Ledwich and Campbell were, in fact, quite at odds politically. Where Campbell was openly critical of English policy in Ireland, Ledwich made it the source of all stability and prosperity. In a short digression on the dramatic increase in the population of Ireland since the late seventeenth century, he praised England for 'fostering our manufactures and promoting our industries'.[90] He affected bland optimism about the state of the country, contrasting the late seventeenth century, as a time 'when religious and civil dissensions prevailed', with 'this happy period of liberal sentiments and domestic concord, when the difference of religious opinions excite neither jealousy or acrimony'.[91] In a chapter entitled 'Of the antient forts and castles in Ireland', he wrote of 'our Anglo-Hibernian castles' as 'monuments of the infelicity of former ages, when cruel and domestic wars convulsed and desolated the island'. The Glorious Revolution and 'the cherishing care of the illustrious House of Brunswic [sic]' had put an end to this desolation, bringing 'a regular government and just and equal laws'.[92] In his private correspondence, however, he was far less sanguine. His letters to Joseph Cooper Walker in 1786, just before he began work on *Antiquities of Ireland*, were confined mainly to antiquarian matters, but indicate how politically charged Ledwich felt these to be. He was particularly critical of Walker's enthusiasm for historic Gaelic Ireland and concomitant censuring of the policy of Anglicisation, and warned him about 'carrying antiquarianism to a very dangerous excess':

> You are bound *personally*, *politically*, and *patriotically* to be polite to the English; and it is historically true that they, under providence, humanized the Irish, who otherwise at this day would be perfect barbars [sic] even as it is they are but half civilized.[93]

Appalled at the tenor and tone of Walker's *Historical Essay* on Irish dress (1788), he accused him of adopting at times 'quite the style of Curry and all the scribbling popish friars'.[94] For Ledwich, Catholic antiquaries were divided into those like Sylvester O'Halloran and Theophilus O'Flanagan, whose 'favourite scheme [is] to separate from England, and set up an independent Kingdom', and those like Curry, who wished to recover 'their lost estates'.[95] He denounced O'Conor for allegedly reviving such issues in his memoir of Curry in the second edition of Curry's *Historical and Critical Review of the Civil Wars in Ireland* (1786):

> It is a curious way to conciliate, to tell the Irish they have for six centuries been most barbarously treated and oppressed – and that they have unjustly lost their property! Every man of estate and honour must feel for his ancestors and his fortune. Tis [sic] absurd in the extreme to think that he will look but to the present moment.[96]

This fearful backward glance became more pronounced in the 1790s. The general tendency of conservatives to see the French revolutionaries as the new barbarians, was, in Ireland, accompanied by an uncomfortable awareness of the apparent incompleteness of the civilising process. It can be seen most strikingly in the correspondence of Lord Charlemont, whose cautious support for the French Revolution was not to last beyond its first and more moderate phase. In July 1795, he wrote of the wretched state of the peasantry in the west in terms which alluded to, but finally rejected, the Pinkertonian thesis of Celtic barbarism:

> I have said they were barbarous. Such indeed they are, and savage acts of cruelty have been perpetrated by them only to be equalled in French [his]story; and such as might incline us to join with Pinkerton in his idea of the Celts, if misery and oppression and ignorance did not better account for their misconduct. Should we not, however, have endeavoured to relieve, to instruct, and to civilize this uncultivated class of human creatures before we receive them into the bosom of our constitution?[97]

In an undated letter written some time within the following two years, Charlemont, worried by the 'defenceless state of this island' and the 'demonaic strength' of France, had become so alarmed by the disaffection of 'the mob of the south' who had 'imbibed French ideas which they do not understand', that he embraced Pinkerton's hostile characterisation: 'these semi-barbarians have not as yet purged away the savageness of their Celtic origin'.[98] The rebellion shortly afterwards only served to confirm such perceptions.

SEVENTEENTH-CENTURY GHOSTS

Among eighteenth-century historians, David Hume was the most influential proponent of a view of Irish national character as unchangingly barbaric in his magisterial *History of England* (1754–62), which rapidly became the standard work on English history. Hume's references to Ireland, though often very brief, were invariably negative. In the volume on the period from Roman to Tudor Britain, he wrote that the Irish 'from the beginning of time, had been buried in most profound barbarism and ignorance', thus implicitly rejecting the idea of a great Irish civilisation destroyed by aggressive colonisation.[1] Even in the late sixteenth century, he claimed, 'when every christian nation was cultivating with ardor every civil art of life', the 'customs and manners' of the native Irish 'approached nearer those of savages than of barbarians'.[2] However, it was when writing about the Irish rebellion of 1641 that Hume revealed the nature of Gaelic barbarism in its full horror. Describing the massacres allegedly carried out by the insurgents, whom he called 'those more than barbarous savages', Hume dwelt on the incidents of torture and 'wanton cruelty' inflicted on an innocent settler population. He blamed the massacres on 'enraged superstition' combining with natural savagery and 'national prejudices' to sweep away all restraint.[3]

Hume's treatment of the 1641 Irish rebellion, as David Berman has suggested, is best understood in terms of his opposition to religious enthusiasm in general, whether Puritan or Catholic.[4] However, he was also clearly influenced by the considerable Irish colonist literature about the rebellion and especially Sir John Temple's lurid account, *The Irish Rebellion* (1646), new and updated editions of which continued to appear in the eighteenth century. Hume's multi-volume history was written in reverse order. The reign of the Stuarts was published first, reflecting Hume's belief that modern history most deserved the attention of historians and the reading public. Thus, in this first volume, his readers were given concrete proof of the inveterate savagery of the Irish as recently as the previous century; assertions of earlier barbarism could be made in the subsequent volumes without the need for concrete examples. But long before Hume had conceived of his unorthodox chronological narrative, the 1641 rebellion had become a template of Irish barbarism throughout the ages, capable of being projected backwards into the remote past, or indeed forward into the present and future. It was coupled to the earlier colonist writings of Edmund Spenser and Sir John Davies, providing a potent demonstration of the accuracy of their analyses of the native Irish threat. Thus, all representations of Gaelic society, no matter whether of the recent or remote past, were made in the light of 1641 and of the rich literature that it spawned.

The impact of that literature and of the commemoration of the rebellion can be seen not only in accounts and interpretations of 1641 written in the second half of the eighteenth century, but also in the more general antiquarian debate about Irish barbarism. 1641 made it impossible to write a history of the colonial period that could command cross-sectarian respect, as can be seen from the response to Thomas Leland's *History of Ireland from the Invasion of Henry II* (1773), which was deemed a failure by all sides. The much publicised but unfinished histories of that period by Charles O'Conor and Thomas Campbell also underlined the difficulty of writing a narrative history of the more modern period in an increasingly bitter and divided society. Seventeenth-century texts and events reverberated through Irish antiquarian writing in the eighteenth century, not always directly articulated, but as a ghostly echo of disquieting ideas and images. We should begin, however, by noting what happened in 1641.

Rebellion broke out in Ulster on 22 October 1641 and spread quickly to the rest of the country. The northern insurgents' leaders were acting in support of improved property rights and safeguards for religious freedom, and claimed the sanction of Charles I for their political and constitutional challenge. However, on the ground, the rising quickly developed into wholesale violence against settlers, who held the better tenancies and often mortgages taken by their Irish neighbours. Indeed, recent research has shown that rebel indebtedness was a common motive for the attacks on settlers and their homes.[5] Lecky's verdict, over one hundred years ago, that murders were perpetrated through 'lack of discipline, for private vengeance, or out of religious fanaticism'[6], has been supported by this new work, as has his estimate of 4,000 murders and 8,000 settler refugee deaths in 1641–2.[7] Contemporary estimates were much higher: a figure of 154,000 was claimed in 1642 and by 1646 it had almost doubled to 300,000.[8] This exaggeration 'beyond all rational credibility' had much to do with the subsequent propaganda campaign to confiscate Catholic property.[9]

Although the rebellion spread to the rest of the island, events in the northern province provided the focus for the later commemorations and outrage literature. Temple's *Irish Rebellion*, published in 1646, was the most influential of a series of propaganda works devoted to the rebellion in Ulster. Temple had been Master of the Rolls in Ireland in 1641 and, in the subtitle to the book, claimed to have written a 'history of the beginning and first progress' of the rising, as well as a catalogue of 'the barbarous cruelties and bloody massacres which ensued thereupon'. He contended that the massacre of Protestants had been planned as part of the insurrection by the Catholic leadership, with the encouragement of the Catholic clergy, in order to recover Ireland for the pope's interest. His emphasis on the innocence of these Protestants 'peaceably setled [sic] and securely intermixed' among the native population pointed up all the more the 'horrid cruelties' of the latter.[10] He used the official correspondence of Dublin Castle, but more importantly he had access to the 'depositions' – sworn statements collected from survivors in the months immediately after the rebellion – which he cited liberally throughout the text. Partly because it was based on such rich contemporary evidence, Temple's book 'assumed the status of an official interpretation almost from the moment of its publication'.[11]

Perhaps even more importantly, Temple's *Irish Rebellion* had deep psychological resonances for Irish Protestants. Toby Barnard has argued that it was a 'blatant forging of a national legend for the Irish Protestants, reminiscent of those which already memorialized the persecuted Protestants of France, the Low Countries and England'.[12] Similarly, Thomas Bartlett has compared it to Foxe's *Book of Martyrs*, which had given English Protestants 'the memory of a tragic yet heroic shared historical experience' and thus had made 'a vital contribution towards the evolution of national consciousness'.[13] The lessons to be drawn from Temple's *Irish Rebellion* were clear. The first of these was that Irish Protestants had been spared total extirpation only by God's providence. Secondly, Irish Catholics were barbarous by nature, without the possibility of redemption. Editions of Temple continued to appear at times of political crisis throughout the seventeenth and eighteenth centuries, emphasising the continued relevance of its message. In 1724, an amended edition was published in Dublin, containing 'blatantly anti-Catholic invective'[14] and with several vignettes opposite the title-page depicting the carrying out of a number of the most notorious atrocities of 1641 by prosperous-looking figures in eighteenth-century dress.[15] An edition published in 1746, the year of Culloden, changed the subtitle from one specific to events in 1641 to the more universal, 'an History of the Attempts of the Irish Papists to extirpate the Protestants of the Kingdom of Ireland', and added 'Now Reprinted for the perusal of all Protestants as the most Effectual Warning-Piece to keep them upon their Guard against the Encroachments of Popery'. A further edition appeared in Cork in 1766, in the midst of serious agrarian unrest in Munster.[16]

The lesson of Temple's *Irish Rebellion* was soon reinforced by the state. In 1662 the government decreed that 1641 should be remembered officially, by making the 23rd of October (the day of its planned outbreak) part of the Church of Ireland calendar. The parliamentary Act laid down that 'all and every person and persons inhabiting within this realm of Ireland shall yearly, upon the twenty-third day of October, diligently and faithfully resort to the parish church or chappel [sic] accustomed', for a service of thanksgiving. According to the Act, that date had revealed 'a conspiracy so generally inhumane, barbarous and cruel, as the like was never before heard of in any age or kingdom'.[17] By the early eighteenth century, the official commemoration ceremony had become an established ritual:

> In Dublin, the peers and commoners, attended by suitably gowned officers and freemen of the Corporation, the tabarded heralds and robed judges, processed to the churches; in the larger towns, the members of the municipality and the

guilds, properly habited and preceded by mace or sword, went to seat themselves according to office and degree in the Protestant church.[18]

Many of the sermons preached on that day were published; most had as their theme the unchanging nature of Catholicism and the danger it represented. Barnard has called this emphasis the principle on which the 'continuum of Protestant history' rested.[19] It can be seen in the anniversary sermon of one preacher in 1735, when he warned his congregation that 'popery is still the same thing; and differs only from what it was as a lion chained doth from a lion at liberty'.[20] In addition, the sermons reinforced the more general connection between Catholicism and barbarism, by attributing the barbarousness of the everyday life of the native Irish to their religion. Catholicism, one preacher asserted, encouraged 'their wild savage way of living in single cottages and dismal unhabitable [sic] places' and was, therefore, no better than the paganism of primitive tribes.[21] Thus, every 23rd October, a 'rite of exclusion', as Barnard put it, was enacted, which justified, first the promulgation, and later the retention of penal legislation against Catholics.[22]

We know from remarks in the correspondence of Charles O'Conor and his close friend John Curry, a Catholic physician in Dublin, that the 23rd October commemorations were galling for Catholics; O'Conor called it one of the 'holy days set aside for pleasing untruths'.[23] Indeed, in his memoir of Curry, prefixed to the posthumous second edition of the latter's *Historical and Critical Review of the Civil Wars in Ireland* (1786), O'Conor recounted that it was a child's question, 'Are there any of those bloody papists in Dublin?', overheard by Curry outside Christchurch in Dublin, just after the anniversary service on 23 October 1746, which prompted him to begin his investigations of 1641.[24] As Jacqueline Hill has noted, prior to this, the Catholic response to the charge of barbarousness in 1641 was muted. Even after 1691, there was little or no need to make a defence, when there was a general belief, or fear, that the Stuarts could regain the throne, restoring Catholicism as the state religion. It was only after the failure of the 1745 rebellion that the Hanoverian dynasty seemed fully secure, and at that point O'Conor and Curry devised a new campaign to persuade the government of the absence of a Catholic political threat in Ireland.[25] As Curry recognised outside Christchurch in 1646, it was vital to tackle the barbarous stereotype of Catholics derived from 1641 and reinforced annually by commemoration.

Curry rapidly became the Catholic specialist on the 1641 rebellion. In 1747, he published *A Brief Account from the most Authentic Protestant Writers of the Causes, Motives and Mischiefs of the Irish Rebellion on the 23rd day of October 1641*. Adopting the guise of a liberal Protestant, he argued that the Irish rebels had been provoked by Protestant outrages and long-standing bad government. In 1758, his *Historical Memoirs of the Irish Rebellion* continued this theme, and was a rejoinder to the Protestant antiquary Walter Harris, whose *Fiction Unmasked* (1752) had accused Curry of writing *A Brief Account* during the

Jacobite rebellion of 1745–6 in order to incite a fresh Irish uprising.[26] But as well as repudiating Harris, Curry also appealed to David Hume to correct *his* account in further editions and to assign the majority of the outrages to Protestants.[27] This was part of a long-running, and, ultimately, unsuccessful campaign by Curry and O'Conor to get Hume to modify his position.[28]

While O'Conor and Curry were close collaborators, particularly on a series of pamphlets on the Catholic question, they used different, even contrasting, approaches in their historical works.[29] Curry set out largely to defend Catholic conduct in 1641, both in terms of the political decisions of the leadership, and the behaviour of the rebels on the ground. It was because of this overtly apologetic stand that some members, at least, of the Catholic Committee were unhappy about the publication of his *Historical Memoirs of the Irish Rebellion in the year 1641* in 1758, shortly after a number of unsuccessful attempts by the Irish parliament to enact further penal legislation.[30] Curry's defence of the rebels rested on his analysis of the prior iniquitous conduct of government ministers.[31] Similarly, in his later work, *A Historical and Critical Review* (1775), he argued that the massacres of Protestants in Ulster had been preceded by atrocities carried out by Scottish troops on the Catholics of Islandmagee in Co. Antrim.[32] He also tried to discredit the depositions, upon which detailed testimony the Protestant case for Catholic atrocities in 1641 rested. Curry had not seen these documents, which were lodged in Trinity College Library in 1741 on the centenary of the rebellion.[33] Trinity Library was notoriously difficult to gain access to, even for establishment figures such as Vallancey.[34] O'Conor was the first Catholic to use it, on the invitation of Thomas Leland, the librarian, and then only in order to look at the holdings of Gaelic manuscripts.[35] Leland also invited Curry to visit him there, though not actually to consult the depositions, but rather to be shown some discovery he had made relating to the Islandmagee massacre.

Lacking O'Conor's self-confidence and social ease in Ascendancy circles, Curry refused to go on his own to Trinity to meet Leland.[36] He was thus forced to rely exclusively on the accounts of Protestant historians who had examined the depositions, notably Ferdinando Warner, who had been sceptical of their authority.[37] Echoing Warner, Curry dismissed their alleged status as oath-bound statements, and he also made much of the stories of the supernatural which permeated them; of the ghosts of massacred Protestants appearing to the deponents and crying out for vengeance.[38] He argued that the degree of exaggeration and superstition to be found in them rendered them unusable by the scrupulous historian.[39] There is, thus, an interesting parallel between Curry's stance and mode of argument on the depositions, and that of conservative antiquaries, such as Ledwich, on the reliability of the Gaelic annals. Neither had direct access to the contentious documents, save through intermediaries or translators, but both claimed that gross hyperbole ruled out their use as evidence.

Although O'Conor was always very encouraging in his letters to Curry, privately he had reservations about his approach:

> All along he produces proofs of the civil Injuries done the Irish Catholics, and
> while he justifies the Conduct of the latter in various Instances, he makes no
> Mention of their Follies or Imprudence in any.

This was not 'History', he argued, 'which like every true Picture should consist of Shade and Colouring; but it is a mere Justification on one Side, and disguised Invective on the other'.[40] In O'Conor's 'Advertisement' to Curry's
Historical Memoirs, he attempted to rise above what he saw as this spirit of
party; insisting that the role of the historian must be to distinguish the past
from the present, instead of confounding them, as the party historian did.[41]
Yet, while following this precept, he attempted, nevertheless, to undermine
the charge of specifically Catholic savagery, by positing a universal barbarism
to explain both the causes and the nature of the rebellion. Thus, among the
reasons for the many calamities in Irish history were 'public Misrule, barbarous
Manners, private Interests, and the Rage of Parties'.[42] His line of explanation
began with the Anglo-Norman conquest which took place in 'the Days of Barbarity and Ignorance' and in which 'a set of truculent Free-booters' denied the
Irish 'the Benefit of the English Laws, and of all Law'. In the wake of this 'wanton Exercise of *lawless Power*', 'Our People changed from Bad to Worse', but
also 'sought Redress in frequent Insurrections'. The situation was exacerbated
by the Reformation, which intensified the 'rage of Parties', causing 'Protestants
and Papists . . . to load their Adversaries with odious Crimes'.[43] Some years
earlier, in his anonymous preface to an edition of the Earl of Castlehaven's
Memoirs (1753), O'Conor argued that the interaction of religious and political
discord had resulted in 'the Mass of Civil Rage fermented, beyond any Degree
which Heathen Violence, in the worst of Time, could afford'.[44] The emphasis
on 'civil rage' was later echoed in the title of John Curry's last work, which was
an expansion of his earlier writings on 1641: *An Historical and Critical Review
of the Civil Wars in Ireland from the Reign of Queen Elizabeth to the Settlement
under King William* (1775). The earlier emphasis on 'rebellion' was quietly
dropped, in favour of the term 'civil war', which implied that there were two
warring parties, rather than one rebellious Catholic faction.[45] O'Conor also
argued that the Reformation had modified the way in which English writers
had characterised the native Irish since the twelfth century. While the first
colonists imputed 'a peculiar Perverseness of the Irish Nation as a way of jus-
tifying their oppressive conduct', after the Reformation 'the Perverseness so
long imputed to the Irish as a People, was no longer charged on their *Nature*,
but on their *Religion*'.[46]

   Given O'Conor's undoubted skill in presenting the new Catholic case on
1641, it is striking that he himself did not write on the period, beyond the
short pieces referred to here, and in his pamphlets, which, while they rely on
historical arguments, are not proper narratives. This was in spite of his belief
that the history of 1641 was 'of more consequence than five hundred pages of
ancient unimportant History such as I formerly dabbled in'.[47] At this stage, in

the late 1750s, he had become disillusioned with his antiquarian work, to the point where he contemplated giving it up.[48] By 1760, however, his black mood had abated and he had turned back to his former pursuits, but still referred slightingly to his 'old annals' as 'no better than a file of newspapers' and to his work as 'my castle of cards'.[49] Writing to Edmund Burke in 1765, he described himself as 'digging in the rubbish of the ancients . . . of our own island' and contrasted those 'ages of barbarism and ignorance' to 'our own enlightened days of good sense and sound policy'.[50]

However, O'Conor was given a great incentive to return to the 'ages of barbarism and ignorance', when, in 1763, the respected Dublin publisher George Faulkner offered to publish a second edition of the *Dissertations*.[51] Among the changes O'Conor set out to make was the addition of two new chapters, bringing the narrative from the twelfth century right up to the reign of Elizabeth. The first of these, written in full at the draft stage, was entitled 'From the Invasion of Henry 2nd King of England to the End of Bruce's War. 145 Years'. The second, 'From the Conclusion of Bruce's War to the Reformation of Religion under Queen Elizabeth', remained unwritten; he wrote only the title and left the space underneath it blank.[52] In the event, O'Conor decided to end with the victory of Henry II and dropped most of what he had written. In a letter to Curry in September 1764, he complained that he could not make the work 'complete . . . from the want of the leisure and, what is worse, the want of the materials which were not at any time in my power'.[53] Perhaps in response to these difficulties, he conceived a plan of moving to Dublin for eight months of the year, in order to devote himself to 'retirement and study'. By this stage he had given over the running of the main Belanagare estate to his eldest son, Denis. However, his remaining responsibilities for a smaller portion of one hundred acres appear to have prevented such a move.[54]

O'Conor's tactics changed after this failure, when he seems to have decided that a modern history from the pen of a liberal Protestant would be more successful in promoting a favourable view of recent Catholic actions, particularly if O'Conor himself could act as principal research assistant and guide. His first choice was Ferdinando Warner, an English cleric, who had approached him in 1761 for assistance with his planned history of Ireland.[55] While O'Conor's plans for his own modern history were still in place, he seemed relatively uninterested in the Englishman's project, although he answered queries and supplied materials with a usual courtesy. However, by the time the second edition of his *Dissertations* was published, he was writing with a certain alarm of Warner's difficulties in attracting subscribers for the second volume of the *History*, which planned to bring the story up to the reign of Charles I: 'I dread that he will receive no encouragement from Ireland and that he will be disgusted enough to drop his scheme'.[56] Although Warner published an account of the 1641 rebellion in the following year which reduced the quantity of Catholic-perpetrated outrages,[57] O'Conor had already turned his attention to encouraging another Protestant proxy to write a modern history to his liking. Thomas

Leland was chosen and courted, not only by O'Conor, but also by Edmund Burke and by the liberal Protestant circle around George Faulkner, to do for Ireland what the great Scottish historians David Hume and John Robertson had done for England and Scotland respectively: that is, to write a 'philosophic' modern history, giving an ostensibly objective, or non-party, narrative of the colonial period. Leland was a clergyman, Fellow of Trinity College Dublin and Professor of oratory, as well as Librarian, who had already published a number of works on classical history, among them, *A History of the Life and Reign of Philip, King of Macedon* (1758) and *The Orations of Demosthenes* (1763).

O'Conor believed that a 'philosophic' approach would demolish the hitherto dominant hostile accounts of Catholic conduct in the seventeenth century and, when carried out by a respected Irish Protestant such as Leland, would have the merit of far greater political influence than anything that the lowly Catholic Curry could produce. Curry remained sceptical of this strategy. Never comfortable with O'Conor's success in moderate Protestant circles, he did not trust any Protestant to write a history of the seventeenth century which would be favourable to Catholics. Writing to O'Conor in 1770, when Leland had embarked on his project, he told him '[y]our friend Dr Leland preached at Christchurch the 23rd of last [October], but what sort of Sermon it was, I could not hear'. Still not trusting Leland's *bona fides*, he thought the sermon would indicate, perhaps, 'the temperateness or Inflamability [sic] of the Modern Part of his History'. [58] Curry might well have been pleased at Leland's sermon, had it been printed, which was the usual practice with the commemoration sermons given at Christchurch, the place of worship of the lord lieutenant and Dublin Castle. However, in the course of his oration, Leland had lectured his congregation of members of parliament and dignitaries on 'the errors and iniquities of our forefathers', which consisted in 'oppression, avarice, and cruelty; factious discontent and clamour; and indifference and disregard to religion; heinous and crying offences, and such as are the declared object of God's severest vengeance'.[59] Ominously, the customary thanks to the preacher and the order to print the sermon were withheld by parliament, and it appeared only posthumously, eighteen years after its delivery, in his collected sermons.[60] Leland was given, in effect, a powerful warning that it was not acceptable to tamper with the traditional Protestant interpretation of the colonial period, at least not within the highly symbolic realm of the official commemoration of the 1641 rebellion.

Despite his reservations, Curry held back the publication of his last book, *An Historical and Critical Review of the Civil Wars in Ireland*, in the expectation that Leland's work would provide confirmation of his argument that the rebellion had been triggered by a massacre of Catholics by Scottish soldiers at Islandmagee in Co. Antrim. Burke, who had initially encouraged Curry in this line of argument, together with O'Conor, who had had discussions with Leland about Catholic responsibility for the massacres of 1641 even before this project was mooted, were convinced that Leland would uphold Curry's contention.[61] In spite of Leland's cordial invitation to Curry to come to Trinity to discuss Islandmagee, he did not invite his friends to read his history before it went to print, and they relied on rumours and leaks emerging from the publisher. These confirmed Curry's suspicions; he wrote to O'Conor to warn him that, on 'the Modern Part', Leland wrote 'like a Protestant, which you know he *must* do', and as indeed Leland himself had advised.[62] In the event, Leland wrote less like a Protestant than he might have. He criticised Hume for his claims of Irish barbarism since the beginning of time.[63] On the 1641 rebellion he was more moderate than either Hume or Harris and avoided their extreme language. Like O'Conor, he argued that there was barbarism on both sides; the policy of James I's ministers was designed to alienate the native Irish and provoke them 'yet farther by injustice and oppression', and was 'a barbarous iniquity'. The followers of Phelim O'Neill, leader of the rebellion in Ulster, were 'barbarous', and provoked by defeat 'to a degree of rage truly diabolical'. His account of the massacres, while extremely brief, used vivid language to capture the horror and highlighted the involvement of priests, women and children.[64]

Leland's *History*, perhaps because of this attempted evenhandedness, pleased neither Protestants nor Catholics.[65] It enraged Curry, in particular, because, contrary to expectations, Leland demolished the case he had made for the early occurrence of the Islandmagee massacre, assigning it instead to January 1642, and compounded the injury by having recourse to the depositions in order to do so.[66] Curry, alerted while the book was being printed, rushed out a pamphlet which took issue in advance with Leland's interpretation.[67] His subsequent failure to get a London publisher for his withheld *Historical and Critical Review* highlighted continuing sensitivities about 1641. O'Conor considered it vital that Curry's work should appear in London, as Leland's had done. However, when Edmund Burke was approached to suggest the name of a publisher and to stand as referee for the competence of the work, he refused to help. This reluctance to become publicly involved in a controversial Catholic project can be traced to the previous decade when, at the outset of his political career and a time of agrarian disturbance in Munster, Burke had been heavily censured in the English press for seeming to favour Irish Catholic interests.[68]

Perhaps abandoning all hope of getting a liberal Protestant to write an account that suited his purpose, O'Conor's desire to write a modern history re-emerged at this time. In 1772 he was projecting a third edition of the *Dissertations*, correcting some errors, but also adding a second volume, 'more interesting as coming more home to our own affairs than that about antiquities in which we have now little or no concern'.[69] He gradually amassed the kind of materials which he felt he had lacked in 1764,[70] and, in the 1780s embarked on a study entitled 'The Revolutions of Ireland', a separate work rather than an addendum to the *Dissertations*.[71] This was to be 'an historical view of the laws, manners, and political statement of this country', beginning in the second century, which he now called 'the earliest periods of historical faith', indicating how cautious he had become on the issue of the reliability of the annals for the pre-Christian period. If the question of where to begin was a relatively simple one, where to close the narrative was not. In January 1781 he told his friend Thomas O'Gorman, the genealogist, that he would bring it down to the accession of James I, when, as he termed it, the 'old inhabitants of Ireland . . . [in a great degree] ceased to be a nation.'[72] Two months later, he decided to go as far as 1608, that is, stopping just before the Ulster plantation.[73] By June 1781 he had changed his mind and abandoned caution: he would continue the narrative as far as the Restoration of Charles II, calling it *'periculosae plenum opus aleae'* (a task filled with dangerous chance).[74] In the event, O'Conor was diverted from this project and embarked instead on a 'memoir' on pre-colonial Ireland, in anticipation of Thomas Campbell's combative essay on the same subject.[75] To judge from his letters, he may well have been glad of such diversion, as he complained that gout and rheumatism were preventing him from making progress on the larger project; and he confessed that its very scope was intimidating.[76]

It seems that O'Conor could not get away from the pre-colonial period; as the person who had done most to foster interest in it and to project a positive image of it, he had a considerable stake in its reputation. Whatever the reasons for O'Conor's abandonment of his modern history, it is tempting to wonder how he might have dealt with the sensitive issues revolving around the forfeitures of the previous century and the subsequent land settlement. While the argument about a universal barbarism was an effective tactic against the cultural denigration of the native Irish, it would have been much more difficult to deal in a politic way with the justice, or injustice, of confiscation, given the ever-present fears of Protestants that 'the property they held was still fiercely coveted by the heirs of the dispossessed'.[77] Certainly, early on, O'Conor denied that the confiscations were a significant factor in Catholic rebellion in the seventeenth century. In the 'Advertisement' which he wrote for Curry's *Historical Memoirs of the Irish Rebellion in the year 1641* (1758), he claimed that 'the main Incentive to every Insurrection in Ireland since the Reformation' was the penal laws.[78] This early caution could be said to have abated somewhat, when, in his memoir of Curry, prefacing the second edition of the latter's *Historical and Critical Review* in 1786, he explicitly drew attention to the impact of confiscation. Curry, he wrote, though a man of modest means, was descended from 'an antient Irish family' who lost their considerable lands 'in the usurpation of Cromwell' and through later forfeitures for their support of James II, 'in whose service the doctor's grandfather commanded a troop of horse, and fell at the head of it in the Battle of Aughrim'.[79]

In the previous year, O'Conor was consulted by the Catholic peer and member of the Catholic Committee Viscount Gormanston, who was contemplating an appeal to the government to reverse Acts of Attainder against two of his ancestors: the sixth Viscount in 1641 and the seventh in 1691.[80] This action, which came at the urging of the Catholic Committee, was enthusiastically endorsed by O'Conor, since it involved no question of restoration of lands, but only of reputation.[81] O'Conor's optimistic view was that the new government was 'no way interested in party malignity of the seventeenth century, but indeed interested in putting an End to all its Effects', and that it would 'bring us considerable Credit, that at this time an Irish Catholic peer should be restored to all his family honours, without giving up his best principle in Exchange'.[82] He saw no problem in advancing a defence of the conduct of the sixth Lord Gormanston in 1641 as having 'laboured to unite all parties, for the support of Monarchy and Monarch'. However, he cautioned that the case for the seventh Viscount, who was attaindered by order of William III, would have to be made with 'prudence and Discretion', since it 'requires some Delicacy to speak to this last subject with the freedom that the Truth and even the Constitution requires'.[83] The following year, O'Conor was unwillingly involved in a local crisis over seventeenth-century land title, which clearly demonstrated the political risks of raising such issues. His cousin, Alexander O'Conor, revived a family claim to the estate and castle of Ballintubber, Co. Roscommon, taking possession of the latter. The claim was based on legal documents dating from 1662, and raised the prospect of widespread Catholic efforts to overturn the Williamite land settlement and repossess their lands. The alarm was raised in Dublin and troops were sent to Roscommon. The conservative MP George Ogle linked the Roscommon incident to the Rightboy unrest in Munster, and warned that 'the landed property of the kingdom [and] the Protestant ascendancy' were under threat and in need of protection.[84] In response, O'Conor and other leading Catholics of the county met in an attempt to quash the rumours of an insurrection by drawing up an address of loyalty to the lord lieutenant and by publishing a number of resolutions declaring their abhorrence of 'riots and tumults or the revival of any claims to lands or property not supportable by the laws of our country'.[85]

In these fraught political circumstances it is doubtful whether O'Conor would have risked publishing a modern history concluding in the seventeenth century. Even if he had wished to take that risk, he would probably have had difficulty finding a London publisher (always deemed by him to be essential). As Thomas Campbell reported, following his tour of London publishers in 1786, there was a great suspicion about works of Irish history, following the extravagances of O'Halloran and Vallancey, amongst others.[86] Campbell also planned a modern history at this time, and was actively encouraged by Edmund Burke, who, having been unimpressed by Leland's history, looked to Campbell as another Protestant candidate to write an account that would be favourable to Catholics.[87] In 1787, Campbell visited Burke at his home in Beaconsfield and was given four folio volumes of manuscripts from his library, together with the advice to be 'as brief as possible upon everything antecedent to Henry II'.[88] But Campbell was also under pressure from Samuel Johnson to concentrate on early Christian Ireland, deemed by him to be the most important period in the country's history.[89] *Strictures on the Ecclesiastical and Literary*

History of Ireland (1789) was dedicated to Burke, but, conscious that this was not the work expected by him, Campbell confessed himself torn between the conflicting advice of his two mentors. He implied that this was the first of a two-part project, a 'literary and ecclesiastical study' in response to Johnson's urging, which would be followed by a 'civil and political study', presumably in answer to Burke's wishes, since Campbell maintained that the civil and political arts were developed in Ireland only after the conquest, and even then only imperfectly.[90] However, Campbell never returned to the modern part of the project, and instead embarked on a biography of the poet Oliver Goldsmith, which also was unpublished.[91]

Interestingly, Campbell and O'Conor used the same title for their unfinished modern histories, 'Revolutions of Ireland',[92] and failed to complete them, in part at least because the lure of the pre-colonial period and its controversies proved too strong. In 1784, Campbell privately circulated a printed essay which he called 'an Analysis of the Antiquities of Ireland', intended as part of the introduction to the modern history.[93] Vallancey, when shown the essay by its author, was sufficiently alarmed by it to write 'A Vindication of the History of Ireland', published in the *Collectanea* in 1786.[94] Initially at least, O'Conor was sanguine after reading the piece, in spite of the fact that his 'friend Dr Campbell' had put 'a thorough slight on all transactions in this island anterior to the invasion and revolution under Henry II'. O'Conor's interest and hopes lay with the modern history: 'I have no doubt but Dr Campbell will give a good representation of our affairs from the twelfth century to our own times, and as the subject is important I am glad that it falls under such good hands.'[95] In spite of Campbell's campaign against Vallancey and derogatory remarks about all Catholic antiquaries, O'Conor always wrote politely about him, referring to him even in private correspondence in 1784 as his friend.[96] In turn, Campbell was complimentary about O'Conor in *Philosophical Survey* and still polite in his criticism in *Strictures*, unlike his wholesale scorn towards Vallancey.[97] O'Conor's evident respect for Campbell was probably a measure of his approval of the latter's forthright criticism of the penal laws, particularly since in *Philosophical Survey* he had used the discovery suit brought against O'Conor by his younger brother, Hugh, as an example of the iniquity of this provision of the laws.[98] Campbell may also have found favour through his acquaintance with Samuel Johnson, who had written to O'Conor in praise of his *Dissertations*;[99] on one occasion Campbell had acted as courier for a letter to O'Conor.[100]

Vallancey laboured to convince O'Conor of the serious challenge posed by Campbell's essay, denouncing it as an attempt at 'demolishing all our ancient historical structures with a few well directed blows'.[101] Within a fortnight of his immediate relaxed response, O'Conor was showing more concern, particularly about Campbell's depiction of pre-colonial society. In a letter to the Archbishop of Dublin, John Carpenter, he wrote:

> Dr Campbell . . . represents the People as the most uncultivated Barbarians in Europe til the arrival of Henry 2 here in the twelfth century. He must be opposed; the more the question about the origins and manners and civil oeconomy of the antients of this country is agitated the more the truth will appear, and the critical public will decide.[102]

A further fortnight later, O'Conor's response, an 'essay on the ancient state of this island', was nearly complete, and he was granted permission to dedicate it to the Provost of Trinity College Dublin, John Hely-Hutchinson.[103] Even at this stage, however, his aim was to participate in a debate stimulated by Campbell, not to attack the latter for his views, for fear of jeopardising his 'Revolutions' project: 'In a memoir I am now employed upon, I labour to shew he is mistaken, but *indirectly* without application to the work he is preparing for the public. He is a worthy person, and I shall have no direct controversy with him.'[104] However, due to declining health, O'Conor found the prospect of preparing a final draft of his essay 'distressing' and it remained unfinished, along with his own 'Revolutions' project.[105]

Speculation about the approach and argument of O'Conor's unfinished 'Revolutions' is limited by the absence of either a manuscript and or any substantial discussion of the enterprise in his correspondence. Fortunately, some of the lines of Campbell's modern project can be detected both in his published work and in hints given in his correspondence with Thomas Percy, Bishop of Dromore, and with John Pinkerton, the Scottish Gothicist. He met the latter in London in the summer of 1787 at around the same time as he visited Burke in Beaconsfield.[106] In October of that year he wrote to Percy that, following a letter received from him, he had decided to 'expose the inconsistencies of our "Collectanea" scribes'.[107] This exposure took the form of a 'Sketch or Summary View of the Ecclesiastical and Literary History of Ireland', published in the *Dublin Chronicle*, under the Spenserian pseudonym Ierneus, from December 1787 to March 1788. The 'Sketch' was subsequently incorporated into *Strictures*, together with an amended version of 'An Historical Sketch of the Constitution and Government of Ireland . . . down to the year 1782', which had first appeared in Richard Gough's edition of Camden's *Britannia* (1789).[108] It also reprinted many of the scurrilous letters mocking Vallancey by Ledwich and Beauford, first published pseudonymously in the *Dublin Chronicle*.[109] *Strictures*, therefore, was far from the coherent narrative work expected of Campbell by Johnson and Burke. Neither wholly medieval nor modern in focus, it was almost as rambling and digressive as the works of Vallancey that it jeered at. Thus, for example, he interrupted an account of the Irish church in the reign of Henry II to meditate on the conduct of the Jacobite army in 1690.[110]

Campbell called the 'Historical Sketch of the Constitution and Government of Ireland' 'the skeleton of the history I mean to publish'.[111] It was intended primarily to advance the union cause, Campbell stating in 1788 that he had 'long been of the opinion that the Protestant Ascendancy (in so few hands) is very insecure and precarious, till a thoro' incorporation of the islands is effected'.[112] He also appended a list of the 'Revenues of Ireland' to prove the 'sufficiency of the hereditary revenue for the support of the establishments', thus removing the need for a separate Irish parliament: 'for the expediency of a Union can never become popular in Ireland, till the nation is convinced that a King of England has resources sufficient for governing Ireland, without any new aids from his Parliament here'.[113] Although Campbell began by dismissing the claims for a parliamentary tradition in pre-colonial Ireland,[114] his real concern in this 'Sketch' was with the modern 'patriot' faction from Molyneux to Grattan, which he attempted to undermine by denying that the Irish parliament, at any date prior to 1782, had powers to legislate; the operation of Poynings Law (1494) had made it 'little more than the register of royal edicts'.[115] He argued by implication that the reforms of 1782 were not a return to previous arrangements but rather the creation of a new constitutional position for the Irish parliament. In spite of his unionism and opposition to Grattan and the 'patriots', Campbell made it clear that he welcomed this change. The reforms had removed the 'mortifying' distinctions between the Irish and British legislatures, and the latter had 'happily' given up the doctrine of the subordination of the Irish parliament.[116] Campbell's highly individual brand of unionism seems to have incorporated support for basic 'patriot' aims.

There are other discordant notes in *Strictures* which reinforce the sense that Campbell's politics were not only complex but contradictory. He devoted a long footnote to the career of Hugh O'Neill, which had first appeared in the 'Sketch' in the *Dublin Chronicle* in March 1788. This seems to have been the abstract of a planned full life of O'Neill, for which he had borrowed Charles O'Conor's copy of the Annals of the Four Masters (*Annála Ríoghachta Éirinn*), but which he abandoned at an early stage.[117] Campbell's O'Neill was a tragic hero, 'a compound of vice and virtue in the extreme'; a proud and ambitious man, the first to use religion as a pretext for rebellion, but also a 'great man' who 'united all Ireland in one great cause, the cause of freedom'. Using Keating's distinction between nobles and commoners, Campbell denied that O'Neill was uncivilised. He had been 'bred up under the best masters in England' and while he lead an army of 'barbarians', 'it would be an injustice to his memory to call him a barbarian'. He finished by describing the 'painful march across the kingdom' to Kinsale by O'Neill and his 'ragamuffin troops, half starved, half naked, and not half armed', and in spite of O'Neill's defeat there, concluded with a rhetorical flourish: 'deny O'Neill the praise of an Hannibal, if you can'.[118] If this portrait and its emphasis on native Irish heroism in the face of 'oppression from without'[119] seems out of kilter with Campbell's own fears for the survival of Protestant Ascendancy, it does fit in with one of Campbell's sub-themes in *Strictures*, that is, the military valour of the native Irish.

While Campbell quoted with approval Hume on the barbarism of the native Irish in the twelfth century, he deplored the latter's derogatory remarks about their military skills, accusing him of 'frequently going out of his road in search of opportunities to depreciate the Irish'.[120] Similarly, he attacked Voltaire for claiming 'a *natural* inferiority to England in the genius of Ireland' and insisted that 'the Irish want not talents for the arts of either peace or war', but that these talents 'have, at no period, been improved to that high degree of which they are so susceptible'.[121] In a surprising peroration on the bravery of the Irish Jacobite forces in 1688–90, he deliberately distinguished between 1641 and the Jacobite wars, asserting that the latter could 'never be called a rebellion, because undertaken in [*sic*] behalf of the King upon the throne, who shewed himself as unworthy to reign over them, as they were prodigal of their blood in his support'.[122] In his emphasis on Irish loyalty to James, Campbell echoed the earlier arguments of Catholic apologists that Irish Catholics in the previous century, far from being disloyal, had shown perhaps excessive devotion to their sovereign.[123]

Is it possible to resolve the contradictions apparent in Campbell's position? He appeared a firm adherent to the theory of native Irish barbarism and yet an opponent of most of the penal laws. Outspoken critic of English rule in Ireland – at one point in his peroration on Hugh O'Neill he stated that 'it should never be forgotten, that Ireland was at all times, more sinned against than sinning'[124] – but also an enthusiast for union. Some of the less fundamental contradictions can be explained. For example, his concern to establish the military valour of the native Irish was compatible with his equally strong emphasis on their lack of civility, for bravery on the field of battle was a trait long associated with barbarism.[125] His point was that policies should be put in place to improve the native Irish rather than to penalise them:

> Every page in the history of Ireland . . . points to the execution of some great plan for the illumination of a people, whose genius, like the rude and rough gem, is either unknown or despised; and yet, if polished, would not only shine but sparkle.[126]

But overarching these concerns, most of them visible in Campbell's early writing, was his realisation by 1788 that the security of Protestant Ascendancy was under threat and that, in spite of the history of English misrule in Ireland, a union was the only possible safeguard against the menace of a resurgent barbarism. His own interests as an Anglican clergyman ensured that he would uphold the Protestant constitution of church and state.

Given these fears, it might be expected that the 1641 rebellion would figure prominently in the works of Campbell, and of Ledwich who was equally apprehensive, but the opposite is the case. Granted, in *Philosophical Survey*, Campbell argued that the rebellion had been caused by English policy from the reign of Elizabeth, in particular by religious oppression and the confiscation of estates on the pretext of invalid title, and blamed the two Lords Justice, Parson and Borlase, 'men of narrow, puritanical principles' who did everything to precipitate 'these poor people' into rebellion.[127] However, in his more controversial *Strictures*, Campbell referred only briefly to the 1641 rising as 'the most formidable and bloody rebellion, which ever raged, perhaps in any country' and then purely in the context of Irish military prowess.[128] Similarly, Ledwich, for example, in his 'History of the Antiquities of the Irishtown and Kilkenny', mentioned only in passing 'the grand rebellion' of 1641 and declined to elaborate, on the basis that '[t]he causes leading to this dire event, and the transactions consequent thereon, have been minutely detailed by many writers'.[129] The absence of 1641 in their writings would tend to support Jacqueline Hill's contention that by the early 1780s the rebellion had ceased to loom large in Protestant consciousness.[130] In the case of Ledwich, however, there is also some evidence that attempts were made to keep him away from material on the rebellion. In 1775 or 1776, he had obtained access to the papers of David Rothe (1573–1650), Catholic Bishop of Ossory from 1620 to 1650, by permission of James Laffan, the executor of the recently dead successor to Rothe's episcopal see who had held the papers. Although he believed Ledwich to be 'honest', Laffan did not give him any material relating to the rebellion of 1641, as he had not vetted it first. Ironically, he seems to have sent the material instead to John Curry, whom Ledwich later excoriated as a 'dangerous' writer who threatened the 'fate of Protestantism'.[131]

The 1641 rebellion and its ghosts returned to haunt Protestants in 1798. It was as if the dark prophecies which had been retailed in church every 23rd of October for over one hundred and thirty years had been fulfilled.[132] As Hill has argued, 1798 'put new life into the "massacre" tradition and its literature', although no new edition of Temple's *Irish Rebellion* was published between 1766 and 1812.[133] Instead, Richard Musgrave, member of parliament for Waterford and also of the Orange Order, compiled, with great dispatch, a monumental history of 1798 which was modelled closely on Temple's.[134] His *Memoirs of the Different Rebellions in Ireland from the Arrival of the English: also, a Particular Detail of that which broke out the 23d of May, 1798* (1801) signalled in its title that the recent rebellion fitted into an established pattern, and its extended treatment consciously followed the template established for 1641, in that it was based on a large number of sworn affidavits, many of these collected by Musgrave himself from Protestant eye-witnesses and victims, who gave testimony of the 'dreadful barbarities' perpetrated by the rebels.[135] Musgrave's basic thesis was identical to Temple's: the rebellion was an attempt by Catholics to achieve 'the extirpation or expulsion of the protestants [and] the exclusive occupation of the island for themselves', although he also maintained that 'separation from England' was the constant aim of Catholics 'from the beginning of Elizabeth's reign to the late rebellion'. The sole motivating force behind this and all previous rebellions was religious bigotry, and particularly the doctrinal influence which the pope exerted over Irish Catholics through his emissaries, the clergy, who together with the rebellion leaders, had invoked 'the popish multitude to rise against their sovereign and their protestant fellow subjects'. The dogma of exclusive salvation for Catholics, which 'narrows the channels of infinite mercy', engendered in 'the lower class of people an uncharitable aversion, a cruel and unrelenting spirit of persecution, against protestants'.[136] In addition, because 'popery . . . teaches and sanctions treason to a protestant state', so long as the peasantry adhered to that religion they would remain 'traitorous towards the state'. Furthermore, in view of the fact that the contemporary pope had become 'a mere engine in the hands of Buonaparte, it behoves the government of England to guard more vigilantly than ever against the malignant spirit of popery'.[137] Musgrave's tract was an updated argument against any further repeal of the popery laws, and in favour of measures to eradicate Catholicism from Ireland. But in this latter regard, he had nothing new to offer, only the reintroduction of the charter schools as a proselytising tool, and a revival of the seventeenth-century policy of establishing Protestant urban settlements, on the lines of Derry and Bandon.[138]

While Musgrave did not rehearse in detail the alleged massacres of 1641, Temple's history was the unacknowledged model for his atrocity narrative. As in Temple, Irish Protestants were entirely innocent and upright, 'the most loyal, liberal and humane body of people in Ireland'. The rebels were made up of 'the lowest order of the people, whose minds are perverted by bigotry' and whose actions matched those of 1641 in alleged ferocity, including the drinking of the blood of their victims.[139] He also highlighted instances in the recent rebellion which appeared to be an exact re-run of 1641: 'The county of Wexford was desolated in the year 1641; and the houses of the bishop of Ferns and Mr. Ram of Ramsfort, were destroyed as well in the rebellion of that period as in the late one', and included the 1641 affidavits in support.[140] It seems entirely fitting that the only contemporary antiquary whose work featured in this extended catalogue of barbarism was Edward Ledwich. In the 'Introductory Discourse' Musgrave opened with an affirmation of the independence of the early Irish church from Rome, supported by reference to the 'learned' author of *Antiquities of Ireland*. The harnessing of Ledwich to a work of this nature underlined the conservative political dimensions of all his antiquarian researches.[141] Ledwich, however, also featured in Musgrave's *Memoirs of the Different Rebellions* in another guise. As Justice of the Peace in Queen's County, he took an affidavit from a Protestant farmer in 1784, recounting his abduction by 'white boys' one night, who severed his ears 'with circumstances of great barbarity' and left him buried up to his chin in a grave lined with furze.[142] In the light of such contemporary horrors, it is no wonder that fears of barbarism continued to haunt the work of Protestant, and indeed Catholic, antiquaries.

ASCENDANCY, REBELLION AND THE COLLAPSE OF THE ANTIQUARIAN ENTERPRISE:
the Royal Irish Academy, 1785–1800

In the series of 'golden ages' around which Irish narratives of the past have been built, the myth of 'Grattan's Parliament' stands out. It is distinguished from others by the brevity and exactitude of its time span (from 1782, when the Irish parliament was granted a measure of formal independence, until the dissolution of that body under the Act of Union in 1800), and it is also unique in having emerged within only a decade or two of its traumatic terminal date.[1] It featured claims of enhanced self-government, of brilliant politics informed largely by a liberal spirit, and of unprecedented economic prosperity. In recent decades, however, the myth has been challenged in all of these areas, and shown to be based mainly on the exaggerated claims made by politicians of the time and by none more so than Henry Grattan himself who set out to consolidate his own reputation, to the extent of rewriting his most famous parliamentary speeches years later, thereby achieving immortal fame as the myth incarnate.[2] Historians now argue for a very different reading of the 1780s and 1790s. J.J. Lee's bravura sketch of it as a period of political repression and economic decline has found support in a number of studies of major and related crises that cumulatively ensured the dominance of a reactionary 'Protestant Ascendancy' ethos rather than of Grattanite liberalism.[3] These crises had deeper roots and consequences than the purely political ones of more traditional accounts, such as the challenge of the Volunteer convention, conflicts over the Regency and the failure of Pitt's commercial propositions. They centred instead on the revival of the seventeenth-century fear of the native Irish threat, as a demographic crisis and economic modernisation combined with the relaxation of the penal laws to bring Catholics more and more into competition with Protestants.[4] This led to conflict in the areas of land tenure and employment, in particular, but even the Protestant monopoly of the political process seemed in danger. At all levels a more assertive Catholicism was prepared to exploit new circumstance, and provoked a more extreme Protestant reaction.

The 'golden age' had barely begun when the Rightboy disturbances of 1784–6, and especially the attack on the tithe system, convulsed politics and led to a 'paper war' between liberal and conservative Protestants, while a less inhibited Catholic polemic confirmed the fears of the latter.[5] Under a more dynamic bourgeois leadership, the Catholic Committee became increasingly radical and further confirmed the threat it posed by the summoning of a national Catholic Convention in 1792. In the following year its eager acceptance of the Catholic franchise showed how limited its radicalism was, and disgusted its Protestant allies in the United Irish organisation.[6] However, the extension of the vote to Catholic forty-shilling freeholders, together with their arming in the new militia, further destabilised the political system during 1793–4 and gave a major boost to the 'Protestant Ascendancy' element.[7] The years following were characterised by the rival sectarian violence of Catholic Defenders and Protestant Orangemen, destroying the bourgeois radical dream of 'United Irishmen'.[8] Thus the rebellion of 1798 now appears less a sudden eruption than the culmination of a series of increasingly violent and sectarian crises.[9] These, resulting in ever more polarised politics, and ever more fearful state repression, made it increasingly difficult to sustain the tendency among antiquaries towards developing shared historical perspectives. More slowly and unevenly, but as inevitably, the collapse of the antiquarian agenda mirrored that of the Grattanite whigs.

The commitment of most liberal Protestants to religious toleration had always been a limited one, part of their overall strategy for achieving 'legislative independence' rather than something embraced for its own sake.[10] In the immediate aftermath of 1782 the conservatism of the 'patriot' leadership on this issue was apparent, particularly in the conflict between the politicians and the more radical elements in the Volunteer movement. Many prominent 'patriot' politicians, such as Henry Flood and the commander-in-chief of the Volunteers, Lord Charlemont, who supported parliamentary reform and, in theory at least, further Catholic relief, baulked at extending the electoral franchise to Catholics and at allowing them to bear arms. James Kelly argues that the agrarian disturbances in Munster from 1784 weakened the reformist tendency by raising fears for the security of the constitutional settlement.[11] The Rightboy protest was primarily directed against the tithe system, and involved intimidation on a massive scale. However, like earlier disturbances in this area, such as the Whiteboy campaign in the 1760s, the objectives were essentially conservative; protest was directed at the level of tithes and not at the principle, and included Catholic as well as Protestant dues.[12] At the outset, both the administration and liberal Protestants were prepared to countenance tithe reform, but the extent and extremity of the outrages allowed a conservative Protestant regrouping to take place and to fight what they saw as a threat to the privileges of the established church.[13] In essence, this was a dispute between Protestants which used the agrarian disturbances in Munster as either a proof of the need for reform or for its opposite. Opponents of further reform and toleration measures played successfully on traditional Protestant fear of popery and argued that the Rightboys were attempting to overturn the Protestant establishment in church and state. The most effective of these pamphleteers was Richard Woodward, Bishop of Cloyne in Munster and author of *The Present State of the Church of Ireland* (1786), which went through an astonishing six editions in a fortnight. His forceful analysis bound 'the most deeply felt fears of Irish Protestants into a conservative ideology centring on the concept of "Protestant ascendancy"', which he equated with control of land, preservation of the British connection, and the maintenance of Protestant domination of existing constitution in church and in state.[14] Kelly sees the supplanting of the older and more neutral term 'Protestant interest' by 'Protestant Ascendancy' as evidence of the hardening of opinion in the 1780s and of the vulnerability of the Protestant élite. He concludes that the Rightboy disturbance caused the eclipse of a briefly triumphant liberal or reformist Protestantism and its replacement by a resurgent conservatism.[15]

This was the climate in which the Royal Irish Academy was established, thus initiating significant Protestant sponsorship of the study of Gaelic culture and antiquities. It also provides the context for many of the most influential Protestant publications on antiquities of the century and, not surprisingly, they reflect its divisions and controversies. The pro-Gaelic works of Joseph Cooper Walker and Charlotte Brooke were balanced by those of Thomas Campbell and Edward Ledwich, which offered a conservative and hostile perspective on the Gaelic past. However, the publication dates of these works do not show a simple eclipse of the liberal view. Walker's *Historical Memoirs of the Irish Bards* appeared in 1786, the highpoint of the Munster disturbances, but Brooke's *Reliques of Irish Poetry* was published in 1789, the same year as Campbell's *Strictures*, and also when Ledwich was producing his *Antiquities of Ireland* in separate numbers. Moreover, even as this latter was being published, a rejoinder was under way from William Webb, almost certainly a Quaker, who denied being 'a votary of any particular hypothesis' and was motivated by 'curiousity' rather than 'controversy'.[16] While Webb deplored the manner in which Ledwich, Campbell and Beauford argued their case 'by ill-placed invective, and too frequently by personal allusion', his main target was John Pinkerton's *Dissertation on the Origins and Progress of the Scythians or Goths* (1789) which, he alleged, had been received and adopted uncritically in Ireland, presumably by these same writers. Pinkerton had transgressed by his 'total perversion of Celtic history' which came from his enslavement 'to prejudices, the meanest and most ridiculous', in spite of his much-vaunted claims to impartiality.[17] Webb's intention was to reclaim as Celtic 'a large proportion of those nations, which [Pinkerton] has ranged under the Gothic standard'.[18] On the origins question, Webb tended towards the synthetic model put forward by Thomas Barnard, positing successive oriental and Gothic colonisations of Ireland, and he was a follower of the early Vallancey's *Essay on the Irish Language*, regretting that the latter was now traversing the globe in his efforts to extend further 'his scheme of Irish antiquities'.[19] On the related issue of the authenticity of the annals as a repository of early Irish history, Webb echoed Leland's argument that they were being measured by a standard far higher than that applied to the older records of other peoples.[20] He called them 'genuine national records' and urged their publication, along with an improved translation of Keating's *Foras Feasa*, so that it could not be assumed that antiquaries were fearful of public scrutiny.[21]

A further defence of Gaelic tradition was mounted by James Hely, a Church of Ireland clergyman and kinsman of John Hely-Hutchinson, the liberal provost of Trinity College Dublin, in the form of a translation from the Latin of Roderic O'Flaherty's *Ogygia* (1685), which was published in 1793. The lengthy list of subscribers included a very large number of peers and bishops, and a smattering of MPs (among them Henry Grattan and John Foster), United Irish members (Napper Tandy and Archibold Hamilton Rowan), and antiquaries such as Thomas O'Gorman, Sylvester O'Halloran and Charles Vallancey. The fact that Charles O'Conor was listed, even though he had died in 1791, is perhaps an indication that there had been a delay in the publication of this work.[22] Hely's opening address to 'The Irish nation' combined a patriot eulogy of 'my country', which was no longer 'made to slumber over her rights and her interests', with a defence of O'Flaherty as a preserver of 'many facts, which are certainly authentic, and which will enable a modern . . . to obtain a good idea of the state of society in this kingdom, in the times of paganism and idolatry'.[23] Apart from criticising O'Flaherty's excessively early dating of the Milesian landing, Hely endorsed his findings, including the knowledge of letters in pre-Christian times. He acknowledged the help of O'Conor 'whose memory must be revered by this country', and defended Vallancey as skilled in 'the ancient language of this island' and oriental history. The efforts of the latter's detractors to detect mistakes in his etymologies were actually designed to fill 'volumes with the superior savageness of our old inhabitants'; an indication of how clearly the conservative antiquarian political agenda was understood.[24]

Among Protestant antiquaries, therefore, the liberal ethos which had promoted research in the Gaelic past was not immediately crushed by the Rightboy disturbances and ensuing debate, but it was now operating in a more highly charged climate. A striking manifestation of this was both the bequest in the will of the 'patriot' politician, Henry Flood, who died in 1791, endowing a Chair of Gaelic at Trinity College Dublin, and the family's response to it. It was ultimately held to be void as contrary to the statute of Mortmain, but counsel for Flood's relatives also adopted the highly political argument that the bequest contravened the sixteenth-century 'Act for English order, habite and language' (28 Henry VIII *c*. 15), which equated loyalty with Anglicisation. In response, the defence maintained that Flood had intended to endow the philological study of Gaelic and that the chair would not contribute in any way to its revival as a spoken language.[25] Thus, while some Protestant support of the Gaelic heritage continued in the 1790s, the old colonial linking of Gaelic culture to sedition was also being forged anew.

Catholic antiquaries in the 1780s were also affected by these changes in the political climate, and this may account for their relatively low profile during the period, thus following the dominant pattern of Catholic politics until the 1790s. The Catholic Committee abstained from the divisive debate over parliamentary reform in 1783–4, and thereby minimised the damage inflicted to their cause. Similarly, the Munster bishops were quick to denounce the Rightboy agitation and to do what they could to defuse the situation by reducing Catholic priestly dues. The Catholic leadership maintained this moderate and low-key stance, until the appearance of inflammatory pamphlets by Duigenan and Woodward in the winter of 1786–7. These claimed that the disturbances were fomented by the clergy and were part of a concerted plot to overthrow the Protestant establishment. In response, a number of pamphlets by lay and ecclesiastical Catholic leaders were published in 1787, provoking a wide-ranging exchange with conservative Protestants.[26]

Antiquarian publications by Catholics in the 1780s were few in number and included no substantial works comparable to those of the previous decade, such as, for example, Sylvester O'Halloran's two-volume *General History of Ireland* (1778). Most of them appeared in the form of contributions to Protestant-sponsored journals, indicating not only a sense of political caution, but also a shift in the control of antiquarian research from Catholic to Protestant hands. Between 1783 and 1784, O'Conor published three essays on pre-Christian Ireland in Vallancey's *Collectanea de Rebus Hibernicis*; these were designed to provide support for Vallancey in the face of Ledwich's challenge rather than to break new ground.[27] Sylvester O'Halloran, in his last excursion into print on antiquarian matters, presented an English translation of a 'Martial Ode' in Gaelic to the Royal Irish Academy which was published in the second volume of their *Transactions* in 1788.[28] He also read a paper, on the ancient armies of Ireland, to the Academy in February 1786, just as hardline Protestants were beginning their attack on the Rightboy campaign as sedition.[29] O'Halloran's celebration of the martial qualities of the native Irish was more appropriate to the relatively peaceful and conciliatory atmosphere of the 1770s, and this may account for its non-appearance in the Academy's journal.

Charles O'Conor provides the most complex example of the impact of political events on Catholic antiquarian writing at the time of the establishment of the Royal Irish Academy. As a member of the Catholic Committee, he was a formulator of its policy of moderation and discretion. In October 1784, on the subject of parliamentary reform, he urged that Catholics should stay out of the debate between liberal and conservative Protestants:

> Let those who have an eligible right to sit in Parliament labor to reform what is amiss in our civil constitution. We who are excluded from such a right should avail ourselves of the negative right left us, that of being silent and passive.[30]

However, he had even more cause than his colleagues to chafe at the remaining penal laws and to resent arguments in their support. In 1777 his younger brother, Hugh, taking advantage of one such law, had converted to

Protestantism and sued Charles for his lands at Belanagare. In 1779, a second 'discovery suit' was brought against Charles which sought to have the estate divided equally between him and his brothers. The case dragged on for almost six years until 1783, and was eventually settled out of court at great financial and physical cost to O'Conor.[31]

This may have been another factor in his failure to complete his 'Revolutions of Ireland' project. This ambitious work was begun in the more hopeful political atmosphere after the first Catholic Relief Act of 1778, and before the extent of the threat from Hugh was apparent. It is interesting to note that he extended the chronological range of the project as expectations of further toleration measures grew. While he had certain reservations about the wisdom of writing about the seventeenth-century revolution, his main anxiety was that, at seventy, he was too old and infirm for such a challenging assignment.[32] Others were less sanguine, notably Charles Vallancey, who was particularly sensitive to the political implications of such work. Vallancey's own researches at this point were directed away from Catholic concerns and towards the wider (and wilder) reaches of orientalism, and he was sufficiently worried by the tenor of O'Conor's work, as reported to him, that he approached the Chief Secretary, Thomas Orde in late 1784, with a view to applying some subtle pressure on O'Conor to modify his account:

> I wish this gentleman could be made a real friend to Government; he has been many years employed in writing the history of Ireland, and he tells me it will be ready for publication in the course of next year – a douceur properly applied might engage him to soften his style, when treating of his brethern, the Catholicks, or of the Irish Rebellions and the fatal consequences to them . . . [33]

Such a *douceur* would not have been unprecedented, as one of the most influential Catholic propagandists of the time, the Capuchin friar Arthur O'Leary, was awarded a pension for similar reasons from Dublin Castle in 1780 and again in 1784 (in spite of which he was the leading Catholic polemicist in the 'paper war' of 1786–7).[34] Vallancey also applied direct pressure on O'Conor to organise a loyal address by Catholics deploring the clamour for parliamentary reform, representing this as the wish of the Chief Secretary. When O'Conor declined politely but firmly, on the basis that 'the strongest assurances' of loyalty had been given many times, Vallancey ceased corresponding with him for over two months.[35]

Such reminders of O'Conor's fragile position *vis-à-vis* the Protestant élite, particularly in troubled times, may have been an inhibiting factor on his work. His comment in 1784 that the attention of the public was 'so much employed on the modern state of our island that it supersedes every thought of its antient state', also applied to himself.[36] He, along with other Catholics, was at last drawn into the controversy over the Munster disturbances by Richard Woodward's skilful polemic on alleged Catholic plots to overthrow the established church. O'Conor drew up a reply for the use of the Catholic Committee, which has not survived. The covering letter to Charles Ryan communicated his unease: 'If you think the whole should be suppressed, be it so. I shall be happy in finding that the little assistance I could give is not wanted.'[37]

O'Conor's one open foray into contemporary politics in this period was an unusual and, especially in the circumstances, a surprisingly daring one. In 1786, new editions of his friend John Curry's *Historical and Critical Review of the Civil Wars of Ireland* were published in London and Dublin, with a biographical sketch of Curry (dead since 1780) by O'Conor. To rake up again the events of the previous century at a time of great Protestant insecurity seems somewhat hazardous. In his account of Curry's life, O'Conor assured the public that 'the intention of the author in the following work was solely to instruct, not to misrepresent, to conciliate, not to irritate' and 'to remove the false grounds of a torrent of invectives, which have borne down repeatedly on our good sense'. But in giving Curry's family background he reinforced the idea of existing Catholic grievance at the loss of their lands.[38] Furthermore, he pointed out that because of the penal laws Curry had been forced to go to Paris to study medicine, and that his sons 'by the like impolitic penal law' had to emigrate to the continent to seek employment in the 'imperial army'.[39] Such uncharacteristic forthrightness may reflect O'Conor's own recent experiences with the popery laws, but its force was greater than intended, because O'Conor had envisaged a less contentious context for his remarks.

There is only one letter mentioning the publication in O'Conor's extant correspondence, but it is clear from this that the new edition was the initiative of the Catholic Committee, rather than of O'Conor acting on his own, and that it was a botched propaganda effort, perhaps intended as the Committee's contribution to the 'paper war'. O'Conor co-operated with another member, Thomas Braughall, who had agreed with him that some parts (unspecified) of Curry's book were 'not proper to be exposed to the public at present [and] should be rescinded'. However, the secretary of the Committee, Martin Gaven, failed to produce a modified text, leaving O'Conor in the invidious position of appearing to be the instigator of a controversial work, seeking to revive old claims and fears.[40] An example of the criticism directed at him can be seen in the correspondence of Edward Ledwich:

> Is this a time to talk of the oppressions of the English[?] . . . yet in O'Conor's preface we are told, the present generation have nothing to do with past times. What end could he then serve in laying before the public this long catalogue of English cruelties . . . [41]

This bruising experience seems to have marked the end of O'Conor's career as a publicist for the Catholic Committee and a final retreat into the world of scholarship. He understood the impact it would have on both his friends and adversaries among the Protestant intellectual élite.[42] Since 1785,

Walker and Vallancey had been attempting to procure a government pension for him in order to complete his 'memoir' on the ancient state of Ireland; the delay in securing it may have been connected with his indiscretion on this occasion. O'Conor's sinecure of one hundred pounds per annum was eventually granted in 1788 by the newly appointed Lord Lieutenant, the Marquis of Buckingham, in return for a promise to leave his papers to the Royal Irish Academy.[43] The episode underlines the insecurity of O'Conor's position in the Dublin literary establishment. On the one hand, he was a respected scholar whose library was to be housed in the new and prestigious learned society. On the other, his work on the less remote periods was feared even by Protestant supporters as inflammatory, and recognised by himself as a threat to his acceptance in their society.

The diffusion of the 'Protestant Ascendancy' ethos also had an impact on Protestant research, even when that focused on the pre-colonial period, particularly since one aspect of the 'paper war' involved a discussion of the continued use of the Irish language among the poor. Woodward had declared that 'it should be the object of Government . . . to take measures to bring it into entire disuse', and while he was countered by one disputant who replied that such a proposal 'would come with a better grace from the leader of Goths and Vandals . . . than from the Bishop of a large diocese, in a philosophic age', others supported Woodward's position.[44] The resulting stresses and strains can be seen particularly clearly in the internal workings of the Royal Irish Academy, which was set up in 1785, just as the Munster disturbances were beginning to have an impact on public opinion. This institution, and more especially its antiquities section, was imbued with the same liberal spirit which lay behind the productions of Joseph Cooper Walker and Charlotte Brooke. It included Charles O'Conor among its foundation members, one of two Catholics so honoured. However, its efforts to promote sympathetic understanding of the Gaelic past, and particularly of its literary heritage, was overwhelmed by growing Protestant fears about the political legacy of that world.

Representative and supportive institutions for antiquarianism were relatively slow to develop in the peripheral areas of the British state. The Society of Antiquaries had been established in London in 1717, while the Society of Antiquaries of Scotland and the Royal Irish Academy were founded only in 1780 and 1785 respectively. In the timing of their establishment, the Dublin and Edinburgh societies were part of the trend towards the setting up of provincial learned bodies, such as the Lunar Society of Birmingham (1766), the Manchester Literary and Philosophical Society (1781) and the Newcastle-on-Tyne Literary and Philosophical Society (1793).[45] The Edinburgh-based Society of Antiquaries was the first attempt at giving Scottish antiquarianism an institutional expression, but there had been three previous unsuccessful attempts in Ireland. These earlier societies shared a common weakness – a lack of financial support – which stemmed from the small size of the Dublin élite. The two earliest Irish antiquarian bodies, the solely

Protestant Physico-Historical Society (1744–52) and the Select Committee on Antiquities of the Dublin Society (1772–4) (which had Charles O'Conor and the Catholic Archbishop Carpenter as corresponding members), were wound up due to declining attendance at meetings and a consequent difficulty in the collection of membership subscriptions.[46] The second of these published no proceedings, but the Physico-Historical Society sponsored the county surveys of Charles Smith.[47] The third body, the Hibernian Antiquarian Society (1779–83), did not rely on subscriptions since it had the backing of a wealthy patron, William Burton Conyngham, and could function with a membership of only seven people (again, including O'Conor). However, the smallness of this group also presented problems, given the controversial nature of Irish antiquarianism and the explosive relationship between two of the seven, Charles Vallancey and Edward Ledwich. The society foundered amidst the controversy over their rival theories of Irish origins rehearsed in the pages of Vallancey's journal, *Collectanea de Rebus Hibernicis*, which he had put at the disposal of the new antiquarian body in 1779.[48]

The Royal Irish Academy had numerous advantages over these earlier bodies. It began with a membership of eighty-eight, growing by 1790 to one hundred and thirty-eight. Covering science and what was then commonly referred to as 'polite literature' as well as antiquities, it had a broader mix of people and wider aims. Each section had its own committee, elected annually, which decided on activities and publications, but the decision-making process also involved the Council and the general membership of the Academy voting together.[49] This meant that the tensions among antiquaries were, to a large extent, diluted in the larger institution. The Academy had its origins in a small society, the Neophilosophers, consisting of seven Fellows of Trinity College Dublin, including Mathew Young, whose study of Macpherson's Ossian was published in the first volume of the *Transactions of the Royal Irish Academy*.[50] Within months, however, it was decided to approach Lord Charlemont and seek his support for a much larger body on the lines of the Royal Society, and that was readily given. The first meeting of the Academy was held in Charlemont's town house on 18 April 1785. A constitution and by-laws were quickly drawn up, modelled on those of the Royal Society, giving significant power to a council of twenty-one, in order to prevent 'factious proceedings'.[51] To mark the distinctive national identity of the new body, it was decided to hold the principal meeting of the year on the eve of St Patrick's Day; the previous day being chosen 'from an apprehension that our devotion to the memory of our tutelar saint might render our heads less cool than became an assembly of philosophers'.[52] In the same historical vein, the royal charter, granted in January 1786, referred explicitly to the 'kingdom of Ireland, which was in ancient times famous for its schools and seminaries of learning'.[53]

But if Ireland's early Christian golden age was used to frame the Academy historically, recent political developments, notably the achievement of legislative independence, were equally important in providing its members with a sense of purpose. This can be seen clearly in the 'Preface' to the first volume of the Academy's *Transactions* (1787), an exposition of the body's origin and aims by Robert Burrowes, who was a Fellow of Trinity College Dublin. Referring to the 'peculiar circumstances [which] have now given to Ireland an importance in the political scale', Burrowes argued that 'well directed industry alone' could maintain that new status. The Academy's overall aim was to promote the advancement of knowledge and, by practical means, namely 'the cultivation of useful arts and sciences', to support Ireland's growing political stature. The study of polite literature and antiquities was seen as germane to the project, both 'to civilize the manners and refine the taste of its people' and to 'awaken a spirit of literary ambition, by keeping alive the memory of its antient reputation for learning'.[54] The overall political focus of the Academy was reinforced by Burrowes's outline of the reasons for the failure of colonial Ireland to excel in the pursuit of scientific or literary endeavour. Behind all of these was the conquest, which he referred to tortuously as 'the important changes which took place in the government upon the invasion by Henry II'. This did not permit 'the nation to apply itself immediately to the peaceful employments of literary enquiry', while the resultant influx of settlers created 'two classes of inhabitants entirely dissimilar in their inclinations and habits, and afterwards more widely separated by a difference in religion', who could not lay aside 'their mutual enmity, and unite in the pursuit of speculative science'. Thus, the key to Ireland's state of 'comparative ignorance and inferiority' was 'the connection of this kingdom with England', which had gradually enticed away 'its men of genius'.[55]

The 'patriot' agenda of the Academy was most visible in the first volume of the *Transactions*. Charlemont, its president, contributed what might seem an innocuous essay on 'The Antiquity of the Woollen Manufacture in Ireland, proved from a Passage of an Antient Florentine Poet', but that industry and its control by English legislation had spurred William Molyneux into writing what was seen as the manifesto of Irish 'patriot' ideology in 1698, *The Case of Ireland being bound by Acts of Parliament in England, stated*. Furthermore, Charlemont not only argued that Ireland was 'possessed of an extensive trade in woollens at a very early period', but also conjectured as 'by no means impossible' that the English woollen industry established in the fourteenth century under the aegis of Edward III was modelled on that of Ireland. He expressly included 'the native Irish' in this trade, 'the English settlers being too few, and too much occupied by perpetual broils, to be alone equal to an extensive manufacture'. His aim, in part, was to refute the negative aspersions cast on 'a people, who, however erroneously, we are taught to believe were at this period little removed from a state of absolute barbarity', by reversing the direction of the civilising process, from Ireland to England.[56]

Charlemont's 'deep personal commitment to the politics of Irish patriotism', as well as his self-image as 'an Irishman' for whom 'love [of] my country is the ruling passion of my heart', made him the ideal figurehead for an institution which saw itself as part of a new political movement to bring about progress and prosperity.[57] Consciousness of the achievement of legislative independence, and perhaps also of the vexed question of parliamentary reform, may have spurred the Committee of Antiquities of the Academy to relay a set of queries relative to Ireland's earliest form of kingship and of parliamentary assembly to Charles O'Conor's friend the genealogist Thomas O'Gorman. The second of these queries had a contemporary ring:

> Of what ranks of the People were the States general of the Nation composed before and after the preaching of the Gospel? By whom and after what manner were they elected in their different Ranks? Who in particular represented the Artists and Plebians [sic]?

O'Gorman's reply, based no doubt on his long residence in France, was to make direct parallels with the French provincial estates, which 'observe the same Customs with the Antient States of Ireland'.[58]

While each of the three sections were given equal representation on the Council, with seven members each, there is no doubt that scientific matters were more prominent in the Academy's affairs. In a survey of the first eight volumes of the *Transactions*, R.B. McDowell has shown that twice as many science contributions were published as those of antiquities and polite literature together.[59] There is some evidence that the scientists were uncomfortable with Celticist enthusiasm and joined together with sceptics in the other two sections in order to trim its excesses. When Burrowes's 'preface' was presented to the Council in draft form, there were complaints that it was 'such a rant on the heroism, genius, learning and arts of Ireland as would have given a *coup de grâce* to our reputation'.[60] This criticism was supported by the chemist Richard Kirwan and by Thomas Percy, Bishop of Dromore and friend of Edward Ledwich and Thomas Campbell. In spite of this opposition, the Council voted to accept the draft for publication, but at its next meeting it was persuaded by Kirwan to insist that a substantial segment relating to 'the antient State of Literature in Ireland' be omitted.[61] Burrowes was asked to modify that part to form an introductory essay for the antiquities section of volume one of the *Transactions*, but, in spite of a number of reminders to him, he did not produce it.[62] The compromise decision to corral the Celticist enthusiasm of some Academy members into the antiquities section shows the general sensitivity to any risk of incurring ridicule of the institution as a whole and its scientific endeavours in particular.

The minutes of Council meetings indicate, moreover, that while that body exercised a veto over all papers submitted for publication in the *Transactions*, those on antiquarian subjects were more likely to come to ballot than any others. Lessons may well have been learnt from the mistakes of the Hibernian Antiquarian Society and in particular its journal, *Collectanea de Rebus Hibernicis*, which had been the fief of Vallancey when the society collapsed. Only one paper on the vexed and central question of origins was published in the *Transactions*, 'An Enquiry concerning the Original of the Scots in Britain', by Thomas Barnard, a founder member and Church of Ireland bishop. This attempted a synthesis of the rival Irish and Scottish theories, as put forward by O'Conor and Macpherson, but did not address the dispute between Irish antiquaries over Gothic and oriental models.[63] Sylvester O'Halloran's translation of a Gaelic poem, *Rosc Catha*, which appeared in the second volume in 1788, was referred back by Council to the Committee of Antiquities for changes to be made, including the omission of an introductory passage which repeated some of the inflated claims for early Irish civility made in his books.[64]

In spite of such caution, the *Transactions* could not avoid controversy altogether, though the Academy might not have anticipated it arising from Theophilus O'Flanagan's contribution on the Callan ogham stone, the leading feature in the antiquities section of the first volume, which raised once again the issue of the early use of letters in Ireland.[65] O'Conor's contention that the pre-Christian Irish had a literate culture received a boost in 1772 by the publication of Vallancey's *Essay on the Antiquity of the Irish Language*, which discerned a close affinity between Phoenician and Irish. O'Conor seemed to hope that this did away with the need to provide material evidence in the form of documents or inscriptions. He wrote confidently that the antiquity of the Irish language, as proved by Vallancey's discovery, 'forms, so to speak, a most authentic inscription of itself'.[66] But this curious idea of Gaelic providing its own internal evidence of having long been a written language was not taken up by others. Instead, Vallancey, like O'Conor had done earlier, turned to ogham as potential corroborative evidence for the tradition of a literate early Irish civilisation. In 1781, he tried to interest the English antiquary Thomas Astle in ogham and also sent him extracts from Irish manuscripts, which Astle included in *The Origin and Progress of Writing* (1784), while making plain his disbelief in Irish claims for the early use of letters.[67]

In the same year, ogham became the focus of much interest when Vallancey read a paper to the Society of Antiquaries in London on an ogham inscription recently discovered on a mountain in Co. Clare. The title of Vallancey's paper underlines the extent to which, by the 1780s, Macpherson's Ossian had come to shape perceptions of early Ireland: 'Observations on the Alphabet of the Pagan Irish and of the Age in which Finn and Ossin lived'. Vallancey claimed that he discovered the location of this ogham stone from 'an ancient Epic poem' describing the death of 'a great Chieftain named Conan Colgac' and giving his burial place. In 'an ancient Irish manuscript' he had found mention of an ogham inscription on the tomb of Conan and his death dated to AD 295; in other words the century in which Macpherson located *Fingal* and *Temora*. Mindful of the attacks on Macpherson for withholding the Gaelic originals of his poems, Vallancey gave an extract and his own translation:

> The fierce champion Conán was not present at the bloody battle of Gabra, for
> on the Beltine (1st day of May) of the preceding year, the dauntless hero was
> murdered by the *Fiana Finn*, at an assembly met to worship the sun . . . his grave
> was dug on the north west side of the black mountain of Callán, and his name
> is inscribed in Ogham on a hewn stone.

The inclusion of (and drawing attention to) a reference to sun worship was a
characteristic touch, and a reminder that Vallancey was following his own orientalist track. However, he chose here to emphasise less esoteric concerns,
namely 'that the ancient Irish had an alphabetical character before the arrival
of St Patrick. Secondly, the period in which Ossin and Finn lived.'[68] Vallancey
stated that he had sent Theophilus O'Flanagan to look for the stone, and
included a letter from the latter giving a translation of the inscription as he
found it: 'Beneath lies Conan Colgac the long footed.'[69]

The Academy gave their full backing to the discovery. At their first meeting, in June 1785, the Antiquities Committee paid eight guineas to O'Flanagan to make a further trip to Mount Callan to find 'a remarkable Ogham
inscription reported to be present there'.[70] However, following the publication
of O'Flanagan's findings in the *Transactions*, doubts began to be raised about
the Callan ogham, in terms of the authenticity of the inscription and the interpretation of it. It became part of the disputed terrain of Irish antiquities in the
period of the greatest polemical and sectarian writing. For almost a century the
Mount Callan ogham stone was something of a *cause celèbre* among antiquaries, and coloured general attitudes to such stones. Among the next generation
of scholars, who branded the Mount Callan find as forgery, John O'Donovan
was reluctant to acknowledge that any ogham stone he encountered could be
genuine, while Eugene O'Curry ignored the topic of ogham as far as was prac-
ticable in his works.[71] In many ways the controversy resembled the Ossian
dispute, with doubters taking up positions of extreme scepticism, akin to that
of Samuel Johnson who had alleged that there were absolutely no Gaelic manuscript remains in Scotland which Macpherson might have consulted.[72]

The controversy has been investigated by Siobhán de h-Óir who has made
a study of late ogham inscriptions, known as 'scholastic oghams', to which
class the Callan ogham belonged. Early or 'classic' oghams date from the fourth
to the middle of the seventh centuries, and are found running vertically on
pillar stones which probably served as memorials to the dead.[73] Scholastic
oghams date from the late eighth century to the middle of the nineteenth century, are found mostly in manuscripts and therefore often run horizontally.
According to de h-Óir, the Mount Callan ogham stone had all the traits of this
later class, being cut on a slab rather than a pillar, with vowels marked differ-
ently and dots dividing the words. Moreover, the language of the inscription
is modern Irish, and she suggests that it was carved shortly before it was first
mentioned in print, in an obscure guidebook to Clare by a local antiquary,
John Lloyd, in 1780.[74] De h-Óir placed the carving of the Callan ogham in the

context of the Ossian vogue. The site chosen was a suitably gloomy mountain landscape, dubbed by a local poet *Callan cíordhubh* (black-ridged Callan). She suggested that the subject was either Conán Mac Morna, a minor character in the Fionn cycle, or Conán Cinn tSléibhe, the chief character in *Feis Tighe Chonáin*, which was a frame-work tale for the re-telling of many of Fionn Mac Cumhaill's adventures. The most obvious culprits for the forgery are Lloyd or O'Flanagan, who were close enough to Gaelic tradition to know ogham and had enough Irish to compose the verse.[75] A market existed in Dublin for antiquarian discoveries, as the Royal Irish Academy was collecting its own 'cabinet of curiosities', one of the marks of a learned society. Furthermore, the first manuscript presented to the Academy in 1785 was the Book of Ballymote, a fourteenth-century compilation which contained many examples of ogham.[76]

The Mount Callan ogham initially made O'Flanagan's reputation and gained him an entry into Academy circles; he was employed as scribe and translator there from 1786.[77] He was an unusual figure – a Catholic Gaelic speaker from Co. Clare, son of an Irish teacher and scribe, who knew classical Irish, Latin and Greek, and who, in spite of his religion, was accepted as a student at Trinity College Dublin in 1784, which at that time, under the provostship of John Hely-Hutchinson, was not enforcing the Catholic ban.[78] In his paper, O'Flanagan took credit for tracking down the manuscript references to Conán's, and recounted how he and a Mr Burton found the inscription on the mountainside.[79] By reading from right to left as well left to right, O'Flanagan produced five different translations of the ogham, which were in addition to one he gave to Vallancey in 1784 after his first sighting of it. These were as follows:

1. Beneath this sepulchral monument is laid Conan the fierce, the nimble-footed.
2. Obscure not the remains of Conan the fierce, the nimble-footed!
3. Long let him be at ease on the brink of this lake, beneath this hieroglyphic, darling of the Sacred!
4. Long let him be at ease on the brink of this lake, who never saw his faithful clan depressed!
5. Hail, with reverential sorrow, the drooping heath around his lamentable tomb!

According to O'Flanagan, these were not alternative interpretations, but were elements of a continuous single reading; the strokes and their arrangement being deliberately open to a variety of meanings. This demonstrated, he believed, the considerable sophistication of this form of writing, which, far from being 'primitive hieroglyphics', was the 'obscure' script of the druids and bards, and thus strong proof of the claim for the early use of letters in Ireland.[80]

Significantly, however, O'Conor was unenthusiastic about the discovery and was sceptical that a fourteen-hundred-year-old inscription could survive in a legible form.[81] He did not feel competent to decipher the ogham[82], expressed doubts about the chronology used by O'Flanagan to date it, and was aware that there were a number of figures in the traditional tales called Conán, to whom it might refer.[83] He applied much the same criticism to O'Flanagan as he had used earlier against Macpherson, namely that he was guilty of anachronism in mixing up heroes and princes from different ages.[84] O'Conor was gloomy about the reception of O'Flanagan's paper: 'critics will laugh. What is worse, the publishing of such improbabilities in print will only add to the little credit given to any part of our history antecedent to the reception of Christianity.'[85] This prediction proved accurate, but as with Macpherson's Ossian, O'Conor was mistaken in believing that the details of chronology and anachronism would be instrumental in determining the critical reception of O'Flanagan's Mount Callan ogham paper. In *Antiquities of Ireland* (1790), Ledwich, the most prominent sceptic, ignored the historical context and instead focused on the carving and the methods used by O'Flanagan to decipher multiple readings of it. He branded the discovery 'one of the boldest, most artless and groundless figments offered to the learned world'. The method of deciphering, by which the lines were read from either direction, was 'a form of literary conjuring'.[86] Like O'Conor, he was doubtful that the carving could have been fully preserved in such an exposed location, and used a characteristic heavy irony to mock the claim, imagining its supernatural protection as the work of a 'venerable Druid who . . . washed the stone with a magic composition of Mistletoe, Samolus and Selago; and in a fine prophetic phrenzy, predicted the amazing discoveries of Irish Antiquaries in the eighteenth century.' According to Ledwich, ogham writing was no different from the runes found in the Scandinavian countries, which were based on the Roman alphabet: 'In a word, these wonderful Irish Ogums were nothing . . . but a stenographic . . . contrivance, common among the semibarbarians of Europe in the middle ages, and very probably derived from the Romans.'[87]

Thus, while the larger structure of the Academy gave the antiquaries some financial security and lessened the risk of dissolution through internecine feuding, its foundation at a time of growing political and sectarian tension meant that such Protestant sponsorship of investigations into Gaelic heritage was bound to generate unease in conservative circles. The difficulties facing the Academy antiquaries can be seen even more clearly in the fortunes of their major project: to collect, translate and publish medieval Gaelic manuscripts. Up to the mid-eighteenth century the work of manuscript collection and translation had been carried out by and for individuals, some Protestant (like Arthur Brownlow and Anthony Raymond), others Catholic (Charles O'Conor and John Fergus).[88] Trinity College began to extend its manuscript holdings when Thomas Leland was librarian in the 1760s, a phase culminating in the donation of the Sebright collection (engineered by Trinity graduate Edmund Burke) in 1786.[89] Purchases and donations of private collections led to other major holdings in the Bodleian Library and the British Museum.[90] Such institutionalisation was vital to the preservation of manuscript material and the development of scholarship, but it also further distanced the material from the culture which had produced it. The emphasis on translation is equally significant in this regard. Royal Irish Academy antiquaries, however great or sympathetic their interest in Gaelic sources, did not have even the basic linguistic competence to read them (O'Conor being the only significant exception) and instead employed the remnants of the Gaelic scholarly tradition, whose social position and, sometimes, education, as much as their religion, excluded them from the charmed circle of the scholarly élite.

The initial holding of manuscripts was small (even by 1831 the R.I.A. had only four Gaelic manuscripts), but there was considerable co-operation between the Academy and the library of Trinity College Dublin, which remained the library of Academy antiquaries down to the mid-nineteenth century.[91] The Academy also appointed an agent in Rome to search for manuscripts; this was Charles O'Conor, grandson of the antiquary, who was training for the priesthood. This did not go smoothly, since it appears that the Academy was reluctant to address the pope directly by letter in order to get permission for O'Conor to search the Vatican archives.[92] One of the first actions of the Academy antiquaries was to hire the services of Maurice O'Gorman, who had earlier been employed by Trinity library and by Vallancey.[93] However, O'Gorman's alcohol problem interfered with his work and he was replaced by Theophilus O'Flanagan in December 1786.[94] While O'Gorman had been hired at a salary of only twelve guineas per annum 'as a compensation for his trouble', O'Flanagan was to be paid one hundred pounds, in quarterly instalments, to translate such Irish manuscripts as Vallancey decided on.[95] The commitment of such a large sum of money indicates the importance accorded to this translation work and the impression made on Academy members, particularly Vallancey, by O'Flanagan, who the following year was made a scholar of Trinity College.[96] But the high hopes entertained were unrealistic and soon disappointed, for O'Flanagan made no progress and payments to him were stopped some time early in 1788.[97] However, he was then commissioned to make an English version of the Brehon laws tracts in Trinity library and, under pressure to produce results, within a week had presented a 'Glossary of the Language in which the Brehon Laws are composed' to the Council, who proposed sending it to Charles O'Conor for an assessment.[98] O'Conor was in Dublin at that time and sat in on a meeting of the Antiquities Committee on the same day.[99] There is no record of his response to the Council on this question, but it is clear from his private correspondence that he believed the translation of the Brehon laws to be an impossible task, because of the scale of the linguistic difficulties involved. He felt that the various chronological records, or annals, were in more urgent need of attention, while there were still Gaelic speakers who could decipher their less specialised old Irish.[100] If he made this clear to his Academy friends, they ignored his advice. A project to translate the ancient laws of Ireland had more kudos and fewer risks of political embarrassment for

Protestants than what Campbell and Ledwich referred to as 'meagre annals', which went up to relatively modern times.[101]

The Academy did not consult O'Conor formally on the law tracts again, and instead appointed a committee consisting of enthusiastic amateurs – Vallancey, Mathew Young of Trinity College and Joseph Cooper Walker – to supervise O'Flanagan's work. But their inability to make any assessment of its quality, or even content, can be seen in the Council resolution of April 1789 that he should furnish 'a Translation of the first Volume of Brehon Laws, producing an Attestation, that this production is really a translation'.[102] In spite of this, the committee reported in May 1789 that O'Flanagan 'has not fulfilled his engagement with the Academy', but he was, nevertheless, retained on the project, and the Academy still had hopes of publishing his work in February 1790.[103] O'Flanagan continued to receive money on account (albeit at a reduced rate), and in 1795 it was suggested by the Protestant liberal Lawrence Parsons that he might be paid to translate the Annals of Innisfallen.[104] The reluctance to sack O'Flanagan is curious, as there were other Gaelic scholars available. For example, in November 1790 the lexicographer Peter O'Connell submitted a specimen translation of 'an Irish Treatise on the seven orders of the Irish Bards' together with 'a Memorial in Irish praying to be employed by the Academy'.[105] It could be that a scribe and translator with a Trinity B.A. made a more acceptable employee of the Academy. Equally, they may have been wary of sacking a Trinity scholar who enjoyed the support of the provost, himself a leading Academy member.[106] For whatever reason, it was not until 1797 that a replacement scholar was engaged: Patrick Lynch, a hedge-school master originally from Co. Clare, who kept a school in Carrick-on-Suir, Co. Tipperary in the early 1790s.[107] He was hired as translator of the Book of Ballymote, the first manuscript acquired by the Academy.[108] Significantly less money was allocated by Council for the translation; this was influenced no doubt by past dealings with O'Flanagan, but may also have to do with a general waning of enthusiasm for the project, and with the growing financial crisis in the Academy.[109] Council stipulated that 'a sum not exceeding two guineas be given to Mr Lynch by Payments of half a guinea weekly on his producing eight pages of the Book of Ballymote weekly'.[110] This was quickly doubled to a guinea a week when it was decided that he should also translate the Annals of the Four Masters.[111]

This belated commitment to the translation of annals is further proof that Protestant antiquarianism was not overwhelmed in any simple way by the juggernaut of 'Protestant Ascendancy'. While historical *interpretation* diverged increasingly on religious lines, projects of *collection* and *translation* could be sustained. In part, this can be explained by the support of prominent political figures, notably Burke, whose stature had grown, even among conservative Protestants, after the appearance of *Reflections on the Revolution in France* (1790).[112] More generally, such scholarly endeavour was relatively value-free; conservative as well as radical interpretations could be made of such materials if successfully translated and published. Unlike O'Flanagan, Lynch actually produced translations over a period of two months which were read before Council.[113] There is no record in the various minutes of the Academy that a decision was taken to abandon the translation project, but it was not mentioned after April 1797; no doubt partly as a result of the general political situation. The outcome of this expending of precious resources was a string of incomplete and unpublished translations, and by 1800 the Academy was no nearer to producing English versions of Gaelic manuscripts than when it began.

A similar silence and sense of failure hangs over the essay competitions on Gaelic culture organised by the Antiquities Committee in the 1790s, which attracted few entries, none of which was awarded a prize. The choice of topics seem to have been connected to the translation project, and may illuminate its eventual abandonment. The first competition, announced in 1792, was on the theme 'An Historical Enquiry into the Ancient and Present State of the Irish Language; with the Causes and Remedies of the Obscurity of Ancient Irish Manuscripts'.[114] Only three entries were received but, despite this, a verdict on them was not reached for over five years until 1798, when it was decided not to award the prize. Two of the essays were deemed unworthy by 1794,[115] but the third, by the Gaelic scholar Richard MacElligott of Limerick, was discussed on three occasions, and eventually referred to Vallancey and Mathew Young. The decision not to award the prize to MacElligott was taken finally in April 1798, during the run-up to the outbreak of rebellion in Wexford, when presumably the Academy was particularly unwilling to be seen publicly to sponsor native Irish culture.[116] The later competitions were even less successful, as there is no record of any entries having been received. The sequence of themes is interesting in itself, as it implies a growing disenchantment with the value of Gaelic sources and the possibility of ever understanding them. From 'the Causes and Remedies of the Obscurities of Ancient Irish Manuscripts' of the first competition, they progressed to the 'Authenticity and Value of Irish Manuscript Histories of Ages, prior to Henry II' (1795). The third topic was 'What proofs are extant of a state of civilization in Ireland superior to that of the adjacent Countries, at any period prior to the Reign of Henry II?' This competition was announced in May 1799, and it perhaps most directly highlights the disillusionment with the Gaelic heritage which had been caused by '98.[117] In calling into question the existence of a civil society 'at any period' prior to colonisation, it implied a repudiation even of the still widely accepted idea of Ireland as a haven of learning and sanctity in early Christian times, which had been made an explicit part of the Academy's foundation charter.

The growing fear of Protestant antiquaries at the state of lawlessness in the country also reflected their personal experience, and can be seen in their correspondence from the late 1780s. Thomas Campbell, whose parish, Clogher, was in the north where the Catholic secret society of the Defenders operated, was particularly fearful. He favoured a policy of compromise on the tithe issue 'whilst the country is yet quiet', and freely confessed to writing 'under the impression of fear', rather than from any principle.[118] His anxiety was intensified when the Militia Act was passed in 1793, provoking anti-militia riots around the country. Thomas Bartlett has argued that these disturbances mark the breakdown of Irish society, and of the 'moral economy' or consensus between rulers and ruled.[119] Campbell's letters lend support to this analysis, but also further modify the characterisation of him as an arch-conservative Protestant. Although he was opposed to the 'machinations of the Roman Catholics' and the more energetic campaign of the Catholic Committee from 1792, his response to the militia disturbances was complex.[120] The raising of the militia by ballot had fanned the embers of 'that cursed democratic rage', but he sympathised with the 'common people, whose consternation at the apprehension of the ballot, and . . . of being torn away from their wives and children, I compare to nothing but the trepidation of small birds under the kite hovering over them'. He objected to the way in which the sub-governors, who had the responsibility for choosing those eligible for service, always exempted the rich freeholders, thereby 'throwing the burden of protecting property upon the poor, who had little or none'. Campbell, who was himself a sub-governor, resigned in protest at this policy. His belief that the law should be construed 'in the manner most conducive to the peace and happiness of the country' stands in contrast to the nostrum of Edward Ledwich that it was 'a happy thing for the country that Government sees its peace can only be secured by severity. It was so since the English landed here in 1169, and will ever be so.'[121]

It is significant, however, that Ledwich was writing in 1803 after the rising of Robert Emmett, whereas Campbell, who died in 1795, did not live to see his moderation tested by the 1798 rebellion. Joseph Cooper Walker, like Thomas Campbell, lived in a part of the country where unrest and violence were endemic in this period. His small estate at Enniskerry in Co. Wicklow was in a picturesque location, and in his own description of March 1797 epitomised early romantic ideas of landscape.[122] Yet by May he reported that 'the spirit of sedition' had reached the borders of the county and recorded his alarm in June when a pike, the main weapon of the rebels, was found near his garden; he moved back to Dublin shortly afterwards.[123] Indeed the violence touched the Academicians more directly when in 1797 William Hamilton was murdered. Hamilton was the author of *Letters on the coast of Co. Antrim* (1786), a county survey that examined the antiquities as well as the geology of the area and that reflected a Protestant 'patriot' perspective, upholding the idea of pre-colonial Gaelic civility and criticising England's role in Ireland from the twelfth century.[124] In the 1790s he moved to Donegal, where he was both a rector and local magistrate with a reputation for strong law-and-order policies which made him very unpopular in the locality. He was murdered by a mob in particularly horrific circumstances in March 1797, when they stormed a house where he was staying and the terrified servants thrust him out onto the lawn where he was killed.[125] The memory of his death lived on in the minds of many long into the nineteenth century as a symbol of the savageness of the period.[126]

It is unfortunate that we have no similar sources for the private thoughts of Catholic antiquaries in this period, to shed light on their adaptations to the political situation. The few works by Catholics that were published in the 1790s indicate an understandable cultural defensiveness, but also a lack of creativity. The death of Charles O'Conor in 1791 was the end of an era, and not only for Catholic antiquarianism. After his failure as translator of Gaelic manuscripts, Theophilus O'Flanagan embarked on another project, an English version of John Lynch's seventeenth-century attack on Giraldus Cambrensis in Latin, *Cambrensis Eversus* (1662). His *Cambrensis Refuted* appeared in 1795, and was a translation of the prefatory address and first three chapters of Lynch's work, as a kind of prospectus to gather subscriptions for publishing the remainder. In a long preface, O'Flanagan argued that this seventeenth-century work was worth translating, because 'the circumstances of his time and our own correspond so exactly, that although he published this work nearly a century and a half ago, his remarks and his arguments bear apposite application at this day'.[127] This insistence that a seventeenth-century Catholic work of cultural defence was perfectly applicable to the contemporary situation, was the mirror of the claim by the Protestant conservatives, Ledwich and Campbell, that the classic colonial texts by Spenser and Davies had not been superseded.[128]

O'Flanagan's aims were indeed similar to those of Lynch, in that he wished to attack the 'followers' of Cambrensis, referring explicitly to Edward Ledwich, who 'degrade the character of our nation'.[129] But in terms of tactics and tone, O'Flanagan's approach was updated to take account of the more aggressive Catholic campaigning of the 1790s. Thus, while Lynch had dedicated the book to Charles II in the language of 'fawning' flattery, O'Flanagan addressed Henry Grattan, his chosen dedicatee, as an equal, telling him that this book had 'a peculiar claim' on his 'patronage and protection', and that Catholics looked forward to his 'best exertions' on their behalf.[130] While Lynch had 'pleaded the cause of his communion well', it was no longer necessary to make the case for confessional equality of treatment, 'it pleads so strongly, so ably and so vehemently for itself'.[131] O'Flanagan made crucial interventions in Lynch's text, by using extensive footnotes to comment on and to update the thrust of the argument, in ways which were confrontational and far from the methods of Charles O'Conor's generation. Significantly, O'Flanagan, while praising O'Conor's scholarship, regretted that his 'meek genius and benevolent wisdom' had brought 'the scurrilous invective of insolent imposters' on him.[132]

It is clear that O'Flanagan was motivated mainly by hatred towards his own personal nemesis, Ledwich, 'a scurrilous and insulting defamer' who had mocked his multiple readings of the Callan ogham stone, and, in a phrase revealing of the hurt he felt, then pursued him 'into the recess of his closet, to

insinuate to the world' that his failure to translate the law tracts was due to ignorance. He maintained, rather pathetically, that he was ready 'to prove his com-
petency if the public will give encouragement', but lamented that 'to even know
the language, or to be more than superficially acquainted with the ancient history of this country, has been long considered . . . an ungenteel and inelegant
accomplishment'. On the basis that attack was a better form of defence,
O'Flanagan dismissed Ledwich as 'utterly unacquainted with the subject which
he presumes to handle, and the story of the people whom he traduces', and
asserted his own *bona fides* as 'a native antiquarian, versed in the history, language, and literature of his country'.[133] In this exercise in contrasts, it was Ledwich who appeared uneducated, since he knew no Irish: 'no man ever rested
in grosser ignorance of anything, than he does of this language'; a crime which
he compounded by pretending 'an acquaintance with it'.[134] While O'Conor had
always encouraged, and at times deferred to, Protestant élite investigations into
the Gaelic world, O'Flanagan dismissed them all, with the exception of 'the
respectable exertions' of Vallancey, who, as late as 1808, was acting as his
patron.[135] Thus, he characterised Daniel Beaufort's topographical account of the
country, *Memoir of the Map of Ireland* (1792), which included a glossary of Irish
place names, as 'a paltry performance, that disgusts by its nonsense even the
most superficial in the knowledge of our language'.[136]

Even more significantly, those, like Ledwich, who were overtly sceptical of
the Gaelic tradition, who 'labour to annihilate the ancient renown, and . . . the
independent dignity, of Ireland', were branded as outsiders who merely 'call
themselves natives of Ireland' and 'artfully affect' a knowledge of the language
and history of the country 'of which they are not possessed'. Their aims were
wholly political, in that they wished 'to attach to this great and independent
nation the disgraceful character of a vassal colony'.[137] O'Flanagan also targeted
Ledwich as clergyman, using Lynch's text as a foil, and highlighting the failure
of the Church of Ireland to engage in a proselytising campaign, in imitation of
'the salutary example of the dignitaries of Scotland and Wales, who have translated the scriptures, and the liturgy of their several churches, into the language
of the people of their ministry'. The successors of Bedell, he alleged, did not
do so, because they were engaged in *'more important concerns'*, namely, the
expropriation of Catholic lands: 'The Irish had estates to lose, and therefore
their religion was of no consideration, farther than it tended to deprive them
of their properties!'[138] Thus, O'Flanagan's attack on Ledwich for his antiquarian malfeasance broadened into a critique of the penal laws and the land settlement, linking emancipation and forfeited estates in a way that would surely
have appeared as political folly to Charles O'Conor. In choosing a seventeenth-
century Catholic work as the medium through which to reply to Ledwich,
O'Flanagan recognised that the intensifying Protestant–Catholic dispute of the
1790s was being recast in the terms of its seventeenth-century antecedents.

A similar abrasiveness and political forthrightness occurred in the biography of Charles O'Conor written by his grandson and namesake in 1796. The

Revd Charles O'Conor had studied with his grandfather before going to Rome for his theological training, and on his return in 1789 was appointed to the parish of Castlerea, Co. Roscommon.[139] His plan of a biography was welcomed with enthusiasm by O'Conor's friends, and he had no trouble in procuring his grandfather's letters from correspondents.[140] However, the first volume of *Memoirs of the Life and Writings of the late Charles O'Conor of Belanagare* was withdrawn from sale almost immediately after publication and the second was cancelled at the printing stage. This was done by the author at the behest of his brother, Matthew, who took exception to the first volume as highly inaccurate. A later study of the work revealed that Charles had taken great liberties with his grandfather's letters, making changes and running them together; and in one instance combining two letters by different authors.[141]

One of his strongest supporters initially was Joseph Cooper Walker, but when the advertisement seeking subscribers appeared, he was dismayed to find that the grandson highlighted O'Conor's propaganda against the penal laws, rather than his quiet scholarship. Again, the language used in recounting his grandfather's activities was of the aggressive style characteristic of the decade: 'He was the first who dared publicly to question the justice or the expediency of the penal code; and the first to arraign at the bar of reason, that degrading monopoly of freedom, which compelled the Irishman to degenerate into persecuting sectarist [sic].'[142] Walker was listed as a receiver of subscriptions in the 'Advertisement', but he wrote to O'Conor in August 1795, withdrawing the offer on the basis that he now felt it would be 'a party work' by an 'angry champion of your church', and that it was 'not a time to agitate the public mind' when it was 'already in a state of fermentation'. He took particular exception to O'Conor's statement that Catholics were the victims of religious 'persecution', preferring the term 'oppression', and alleging, in a tone of approbation, that 'they bore the Yoke with a meekness becoming the Servants of Christ'. But what galled him most was to be associated with a work calling for the vote for Catholics. He believed that by this stage they partook 'with the Protestants of every *solid* advantage of our glorious Constitution'. The legislature, he maintained (and affected a confidence that the Revd O'Conor would share this view), 'ought to be in the hands of men professing the established Religion'.[143] Walker had been at ease with the grandfather, whose manner and style was of the earlier, more openly deferential but subtly insistent phase of Catholic writing; this new confrontational form was anathema to him.

Walker's comment on the *Memoirs* in 1800, that 'it breathes the spirit of bigotry, broaches dangerous doctrines, and reflects with acrimony on the English settlers, and the Irish parliament', is an indication of how far he had moved from the 'patriot' position of his *Historical Essay* (1788) which was overtly critical of colonial policy in the past.[144] Having moved away from Irish antiquarianism in the 1790s and into the more tranquil waters of Italian literature (although he continued to serve on the Antiquities Committee of the Royal Irish Academy), Walker made one further contribution in 1806, which amounted to an open rejection of the liberal view for which he is best remembered. His essay 'On the Origin of Romantic Fabling in Ireland' argued that much of the writing of Gaelic historians was embellished by 'romance', a genre which had spread from the Orient into Europe and was brought to Ireland by 'the See of Rome . . . to invigorate superstition, by furnishing fresh supplies of holy legends'. A postscript assured the reader that he was not concerned with the oriental origins theory: 'I have studiously avoided every assertion, or conjecture, that could lead to controversy. I have no system to support.'[145] This unwillingness to be seen as a participant in antiquarian controversy was also made clear in a reference to his *Historical Memoirs of the Irish Bards*, which explained its enthusiasm as a product of youth, then deliberately invoked, while rejecting, the term 'retraction':

> I hope my candour, on this occasion, will not be mistaken for retraction. Although my crude productions on the subjects of the history and antiquities of Ireland, glow with all the warmth of youthful enthusiasm, it will not, I trust, be found, that I was led into wilful misrepresentation.

While he may indeed have 'erred', it was 'inadvertently' on his part and he now blamed his 'authorities', unnamed but presumably O'Conor, Vallancey and O'Halloran, on whom he had heaped praise in *Historical Memoirs* – truly a case of *trahison des clercs*.[146]

Walker continued to collect Gaelic poetry and tales, adding to the material gathered by his protégée, Charlotte Brooke, for her *Reliques of Irish Poetry*, which he had inherited after her death in 1793.[147] In 1809, when he discussed his collection with the English antiquary Francis Douce, who sent him the tale of 'Oisín in *Tír na nÓg*', his main interest was in the question of whether Oisín was said to have ridden a winged horse.[148] This transfer of interest from the producers, or bards, to the motifs which they used, marks another step away from the narrow judgements of either 'truth' or 'fable' in relation to Gaelic sources, and towards an appreciation of their literary qualities. However, for the Protestant Walker, it was also a way of continuing to study such material without reference to the political situation or to the language of the ordinary people. It is clear that his hobby was conducted through contacts such as Douce or Ascendancy figures like the Countess of Moira, who had 'a large collection of Irish romances with literal translations', rather than by commissioning field work among the poor who still recounted such tales.[149]

In some ways, Walker's change of direction after 1798, away from troublesome and dangerous 'history' towards 'romance', had echoes of Charles Vallancey's rejection of Catholic historical concerns in the 1780s. But in spite of Vallancey's immersion in a version of orientalist mythology which merely used Gaelic tradition as a departure point, his reputation suffered greatly after the 1798 rising. Writing to John Pinkerton, Walker summed up the association being made: 'Vallancey must, as you suppose, be hurt at the conduct of those whose champion he has been.' Walker pointed out, as a 'consolation' to the General, that 'the rebellion began amongst, and was for a considerable time confined to, the descendants of the English and other nations that settled in the counties of Dublin, Wicklow, and Wexford', where Irish was in greater decline as a spoken language. But, as he observed, '[l]atterly, indeed, the Milesians have rallied round the standard of rebellion'.[150] The traditional connection between Gaelic and sedition was thus reaffirmed by the rebellion. However, this generally held view of Vallancey was mistaken. As I have argued in Chapter Two, he was far from being the people's 'champion'. As Chief Engineer he was responsible for building the fortifications around Cork harbour and, following the abortive French invasion of 1796, he drew up a scheme for the military defence of Dublin port and of those in the south of the country.[151] Like Walker himself, indeed, Vallancey was still being perceived in terms of an earlier liberalism which he had long abandoned.

It proved impossible for the antiquities section of the Royal Irish Academy to sustain through the 1790s the level of activity and of collegiality that had characterised its early years. The declining attendance at general meetings of the Academy, which Richard Kirwan complained about in 1792, was also reflected in the Antiquities Committee.[152] From 1792, the minutes of these committee meetings record the regular participation of only a small minority of members, and often no business was transacted.[153] In January 1798 Vallancey reported that political tensions in the general body were coming to a head: 'parties begin to trouble our meetings – and some of our best members abscond on that account – we must have a Secretary at Salary or we shall split asunder.'[154] Following the rebellion and its suppression, the Antiquities Committee continued to be elected on an annual basis, but it became virtually moribund. No business at all was transacted between 1802 and 1805, and finally in May 1810 it was decided to disband the Committee, thus bringing to an end a remarkable phase of Protestant-led writing and research into the pre-colonial past.[155]

EPILOGUE:
A Farewell to the Milesians?

In January 1799, Vallancey wrote to Walker of his disillusionment with the Royal Irish Academy, which no longer 'relish[ed] Oriental Subjects', adding that he was 'too old to think of publishing more, than may be squibbed [*sic*] off in a periodical work'.[1] He transferred his undiminished energies to the Dublin Society (later the Royal Dublin Society), where he became librarian, and devised ambitious expansion plans for this older learned society, whose emphasis on the practical application of science appealed to another part of a complex man.[2] He continued to publish his orientalist speculations in *The Oriental Collections*, a periodical established in 1797 in London.[3] When this ceased publication in 1801, Vallancey made one further attempt to publish a full work. His *Prospectus of a Dictionary of the Language of the Aire Coti, or, Ancient Irish* (1802) was over-long and rambling, and is noteworthy mainly for introducing the idea that phallus worship was practised in early Ireland, which he did with apologies to the reader and to 'our English reviewers'.[4] In spite of, or perhaps because of, this theory, sufficient subscriptions were not forthcoming and Vallancey's dictionary was never published. Many of the ideas in the *Prospectus*, however, were developed at greater length in volumes six and seven of *Collectanea de Rebus Hibernicis*, published in 1804 and 1807, and revived by him for the purpose.[5]

Vallancey's final and unpublished essay was written as a self-conscious valedictory piece. Entitled 'A Farewell to the Milesians', he proposed 'in this small volume to make a final close of my remarks on Irish history.' What followed was merely another confused composite of all his many ideas on the identity of the oriental colonists of Ireland, and involved no retrospective overview of his own writing, or of the controversies in which he had been engaged.[6] From start to finish, Vallancey was an unreflective enthusiast. He died in 1812 at the age of 91, leaving the 75-year-old Edward Ledwich as one of the last survivors of that generation of antiquaries.[7] Thus, infirmity and death, as well as political events, were responsible for the marked decrease in antiquarian activity from the early 1790s. However, patterns had been set in place and from then on Gaelic scholarship tended to be associational in its structures and to have significant élite Protestant participation. Throughout the nineteenth century a succession of learned societies were founded with the aim of studying, translating and publishing Gaelic literature. All had absorbed a lesson from the Royal Irish Academy and recognised a political dimension to the undertaking by explicitly forbidding political or religious discussions during proceedings.[8]

The first of these, the Gaelic Society, differed markedly from both its pre-decessors and successors, in that it had a socially less elevated, and predomi-nantly Catholic, membership and consequently kept its affiliation fees low, so as 'to ensure the co-operation of talents and genius in the humbler walks of life'.[9] Among its officers were Theophilus O'Flanagan, Richard McElligott and Patrick Lynch, all of whom had either sought, or been in receipt of, Royal Irish Academy patronage, rather than membership.[10] The new society, however, had similar ambitious objectives to its eighteenth-century Protestant predecessors: 'to publish every Fragment existing in the Gaelic language' and to preserve 'the only language left untaught or unstudied, which can be of use to the Classic Scholar, the Historian and the Antiquarian, of all Europe'.[11] Their *Transactions* began in impressive style with the first translation from the original of the leg-end, 'Deirdri, or, the lamentable fate of the sons of Usnach . . . one of three tragic stories of Eirin'. Translated by O'Flanagan, it was a contribution to the still lingering Ossian controversy, since Macpherson had adapted the tale for one of his poems, 'Darthula'.[12] O'Flanagan's hope that his translation would enable the reader 'to judge of the vast liberties taken with the original by Mr Macpherson', articulated the same cultural defensiveness that had charac-terised the initial Catholic response over forty years before.[13]

This antiquarian initiative was as unsuccessful and short-lived as many of its eighteenth-century antecedents, and no further volumes of *Transactions* appeared.[14] However, one of its objectives was partly fulfilled in 1811 when William Haliday, vice-president of the Gaelic Society and author of an Irish grammar, produced the first volume of a fresh translation of Geoffrey Keating's *Foras Feasa*. This was a dual-language edition, reflecting the influence of new thinking about translation. But Patrick Lynch's introduction simply rehearsed the dominant eighteenth-century view that Keating's work was the embodi-ment of Gaelic tradition – a source rather than an interpretation. Its title, *A Complete History of Ireland*, was even further from the real meaning of *Foras Feasa ar Éirinn* ('compendium of wisdom about Ireland') than O'Connor's 1723 *General History of Ireland*. Lynch also claimed that Keating's history was 'a lasting monument to our national language, as spoken from the earliest ages of Christianity, till the middle of the seventeenth century'.[15] In fact, Keating avoided classical Irish and developed a contemporary prose style; his was a modernising stance, but this went largely unrecognised until well into the nineteenth century. At the other end of the spectrum, Edward Ledwich pub-lished a second and expanded edition of his *Antiquities of Ireland* in 1804, and reported combined sales from the two editions of a massive 2,200 copies – proof of the large market for Gothicist Ascendancy history, post-Union.[16]

The persistence of earlier modes of thinking well into the new century is even clearer in the revival of the Antiquities Committee of the Royal Irish Academy in 1839. On the Committee was William Betham, whose paper on 'The Affinity of the Phoenician and Celtic Languages' was a reprise of the ideas of Charles Vallancey, or as Joseph Leerssen termed it, 'the last weird flowerings of the decaying system within which he worked'.[17] Also present at this first recorded meeting of the revitalised Committee was George Petrie, one of the most important of the new generation of Protestant antiquaries, whose modern professional approach was shortly to eclipse Betham's old-style speculations. Petrie's essay on the 'Round Towers of Ireland', published in the Academy *Transactions* for 1845, was the first scholarly contribution to the debate on these still perplexing structures and signalled the beginning of the specialist discipline of archaeology in Ireland.[18] Although not himself a Gaelic scholar, Petrie could call on the services of John O'Donovan and Eugene O'Curry, employed by him in the antiquities section of the Ordnance Survey. Here, finally, were two scholars, sufficiently rooted and versed in the native tradition, who had (by the standards of the time) enough expertise in old Irish and the stamina and discipline to translate both the Annals of the Four Masters and the Brehon law tracts, however inadequate these translations now appear.[19] But this new professionalism in the areas of linguistic expertise and archaeology did not extend to an abandonment of the romantic antiquarian version of the Gaelic past with its origin myths and golden ages. Vallancey's 'Farewell to the Milesians' was premature in general terms. New editions of Charlotte Brooke's *Reliques of Irish Poetry* (1816), Walker's *Historical Memoirs of the Irish Bards* (1818) and several editions O'Halloran's *History of Ireland* (1803, 1819, 1820) attest to a continuing interest in this tradition, and ensured its influence.[20]

The pervasiveness of such romantic historical perspectives can be seen in *The Nation* newspaper in the 1840s, and especially in the writings of Young Ireland's main ideologue, the Protestant Thomas Davis. Writing under the penname 'the Celt', he proposed a long list of 'historical subjects' suitable for a new 'national art', headed by 'the Landing of the Milesians', and his ballad, 'Lament for the Milesians', invoked the warrior tradition emphasised by O'Halloran. Conscious of his English father, and the mixture of colonist and native Irish in his mother's family, he recognised that the Milesians were not *his* direct ancestors, but was anxious to proclaim that Protestants were 'heirs of their fame, if not of their race'. In his proposed definition of 'Irish nationality', intended to 'contain and represent the races of Ireland', he combined 'Milesian and Cromwellian', just as his 'songs of the nation' proposed to modernise and Anglicise 'the clumsy ornaments and exaggerations' of bardic poetry, replacing their 'clannish' perspectives with 'national' ones.[21] Davis's call for an inclusive *national* history built on the project of liberal Protestant antiquaries like Walker, and had a literary equivalent in the contemporary productions of Samuel Ferguson, although his versions of Gaelic poetry promoted a conservative and unionist political perspective.[22]

Such manipulation and extension of the Milesian motif points to the continued appeal in Ireland of medieval origin myths long after they had been abandoned in most other European countries.[23] Liberal Protestant intellectuals throughout the nineteenth century were even more concerned to attach themselves to the Gaelic past than their forebears had been, in the interests of developing a cultural role as their political dominance waned. More generally, continued emphasis on origins, on race, and on heroic golden ages reflect a political culture dominated by nationalism, however confused and incoherent. This is in contrast to Scotland, where origin myths ceased to be central to political or literary culture in the nineteenth century. This view came to the fore as early as Scott's *The Antiquary* (1816), in which the fierce disputes between his hero, Oldbuck, who supported Pinkerton's Gothicism, and rivals who adhered to Macpherson's Celticist theories, are mocked as absurd and irrelevant to the new Scotland. Colin Kidd has argued that an origin myth was no longer available to the Scots because it had been comprehensively disproved and discredited by historical scholarship, while the attempts by Macpherson and Pinkerton to create new versions were a failure.[24] However, the Irish experience shows that origin myths and the perspectives of romantic antiquarianism can survive in the face of sustained and authoritative challenges, so long as there is a felt need for them. The factors which shaped Scotland in the nineteenth century were industrialisation and commercialisation rather than the nationalism which was so crucial to Irish political culture as to be intermixed even with land agitation, the growth of modern sporting organisations and literary movements. The origin myth was largely irrelevant to the commercial and modernising ethos of Scottish society and could be laid aside as part of an earlier and more credulous age. One result of the Scottish abandonment of their origin myth was the end of the Hiberno-Scottish controversy which, since the seventeenth century, had played such a vital role in the development of antiquarianism in both countries.

In Ireland, the antiquarian tradition (which had already provided much raw material for early nineteenth-century Irish fiction[25]) was particularly influential as a major basis of the more famous Celtic and literary revival of the end of that century. The main link between the two was Standish O'Grady (1846–1928). Staunchly Protestant and unionist in politics, he nevertheless produced new popular versions of the origin myths and of the glories of primitive Gaelic society. By O'Grady's own account, he discovered this material through reading Sylvester O'Halloran's *History of Ireland* when forced to remain indoors by wet weather during a stay in a 'great house' in the west of Ireland.[26] O'Grady could also call on the new work done by O'Curry, O'Donovan and Petrie; but what most distinguishes his account (apart from his reworking of history as 'romance') was his development of the cult of a military hero, especially in his second volume of his *History of Ireland* (1878–80), subtitled 'Cuculain and his contemporaries'.[27] This echoed Davis and had interesting parallels with the epic poems of the older Protestant unionist Sir Samuel Ferguson, such as *Congal: a Poem in Five Books* (1872). O'Grady's importance lies mainly in his formative influence on the next generation, and particularly on W.B. Yeats, who described the *History* as 'perhaps the most imaginative book written on any subject in recent decades'.[28] In his *Autobiographies*, Yeats wrote: '[O'Grady] made the old Irish heroes, Finn, Oisin, and Cuchulainn alive again . . . Lady Gregory had told the same tales . . . but O'Grady was the first and we had read him in our teens.'[29] Hence his claim, 'When modern Irish literature began, O'Grady's influence predominated'.[30] It was most apparent in Yeats's own reworkings of Celtic mythology.[31]

Thus, at the end as at the beginning of the nineteenth century, the romantic strain of antiquarian writing established during the previous century played a central role in the development of the Anglo-Irish literary tradition as well as in the cultural dimensions of Irish nationalism. Far from being the eccentric, marginal and unscholarly productions of cranks, polemicists and enthusiasts, these are among the most important shaping texts in Irish cultural development. Their impact on historical research – and more especially on popular perceptions of Irish history – continued to be important even into the twentieth century. While historians sought, not always successfully, to escape the pattern established by the antiquaries, the quasi-official nationalist histories of the newly independent Ireland counter-pointed their version of the previous seven hundred years as an unrelenting struggle under English rule, by a romantic celebration of a pre-colonial golden age. It was appropriate and significant that in 1930, P.S. O'Hegarty, the most influential exponent of the nationalist account, published a bibliography of Standish O'Grady's writings.[32] The line from Sylvester O'Halloran through Standish O'Grady to P.S. O'Hegarty is perhaps the mainstream of Irish popular history. All three are considered part of a patriotic, if not nationalist, tradition, though their political views differed greatly. What they had most in common was that in each of their accounts, as in all the writings considered in this study, political perspectives and needs shaped historical narratives.

NOTES

Introduction

1. Sylvester O'Halloran, *Ierne Defended* [1774], reprinted in his *A History of Ireland*, 3 vols (Dublin, 1819), I, pp. 540–41.
2. See J.C. Beckett's remarks in T.W. Moody and W.E. Vaughan (eds), *New History of Ireland IV: Eighteenth-Century Ireland* (Oxford, 1986), pp. lx–lxiii, 468.
3. Stuart Piggott, *Ancient Britons and the Antiquarian Imagination* (London, 1989), pp. 15–17. While Scott satirised what was seen as the arid scholarship of the antiquary in this work, he nevertheless made the antiquarian past central to the type of cultural reconciliation between Scotland and England which he put forward in novels such as *The Heart of Midlothian* (1818).
4. On the development of what he calls 'the antiquarian mentality' from classical times to the nineteenth century, see Arnaldo Momigliano, 'Ancient History and the Antiquarian', *Contributo alla Storia degli Studi Classici* (Rome, [1955] 1979), pp. 67–106.
5. Joseph M. Levine, *Humanism and History: Origins of Modern English Historiography* (Ithaca and London, 1987), pp. 73–8.
6. Ibid., pp. 87–9.
7. Sir Walter Scott, *The Antiquary* in *Novels and Tales by the Author of Waverley*, 12 vols (Edinburgh, 1819), 4, pp. 41–51.
8. Levine, *Humanism and History*, pp. 96–7.
9. Piggott, *Ancient Britons*, pp. 27–8.
10. *Archaeologia*, I (1770), 'Introduction', pp. ii–iii.
11. Thomas Burgess, *An Essay on the Study of Antiquities*, 2nd edn (Oxford, 1782), pp. 6, 25.
12. Thomas Pownall, *A Treatise on the Study of Antiquities as a Commentary to Historical Learning* (London, 1782), quoted in Ann de Valera, 'Antiquarian and Historical Investigations in Ireland in the Eighteenth Century' (unpublished M.A. thesis, University College Dublin, 1978), pp. 2–3.
13. Ibid.
14. Beckett, 'Introduction: Eighteenth-Century Ireland' in Moody and Vaughan (eds), *New History of Ireland IV*, p. lxii.
15. Piggott, *Ancient Britons*, Chapter 5 entitled 'Relapse, Romantics and Stagnation', pp. 123–59.
16. Thomas Leland, *The History of Ireland from the Invasion of Henry II*, 3 vols (London, 1773).
17. For a recent article on the only Presbyterian historian of any note, see Norman Vance, 'Volunteer Thought: William Crawford of Strabane' in D. George Boyce, Robert Eccleshall and Vincent Geoghegan (eds), *Political Discourse in Seventeenth- and Eighteenth-Century Ireland* (Basingstoke and New York, 2001), pp. 257–69.
18. See Chapter 3, below.
19. Diarmaid Ó Catháin, 'John Fergus MD, Eighteenth-Century Doctor, Book Collector and Irish Scholar', *J.R.S.A.I.* 118 (1988), pp. 139–62; Charles O'Conor, 'An Account of the Author' in John Curry, *An Historical and Critical Review of the*

Civil Wars in Ireland, 2 vols (Dublin, 1786), I, pp. iii–viii; J.B. Lyons, 'Sylvester O'Halloran, 1728–1807', *Eighteenth-Century Ireland*, 4 (1989), pp. 65–74.

20. Charles Owen O'Conor, *The O'Conors of Connaught* (Dublin, 1891), pp. 284–91.
21. 'Edward Ledwich', *Dictionary of National Biography*, vol. 11, p. 781; 'Thomas Campbell', ibid., vol. 3, p. 844.
22. Walter Love, 'The Hibernian Antiquarian Society', *Studies*, 51 (1962), pp. 419–21; C.E.F. Trench, 'William Burton Conyngham (1733–96)', *J.R.S.A.I.*, 115 (1985), pp. 40–63; 'Memoir of Joseph Cooper Walker' in Nichols, *Lit. Illus.*, VII, pp. 683–4; Liam Price (ed.), *An Eighteenth-Century Antiquary: the Sketches, Notes and Diaries of Austin Cooper (1759–1830)* (Dublin, 1942); Peter Harbison, *Cooper's Ireland: Drawings and Notes from an Eighteenth-Century Gentleman* (Dublin, 2000).
23. G.L.H. Davies, 'The Making of Irish Geography, Part IV: the Physico-Historical Society, 1744–52', *Irish Geography*, xii (1979), pp. 92–8.
24. Charles O'Conor (S.J.), 'Origins of the Royal Irish Academy', *Studies*, 38 (1949), pp. 325–37.
25. O'Conor to John Curry, 21 May 1756, in *O'Conor Letters*, I, pp. 13–14; Edward Ledwich to Joseph Cooper Walker, 10 Jul. 1788, TCD, ms. 1461(3), fol. 73; Tom Dunne, '"A gentleman's estate should be a moral school": Edgeworthstown in Fact and Fiction' in Raymond Gillespie and Gerard Moran (eds), *Longford: Essays in County History* (Dublin, 1991), p. 103.
26. R.B. McDowell, 'The Main Narrative' in T. Ó Raifeartaigh (ed.), *The Royal Irish Academy: a Bicentennial History, 1785–1985* (Dublin, 1985), pp. 1–13.
27. Piggott, *Ancient Britons*, p. 152.
28. Seamus Deane, *Celtic Revivals* (London, 1985), pp. 20–22; Tom Dunne, 'Haunted by History: Irish Romantic Writing, 1800–1850' in Roy Porter and Mikulas Teich (eds), *Romanticism in National Context* (Cambridge, 1988), pp. 68–91.
29. de Valera, 'Antiquarian and Historical Investigations'.
30. Walter Love, 'Edmund Burke, Charles Vallancey, and the Sebright manuscripts', *Hermathena*, 95 (July 1961), pp. 21–35; *idem*, 'The Hibernian Antiquarian Society', *Studies*, 51 (1962), pp. 419–31. In 1980 a two-volume edition of O'Conor's letters by Robert Ward and Catherine Coogan Ward appeared, thus making this important collection easily available to scholars (Robert E. Ward and Catherine Coogan Ward (eds), *The Letters of Charles O'Conor of Belanagare*, 2 vols (Ann Arbor, Michigan, 1980)). While this pioneering venture has become the standard source both for O'Conor's life and thought, and for Catholic politics in the eighteenth century, it is, unfortunately, marred by repeated and significant mis-readings and mis-transcriptions of the letters it reproduces, and omits a number from the National Library of Ireland and from the Gilbert Collection in the Dublin City Library and Archive. In 1988 an abridged version of the 1980 edition was published, but without rectifying these mistakes (Robert E. Ward, John F. Wrynn and Catherine Coogan Ward (eds), *The Letters of Charles O'Conor of Belanagare: a Catholic Voice in Eighteenth-Century Ireland* (Washington, D.C., 1988)). The policy adopted here has been to quote from the 1980 edition, when a check against the originals confirmed accuracy. In other cases, the reference is to the manuscripts.
31. Love, 'Charles O'Conor of Belanagare and Thomas Leland's "Philosophical" History of Ireland', *Irish Historical Studies*, 13 (1962), pp. 1–25; *idem*, 'Edmund

Burke and an Irish Historiographical Controversy', *History and Theory*, 2 (1962), pp. 180–98.

32.   J.R. Hill, 'Popery and Protestantism, Civil and Religious Liberty: the Disputed Lessons of Irish History 1690–1812', *Past and Present*, 118 (Feb. 1988), pp. 96–129. See also T.O. McLoughlin, *Contesting Ireland: Irish Voices against England in the Eighteenth Century* (Dublin, 1999), pp. 159–60.

33.   Norman Vance, 'Celts, Carthaginians and constitutions: Anglo-Irish Literary Relations, 1780–1820', *Irish Historical Studies*, 22 (1981), p. 219.

34.   F.G. James, 'Historiography and the Irish Constitutional Revolution of 1782', *Eire-Ireland*, 18 (1983), pp. 6–16.

35.   Norman Vance, *Irish Literature: a Social History* (Oxford, 1990), p. 86.

36.   James, 'Historiography', pp. 15–16.

37.   J. Th. Leerssen, *Mere Irish and Fíor-Ghael: Studies in the Idea of Irish Nationality, its Development and Literary Expression Prior to the Nineteenth Century* (Amsterdam and Philadelphia, 1986), pp. 325–444.

38.   The most recent contribution to this debate is John P. Delury, '*Ex Conflictu et Collisione*: the Failure of Irish Historiography, 1745–90', *Eighteenth-Century Ireland*, 15 (2000), pp. 9–37.

39.   S.J. Connolly, *Religion, Law and Power: the Making of Protestant Ireland, 1660–1760* (Oxford, 1992); C.D.A. Leighton, *Catholicism in a Protestant Kingdom: a Study of the Irish 'Ancien Régime'* (Dublin, 1994); Jacqueline Hill, *From Patriots to Unionists: Dublin Civic Politics and Irish Protestant Patriotism, 1660–1840* (Oxford, 1997).

40.   Leighton, *Catholicism in a Protestant Kingdom*, p. 31.

41.   Ibid., p. 37.

42.   Ibid., notes 72 and 73 (p. 168), and also note 63 (p. 180). The reference in all cases is to [William Henry], *An Appeal to the People of Ireland* (Dublin, 1749).

43.   Richard Cox's *Hibernia Anglicana*, though influential in the first half of the eighteenth century, was published in 1689 (Sir Richard Cox, *Hibernia Anglicana: or, the History of Ireland from the Conquest thereof by the English, to the Present Time*, 2 vols (London, 1689–90).

44.   See for example, S.J. Connolly, 'Precedents and Principle: the Patriots and their Critics' in S.J. Connolly (ed.), *Political Ideas in Eighteenth-Century Ireland* (Dublin, 2000), pp. 133–46.

45.   Jacqueline Hill, 'Politics and the Writing of History: the Impact of the 1690s and 1790s on Irish Historiography' in Boyce, Eccleshall and Geoghegan (eds), *Political Discourse in Seventeenth- and Eighteenth-Century Ireland*, pp. 227–31.

46.   Clare O'Halloran, '"The Island of Saints and Scholars": Views of the Early Church and Sectarian Politics in Late Eighteenth-Century Ireland', *Eighteenth-Century Ireland*, 5 (1990), pp. 17–18.

47.   Leighton, *Catholicism in a Protestant Kingdom*, p. 119.

48.   Clare O'Halloran, 'Irish Re-creations of the Gaelic Past: the Challenge of Macpherson's Ossian', *Past and Present*, 124 (Aug. 1989), p. 78; *idem*, 'Golden Ages and Barbarous Nations: Antiquarian Debate on the Celtic Past in Ireland and Scotland in the Eighteenth Century' (unpublished PhD dissertation, University of Cambridge, 1991), pp. 56–7, 196–7. For an interpretation of O'Conor as a nationalist, see McLoughlin, *Contesting Ireland*, pp. 146, 154, 156.

49.   See, for example, Jacqueline Hill, 'Corporate Values in Hanoverian Edinburgh and Dublin' in S.J. Connolly, R.A. Houston, and R.J. Morris (eds), *Conflict,*

Identity and Economic Development in Ireland and Scotland, 1600–1939 (Preston, 1995), pp. 114–24. For an interesting interpretation of eighteenth-century Irish 'patriot' ideology which is European in focus, but nevertheless does not lend complete support to the *ancien régime* hypothesis, see Joep Leerssen, 'Anglo-Irish Patriotism and its European Context: Notes towards a Reassessment', *Eighteenth-Century Ireland*, 3 (1988), pp. 7–24.

50.   Colin Kidd, 'Gaelic Antiquity and National Identity in Enlightenment Ireland and Scotland', *English Historical Review*, cix (1994), p. 1197.

51.   Ibid., pp. 1199–1202.

52.   O'Halloran, 'Golden Ages and Barbarous Nations', pp. 92, 137–9, 292–4; Kidd, *British Identities before Nationalism: Ethnicity and Nationhood in the Atlantic World, 1600–1800* (Cambridge, 1999), pp. 146–81.

Gaels, *Scoti* and Milesians

1.   Daniel Owen Madden (ed.), *The Speeches of the Right Hon. Henry Grattan* (Dublin, 1854), p. 68.

2.   William Donaldson, *The Jacobite Song: Political Myth and National Identity* (Aberdeen, 1988), pp. 5–15; G.H. Jenkins, *The Foundations of Modern Wales, 1642–1780* (Oxford, 1987), pp. 246–8, 406–7; H.A. MacDougall, *Racial Myth in English History: Trojans, Teutons, and Anglo-Saxons* (Montreal and Hanover, New Hampshire, 1982), pp. 7–86.

3.   Anthony Smith, *The Ethnic Origin of Nations* (Oxford, 1987), p. 24; see also Susan Reynolds, 'Medieval *Origines Gentium* and the Community of the Realm', *History*, 68 (1983), pp. 375–90.

4.   Peter Burke, *The Renaissance Sense of the Past* (London, 1969), pp. 7–13.

5.   Colin Kidd, *Subverting Scotland's Past* (Cambridge, 1993), pp. 101–7. On the persistence of the Brutus and Arthurian legends in English histories and chronicles of Ireland, see Andrew Hadfield, *Edmund Spenser's Irish Experience: Wilde Fruit and Salvage Soyl* (Oxford, 1997), pp. 87–101.

6.   G. Clark, 'The Invasion Hypothesis in British Archaeology', *Antiquity*, 40 (1966), p. 172.

7.   Bernadette Cunningham, *The World of Geoffrey Keating* (Dublin, 2000), pp. 31, 108, 119–21.

8.   Mark Scowcroft, 'Leabhar Gabhála. Part I: the Growth of the Text', *Ériu*, 38 (1987), p. 81.

9.   R.A.S. Macalister (ed.), *Lebor Gabála Érenn*, 5 vols (Dublin, 1938–56), 4, pp. 91, 97; see also T.F. O'Rahilly, *Early Irish Mythology* (Dublin, 1946); Scowcroft, 'Leabhar Gabhála. Part I', p. 81. However, more recently John Carey has argued that the text embodies 'the confrontation of the two traditions' of learning, pagan and Christian (John Carey, 'Introduction' in Macalister (ed.), *Lebor Gabála Erenn*, 5 vols (Dublin, [1938–56] 1993), 1, p. 3).

10.   Scowcroft, 'Leabhar Gabhála. Part II: the Growth of the Tradition', *Ériu*, 39 (1988), pp. 13–14.

11.   Carey, 'Introduction', pp. 1, 3–6. In dating the *Leabhar Gabhála* to the eleventh rather than twelfth century I am following Carey.

12.   Scowcroft, 'Leabhar Gabhála. Part I', p. 81; Macalister (ed.), *Lebor Gabála*, I, pp. xxvii–xxix, xii–xviii.

13. Proinsias Mac Cana, 'The Rise of the Later Schools of *Filidheacht*', *Ériu*, 25 (1974), pp. 135–8, 140–41.

14. Mark Scowcroft suggests that the authors of the *Leabhar Gabhála* were intent on securing the title of the Uí Néill dynasty of Ulster to the high kingship (Scowcroft, 'Leabhar Gabhála. Part II', p. 49).

15. Macalister, *Lebor Gabála*, I, p. xxxi.

16. Mac Cana, 'The Rise of the Later Schools of *Filidheacht*', p. 138.

17. Richard Stanyhurst, *De Rebus in Hibernia Gestis Libri Quattuor* (Antwerp, 1584), pp. 17–18. Quoted in Colm Lennon, *Richard Stanihurst. The Dubliner, 1547–1618* (Dublin, 1981), p. 75. Stanihurst moved from uncritical acceptance of the 'Scota' tale to scepticism (ibid.).

18. Bernadette Cunningham, 'Seventeenth-Century Interpretation of the Past: the Case of Geoffrey Keating', *Irish Historical Studies*, 25 (1986), p. 116.

19. See Bernadette Cunningham, 'The Culture and Ideology of the Irish Franciscan Historians at Louvain, 1607–1650' in Ciarán Brady (ed.), *Ideology and the Historians* (Dublin, 1991), pp. 11–30, 222–7.

20. Mícheál Ó Cléirigh, 'Address to the Reader' in his version of the *Leabhar Gabhála*, quoted in Brendan Jennings, *Michael O Cleirigh: Chief of the Four Masters and his Associates* (Dublin and Cork, 1936), pp. 119–21.

21. See Cunningham, 'Culture and Ideology', n. 23, p. 224.

22. *Annála Ríoghachta Éireann: Annals of the Kingdom of Ireland by the Four Masters from the Earliest Period to 1616*, ed. and trans. by John O'Donovan, 7 vols, (Dublin 1851, reprint Dublin, 1990).

23. Geoffrey Keating, *Foras Feasa ar Éirinn; the History of Ireland*, ed. and trans. David Comyn and P.S. Dinneen, 4 vols (Dublin, 1902–14). On the circulation of *Foras Feasa* in manuscript, see Cunningham, *World of Geoffrey Keating*, pp. 173–200.

24. Brian Ó Cuív, 'The Irish Language in the Early Modern Period' in T.W. Moody, F.X. Martin and F.J. Byrne (eds), *New History of Ireland III* (Oxford, 1978), p. 531.

25. Cunningham, 'Seventeenth-Century Interpretation', p. 121.

26. *Idem, World of Geoffrey Keating*, pp. 17–31.

27. Geoffrey Keating, *Eochair-sgiath an Aifrinn . . . an explanatory Defence of the Mass*, ed. Patrick O'Brien (Dublin 1898); Keating, *Trí Bhiorghaoithe an Bháis*, ed. Osborn Bergin (Dublin, 1931); Eoin Mac Giolla Eáin, *Dánta, Amhráin is Caointe Shreathrúin Céitinn* (Dublin, 1900).

28. Brendan Bradshaw, 'Geoffrey Keating: Apologist of Irish Ireland' in Brendan Bradshaw, Andrew Hadfield and Willy Maley (eds), *Representing Ireland: Literature and the Origins of Conflict, 1534–1660* (Cambridge, 1993), p. 167.

29. Ibid., pp. 184–5; Cunningham, 'Seventeenth-Century Interpretation', pp. 126–7.

30. Joseph Th. Leerssen, 'On the Edge of Europe: Ireland in Search of Oriental Roots', *Comparative Criticism*, 8 (1986), p. 98.

31. Keating, *Foras Feasa*, I, pp. 3–7.

32. Anne Cronin, 'Sources of Keating's "Forus Feasa ar Éirinn"', *Éigse*, 4 (1943–4), pp. 235–79; ibid., 5 (1945–7), pp. 122–35; Cunningham, *World of Geoffrey Keating*, pp. 60–82.

33. These were settlements by 'three daughters of the wicked Cain'; by the maiden Banbha, two hundred years before the Deluge, who came with 'thrice fifty women . . . and three men'; by Ceasair, the granddaughter of Noah, who arrived just forty days before the Deluge (Keating, *Foras Feasa*, I, pp. 139–47).

34. Ibid., p. 147.
35. Roderic O'Flaherty, *Ogygia, or, a Chronological Account of Irish Events*, trans. James Hely, 2 vols (Dublin, 1793), II, pp. 2–3.
36. Leerssen, *Mere Irish*, p. 321.
37. O'Flaherty, *Ogygia*, trans. Hely, II, pp. 29. On the Stuarts and the Milesians, see also below.
38. Cunningham suggests the possibility of 'indirect contact' between Keating and Ware in their respective searches for manuscripts (*World of Geoffrey Keating*, p. 81).
39. Nollaig Ó Muraíle, *The Celebrated Antiquary Dubhaltach Mac Fhirbhisigh (c. 1600–1671): his Lineage, Life and Learning* (Maynooth, 1996), pp. 248–50.
40. I am using the English translation of Ware's works in all citations. Walter Harris (ed.), *The Whole Works of Sir James Ware Concerning Ireland*, 3 vols (London, 1739–45), II, pp. 14–16. For Keating, see *Foras Feasa*, I, p. 141.
41. Harris (ed.), *Whole Works of Ware*, II, pp. 14–17.
42. Leerssen, 'On the Edge of Europe', pp. 96–7, 92–3, 96.
43. Ibid., pp. 92–3.
44. These conflicting theories and their adherents will be analysed in Chapter 2.
45. Harris (ed.), *Whole Works of Ware*, II, pp. 1–2.
46. Ibid., p. 18.
47. Leerssen, *Mere Irish*, pp. 336–8; see also Ann O'Sullivan and William O'Sullivan, 'Edward Lhuyd's Collection of Irish Manuscripts', *Transactions of the Honourable Society of Cymmrodorion* (1962), pp. 57–71.
48. Joep Leerssen, 'Celticism' in Terence Brown (ed.), *Celticism* (Amsterdam and Atlanta, GA, 1996), pp.4–5.
49. Cunningham, *World of Geoffrey Keating*, pp. 173–225.
50. Cecile O'Rahilly (ed.), *Five Seventeenth-Century Political Poems* (Dublin, 1952), pp. 50–82, 132–63.
51. Geoffrey Keating, *A General History of Ireland*, trans. Dermod O'Connor (London, 1723).
52. See, for example, Thomas Campbell, *Strictures on the Ecclesiastical and Literary History of Ireland* (Dublin, 1789), p. 103. Campbell acknowledged that the error might have been the translator's.
53. O'Connor was accused of plagiarising the work of others in his translation, and of having absconded with some of the subscription money (Diarmaid Ó Catháin, 'Dermot O'Connor, translator of Keating', *Eighteenth-Century Ireland*, 2 (1987), pp. 69–71; Alan Harrison, *The Dean's Friend: Anthony Raymond 1675–1726, Jonathan Swift and the Irish Language* (Dublin, 1999), pp. 105–48).
54. J.R. Hill, 'Popery and Protestantism, Civil and Religious Liberty: the Disputed Lessons of Irish History 1690–1812', *Past and Present*, 118 (Feb. 1988), pp. 102–3.
55. Dermod O'Connor, translator's preface, in Keating, *General History of Ireland*, p. ii.
56. Ibid., p. i.
57. See Anthony Grafton, *The Footnote* (London, 1997), pp. 204–5.
58. Thomas Comerford, *The History of Ireland* (Dublin, 1752), p. v.
59. Ibid., dedication.
60. de Valera, 'Antiquarian and Historical Investigations in Ireland', p. 99. She has

traced a number of editions or reissues of Comerford's book: 1742, 1752, 1754, 1766 (ibid., pp. 100–101).

61. John K'eogh, *Vindication of the Antiquities of Ireland* (Dublin, 1748), dedication.

62. Ibid., pp. 138–42, 142–8.

63. Ibid., second dedication.

64. Ibid., p. 15.

65. Charles Owen O'Conor, *The O'Conors of Connaught* (Dublin, 1891), pp. 284–91.

66. Catherine A. Sheehan, 'The Contribution of Charles O'Conor of Belanagare to Gaelic Scholarship in Eighteenth-Century Ireland', *Journal of Celtic Studies*, 2 (1958), pp. 219–22.

67. O'Conor to John Fergus, 10 Oct. 1731, in *O'Conor Letters*, I, p. 3. See also Diarmaid Ó Catháin, 'John Fergus MD, Eighteenth-Century Doctor, Book Collector and Irish Scholar', *J.R.S.A.I.*, 118 (1988), pp. 142–3.

68. Leerssen, *Mere Irish*, p. 371.

69. Charles O'Conor, *Dissertations on the Antient History of Ireland* (Dublin, 1753), p. v; O'Flaherty, *Ogygia*, trans. Hely, II, p. 102. Ware's claim of pre-Christian literacy was upheld by his editor, Harris, and further boosted by copious detail on ogham writing derived from O'Flaherty and others (Harris (ed.), *Whole Works of Ware*, II, pp. 18–23).

70. For a recent scholar's hypothesis that there was literacy in Latin and Gaelic prior to the spread of christianity in Ireland, see Anthony Harvey, 'Early Literacy in Ireland: the Evidence from Ogam', *Cambridge Medieval Celtic Studies*, 14 (Winter 1987), pp. 9, 13–15.

71. Donald Harden, *The Phoenicians* (Harmondsworth, 1980), pp. 105–13; *Oxford Classical Dictionary* (Oxford, 1970), p. 47.

72. O'Conor, *Dissertations* (1753), pp. 165–6, ix–x.

73. This resembled the account given by Roderic O'Flaherty, where the landing date was given as 2924 AM (year of the world), which by O'Flaherty's own figures worked out as 1015 BC; O'Flaherty was slightly less precise on the number of ships than O'Conor, claiming there were 'about one hundred and twenty sail' (O'Flaherty, *Ogygia*, trans. Hely, II, pp. 29–30, 33). Keating gave the number of ships as thirty, with thirty warriors in each, and the landing date as 1308 BC (Keating, *Foras Feasa*, II, 75–7, pp. 81–3).

74. O'Conor, *Dissertations* (1753), p. 19.

75. Ibid., pp. 14–15.

76. Ibid., p. ix–x.

77. Ibid., p. 35.

78. F.E. Manuel, *Isaac Newton: Historian* (Cambridge, 1963), Chapters 2–5.

79. O'Conor, *Dissertations* (1753), p. 19. O'Conor's friend John Fergus claimed that he had first noticed the similarities between the Newton chronology and that of the *Leabhar Gabhála*, but O'Conor denied this (see O'Conor to John Curry, 5 Nov. 1757, in *O'Conor Letters*, I, p. 45).

80. O'Conor, *Dissertations* (1753), pp. 20–21.

81. Ibid., p. 21.

82. Ferdinando Warner, *The History of Ireland* (London, 1763), pp. 117–18.

83. James William Johnson, 'Chronological Writing: its Concepts and Development', *History and Theory*, 2 (1962), pp. 124–5.

84. O'Conor, *Dissertations* (1753), pp. 135–6.

85. O'Conor, *Dissertations on the History of Ireland* (Dublin, 1766), p. x. Privately, he said that Keating 'ought not to be trusted in a single line where he is not supported by our old Annals'. (O'Conor to George Faulkner, 8 Aug. 1763, in *O'Conor Letters*, I, pp. 167–8).

86. Harris, *Whole Works of Ware*, II, p. 18.

87. Harris, 'An Essay on the Defects in the Histories of Ireland, and Remedies proposed for the Improvement thereof' in Walter Harris (ed.), *Hibernica* (Dublin, 1747–50), part 1, p. 138.

88. Ibid., pp. 137–8, 141.

89. Keating, *Foras Feasa*, II, p. 143; Harris, 'Essay on the Defects in the Histories of Ireland', p. 141.

90. Ibid.

91. See below, Chapter 6.

92. David Hume, *The History of England from the Invasion of Julius Caesar to the Accession of Henry VII*, 8 vols (London, 1762), I, pp. 1–2.

93. Hume, *The History of England from the Invasion of Julius Caesar to the Revolution in 1688*, 8 vols (London, 1778), VIII, pp. 471–3.

94. T.C. Smout, *A History of the Scottish People 1560–1830* (London, 1989), p. 311.

95. William Matthews, 'The Egyptians in Scotland: the Political History of a Myth', *Viator*, I (1970), pp. 289–306; E.J. Cowan, 'Myth and Identity in Early Medieval Scotland', *Scottish Historical Review*, 63 (1984), pp. 111–35.

96. Matthews, 'Egyptians in Scotland', pp. 291–2.

97. John Bannerman, 'The Scots of Dalriada' in Gordon Menzies (ed.), *Who are the Scots?* (London, 1972), pp. 66–7.

98. T.I. Rae, 'Historical Scepticism in Scotland before David Hume' in *Studies in the Eighteenth Century*, 2, ed. R.F. Brissenden (Canberra, 1973), p. 207.

99. Roger A. Mason, 'Scotching the Brut: Politics, History and National Myth in Sixteenth-Century Britain' in Roger A. Mason (ed.), *Scotland and England 1286–1815* (Edinburgh, 1987), pp. 60–84.

100. See Breandán Ó Buachalla, 'Na Stíobhartaigh agus an tAos Léinn: Cing Séamas', *Proceedings of the Royal Irish Academy*, 83c (1983), pp. 81–134; *idem*, 'James our True King: the Ideology of Irish Royalism in the Seventeenth Century' in D.G. Boyce, Robert Eccleshall and Vincent Geoghegan (eds), *Political Thought in Ireland since the Seventeenth Century* (London and New York, 1993), pp. 9–35; Pádraig Breathnach, 'Metamorphoses 1603: Dán le hEochaidh Ó hEoghusa', *Éigse*, 17 (1977/8), pp. 169–80. For the claim that Charles I was a Milesian king, see Keating, *Foras Feasa*, I, pp. 205–9.

101. Colin Kidd, *Subverting Scotland's Past*, pp. 26–8.

102. Leerssen, *Mere Irish*, pp. 303–5, 392; Norman Vance, *Irish Literature: a Social History* (Oxford, 1990), pp. 23–5.

103. Kidd, *Subverting Scotland's Past*, pp. 101–7.

104. Hector Boece, *Scotorum Historiae* (Paris, 1527).

105. Thomas Innes, *A Critical Essay on the Ancient Inhabitants of the Northern Parts of Britain, or Scotland*, 2 vols (London, 1729), I, pp. 137–9, vi–vii, xv–xvi, xlv–xvi. On Buchanan, see Kidd, *Subverting Scotland's Past*, pp. 19–21.

106. Rae, 'Historical Scepticism', pp. 217–20.

107. William Donaldson, *The Jacobite Song* (Aberdeen, 1988), p. 14.

108. Innes, *Critical Essay*, I, pp. xvi–xviii, 145.

109. Ibid., pp. 165–6.

110. On Macpherson, see below; on Pinkerton, see Chapter 2.

111. Innes, *Critical Essay*, I, pp. 197–8, 187–8.

112. Ibid., II, pp. 506–7.

113. James Macpherson, *Temora* (London, 1763), pp. iv–v, iii, vii–x.

114. James Macpherson, *An Introduction to the History of Great Britain and Ireland* (London, 1771), pp. 25–35.

115. Ibid., pp. 90–91.

116. Ibid., pp. 137–9.

117. Macpherson, *Fingal* (London, 1760), preface; Macpherson, *Introduction*, pp. 54, 132–50. Sebastian Mitchell argues that Macpherson's account was 'effectively a colonial narrative with Scotland cast in the role of the mother country and Ireland as its subservient dependent other'. (Sebastian Mitchell, 'James Macpherson's "Ossian" and the Empire of Sentiment', *British Journal for Eighteenth-Century Studies*, 22 (1999), pp. 167–8).

118. On Campbell and Ledwich, see Chapter 2.

119. Charles O'Conor, *A Dissertation on the First Migrations and Final Settlements of the Scots in North-Britain: with Occasional Observations on the Poems of 'Fingal' and 'Temora'* (Dublin, 1766), pp. 13–14, 22, 42–3, 19–20. This was bound with *Dissertations on the History of Ireland* (1766), but had its own title page and was paginated separately.

120. *Idem, Dissertation on the First Migrations and Final Settlements of the Scots*, p. 43.

121. Ibid., pp. 15–19.

122. Ibid., p. 23.

123. Ibid., p. 62; O'Conor to Charles Vallancey, 29 Nov. 1771, in *O'Conor Letters*, I, p. 293.

124. See Walter D. Love, 'Charles O'Conor of Belanagare and Thomas Leland's "Philosophical" History of Ireland', *Irish Historical Studies*, 13 (1962), pp. 1–25.

125. Thomas Leland, *The History of Ireland from the Invasion of Henry II with a Preliminary Discourse on the Antient State of that Kingdom*, 3 vols (London, 1773), I, pp. v–vi.

126. Leland to O'Conor, 9 May 1772, R.I.A., Stowe ms. B1.2. Barnard's essay was published in the first volume of the *Transactions of the Royal Irish Academy* (1787).

127. In the general catalogue of the National Library of Ireland, Dublin, this work is presumed to be by Leland because it came from the same publisher who handled his *History of Ireland* and contains an advertisement for the latter at the back.

128. [Thomas Leland], *An Examination of the Arguments contained in a late Introduction to the History of the Antient Irish, and Scots* (London, 1772), pp. v, viii.

129. Ibid., p. 29.

130. Ibid., pp. 24–5.

131. Ibid., pp. 25–6.

132. Ibid., pp. 32–3, 21. For O'Conor's emphasis on Macpherson's inaccuracies and false chronologies, see his *Dissertation on the First Migrations and Final Settlements of the Scots*, pp. 24–42. See also O'Conor's annotated copy of Macpherson's *Fingal* in the R.I.A.

133. [Leland], *Examination*, pp. 54–5.

134. Ibid., pp. 25–6.
135. Thomas Barnard, 'An Enquiry concerning the Original of the Scots in Britain', *Transactions of the Royal Irish Academy*, 1 (1787), antiquities section, p. 26.
136. Ibid., p. 29.
137. Ibid.
138. William Molyneux, *The Case of Ireland's being bound by Acts of Parliament in England, Stated* ([1698] reprint Dublin, 1977), pp. 30–31. For the argument that Molyneux rejected a royal, but not an aristocratic, conquest of Ireland, see Jacqueline Hill, 'Ireland without Union: Molyneux and his Legacy' in John Robertson (ed.), *A Union for Empire: Political Thought and the British Union of 1707* (Cambridge, 1995), pp. 277–81.
139. See, for example, a long passage on the iniquities of English rule in Ireland and on consequent Irish rebelliousness, which was omitted from the second edition (O'Conor, *Dissertations* (1753), pp. 59–63).
140. Compare *Dissertations* (1753), p. 19, with *Dissertations* (1766), pp. 12–13.
141. O'Conor, *Dissertations* (1753), pp. 20–21.
142. Ibid., pp. xx, 22.
143. William O'Sullivan, 'The Irish Manuscripts in Case H in Trinity College Dublin catalogued by Matthew Young in 1781', *Celtica*, 11 (1976), pp. 230–31. He presented these to O'Conor in 1764, presumably after he had abandoned the project (ibid.).
144. O'Conor to Francis S. Sullivan, 25 Jul. 1763, in *O'Conor Letters*, I, p. 165.
145. O'Sullivan, 'Irish Manuscripts in Case H', p. 231–2. Some of Sullivan's translation can be seen in R.I.A., ms. 24/D/18.
146. O'Conor to Curry, 15 Sept. 1763, in *O'Conor Letters*, I, p. 174.
147. O'Conor to Thomas O'Gorman, 13 Jul. 1781, in ibid., II, p. 170.
148. O'Gorman to Sir Lucius O'Brien, enclosing part of Sullivan's translation, 12 Jul. 1781, R.I.A., ms. 24/D/18, pp. 3–7.
149. O'Conor to O'Gorman, 31 May 1783, 8 Nov. 1783, in *O'Conor Letters*, II, pp. 189, 198–9.
150. Charles O'Conor, 'Third Letter to Colonel Vallancey', *Collectanea*, IV, no. xiii [1784], p. 108; O'Conor to Hugh MacDermot, 12 June 1776, in *O'Conor Letters*, II, p. 87.
151. For example, in a letter dated 1779 he admitted that he could only understand parts of a Gaelic manuscript which he termed an 'Abstract of the Teagusg Flatha of Cormac O Cuinn' (O'Conor to [Charles Vallancey], [12 Mar. 1779], in ibid., p. 136).
152. Leerssen, *Mere Irish*, p. 420.
153. Minute Book of the Select Committee of Antiquities, 12 Jun. 1772, R.I.A., ms. 24/E/7.
154. Among its members were: Vallancey, Thomas Leland, Richard Woodward, Dean of Cloyne, and Thomas Percy, Bishop of Dromore. Shortly before the Committee disbanded, in Feb. 1774, a third Catholic, Sylvester O'Halloran was made a corresponding member (ibid., *passim*.).
155. O'Conor to Denis O'Conor, 9 Mar. 1773, in *O'Conor Letters*, II, p. 42.
156. Charles O'Conor (S.J.), 'Origins of the Royal Irish Academy', *Studies*, 38 (1949), p. 332; Minute Book of the Select Committee of Antiquities, 5 May 1773, R.I.A. ms. 24/E/7.

157. O'Conor to Curry, 25 Mar. 1772, Clonalis, ms. 8.3.HS 026.

158. O'Conor to Carpenter, 9 Feb. 1773, ibid.

159. O'Conor to Curry, 25 Mar. 1772, ibid.

160. O'Conor to Carpenter, 9 Feb. 1773, ibid.

161. Joep Leerssen, *Remembrance and Imagination: Patterns in the Historical and Literary Representation of Ireland in the Nineteenth Century* (Cork, 1996), pp. 100–108. See also Damian Murray, *Romanticism, Nationalism and Irish Antiquarian Societies, 1840–80* (Maynooth, 2000), pp. 23–5, 28–32.

162. Sylvester O'Halloran, 'The Poems of Ossine, the Son of Fionne MacComhal, Reclaimed. By a Milesian', *Dublin Magazine*, Jan. 1763; *idem*, 'A Letter to Mr Macpherson, occasioned by his Dissertation on the Poems of *Temora*. By a Milesian', ibid., Aug. 1763. O'Halloran's contribution to the Ossian debate will be considered in Chapter 4.

163. O'Halloran, *Insula Sacra: or the General Utilities Arising from some Permanent Foundation, for the Preservation of our Antient Annals Demonstrated, and the Means pointed out* (Limerick, 1770), pp. i–ii.

164. O'Halloran, *An Introduction to the Study of the History and Antiquities of Ireland: in which the Assertions of Mr Hume and other Writers are occasionally considered* (London, 1772), pp. 331, 55.

165. Ibid., p. vii.

166. Ibid., p. 298.

167. Keating, *Foras Feasa*, II, pp. 67–9.

168. O'Halloran, *A General History of Ireland*, 2 vols (London, 1778), pp. xli–xlii. It is doubtful whether his knowledge of the language extended to the classical or old Irish in which the annals were written.

169. Hume, *History of England* (1762), I, pp. 1–2.

170. O'Halloran, *Introduction*, pp. 59, 62, 69.

171. Ibid., p. 81.

172. Clare O'Halloran, 'Irish Re-creations of the Gaelic Past: the Challenge of Macpherson's Ossian', *Past and Present*, 124 (Aug. 1989), pp. 79–80.

173. O'Conor to O'Halloran, 25 Jan. 1769, R.I.A., Stowe ms. BI.1a; O'Conor to O'Halloran, n.d. [Jan. 1769], 10 Feb. 1769, 28 Mar. 1769, R.I.A., Stowe ms. BI.2.

174. O'Conor to Curry, 26 Nov. 1771, 26 May 1772, in *O'Conor Letters*, I, p. 291, ibid., II, p. 19; O'Conor to Vallancey, 29 Nov. 1771, in ibid., I, p. 292.

175. O'Halloran to O'Conor, 9 Mar. 1776, R.I.A., ms. 3/D/8, fols. 21–2.

Phoenicians and Goths

1. Raymond Schwab, *The Oriental Renaissance* (New York, 1984), pp. 21–41; Edward Said, *Orientalism* (Harmondsworth, 1985).

2. Samuel Kliger, *The Goths in England* (New York, 1972), pp. 1–6.

3. J.H. Andrews, 'Charles Vallancey and the Map of Ireland', *Geographical Journal*, 132 (1966), pp. 48–61; Monica Nevin, 'The Defence of the Southern Part of Ireland by General Vallancey, Chief Engineer', *J.R.S.A.I.*, 125 (1995), pp. 5–9.

4. Charles Vallancey to Charles O'Conor, 25 Apr. 1772, R.I.A., Stowe ms. BI.2.

5. For the history of this scholarship, see Maurice Sznycer, *Les Passages Puniques et Transcription Latine dans le 'Poenulus' de Plaute* (Paris, 1967), pp. 11–14.

6. Vallancey to O'Conor, 14 May 1772, R.I.A., Stowe ms. BI.2.

7. N.L.I., ms. G135, pp. 39–40. On O'Flanagan's role as translator and scribe for Vallancey and the Royal Irish Academy from the 1780s, see Chapter 7 below.

8. Vallancey to O'Conor, 20 Jan. 1771, 25 Apr. 1772, R.I.A., Stowe ms. BI.2.

9. James Parsons, *Remains of Japhet* (London, 1767), pp. viii, x, xix–xx.

10. Ibid., p. x.

11. *Dictionary of National Biography*, XV, pp. 403–4.

12. Parsons, *Remains of Japhet*, pp. vii, 125, xv, 145–55.

13. See Shearer West, 'Polemic and the Passions: Dr James Parsons' *Human Physiognomy Explained* and Hogarth's Aspirations for British History Painting', *British Journal for Eighteenth-Century Studies*, 13 (1990), pp. 73–6. On Parsons, see also J.G.A. Pocock, *Barbarism and Religion: vol. ii Narratives of Civil Government* (Cambridge, 1999), pp. 357–62.

14. For example, he quoted a long passage from Parsons in an essay on pagan religion written in 1783 (Vallancey, Preface, *Collectanea*, III, no. 12 [1783], p. cli).

15. Charles Vallancey, *An Essay on the Antiquity of the Irish Language. Being a Collation of Irish with the Punic Language* (Dublin, 1772), pp. 1–2.

16. Ibid., p. 2.

17. Ibid., p. viii.

18. Michael Lort to Thomas Percy, 19 Aug. 1784, in Nichols, *Lit. Illus.*, VII, pp. 465–6.

19. Vallancey, *Essay*, p. 3.

20. Joseph Leerssen, 'On the Edge of Europe: Ireland in Search of Oriental Roots 1650–1850', *Comparative Criticism*, 8 (1986), pp. 100–102.

21. Norman Vance, 'Celts, Carthaginians and constitutions: Anglo-Irish Literary Relations, 1780–1820', *Irish Historical Studies*, 22 (1981), pp. 226.

22. He believed that penal law reform in the area of property rights would ensure the unity of Catholic and Protestant against a foreign invader (Vallancey to O'Conor, 6 Nov. 1771, R.I.A., Stowe ms. BI.2).

23. Vallancey, Preface, *Collectanea*, III, no. xii [1783], p. lxxi.

24. Vallancey, *A Vindication of the Ancient History of Ireland* (Dublin, 1786), reprinted in *Collectanea*, IV, no. xiv [1786], pp. xi–xii.

25. Vallancey, 'Fragments of the Brehon laws of Ireland', ibid., III, no. x [1782], p. xliii. On the Brehon laws, see Chapter 5.

26. See Gerard O'Brien, 'The Grattan Mystique', *Eighteenth-Century Ireland*, 1 (1986), pp. 177–94.

27. Vallancey, *Prospectus of a Dictionary of the Language of the Aire Coti* (Dublin, 1802), pp. lii–liii.

28. Brian Ó Cuív, 'Irish Language and Literature, 1691–1845' in T.W. Moody and W.E. Vaughan (eds), *New History of Ireland IV* (Oxford, 1986), p. 416.

29. See for example Joep Leerssen, *Mere Irish and Fíor-Ghael* (Amsterdam and Philadelphia, 1986), p. 427. See also *idem*, 'Antiquarian Research: Patriotism to Nationalism' in Cyril Byrne and Margaret Harry (eds), *Talamh an Eisc: Canadian and Irish Essays* (Halifax, Nova Scotia, 1986), p. 79.

30. Vallancey, *A Grammar of the Iberno-Celtic, or Irish Language* (Dublin, 1773), pp. xxix–xxxi (*recte* xxi–xxiii).

31. As late as 1802 he lamented in private that while the Methodists were interested in preaching through Irish, only the Church of Ireland 'lies like a lump of dough,

nibbled on all sides and takes no pains to save herself'. (Vallancey to Sir Joseph Banks, 14 Nov. 1802, R.I.A., 12/R/25).

32.   Vallancey, note, n.s, n.d., c. 1787, N.L.I., ms. 15,883 (15). This is unmistakeably in Vallancey's handwriting.

33.   Vallancey, *A Grammar of the Iberno-Celtic, or Irish Language* (Dublin, 1773), p. ii, i. On the survival of one of the 'obscene and abominable' mating rituals of the 'idolatrous Jews' in 'the south of Ireland', see idem, 'Conclusion. Miscellaneous', *Collectanea*, III, no. xii (1783), pp. 597–9.

34.   Ibid., p. cxxxvii.

35.   Vallancey to Thomas Burgess, 2 Jan. 1784, N.L.I., ms. 3,899.

36.   Vallancey, *Grammar* (1773), 'Dedication', n.p.; ibid., 'Preface', p. ii.

37.   For an early appreciation of Vallancey's links with British Indianists, see my 'An English Orientalist in Ireland: Charles Vallancey (1726–1812)' in Joep Leerssen, A.H. van der Weel and Bart Westerweel (eds), *Forging in the Smithy: National Identity and Representation in Anglo-Irish Literary History* (Amsterdam and Atlanta, GA, 1995) pp. 161–73.

38.   Thomas Trautmann, *Aryans and British India* (Berkeley, Los Angeles, London, 1997), p. 42. See Colin Kidd, *British Identities before Nationalism* (Cambridge, 1999) for a further exploration of the importance of Mosaic ethnology for identity formation in Britain and Ireland in the early modern period.

39.   Trautmann, *Aryans and British India*, pp. 42–4.

40.   Ibid., p. 74.

41.   Hans Aarsleff, *The Study of Language in England, 1780–1860* (Minneapolis and London, [1967] 1983), pp. 115, 119–21. The first quotation is from a memoir of Jones by his friend John Shore, Lord Teignmouth, the second from a letter by Jones. Both are to be found in Lord Teignmouth (John Shore), *Memoirs of the Life, Writings, and Correspondence of Sir William Jones* in *The Works of Sir William Jones*, 13 vols (London, 1807), II, pp. 27, 120.

42.   Aarsleff, *Study of Language*, p. 119. On native Irish law, see Chapter 5 below.

43.   Schwab, *Oriental Renaissance*, pp. 11–20.

44.   Vallancey to Thomas Orde, 2 Oct. 1784, N.L.I. ms.16,350, p. 40.

45.   Vallancey, *A Grammar of the Iberno-Celtic, or Irish Language. The Second Edition with many Additions* (Dublin, 1781), dedication, p.1.

46.   Trautmann, *Aryans and British India*, p. 44; Aarsleff, *Study of Language*, pp. 128–9.

47.   Jacob Bryant, *A New System, or, an Analysis of Ancient Mythology*, 3 vols (London, 1774–6), I, pp. xii–xiii.

48.   Vallancey, *Vindication*, p. 23.

49.   Ibid., p. xlvi.

50.   Ibid., p. 50.

51.   Abraham Anquetil-Duperron, *Législation Orientale* (1778); Sir William Jones, *The Mohamedan Law of Succession* (1782).

52.   Vallancey, 'A Continuation of the Brehon Laws of Ireland', *Collectanea*, III, no. x [1782], p. xii.

53.   Vallancey, 'Editor's Preface', ibid., I (1786), p. viii.

54.   According to William O'Reilly in a recent excellent paper, Vallancey applied, but was not chosen, for military service in India, after graduating from Woolwich (William O'Reilly, 'Charles Vallancey: Cartography and the Archaeology of

Orientalism', paper delivered at a seminar at the Centre for Human Settlement and Historical Change, N.U.I. Galway, 17 May 2003).

55. Trautmann, *Aryans and British India*, p. 31.

56. Ibid., p. 93.

57. Vallancey, *Grammar* (1773), p. iii. For Vallancey on the Mosaic ethnology, see ibid., pp. xiv–xvi.

58. Aarsleff, *Study of Language*, pp. 115–19.

59. Sir William Jones, 'Sixth Anniversary Discourse to the Asiatick Society' (1789) in *The Works of Sir William Jones*, 13 vols. (London, 1807), III, pp. 123–4, 134–5. See also his earlier 'Third Anniversary Discourse' (1786) in ibid., pp. 34–5.

60. Vallancey, *Vindication*, p. 365. See copy (in Vallancey's hand) of Sir Geo. Yonge's letter to Vallancey, n.d., in which Yonge gives a summary of Jones's 'Sixth Discourse' and his use of ogham (N.L.I., ms. 1415, p. 211).

61. Jones to Joseph Cooper Walker, 11 Sept. 1787, in Garland Cannon (ed.), *The Letters of Sir William Jones*, 2 vols. (Oxford, 1970), II, pp. 770–71.

62. Ibid., note, p. 771.

63. Joseph Cooper Walker to Lord Charlemont, 5 May 1788, R.I.A., ms. 12/R/15.

64. Jones to the second Earl Spencer, 10 Sept. 1787, in Cannon (ed.), *Letters of Sir William Jones*, II, pp. 768–9. In a letter to Sir Joseph Banks, President of the Royal Society, Vallancey later claimed, long after the death of Jones, that he had been 'convinced that the ancient inhabitants of Ireland or Eirin, were originally from Iran and Eirin and Iran were synonymous names' (Vallancey to Sir Joseph Banks, 17 June 1802, R.I.A., ms. 12/R/25).

65. Trautmann, *Aryans and British India*, p. 75.

66. Thomas Maurice, *A Dissertation on the Oriental Trinities* (London, 1801), pp. 21–2, 287–91; Schwab, *Oriental Renaissance*, p. 339; Trautmann, *Aryans and British India*, p. 80.

67. Thomas Maurice, *Sanscreet Fragments, or Interesting Extracts from the Sacred Books of the Brahmins, on Subjects Important to the British Isles* (London, 1798), pp. 8–9, 55.

68. Ibid., pp. 62–4.

69. Ibid., p. 53. To judge by the one reference to Maurice to be found in Vallancey's correspondence, they were not close: 'Maurice is a strange man[,] he acknowledges no letters – his last Vol. on the British is so similar to several parts of my Vindication, one would think he had read it – he certainly had not – I have written to him many letters – he has answered but one, which I believe Ouseley obliged him to do' (Vallancey to Walker, 26 Oct. 1797, T.C.D., ms. 1461(4), fol. 67).

70. Schwab, *Oriental Renaissance*, p. 339.

71. Francis Wilford, 'An Essay on the Sacred Isles in the West, with other essays connected with that work', *Asiatick Researches*, viii (1805), pp. 265–6.

72. Wilford, 'Origin and Decline of the Christian Religion in India', *Asiatick Researches*, x, (1808), pp. 59–69.

73. Trautmann, *Aryans and British India*, pp. 90–91; Wilford, 'An Essay on the Sacred Isles in the West', pp. 265–6.

74. Trautmann, *Aryans and British India*, p. 95.

75. Wilford, 'An Essay on the Sacred Isles in the West', *Asiatick Researches*, xi, pp. 132, 140. Trautmann maintains that Wilford's Purānic researches figure largely

in Vallancey's subsequent writings, notably *The Ancient History of Ireland, proved from the Sanskrit books of the Bramins of India* (Dublin,1797) (Trautmann, *Aryans and British India*, pp. 95–6).

76. Francis Wilford, 'An Essay on the Sacred Isles in the West', *Asiatick Researches*, xi (1810), p. 152.

77. Trautmann, *Aryans and British India*, pp. 91–3.

78. It is clear from these that he was very poor and had an alcohol problem. See, for example, Vallancey to O'Conor, 31 Mar. 1772, complaining that O'Gorman is 'rather a stumbling Block than an Assistance' to him, owing to his drunkenness (R.I.A., Stowe ms. BI.2). See also William O'Sullivan, 'The Irish Manuscripts in Case H in Trinity College Dublin catalogued by Matthew Young in 1781', *Celtica*, 11 (1976), p. 234 n. O'Conor also believed that O'Gorman was 'unfit' to be a scribe owing to his limited competence in classical Irish, 'being almost ignorant of the obsolete terms and phraseology of our old annalists' (O'Conor to Thomas O'Gorman, 17 Jan. 1781, *O'Conor Letters*, II, p. 159).

79. O'Conor to Curry, 21 Dec. 1771, ibid., I, p. 297.

80. Vallancey to O'Conor, 31 Mar. 1772, R.I.A., Stowe ms. BI.2.

81. O'Conor to John Curry, 7 May 1772, in *O'Conor Letters*, II, p.16.

82. O'Conor, 'Remarks on the Essay on the Antiquity of the Irish Language. Addressed to the Printer of the London Chronicle, in the year 1772', reprinted in *Collectanea*, II, no. viii [1781], pp. 337–9.

83. O'Conor to O'Gorman, 6 Aug. 1783, in *O'Conor Letters*, II, p. 194.

84. Vallancey to O'Conor, 1 Aug. 1772, R.I.A., Stowe ms. BI.2.

85. Vallancey to O'Conor, 25 Apr. 1772, ibid.

86. O'Conor to Vallancey, 4 Dec. 1773, in *O'Conor Letters*, II, p. 57.

87. O'Conor to Vallancey, 16 Sept. 1774, in ibid., p. 72.

88. O'Conor to Thomas O'Gorman, 14 Mar. 1781, in ibid., p. 162.

89. O'Conor to Vallancey, c. 25–30 Sept. 1784, 13 Oct. 1784, N.L.I., ms. 16,350, pp. 20, 41. These letters are not included in *O'Conor Letters*.

90. O'Conor to Thomas O'Gorman, 16 Jul. 1786, in *O'Conor Letters*, II, p. 249.

91. Trautmann, *Aryans and British India*, pp. 96–7.

92. See note 33 above.

93. The *Essay* appeared in a second edition in *Collectanea*, II, no. viii (1781); a third edition was published in London in 1818 and reissued in London in 1822. The Punic-Gaelic collation was published in French in 1787. There were two editions of the *Grammar.*

94. R.B. McDowell and D.A. Webb, *Trinity College Dublin, 1592–1952* (Cambridge, 1982), pp. 9–10.

95. Vallancey to O'Conor, 1 Aug. 1772, R.I.A., Stowe ms. BI.2.

96. Vallancey to O'Conor, 31 Aug. 1772, ibid.

97. O'Halloran, *A General History of Ireland*, 2 vols (London, 1778), I, pp. i, 1.

98. Ibid., p. 156.

99. Ibid., p. 155–6.

100. Walter Love, 'The Hibernian Antiquarian Society', *Studies*, 51 (1962), pp. 425–9.

101. Ibid. For more on this society, see below, Chapters 4 and 5.

102. Vallancey, *Vindication*, pp. 462 ff. (not paginated).

103. See Walter D. Love, 'Edmund Burke and an Irish Historiographical Controversy', *History and Theory*, ii (1962), pp. 187–92.

104. Daniel Beaufort, *Memoir of a Map of Ireland, illustrating the Topography of that Kingdom* (London, 1792).

105. Beaufort to Grimar Thorkelin, 16 Jan. 1790, Edinburgh, Edinburgh University Library, ms. La.III.379, no. 35.

106. Beaufort to Walker, 13 Mar. 1790, T.C.D., ms. 1461(1), fol. 36.

107. Walker, incomplete essay on Irish poetry, n.d. [*c.* 1790], R.I.A., ms. 4/A/27.

108. Hamilton to Charlemont, 14 April [*c.* 1785], R.I.A., ms. 12/R/21.

109. William Hamilton, *Letters concerning the Northern Coast of the County of Antrim* (Dublin, 1786).

110. Flood's will is printed in Sir Lawrence Parsons, *Observations on the Bequest of Henry Flood esq. to Trinity College, Dublin* (Dublin, 1795), pp. 7–12.

111. See Chapter 7, below.

112. Parsons, *Observations on the Bequest*, pp. 55–6.

113. James Kelly, *Henry Flood: Patriots and Politics in Eighteenth-Century Ireland* (Dublin, 1998), pp. 435–6.

114. The term 'Gothic' was used from the seventeenth century to denote all the Germanic tribes including the Saxons (Kliger, *The Goths in England*, pp. 1–3).

115. Hugh MacDougall, *Racial Myth in English History* (Montreal and Hanover, New Hampshire, 1982), pp. 31–41; Kidd, *British Identities*, pp. 99–109.

116. MacDougall, *Racial Myth*, pp. 53–9; J.G.A. Pocock, *The Ancient Constitution and the Feudal Law* (2nd edn: Cambridge, 1987), pp. 30–55; Kidd, *British Identities*, pp. 75–88.

117. Christopher Hill, 'The Norman Yoke', *Puritanism and Revolution* (Harmondsworth, 1990), pp. 58–98.

118. MacDougall, *Racial Myth*, pp. 22–7; Kidd, *British Identities*, pp. 89–90.

119. Ibid., pp. 91–97.

120. Hill, 'Norman Yoke', pp. 98–106.

121. T.C. Smout, 'Problems of Nationalism, Identity and Improvement in Later Eighteenth-Century Scotland' in T.M. Devine (ed.), *Improvement and Enlightenment* (Edinburgh, 1989), pp. 11–12. On Scotland's 'ancient constitution' see Colin Kidd, *Subverting Scotland's Past* (Cambridge, 1993), pp. 101–28; *idem*, *British Identities*, pp. 123–45.

122. See Chapter 3, below.

123. William Molyneux, *The Case of Ireland's being Bound by Acts of Parliament in England, Stated* (Dublin, 1698, repr. Dublin, 1977), pp. 71, 132.

124. John Macpherson, *Critical Dissertations on the Origins, Antiquities, Language, Government, Manners and Religion of the Ancient Caledonians* (London, 1768). See Kidd, *British Identities*, pp. 200–204.

125. Leah Leneman, 'A New Role for a Lost Cause: Lowland Romanticisation of the Jacobite Highlander' in Leah Leneman (ed.), *Perspectives in Scottish Social History* (Aberdeen, 1988), pp. 107–24.

126. Address by the Earl of Buchan to the Society of Antiquaries in Scotland, 14 Nov. 1787, reported in the *Dublin Chronicle*, 3–5 Apr. 1788. On Buchan's acquaintance with Vallancey, see Thomas Percy to John Pinkerton, 11 Feb. 1786, *The Literary Correspondence of John Pinkerton*, 2 vols (London, 1830), I, pp. 113–15.

127. Mr Dempster to Pinkerton, 18, 22 and 28 Jul. 1789, ibid., pp. 218–22. By the end of this exchange Dempster appeared to have been convinced by Pinkerton that all the inhabitants of Scotland were Goths.

128. Alexander Stewart, *Elements of Gaelic Grammar* (2nd edn, Edinburgh, 1812), p. 129.

129. Leneman, 'A New Role for a Lost Cause', pp. 123–4, note; Hugh Trevor Roper, 'The Invention of Tradition: the Highland Tradition of Scotland' in Eric Hobsbawm and Terence Ranger (eds), *The Invention of Tradition* (Cambridge, 1985), pp. 26–34.

130. John Pinkerton, *A Dissertation on the Origin of the Scythians or Goths* (1787), reprinted in *An Enquiry into the History of Scotland*, 2 vols (London, 1789), II, pp. 222–3.

131. John Pinkerton, *Select Scottish Ballads*, 2 vols (London, 1783); *idem, Ancient Scottish Poems*, 2 vols (London and Edinburgh, 1786). See also Patrick O'Flaherty, 'John Pinkerton (1758–1826): Champion of the Makars', *Studies in Scottish Literature*, 13 (1978), pp. 159–95.

132. On Pinkerton and on Scottish Gothicism in general, see Colin Kidd, 'Teutonist Ethnology and Scottish Nationalist Inhibition, 1780–1880', *Scottish Historical Review*, lxxiv (1995), pp. 45–68.

133. Pinkerton, *Enquiry*, II, pp. 49–51.

134. Ibid., I, pp. 233–4.

135. Ibid., p. 208.

136. Ibid., p. 75.

137. Ibid., II, p. 48.

138. Pinkerton, *Enquiry* (2nd edn: Edinburgh, 1814), pp. iii, 137.

139. Ledwich to Joseph Cooper Walker, 22 Oct. 1787, T.C.D., ms. 1461(2), fol. 282.

140. Beauford to Walker, 1 Oct. 1789, T.C.D., ms. 1461(3), fol. 176.

141. Campbell to Percy, 25 Oct. 1787, in Nichols, *Lit. Illus.*, VII, pp. 770–71.

142. Ledwich to Walker, [?16 Feb. 1786], T.C.D., ms. 1461(2), fol. 95.

143. Ledwich to Walker, 19 Jun. 1786, ibid., fol. 120; Ledwich to Walker, 29 Apr. 1786, ibid., fol. 103.

144. John Curry, *Historical Memoirs of the Irish Rebellion in the year 1641* (London, 1758); *idem, An Historical and Critical Review of the Civil Wars in Ireland* (Dublin, 1775).

145. Ledwich to Walker, 13 May 1786, T.C.D., ms. 1461(2), fol. 107. Curry died in 1780; the book to which Ledwich referred was a new edition of Curry's *Historical and Critical Review*, with a short biographical sketch of him by Charles O'Conor, which was published in 1786.

146. Ledwich to Walker, 13 Mar. 1787, T.C.D., ms. 1461(2), fol. 209.

147. James Kelly, 'The Genesis of "Protestant Ascendancy": the Rightboy Disturbances of the 1780s and their Impact upon Protestant Opinion' in Gerard O'Brien (ed.), *Parliament, Politics and People* (Dublin, 1989), pp. 93–127; *idem*, 'Conservative Political Thought in Late Eighteenth-Century Ireland' in S.J. Connolly (ed.), *Political Ideas in Eighteenth-Century Ireland* (Dublin, 2000), pp. 197–206.

148. Ledwich to [? William Burton Conyngham], 13 Apr. 1779, N.L.I., ms. 1415, pp. 125–7.

149. Ledwich to [? Burton Conyngham], 1 May 1779, ibid., p. 129.

150. Ledwich, 'An Essay on the Study of Irish Antiquities', *Collectanea*, II, no. vi [1781], pp. 86, 94–5.

151. On Barnard, see Chapter 1, above.

152. Vallancey, 'Some Remarks on the Round Towers of Ireland', *Collectanea*, III, no. x [1782], pp. 191–7.

153. Ledwich, 'A Dissertation on the Round Towers in Ireland', ibid., II, no. vi [1781], pp. 141, 129–31, 120.

154. For this reason, J.R. Hill's categorisation of Ledwich as a 'sceptical' historian, on the lines of William Robertson of Scotland, is inaccurate (Hill, 'Popery and Protestantism, Civil and Religious Liberty: the Disputed Lessons of Irish History 1690–1812', *Past and Present*, 118 (Feb. 1988), pp. 119–21). He has been described more subtly as 'a curious mixture of enlightened scepticism and historical romanticism' (Donal McCartney, 'The Writing of History in Ireland, 1800–30', *Irish Historical Studies*, 10 (1957), p. 349).

155. Ledwich to Walker, n.d., T.C.D., ms. 1461(7), fol. 154.

156. Ledwich, 'The History and Antiquities of Irishtown and Kilkenny', *Collectanea*, II, no. ix [1781], pp. 349–51.

157. John Whitaker, *The Genuine History of the Britons Asserted. In a Full and Candid Refutation of Mr Macpherson's Introduction to the History of Great Britain and Ireland* (Dublin, 1773), pp. 1–2, 2–3.

158. Whitaker, *History of Manchester*, 2 vols (London, 1771–5) I, pp. 433–7.

159. Ledwich, *Antiquities of Ireland* (Dublin, 1790), pp. 9–10.

160. Ibid., pp. 15–6.

161. Ibid., pp. 12–13.

162. On earlier versions of this theory put forward by William Molyneux and Sir Richard Cox, see Jim Smyth, '"Like Amphibious Animals": Irish Protestants, Ancient Britons, 1691–1707', *Historical Journal*, 36 (1993), pp. 789–91.

163. Thomas Campbell, *A Philosophical Survey of the South of Ireland* (London, 1777), p. 61. The reference is to Davies' 'Historical Relations', probably meaning a collection of Davies' writing, similar to another published in Dublin in 1787 under the title, *Historical Tracts by Sir John Davies*.

164. Campbell, *Philosophical Survey*, pp. 67–8, 69. Edmund Spenser, *A View of the Present State of Ireland*, ed. W.L. Renwick (Oxford, 1970), p. 41.

165. Campbell to Richard Gough, 9 Feb. 1788, in Nichols, *Lit. Illus.*, VII, pp. 800–802. For more on Campbell's political attitudes, see below, Chapter 6.

166. Campbell, *Philosophical Survey*, pp. 236, 237.

167. Ibid., pp. 238–9.

168. This episode is dealt with in detail in Love, 'Edmund Burke and an Irish Historiographical Controversy'. On Campbell's modern history project, see below, Chapter 6.

169. Although *Strictures* was based to a large degree on the 'Sketch', they are by no means identical as has been alleged (Walter Love, 'Edmund Burke', p. 188).

170. *Dublin Chronicle*, 24–27 Dec. 1787; 26–28 Feb. 1788. For Ledwich, see note 159 above.

171. Ledwich to Richard Gough, 22 Mar. 1787, in Nichols, *Lit. Illus.*, VII, pp. 844–5.

172. Ledwich to Walker, 13 Mar. 1787, T.C.D., ms. 1461(2), fol. 210.

173. Ledwich to Percy, Aug. 1799, in Nichols, *Lit. Illus.*, VII, 819–20.

174. Beaufort to Walker, 13 Mar. 1790, T.C.D., ms. 1461(1), fol. 36.

175. W.G. Strickland, *A Dictionary of Irish Artists*, 2 vols ([1913] repr. Shannon, 1989) I, pp. 51–3.

176. Ledwich to Walker, 11 Mar. 1786, T.C.D., ms. 1461(2), fol. 97; Ledwich to Percy, 14 Feb. 1807 in Nichols, *Lit. Illus.*, VII, 842–3.

177. Ledwich to Percy, 28 Aug. 1802, ibid., pp. 822–4. The manuscript history is in T.C.D. His Ossian essay is missing, but details from it are quoted in ibid. Percy's

friend Robert Anderson, author of *Lives of British Poets*, bought the Ossian essay from Beauford for twenty pounds, and intended putting it in a new edition of Macpherson's Ossian, which apparently was not published.

178. O'Conor to Thomas O'Gorman, 31 May 1783, in *O'Conor Letters*, II, p. 189.
179. Ledwich hinted to Walker that his 'credit' would be 'somewhat at stake' if he proposed Beauford for membership of the R.I.A. (Ledwich to Walker, 25 Jul. 1787, T.C.D., ms. 1461(2), fol. 256).
180. William Beauford, 'Druidism Revived', *Collectanea*, II, no vii [1781], pp. 176, 181.
181. Beauford, 'Of the Origin and Language of the Irish', ibid., no. viii [1781], pp. 223–4.
182. Beauford, 'The Antient Topography of Ireland', ibid., III, no. xi (1783), pp. 391–3.
183. Campbell, *Strictures*, pp. 62–4.
184. See Leerssen, *Mere Irish*, Chapter 2, 'Ireland in English Representations', especially pp. 72–84.
185. The correspondence is printed in Nichols, *Lit. Illus.*, VII, pp. 798–809, 844–56. William Camden, *Britannia*, ed. Richard Gough, 3 vols (London, 1789). The edition included new material contributed by Gough and his consultants.
186. Campbell to Gough, 9 Feb. 1788, in Nichols, *Lit. Illus.*, VII, pp. 800–802.
187. Dacre to Gough, 7 Jan. 1784, in ibid., pp. 798–9.
188. Campbell to Gough, 9 Feb. 1788, ibid., pp. 800–802.
189. Campbell to Gough, 15 Apr. 1788, ibid., p. 805.
190. Campbell to Gough, 28 Apr. 1788, ibid., pp. 806–7; Campbell, *Survey*, pp. 341–72. For more on Campbell's analysis of English policy, see below, Chapter 6.
191. Campbell to Gough, 28 Apr. 1788, in Nichols, *Lit. Illus.*, VII, pp. 806–7.
192. See for example his account of dining in London with Pinkerton (Campbell to Percy, 25 Oct. 1787, in ibid., pp. 770–71).
193. Campbell's diary of this and six other visits to England (and one to France in 1787) was first published in 1854 and re-edited in 1947 (*Dr Campbell's Diary of a Visit to England in 1775*, ed. James L. Clifford (Cambridge, 1947)).
194. 'Memoir of Thomas Campbell' in Nichols, *Lit. Illus.*, VII, pp. 759–60.
195. Campbell to Thomas Percy, 25 Oct. 1787, in ibid., p. 770. See also Toby Barnard, 'Protestantism, Ethnicity and Irish Identities, 1660–1760' in Tony Claydon and Ian McBride (eds), *Protestantism and National Identity: Britain and Ireland c. 1650–c.1850* (Cambridge, 1998), p. 213.
196. J. Warburton, J. Whitelaw and R. Walsh, *History of the City of Dublin*, 2 vols. (London, 1818), II, p. 920.
197. [Edward Ledwich], *Antiquitates Sarisburienses* (Salisbury, 1771). A letter from Ledwich to Walker confirms that he wrote on Salisbury (Ledwich to Walker, 26 Jun. 1786, T.C.D., Ms. 1461(2), fol. 124).
198. On Ledwich's move to Dublin, see Ledwich to Joseph Cooper Walker, [Mar. 1790], [? Oct. 1791], T.C.D., ms 1461(3), fols. 205, 238
199. Ledwich to [?Burton Conyngham], 26 Nov. 1778, 13 Apr. 1779, N.L.I., ms. 1415, pp. 120, 125–7; Ledwich to Walker, 9 Jul. 1785, T.C.D., ms. 1461(2), fol. 35.
200. Ledwich to Walker, 29 Feb. [1788], T.C.D., ms. 1461(3), fol. 12.

201. Ledwich ['Mediocriter'] to the editor of the *Dublin Chronicle*, 12 Mar.[1788], T.C.D., ms. 1461(3), fols. 19–20. An edited version of the letter was published in the *Dublin Chronicle*, 18–20 Mar. 1788.

202. *The Monthly Review* (Dec. 1787), p. 427. See also Harry White, *The Keeper's Recital: Music and Cultural History in Ireland, 1770–1970* (Cork, 1998), pp. 23–5.

203. Ledwich ['Mediocriter'] to the editor of the *Dublin Chronicle*, 12 Mar.[1788], T.C.D., ms. 1461(3), fols. 19–20. On the growing tendency for Irish Protestants to feel insulted by such derogatory references to Ireland, see also David Hayton, 'Anglo-Irish Attitudes: Changing Perceptions of National Identity Among the Protestant Ascendancy in Ireland, ca. 1690–1750', *Studies in Eighteenth-Century Culture*, 17 (1987), pp. 148–9.

204. *The Monthly Review* (Dec. 1787), pp. 435–6, 438.

205. O'Conor's letter attacking Hume was published in *Gentleman's Museum* (April–May 1763); he sent his letter in support of Vallancey's *Essay on the Antiquity of the Irish Language* to the *London Chronicle* (See 'The Known Works of Charles O'Conor' in *O'Conor Letters*, I, pp. 299–304).

206. Ledwich ['Mediocriter'] to the editor of the *Dublin Chronicle*, 12 Mar.[1788], T.C.D., ms. 1461(3), fols. 19–20.

207. Ledwich to Walker, 20 Nov. 1786, T.C.D., Ms. 1461(2), fol. 163.

208. See for example, Ledwich to Gough, 22 Mar. 1787, 18 Sept. 1787, in Nichols, *Lit. Illus.*, VII, pp. 844–5, 850–51.

209. Ledwich to Gough, 18 Sept. 1787, ibid., pp. 850–51.

210. Gough to Ledwich, 24 Nov. 1787, ibid., p. 853; Edward Ledwich, 'Observations on our Antient Churches', *Archaeologia*, 8 (1787), pp. 165–94.

211. Gough to Ledwich, 24 Nov. 1787, in Nichols, *Lit. Illus.*, VII, p. 853.

212. Ledwich's copy of Camden's *Britannia*, ed. Richard Gough, is in the Joly Collection in the National Library of Ireland, Dublin. See Michael Hewson, 'Edward Ledwich's Gift', *The Long Room*, 30 (1985), pp. 29–31.

213. See Warburton, Whitelaw and Walsh, *History of the City of Dublin*, II, p. 920.

214. Ledwich's copy of Camden's *Britannia*, ed. Richard Gough, p. 224 (N.L.I., Joly Collection). Given Ledwich's birth in 1738, it is unlikely that his great-great-grandfather could have fought at the Boyne – he probably meant great-grandfather.

215. The name Ledwich does not appear in the extant convert rolls (Eileen O'Brien (ed.), *The Convert Rolls* (Dublin, 1981)).

216. Ledwich, 'History of the Antiquities of Irishtown and Kilkenny', in *Collectanea*, II, no. ix [1781], pp. 366–7.

217. See for example, Campbell, 'Sketch', *Dublin Chronicle*, 13–15 Mar. 1788.

218. Ledwich to Walker, 7 Mar. 1787, T.C.D., ms. 1461(2), fol. 202. See also Chapter 5, below. For further examples of Protestants tracing their 'complicated ancestry', see Barnard, 'Protestantism, Ethnicity and Irish Identities', pp. 214–16.

219. Fitzgibbon's father converted in 1731 (Ann C. Kavanaugh, *John Fitzgibbon, Earl of Clare* (Dublin, 1997), p. 10).

220. Ibid., pp. 363–6; See also A.P.W. Malcolmson, *John Foster: the Politics of the Anglo-Irish Ascendancy* (Oxford and Belfast, 1978), pp. 5, 357–9.

221. Kavanaugh, *Fitzgibbon*, pp. 364–5.

222. Ibid., p. 201.

223. In 1790 a pseudonymous satire on Vallancey was published (J. Hastler, *The Antiquities of Killmackumpahaugh* [Dublin, 1790]).

Island of Druids, Saints and Scholars

1. Stuart Piggott, *The Druids* (London, 1968), p. 24.
2. Ibid., pp. 28–30.
3. A.L. Owen, *The Famous Druids* (Oxford, 1962), p. 109.
4. Ibid., pp. 28–30.
5. Caesar, *The Conquest of Gaul*, trans. S.A. Handford (Harmondsworth, 1951), p. 32.
6. For a survey of classical writing on the druids, see Owen, *The Famous Druids*, pp. 15–26.
7. Quoted in ibid., pp. 39–40.
8. Piggott, *The Druids*, pp. 32–3.
9. Owen, *The Famous Druids*, pp. 114–15.
10. J.A.I. Champion, '"Manuscripts of Mine Abroad": John Toland and the Circulation of Ideas, c.1700–1722', *Eighteenth-Century Ireland*, 14 (1999), p. 13.
11. J.G. Simms, 'John Toland (1670–1722), a Donegal Heretic', *Irish Historical Studies*, 16 (1969), pp. 304–20, reprinted in J.G. Simms, *War and Politics in Ireland, 1649–1730*, eds D.W. Hayton and Gerard O'Brien (London and Ronceverte, 1986), pp. 31–3. All references are to the latter publication.
12. John Toland, *Christianity not Mysterious* (London, 1696), pp. 147–8.
13. Peter Browne, *A Letter in Answer to a Book intituled, Christianity not Mysterious* (Dublin, 1697), p. 96, quoted in Simms, 'John Toland', p. 36. See also David Berman, 'Enlightenment and Counter-Enlightenment in Irish Philosophy', *Archiv für Geschichte der Philosophie* (1982), pp. 151–2.
14. Berman, 'The Culmination and Causation of Irish Philosophy', ibid., p. 266.
15. John Leland, *View of the Principal Deistical Writers*, 3 vols (London, 1754–7).
16. Berman, 'Culmination and Causation', pp. 269–70.
17. Jonathan Swift, *An Argument Against Abolishing the Christian Religion* (1711), quoted in Berman, 'Culmination and Causation', p. 269. Swift was adverting to the rumour, possibly true, that Toland was the illegitimate son of a priest and a prostitute.
18. It was given the running head 'History of the Druids' in *A Collection of Several Pieces* (1726) and was later published as *History of the Druids* (Montrose, 1814).
19. John Toland, 'A Specimen of the Critical History of the Celtic Religion and Learning: containing an Account of the Druids, in *A Collection of Several Pieces of Mr John Toland*, 2 vols (London, 1726), I, p. 8. Hereafter 'Specimen'.
20. Robert Sullivan, 'John Toland's Druids: a Mythopoeia of Celtic Identity', *Bullán*, 4 (1998), pp. 19–42; Richard Kearney, 'John Toland: an Irish Philosopher?' in Philip McGuinness, Alan Harrison and Richard Kearney (eds), *John Toland's 'Christianity not Mysterious': Texts, Associated Works and Critical Essays* (Dublin, 1997), pp. 207–222.
21. Toland, 'Specimen', pp. 79, 23. But see J.A.I. Champion's suggestive arguments that 'Toland's Celtic identity was pan-British' and that his aim in promoting 'the remnants of Celtic history' was to subvert 'the commonplace privileging of classical antiquity' (J.A.I. Champion, 'John Toland, the druids and the politics of Celtic scholarship', *Irish Historical Studies* 32 (2001), pp. 330–33).
22. Ibid., pp. 36–7, 51. Alan Harrison speculates that it is 'quite possible' that Toland had a first-hand acquaintance with such texts (Harrison, 'John Toland

(1670–1722) and Celtic Studies' in C.J. Byrne, Margaret Harry and Pádraig Ó Siadhail (eds), *Celtic Languages and Celtic Peoples* (Halifax, N.S., 1992), pp. 560–1).

23. Ibid., p. 567.
24. Toland, 'The Relation of an Irish Manuscript of the Four Gospels', *Nazarenus* (London, 2nd edn, revised 1718). See Harrison, 'Toland and Celtic Studies', p. 563. See also below.
25. Ibid., pp. 557–8.
26. Toland, 'Specimen', p. 45.
27. Ibid., p. 46.
28. Ibid., pp. 48–9.
29. Ibid., p. 57.
30. Ibid., p. 12.
31. Ibid., pp. 21, 14.
32. Ibid., p. 46.
33. Ibid., p. 51.
34. Sullivan, 'John Toland's Druids', p. 33.
35. On Toland's anti-Catholicism, see Philip McGuinness, 'John Toland and Irish Politics' in McGuinness, Harrison and Kearney (eds), *John Toland's 'Christianity not Mysterious'*, pp. 280–81.
36. Toland, 'Specimen', pp. 50, 54–6. Cf. Geoffrey Keating, *Foras Feasa ar Éirinn; the History of Ireland*, ed. and trans. David Comyn and P.S. Dinneen, 4 vols (Dublin, 1902–14), II, p. 133; on druids, see index under 'druids', ibid., IV, p. 264. On Toland's use of Keating, see David Berman and Alan Harrison, 'John Toland and Keating's History of Ireland (1723)', *Donegal Annual*, no. 36 (1984), p. 27. Toland does not mention Keating in his own work.
37. Ibid., pp. 25–9.
38. Harrison, 'John Toland's Celtic Background' in McGuinness, Harrison and Kearney (eds), *John Toland's 'Christianity not Mysterious'*, pp. 255–6.
39. Compare Keating, *Foras Feasa*, I, pp. 203–5, with idem, *The General History of Ireland*, trans. Dermod O'Connor (London, 1723), pp. 42–3.
40. Compare *Foras Feasa*, II, pp. 319–21, with *General History*, pp. 263–5.
41. Keating, *General History*, p. 212.
42. Keating, *Foras Feasa*, II, p. 247.
43. Keating, *General History*, p. 215.
44. Fiona Stafford, *The Sublime Savage: James Macpherson and the Poems of Ossian* (Edinburgh, 1988), pp. 156–7.
45. Review of Macpherson's *Fingal*, *Annual Register* (1761), p. 278.
46. James Macpherson, *Fingal* (London, [1761] 1762), pp. v–vi.
47. Ibid., p. iv.
48. Charles O'Conor, *Dissertations on the Antient History of Ireland* (Dublin, 1753), pp. v–vi, 95. For the origins and development of this belief, see Owen, *The Famous Druids*, pp. 59–82.
49. O'Conor, *Dissertations* (1753), pp. v–vi, 95–103.
50. O'Conor, *Dissertations on the History of Ireland* (Dublin, 1766), pp. 96, 200.
51. D.S. Thomson, 'Bogus Gaelic Literature c. 1750–c. 1820', *Transactions of the Gaelic Society of Glasgow*, 5 (1958), pp. 180–81.
52. John Smith, *Galic Antiquities* (Edinburgh, 1780), pp. 10–11, 33.

53. Ibid., p. 34; Sylvester O'Halloran, *Introduction to the Study of the History and Antiquities of Ireland* (London, 1772), p. 10.

54. Chapters 2, 3, 4, and 9 (ibid.).

55. Ibid., pp. 17, 21–2. For Keating, see *Foras Feasa*, II, p. 63.

56. O'Halloran, *Introduction*, p. 19. On O'Halloran's use of classical sources, see for example, ibid., pp. 10–11, where Caesar, Strabo, Pliny and Tacitus are cited. O'Halloran did not refer to Keating in his treatment of the druids, but on other issues cited him extensively (ibid., pp. 113, 125, 128, 138 and 153).

57. Ibid., p. 20.

58. Smith, *Galic Antiquities*, pp. 83–4. Smith later wrote a life of St Columba, founder of the monastery of Iona: *The Life of St Columba* (Edinburgh, 1798).

59. Keating, *Foras Feasa*, III, pp. 16–21.

60. Ibid., II, pp. 344–5.

61. Ibid., II, pp. 132–3; ibid., III, pp. 31–3.

62. O'Conor, *Dissertations* (1766), p. 198.

63. Bridget McCormack, *Perceptions of St Patrick in Eighteenth-Century Ireland* (Dublin, 2000), pp. 30–31.

64. Toland, 'Specimen', pp. 57–8.

65. O'Halloran, *Introduction*, pp. 25, 38.

66. Joseph Cooper Walker, *Historical Memoirs of the Irish Bards*, 2 vols (Dublin, [1786] 1818), I, p. 67.

67. Walter Harris in *The Whole Works of Sir James Ware*, ed. Walter Harris (Dublin, 1739–45), I, p. 6; Thomas Campbell, *Strictures on the Ecclesiastical and Literary History of Ireland* (London, 1790), p. 85.

68. McCormack, *Perceptions of St Patrick*, pp. 69–70; J. R. Hill, 'National Festivals, the State and "Protestant Ascendancy" in Ireland, 1790–1829', *Irish Historical Studies*, 24 (1984), pp. 31–2.

69. Harris in *Whole Works of Sir James Ware*, I, p. 4.

70. McCormack, *Perceptions of St Patrick*, pp. 71–3; James Kelly, '"The Glorious and Immortal Memory": Commemoration and Protestant Identity in Ireland 1660–1800', *Proceedings of the Royal Irish Academy*, 94c (1994), p. 48.

71. Benignus Millett, 'Irish Literature in Latin, 1550–1700', in T.W. Moody, F.X. Martin and F.J. Byrne (eds), *New History of Ireland III* (Oxford, 1976), pp. 577–9.

72. James Ussher, *A Discourse of the Religion Anciently Professed by the Irish and British* (4th edn: London, 1687), epistle.

73. John McCafferty, 'St Patrick for the Church of Ireland', *Bullán*, 3 (1997–9), pp. 97, 92, 98.

74. Alan Ford, 'James Ussher and the Creation of an Irish Protestant Identity' in Brendan Bradshaw and Peter Roberts (eds), *British Consciousness and Identity: the Making of Britain, 1533–1707* (Cambridge, 1998), p. 206.

75. O'Conor, *Dissertations* (1766), p. 202.

76. See for example, Keating, *Foras Feasa*, II, pp. 342–9; III, pp. 32–7.

77. O'Conor, *Dissertations* (1766), p. 200.

78. O'Halloran, *Introduction*, pp. x, 32–5, 169–70.

79. Ibid., pp. 170, 182, 220; Edward Gibbon, *The History of the Decline and Fall of the Roman Empire*, ed. David Wormersley, 3 vols (London, 1995 [1776–88]), II, pp. 416–48.

80. O'Halloran, *Introduction*, pp. xix.

81. Vincent Geoghegan, 'A Jacobite History: the Abbé MacGeoghegan's *History of Ireland*', *Eighteenth-Century Ireland*, 6 (1991), pp. 37–9.

82. 'les plus brillants de toute l'Histoire ancienne et moderne de ce peuple', James MacGeoghegan, *Histoire de l'Irlande*, 3 vols (Paris, 1758–62), I, p. xi. All translations from this work are by C.O'H.

83. Thomas Leland, *The History of Ireland from the Invasion of Henry II with a Preliminary Discourse on the Antient State of that Kingdom*, 3 vols (London, 1773), I, pp. xix–xxiv.

84. Campbell, *Strictures*, p. 4.

85. Ibid., pp. 152–3.

86. Sir James Ware, *De Scriptoribus Hiberniae* (Dublin, 1639); Walter Harris (ed.), *Whole Works of Sir James Ware*, III.

87. Campbell, *Strictures*, pp. 152–3.

88. O'Halloran, *Introduction*, pp. 365–84.

89. Edward Ledwich, *Antiquities of Ireland* (Dublin, 1790), pp. 167, 164.

90. Hill, 'Popery and Protestantism, Civil and Religious Liberty: the Disputed Lessons of Irish History 1690–1812', *Past and Present*, 118 (Feb. 1988), p. 103.

91. See also Bernadette Cunningham, *The World of Geoffrey Keating* (Dublin, 2000), pp. 224–5.

92. See, for example, MacGeoghegan, *Histoire de l'Irlande*, I, p. 309.

93. Maureen Wall, 'The Quest for Catholic Equality, 1745–78', *Catholic Ireland in the Eighteenth Century: Collected Essays of Maureen Wall*, ed. Gerard O'Brien (Dublin, 1989), pp. 118–22.

94. O'Conor, *Dissertations* (1753), pp. 148–9.

95. O'Conor, *Dissertations* (1766), pp. 205–6.

96. Ibid., pp. 199, 196, 205.

97. Campbell, *Strictures*, p. 97.

98. Ledwich, *Antiquities of Ireland*, pp. 160–61, 366, 370.

99. M. Esposito, 'The Patrician Problem and a Probable Solution', *Irish Historical Studies*, 19 (1956), pp. 131–55. For a recent view of the Patrician problem, see David Dumville et al, *Saint Patrick, AD 493–1993* (Woodbridge, Suffolk, 1993), pp. 39, 59–64.

100. Ledwich to Joseph Cooper Walker, 15 Mar. [1789], T.C.D., ms. 1461(3), fol. 128.

101. Ledwich to Walker, [1789], ibid., fol. 108.

102. Ledwich to Walker, 10 May 1788, ibid., fol. 53.

103. Ledwich to Walker, 1 Dec. 1789, [22 Mar. 1789], ibid., fols. 188, 132.

104. Ledwich, *Antiquities of Ireland*, p. 360.

105. O'Halloran, *A General History of Ireland*, 2 vols. (London, 1778), I, p. xxxi; II, p. 28.

106. As late as 1788 he wrote to Walker that 'Not one proof has hitherto occurred to me of an oriental ever having put his foot on Irish ground' (Ledwich to Walker, [Dec. 1788], T.C.D., ms. 1461(3), fol. 97).

107. Ledwich, *Antiquities of Ireland*, pp. 163–4.

108. Ibid., p. 389.

109. Mervyn Archdall, *Monasticon Hibernicum*, (Dublin, 1786), p. xvii.

110. McCormack, *Perceptions of St Patrick*, p. 20.

111. Ledwich, *Antiquities of Ireland*, p. 356.

112. Campbell, *Strictures*, pp. 142, 145–6.
113. Ledwich, *Antiquities of Ireland*, pp. 174–5.
114. Peter O'Dwyer, *Céli Dé: Spiritual Reform in Ireland 750–900* (Dublin, 1981), pp. 1–4, 16–17.
115. Colin Kidd, *Subverting Scotland's Past* (Cambridge, 1993), pp. 22–4, 63–9.
116. The best review of the Culdee controversy is William Reeves, *The Culdees of the British Islands* (Dublin, 1864), pp. 67–77.
117. Ledwich, *Antiquities of Ireland*, pp. 56–7.
118. Ibid., pp. 174–5, 55, 62.
119. Ford, 'James Ussher and the Creation of an Irish Protestant Identity', pp. 200–202.
120. Ledwich, *Antiquities of Ireland*, p. 70.
121. Ibid., pp. 142, 157.
122. Ledwich to Walker, 11 Dec. 1786, T.C.D., ms. 1461(2), fol. 166.
123. O'Conor, *Dissertations* (1766), p. 206.
124. O'Halloran, *General History of Ireland*, II, p. 28.
125. MacGeoghegan, *Histoire de l'Irlande*, I, pp. 324–7.
126. F.X. Martin, 'Diarmait Mac Murchada and the coming of the Anglo-Normans' in Art Cosgrove (ed.), *New History of Ireland II* (Oxford, 1987), pp. 43–66.
127. O'Conor, *Dissertations* (1753), p. xxxi.
128. O'Conor, *Dissertations* (1766), pp. 230–31. See also n. 74 above.
129. 'favorables à l'ambition et à la cupidité d'une nation voisine', MacGeoghegan, *Histoire de l'Irlande*, I, p. xi.
130. Ledwich, *Antiquities of Ireland*, pp. 413–14.
131. Campbell, *Strictures*, p. 98.
132. Ledwich, *Antiquities of Ireland*, pp. 379–80.
133. Keating, *Foras Feasa*, III, pp. 313–15.
134. See, for example, O'Halloran, *General History of Ireland*, I, pp. xxxii–xxxiii.
135. Ibid., pp. xxxiv–xxxv.
136. MacGeoghegan, *Histoire de l'Irlande*, I, pp. 461–2, 439, 440, 444, 442.
137. O'Conor, *Dissertations* (1766), pp. 279–80.
138. Thomas Leland to O'Conor, 9 May 1772, R.I.A., Stowe ms. BI.2.
139. Ledwich, *Antiquities of Ireland*, p. 448.
140. Ibid., pp. 156–7.
141. Ibid., p. 448.
142. Campbell, *Strictures*, pp. 204–5.
143. William Hamilton, *Letters concerning the Northern Coast of the County of Antrim* (Dublin, 1786), pp. 43–5.
144. See Chapter 2, above.

Ossian and the Irish Bards

1. William Wilde, *Memoir of Gabriel Beranger* (Dublin, 1880), pp. 3, 38, 44–5; Beranger to Vallancey, 26 May 1785, N.L.I., ms. 1415, fol. 61. For a new and informative account of the tour and a selection of Beranger's and Bigari's sketches, see Peter Harbison, *'Our Treasure of Antiquities': Beranger and Bigari's Antiquarian Sketching Tour of Connacht in 1779* (Bray, Co. Wicklow, 2002).
2. Beranger to [William Burton Conyngham], 25 Jun. [1779], N.L.I., ms. 1415, fol. 76.

3. Beranger to Vallancey, 26 May 1785, ibid., fols. 66–7.
4. Bernard Smith, *European Vision and the South Pacific* (New Haven and London, 1985, second printing 1988).
5. Ibid., pp. 41–3.
6. Ibid., pp. 1–2.
7. Bougainville was published in translation in Dublin in 1772 (Louis-Antoine de Bougainville, *A Voyage Round the World. Performed by Order of His Most Christian Majesty, in the Years 1766, 1767, 1768, and 1769* (Dublin, 1772)). See Graham Gargett, 'French Books connected with the French Enlightenment published in Ireland, 1700–1800' in Graham Gargett and Geraldine Sheridan (eds), *Ireland and the French Enlightenment, 1700–1800* (Basingstoke, London and New York, 1999), p. 247.
8. Beranger to Vallancey, 26 May 1785, N.L.I., ms. 1415, fols. 66–7.
9. Beranger to [William Burton Conyngham], 25 Jun. [1779], ibid., fol. 76.
10. Beranger to Vallancey, 26 May 1785, ibid., fols. 72–3.
11. Gilbert White to Thomas Pennant, 9 Mar. 1775, in White, *The Natural History and Antiquities of Selbourne*, ed. William Jardine ([1789] London, 1853), p. 85.
12. A. Grenfell Price (ed.), *The Explorations of Captain James Cook in the Pacific as told by Selections of his own Journals 1768–1779* (New York, 1971), pp. 262–71.
13. Smith, *European Vision*, pp. 118–22. See also Arthur Young's *Autobiography* for an account of a 'Captain Cook' spectacular planned by Sir James Caldwell of Castle Caldwell, on Lough Erne, in 1772. Caldwell enlisted fifty of his labourers whom he deemed most suitable to represent New Zealand 'savages' in one vessel, and an equal number to play Captain Cook and his crew in another (Arthur Young, *The Autobiography of Arthur Young*, ed. M. Betham-Edwards, ([1898], repr. New York, 1967), pp. 69–70).
14. Smith, *European Vision*, pp. 121–3.
15. Giraldus Cambrensis [Gerald of Wales], *The History and Topography of Ireland [Topographia Hiberniae]*, trans. John J. O'Meara (Mountrath, Portlaoise, and Atlantic Highlands, NJ, 1982), pp. 75, 100–103, 117–18.
16. Edmund Spenser, *A View of the Present State of Ireland* [1596], ed. W.L. Renwick (Oxford, 1970); Sir John Davies, *A Discovery of the True Causes why Ireland was never Entirely Subdued* ([London, 1612], repr. Shannon, 1969).
17. John Lynch, *Cambrensis Eversus*, (n.p. [?St Omer], 1662); Geoffrey Keating, *Foras Feasa ar Éirinn; the History of Ireland*, ed. and trans. David Comyn and P.S. Dinneen, 4 vols (Dublin, 1902–14).
18. These were: *Fragments of Ancient Poetry* (Edinburgh, 1760); *Fingal* (London, [Dec. 1761] 1762); *Temora* (London, 1763). For a new edition, see James Macpherson, *The Poems of Ossian and Related Works*, ed. Howard Gaskill with an introduction by Fiona Stafford (Edinburgh, 1996).
19. Derick Thomson, *The Gaelic Sources of Macpherson's 'Ossian'* (Edinburgh and London, 1952), pp. 42, 84. See also, Donald E. Meek, 'The Gaelic Ballads of Scotland: Creativity and Adaptation' in Howard Gaskill (ed.), *Ossian Revisited* (Edinburgh, 1991), pp. 19–48. On literary historians and Macpherson's Ossian, see an excellent article by Howard Gaskill, '"Ossian" Macpherson: towards a Rehabilitation', *Comparative Criticism*, 8 (1986), pp. 113–46.
20. Fiona Stafford, *The Sublime Savage: James Macpherson and the Poems of Ossian* (Edinburgh, 1988), pp. 28–32.

21. S.N. Cristea, 'Ossian v. Homer: an Eighteenth-Century Controversy', *Italian Studies*, 24 (1969), pp. 95, 100–101; Paul Dukes, 'Ossian and Russia', *Scottish Literary News*, 3, no. 3 (Nov. 1973), pp. 17–21; Lois Whitney, 'English Primitivistic Theories of Epic Origin', *Modern Philology*, 21 (1924), pp. 346–8.

22. Eugene E. Reed, 'Herder, Primitivism and the Age of Poetry', *Modern Language Review*, 60 (1965), p. 556. See also Howard Gaskill, 'Herder, Ossian and the Celtic' in Terence Brown (ed.), *Celticism* (Amsterdam and Atlanta, GA, 1996), pp. 257–71.

23. Arthur E. McGuinness, 'Lord Kames on the Ossian poems: Anthropology and Criticism', *Texas Studies in Literature and Language*, 10 (1968), pp. 68–9. On Scottish stadialism, see Ronald L. Meek, *Social Science and the Ignoble Savage* (Cambridge, 1976), pp. 5–36.

24. John Greenway, 'The Gateway to Innocence: Ossian and the Nordic Bard as Myth', *Studies in Eighteenth-Century Culture*, 4 (1975), pp. 161–2.

25. M.M. Rubel, *Savage and Barbarian: Historical Attitudes in the Criticism of Homer and Ossian in Britain, 1760–1800* (Amsterdam, Oxford and New York, 1978), pp. 37, 81, 90–91.

26. Larry Le Roy Stewart, 'Ossian in the Polished Age: the Critical Reception of James Macpherson's Ossian' (unpublished Ph.D dissertation, Case Western Reserve University, 1971), p. 26.

27. See Clare O'Halloran, 'Irish Re-creations of the Gaelic Past: the Challenge of Macpherson's Ossian', *Past and Present*, 124 (Aug. 1989), pp. 91–3.

28. Gerard Murphy, *The Ossianic Lore and Romantic Tales of Medieval Ireland* (Dublin, 1961), pp. 55, 61. 'Ossian' will be used throughout to refer to Macpherson's character; 'Oisín' will refer to the son of Fionn, the hero of the Irish Fionn cycle.

29. See Chapter 1, above.

30. Macpherson, *Fingal*, preface.

31. Macpherson, *Temora*, p. xi.

32. Thomson, *Gaelic Sources*, pp. 59, 14. See also, John MacQueen, 'Temora and Legendary History' in Fiona Stafford and Howard Gaskill (eds), *From Gaelic to Romantic: Ossianic Translations* (Amsterdam and Atlanta, GA, 1998), pp. 69–78.

33. See, for example, James Macpherson, *An Introduction to the History of Great Britain and Ireland* (London, 1771), pp. 137–9

34. See Chapter 1, above.

35. O'Conor to Curry, 15 Oct. 1765, 5 Oct. 1765, Clonalis, ms. 8.3.HS.023. The letter of 5 Oct. 1765 is wrongly transcribed in *O'Conor Letters*, I, p. 196; and from that source in my 'Irish Re-creations of the Gaelic Past', p. 76, fn. 33.

36. Charles O'Conor, *Dissertations on the Antient History of Ireland* (Dublin, 1753), pp. v–vii. The second edition (1766) dropped 'antient' from the title.

37. O'Conor to Vallancey, 29 Nov. 1771, in *O'Conor Letters*, I, pp. 292–3.

38. Charles O'Conor, *A Dissertation on the First Migrations and Final Settlements of the Scots in North-Britain: with Occasional Observations on the Poems of 'Fingal' and 'Temora'* (Dublin, 1766), pp. 23, 20; bound with *Dissertations on the History of Ireland* (1766), but paginated separately.

39. O'Conor, *Dissertation on the First Migrations and Final Settlements of the Scots*, pp. 60–61.

40. Ibid., p. 27.

41. Charles O'Conor, 'Observations on the Heathen State and Ancient Topography of Ireland' in *Collectanea*, III, no. xii [1783], pp. 653–4.

42. Fragment of letter in Charles O'Conor's hand, [c. Nov. 1785], R.I.A. 23/H/39, pp. 17–20. On the Ossian debate in Morgan's *The Wild Irish Girl*, see Tom Dunne, 'Haunted by History: Irish Romantic Writing 1800–1850' in Roy Porter and Mikulas Teich (eds), *Romanticism in National Context* (Cambridge, 1988), pp. 74–5.

43. Charles Owen O'Conor, *The O'Conors of Connaught* (Dublin, 1891), pp. 284–5, 286–91.

44. Charles O'Conor to J.C. Walker, 31 Jan. 1786, D.C.L.A., ms. 203, fol. 27.

45. Stafford, *Sublime Savage*, pp. 6–20.

46. Charles O'Conor, 'Third Letter to Colonel Vallancey', *Collectanea*, IV, no. xiii [1784], p. 108; O'Conor to Hugh MacDermot, 12 Jun. 1776, in *O'Conor Letters*, II, p. 87.

47. O'Conor to Thomas O'Gorman, 17 Jan. 1781, 14 Mar. 1781 and 31 May 1783, in ibid., pp. 159, 162, 189–90. However, this seems to have been only temporary, as by February 1784 the boy was working as a scribe for Thomas O'Gorman (O'Gorman to O'Conor, 28 Feb. 1784, San Marino, Huntingdon Library, Stowe Collection).

48. O'Conor, *Dissertations* (1766), pp. 27–8.

49. Michael Richter, *Medieval Ireland* (London, 1987), pp. 30–31.

50. Roderic O'Flaherty, *Ogygia*, trans. James Hely, 2 vols (Dublin, 1793), II, pp. 102.

51. O'Conor, *Dissertations* (1766), pp. 35, 17.

52. See below, Chapter 7.

53. Charles O'Conor to J.C. Walker, 31 Jan. 1786, D.C.L.A., ms. 203, fol. 27.

54. O'Conor, 'Third Letter to Col. Vallancey', pp. 116–17.

55. O'Conor, 'Second Letter to Col. Vallancey', *Collectanea*, III, no. xii [1783], pp. 665–6.

56. Adam Ferguson, *An Essay on the History of Civil Society* (Edinburgh, 1767); Macpherson, *Temora*, p. xi.

57. Peter Burke, *The Renaissance Sense of the Past* (London, 1969), pp. 87.

58. O'Conor, *Dissertations* (1766), p. xvi.

59. Charles O'Conor, fragment of draft memoir presented to the Select Committee on Antiquities of the Dublin Society, 8 Aug. 1773, Clonalis, ms. 8.4.HL.219.

60. Richard B. Sher, *Church and University in the Scottish Enlightenment* (Edinburgh, 1985), pp. 242–61.

61. Macpherson, *Introduction*, pp. 35, 188–9.

62. Ibid., p. 198.

63. Ibid., pp. 163–6.

64. Macpherson, *Fingal* (London, 1762), p. xv.

65. See also Fiona Stafford, 'Primitivism and the "Primitive" poet: a Cultural Context for Macpherson's Ossian' in Brown (ed.), *Celticism*, pp. 79–96.

66. O'Conor, *Dissertations* (1766), pp. 1–2.

67. O'Conor to George Faulkner, 25 Sept. 1767, in *O'Conor Letters*, I, p. 228.

68. O'Conor's only formal association with the Society was as 'corresponding member' to its Select Committee on Antiquities in 1772 (Charles O'Conor (S.J.), 'Origins of the Royal Irish Academy', *Studies*, 38 (1949), pp. 331–3).

69. On O'Conor's covert purchasing and then improvement of poor land, see O'Conor to Curry, 27 Jan. 1759, 22 Aug. 1759, in *O'Conor Letters*, I, pp. 67, 74–5.

70. Stafford, *The Sublime Savage*, p. 20; O'Conor to John Curry, 23 Jun. 1758, in *O'Conor Letters*, I, pp. 57–8.

71. O'Conor to John Carpenter, 20 Feb. 1781, in ibid., II, p. 161.
72. O'Conor, 'Second Letter to Colonel Vallancey', pp. 653–4; O'Conor to Thomas O'Gorman, 17 Jan. 1781, in *O'Conor Letters*, II, p. 158; Leerssen, *Mere Irish*, pp. 224–9.
73. See Maureen Wall, 'The Rise of the Catholic Middle Class in Eighteenth-Century Ireland', *Irish Historical Studies*, 11 (1958), pp. 91–115.
74. J.B. Lyons, 'Sylvester O'Halloran, 1728–1807', *Eighteenth-Century Ireland*, 4 (1989), pp. 65–6.
75. Miso-Dolos [Sylvester O'Halloran], 'The Poems of Ossine, the Son of Fionne mac Comhal, Reclaimed: by a Milesian', *Dublin Magazine* (Jan. 1763).
76. Ibid.
77. O'Halloran, 'A Letter to Mr Macpherson, occasioned by his Dissertation on the Poems of Temora. By a Milesian', *Dublin Magazine* (Aug. 1763).
78. O'Halloran to O'Conor, 19 Feb. 1765, reprinted in 'The Letters of Sylvester O'Halloran, pt. 1', ed. J.B. Lyons, *North Munster Antiquarian Journal*, 8 (1961), p. 169.
79. O'Halloran to O'Conor, 1 March 1765, in ibid., p. 170.
80. O'Conor, *Dissertations* (1766), p. 48. Later in the same work, O'Conor claimed that the system 'differed widely' from that of contemporary Britain, and linked it more to 'the Gothic Forms so much celebrated (and, perhaps, with little justice) by the writers of the Age we live in' (ibid., pp. 56–7), But that kind of linkage served only to reinforce the point that, without the conquest, early Irish government would anyway have conformed to the British model.
81. Ibid., p. 49.
82. Charles O'Conor, fragment of draft memoir presented to the Select Committee on Antiquities of the Dublin Society, 8 Aug. 1773, Clonalis, ms. 8.4.HL.219.
83. Sylvester O'Halloran, *An Introduction to the Study of the History and Antiquities of Ireland* (London, 1772), pp. 55, 125.
84. Ibid., pp. 5–6.
85. Ibid., pp. 40, 124–5.
86. O'Halloran, *Insula Sacra* (Limerick, 1770), p. 18.
87. See, for example, Charles Forman, *A Defence of the Courage, Honour, and Loyalty of the Irish Nation* (London, 1731); Patrick Abercromby, *The Martial Achievements of the Scots Nation*, 2 vols (Edinburgh, 1711–15).
88. John K'eogh, *Vindication of the Antiquities of Ireland* (Dublin, 1748), pp. 88–93, 96, 98.
89. O'Conor *Dissertations* (1753), pp. xii–xiii, xxiii.
90. O'Halloran to Charles Vallancey, 10 Apr. 1772, N.L.I., ms. 4158, p. 20.
91. O'Halloran, *Introduction*, p. 124.
92. Ibid., pp. 72–3.
93. O'Conor, *Dissertations* (1753), pp. 140–41.
94. On Hume's *History of England*, see below, Chapter 6.
95. O'Halloran to O'Conor, 8 Apr. 1765, 'Letters of Sylvester O'Halloran, pt 1', p. 175; O'Halloran, *Insula Sacra*, p. ii; *idem, Introduction*, p. 333.
96. Macpherson, *Temora*, p. 118.
97. Charles Vallancey, *A Grammar of the Iberno-Celtic* (Dublin, 1773), pp. xxvii–xxviii. Later, he dubbed Ossian a Persian 'prophet' ('Vindication of the Ancient History of Ireland', *Collectanea*, IV, no. 14 (1786), p. 217).

98.   Ludwig C. Stern, 'Ossianic Heroic Poetry', *Transactions of the Gaelic Society of Inverness*, 22 (1897–8), p. 263.
99.   On Scotland, see Kenneth D. MacDonald, 'The Rev. William Shaw: Pioneer Gaelic Lexicographer', *Transactions of the Gaelic Society of Inverness*, 50 (1976–8), pp. 1–2; V.E. Durkacz, *The Decline of the Celtic Languages* (Edinburgh, 1983), pp. 193–4.
100. Joseph Cooper Walker, *Historical Memoirs of the Irish Bards* (Dublin, 1786); Charlotte Brooke, *Reliques of Irish Poetry* (Dublin, 1789); Lady Morgan, *The Wild Irish Girl*, 3 vols (London, 1807).
101. Thomas O'Gorman to O'Conor, 19 Jul. 1781, R.I.A., Stowe ms. BI.2.
102. Seamus Deane, *Celtic Revivals* (London, 1985), p. 20.
103. David Hayton, 'Anglo-Irish Attitudes: Changing Perceptions of National Identity Among the Protestant Ascendancy in Ireland, *ca.* 1690–1750', *Studies in Eighteenth-Century Culture*, 17 (1987), pp. 145–57.
104. Peter Burke, *Popular Culture in Early Modern Europe* (London, 1978), pp. 3–22.
105. O'Conor to Curry, 23 Jul. 1763, in *O'Conor Letters*, I, p. 164.
106. See Chapter 1, above.
107. Thomas Campbell, *A Philosophical Survey of the South of Ireland* (London, 1777), pp. 430–31.
108. Strictly speaking, Charles Wilson's *Select Irish Poems translated into English* (Dublin, n.d., *c.* 1782) was the first book of Gaelic poetry translations, but it did not include the Gaelic originals, and did not have the impact or success of Charlotte Brooke's later *Reliques of Irish Poetry* (1789).
109. William O'Sullivan, 'The Irish Manuscripts in Case H in Trinity College Dublin catalogued by Matthew Young in 1781', *Celtica*, 11 (1976), pp. 238–9, 232.
110. Ibid., p. 241.
111. Mathew Young, 'Antient Gaelic Poems respecting the Race of Fians, collected in the Highlands of Scotland in the year 1784', *Transactions of the Royal Irish Academy*, 1 (1787), antiquities section, pp. 43–4, 48–9. I am not using the terms 'tale', 'ballad' and 'poem' here in a precise modern sense, but rather in the interchangeable way that these writers employed.
112. Ibid., pp. 44–5.
113. Sylvester O'Halloran, 'A Martial Ode', *Transactions of the Royal Irish Academy*, 2 (1788), antiquities section, pp. 7–17.
114. O'Halloran, draft manuscript of the 'Martial Ode', 29 Dec. 1787, R.I.A, ms. 24/H/39. Quotations are taken from an introductory section which was omitted from the published version.
115. Evan Evans, *Some Specimens of the Poetry of the Ancient Welsh Bards* (London, 1764); Edward Jones, *Musical and Poetical Relicks of the Welsh Bards* (London, 1784); Thomas Percy, *Reliques of English Poetry*, 3 vols (London, 1765).
116. Leerssen, *Mere Irish*, p. 424.
117. Walker, *Historical Memoirs of the Irish Bards*, 2 vols (2nd edn, Dublin, 1818), I, pp. xv–xvi. All quotations are taken from this edition.
118. For examples, see ibid., pp. 23, 52–3.
119. On Carolan, see Donal O'Sullivan, *Carolan: the Life, Times and Music of an Irish Harper*, 2 vols (London, 1958).
120. Fragment of letter in Walker's hand, n.d. [? *c.*1785], Clonalis, ms. 8.4.HL.072.
121. Harry White, *The Keeper's Recital* (Cork, 1998), pp. 21–2.

122. Walker to O'Conor, 1 Feb. 1785, Clonalis, ms. 8.4.HL.071. O'Conor himself had used the term 'bard' in the first edition of his *Dissertations* (e.g. p. 60).
123. Fragment of letter in Walker's hand, n.d. [? *c*.1785], Clonalis, ms. 8.4.HL.072. Further queries can be found in Walker to O'Conor, 25 Jul. 1785, San Marino, Huntingdon Library, Stowe Collection.
124. E.H. King, *James Beattie* (Boston, 1977), pp. 15, 17–18, 91, 94.
125. Walker, *Historical Memoirs*, I, pp. 287, 222.
126. Ibid., pp. 309–10, 313, 326–7.
127. Ibid., pp. 9–11.
128. Ibid., pp. 90–91.
129. Ibid.
130. Ibid., pp. 89, 90–91.
131. Ibid., pp. 8–9.
132. Ibid., p. 86.
133. Ibid., p. 224.
134. Ibid., p. 91.
135. Ibid., pp. 11, 9–10.
136. Ibid., p. 11. I have benefited greatly from reading an unpublished paper by Leith Davis ('Harping on the Past: Joseph Cooper Walker's *Historical Memoirs of the Irish Bards*', delivered at ASECS Conference, Notre Dame, Indiana, 1998).
137. Leerssen, *Mere Irish*, p. 422.
138. Leith Davis, 'Birth of the Nation: Gender and Writing in the Work of Henry and Charlotte Brooke', *Eighteenth-Century Life*, 18 (Feb. 1994), pp. 28–30.
139. Henry Brooke, *The Farmer's Letters to the Protestants of Ireland* (Dublin, 1745); idem, *The Tryal of the Roman Catholics of Ireland* (Dublin, 1761).
140. Leerssen, *Mere Irish*, pp. 363–4, 376–7.
141. [Henry Brooke], *An Essay on the Antient and Modern State of Ireland* (Dublin, 1759).
142. Henry Brooke, *A Collection of the Pieces formerly published by Henry Brooke*, 4 vols (London, 1778), IV, pp. 393–414. See Davis, 'Birth of the Nation', p. 31.
143. Aaron Crossley Seymour, 'Memoirs of Miss Brooke', *Reliques of Irish Poetry*, 2nd edn (Dublin, 1816), pp. liii–lv.
144. Charlotte Brooke to Thomas Percy, 6 Jun. [?1788], in Nichols, *Lit. Illus.*, VIII, pp. 250–51.
145. William Beauford to Charlotte Brooke, 9 Apr. 1789, R.I.A., 23/H/39, pp. 21–4.
146. Vallancey to Brooke, 25 Aug. 1788, ibid., pp. 25–6.
147. Charlotte Brooke, *Reliques of Irish Poetry* (Dublin, 1789), p. iii. She also included Vallancey in this tribute, but was clearly influenced more by his early *Essay on the Irish Language* (1772) than by his later work. It has been alleged that Sylvester O'Halloran was Charlotte Brooke's 'godfather' (see, for example, Vance, 'Celts, Carthaginians and Constitutions', p. 221). Given that O'Halloran was a Catholic and Brooke's mother a follower of John Wesley, this seems implausible (on Brooke's mother, see Crossley Seymour, 'Memoirs of Miss Brooke', p. xxv).
148. Davis, 'Birth of the Nation', pp. 34–5.
149. Cheryl Turner, *Living by the Pen: Women Writers in the Eighteenth Century* (London and New York, 1992), pp. 20–23, 26–30.
150. Brooke, *Reliques* (1789), pp. vii–viii.

151. Cathal Ó Háinle, 'Towards the Revival: some Translations of Irish Poetry, 1789–1897' in Peter Connolly (ed.), *Literature and the Changing Ireland* (Gerrard's Cross and Totowa, N.J., 1982), pp. 42–3.
152. Brooke, *Reliques* (1789), p. vi; see also Davis, 'Birth of the nation', pp. 42–3.
153. Brooke, *Reliques* (1789), p. vi.
154. Davis, 'Birth of the Nation', p. 36.
155. Brooke, *Reliques* (1789), p. 140.
156. Ibid., pp. 140, iv–v.
157. O'Halloran, 'Irish Re-creations of the Gaelic Past', pp. 87, 89.
158. See, for example, *Monthly Review*, 4 (1791), p. 45; *Critical Review*, 60 (1790), p. 24.
159. Walker, *Historical Memoirs*, I, pp. 57–8.
160. Ó Háinle, 'Towards the Revival', p. 42.
161. Macpherson, *Introduction*, pp. 219–20, 259, 268–9; Brooke, *Reliques* (1789), pp. 168, 171.
162. Ibid., p. 27.
163. Ibid., pp. iv–v.
164. Ibid., pp. vii–viii.
165. Kate Trumpener, *Bardic Nationalism* (Princeton, New Jersey, 1997), p. 4.
166. O'Conor, *Dissertations* (1753), pp. 60, 63.
167. The poem was by 'Ferflatha O'Gnive, Family Poet of the O'Neills of Clannaboy' (O'Conor, *Dissertations* (1753), pp. 61–3).
168. Walker, *Historical Memoirs*, I, p. 197.
169. Ibid., p. 147.
170. Ibid., pp. 147, 181, 185.
171. Leerssen, 'Antiquarian Research: Patriotism to Nationalism' in Cyril Byrne and Margaret Harry (eds), *Talamh an Eisc: Canadian and Irish Essays* (Halifax, Nova Scotia, 1986), pp. 80–81.
172. Walker to William Hayley, 10 Dec. 1786, D.C.L.A., ms. 146.
173. Brooke, *Reliques* (1789), pp. 237–8.
174. Ibid., p. 238.
175. Ibid., p. 138.
176. Ibid., pp. vii–viii.
177. Ibid., p. 74.
178. Ibid., pp. 53, 99.
179. Ibid., p. 76.
180. Ibid., p. 47.
181. Mary Helen Thuente, *The Harp Re-strung: the United Irishmen and the Rise of Literary Nationalism* (Syracuse, 1994), p. 85.
182. Ibid., p. 25.
183. Quoted in ibid., pp. 30–31.
184. Ibid., pp. 95–6, 10.
185. Quoted in ibid., pp. 54–5.
186. Brooke, *Reliques* (1789), p. 74.
187. Quoted in Thuente, *The Harp Re-strung*, pp. 54–5.
188. Quoted in ibid., p. 55.
189. Ibid., p. 51.
190. Spenser, *A View of the Present State of Ireland*, pp. 50–53.

191. Walker, *An Historical Essay on the Dress of the Ancient and Modern Irish* (Dublin, 1788), pp. 80–81.
192. Ibid., pp. v–vi.
193. Walker to Pinkerton, 31 May 1798, in *The Literary Correspondence of John Pinkerton*, 2 vols (London, 1830) II, pp. 30, 32.

Irish Custom, Law and Lawlessnes

1. Sir Lucius O'Brien to O'Conor, 26 May 1772, R.I.A., Stowe ms. BI.2.
2. David Hayton, 'Anglo-Irish Attitudes: Changing Perceptions of National Identity among the Protestant Ascendancy in Ireland, *ca.* 1690–1750', *Studies in Eighteenth-Century Culture*, 17 (1987), pp. 148–9.
3. Harris, 'An Essay on the Defects in the History of Ireland' in Walter Harris, ed., *Hibernica*, (Dublin, 1747–50), part 1, pp. 135–6.
4. Joseph Leerssen, *Mere Irish and Fíor-Ghael* (Amsterdam and Philadelphia, 1986), pp. 402, 33–9.
5. W.D. Love, 'Edmund Burke, Charles Vallancey, and the Sebright Manuscripts', *Hermathena*, no. 95 (Jul. 1961), pp. 21–3.
6. This is now ms. H.2.15a, Trinity College Library. For a modern edition and translation of the bee judgments see Thomas Charles-Edward and Fergus Kelly (eds), *Bechbretha* (Dublin, 1983). Through the offices of Burke, Sebright eventually presented 28 manuscripts to the library of T.C.D. in 1781, although they remained in Vallancey's possession until 1786 when they were at last lodged in the College library (Love, 'Sebright Manuscripts', pp. 25, 29–31).
7. O'Conor to Thomas O'Gorman, 14 Jul. 1784, *O'Conor Letters*, II, p. 212. In the second edition of *Antiquities of Ireland*, Ledwich quoted from a letter by O'Conor (probably written to Joseph Cooper Walker) which stated that without a 'Law Lexicon' of terms, the law tracts would be impossible to translate (Ledwich, *Antiquities of Ireland* (Dublin, 1804), p. 303).
8. Charles Vallancey, *Essay on the Antiquity of the Irish Language* (Dublin, 1772), pp. 55–61.
9. Vallancey, 'Part of the Ancient Brehon Laws of Ireland', *Collectanea*, I, no. iv [1780], pp. 657–72; *idem*, 'A Continuation of the Brehon Laws, in the Original Irish, with a translation into English', ibid., III, no. x [1782], pp. 1–126; the quotation is from ibid., preface, p. iii. Vallancey also included 'A Dissertation concerning the Ancient Irish Laws, or National Customs, called Gavel-kind and Thanistry', implying that he was the author (ibid., I, no. iii, pp. 215–417; ibid., no. iv, pp. 423–646). It is now believed that this essay was by the Irish Catholic Bishop of Cloyne and Gaelic scholar, John O'Brien (see copy of letter from Thomas O'Gorman to Lucius O'Brien, 12 Jul. 1781, R.I.A. 24/D/18, pp. 3–7; also Diarmaid Ó Catháin, 'An Irish Scholar Abroad: Bishop John O'Brien of Cloyne and the Macpherson Controversy' in Patrick O'Flanagan and Cornelius G. Buttimer (eds), *Cork: History and Society* (Dublin, 1993), pp. 503, 526).
10. D.A. Binchy, 'The Linguistic and Historical Value of the Irish Law Tracts', *Proceedings of the British Academy*, 29 (1943), pp. 195–9.
11. Love, 'Sebright Manuscripts', pp. 34–5.
12. Sir John Davies, *A Discovery of the True Causes why Ireland was never Entirely Subdued* ([1612] repr. Shannon, 1969), pp. 15–16.

13.   Ibid., pp. 102–3, 107–13, 116–21; Hans Pawlisch, *Sir John Davies and the Conquest of Ireland* (Cambridge, 1985), pp. 59–60; Edmund Spenser, *A View of the Present State of Ireland*, ed. W.L. Renwick (Oxford, 1970) p. 13.

14.   Davies, *Discovery*, p. 165.

15.   Spenser, *View*, pp. 5–10; Davies, *Discovery*, pp. 165–73.

16.   Pawlisch, *Sir John Davies*, pp. 60–61.

17.   Davies, *Discovery*, pp.165–6.

18.   O'Conor, *Dissertations on the Antient History of Ireland* (Dublin, 1753), pp. 80–81.

19.   Ibid. (1766), pp. 5, 48. In his manuscript draft O'Conor argued that 'the customs of Tanistry and Election' only produced 'their worst consequences' after Henry II had 'cantonized this Kingdom among ten over grown Feudatories, and excluded the Natives from the Benefit of Law and Property'. This was omitted from the final version (O'Conor, manuscript draft, pp. 170–71, Clonalis, ms. 8.4.LH.219).

20.   *Dissertations* (1766), p. 130.

21.   Ibid., p. 132–3.

22.   Ibid., pp. 133–4.

23.   Ibid., p. 140.

24.   C.D.A. Leighton, *Catholicism in a Protestant State* (Dublin, 1994), p. 123.

25.   Leland to O'Conor, 5 Jan. 1769, R.I.A., Stowe ms. BI.2.

26.   James Macpherson, *Fingal* (London, 1762); *idem*, *Temora* (London, 1763); *idem*, *An Introduction to the History of Great Britain and Ireland* (London, 1771).

27.   [Thomas Leland], *An Examination of the Arguments contained in a late Introduction to the History of the Antient Irish, and Scots* (London, 1772), pp. 11, 14, 15; Geoffrey Keating, *Foras Feasa ar Éirinn: the History of Ireland*, ed. and trans. David Comyn and P.S. Dinneen, 4 vols. (Dublin, 1902–14), I, p. 5.

28.   I have not been able to trace this. Leland may have been thinking of Spenser who asserted that the Brehon law was handed down by tradition (Spenser, *View*, p. 5).

29.   Thomas Leland, *The History of Ireland from the Invasion of Henry II*, 3 vols (London, 1773), I, pp. xxiv–xxix.

30.   Ibid., pp. xxxi–xxxiii, xxxvi–xxxvii.

31.   Ibid., pp. xxxiv–xxxv.

32.   Ibid., p. xxxvii; Fynes Moryson, *An Itinerary* (London, 1617), p. 164. A new edition of the Irish part of this work was published in 1735 under the title *An History of Ireland*, 2 vols. (Dublin, 1735).

33.   Leland, *History of Ireland*, I, pp. xxxvi–xxxvii.

34.   Ibid., pp. xxxiii–xxxiv, xxxvi.

35.   Ibid., pp. xl–xli.

36.   Ibid., II, p. 418.

37.   Edmund Spenser, *A View of the State of Ireland as it was in the Reign of Queen Elizabeth* (Dublin, 1763); Sir John Davies, *A Discoverie of the True Causes why Ireland was never Entirely Subdued* (Dublin, 1761). The printers of Spenser were Ann Watts and Laurence Flin; of Davies: Richard Watts and Laurence Flin. Ann Watts carried on a separate bookselling business and 'was neither wife nor daughter of Richard [Watts]' (Robert Munter, *A Dictionary of the Print Trade in Ireland 1550–1775* (New York, 1988), pp. 287–8).

38.   Davies, *Historical Relations: or a Discovery of the True Causes why Ireland was never Entirely Subdued* (Dublin, 1733), Dedication (n.p.); this was reprinted in Dublin

in 1751. Another edition was published in London in 1747.

39. Davies, *Historical Tracts by Sir John Davies* (Dublin, 1787), Editor's Advertisement (n.p.).

40. W.J. McCormack, *The Dublin Paper War of 1786–1788* (Dublin, 1993).

41. Thomas Campbell, *A Philosophical Survey of the South of Ireland* (London, 1777), p. 61. The reference is to Davies' '*Historical Relations*', probably meaning a collection of Davies' writing, such as that published in 1733, and similar to another published in Dublin in 1787 under the title *Historical Tracts by Sir John Davies* (see notes 38, 39, above).

42. Campbell, *Strictures on the Ecclesiastical and Literary History of Ireland* (Dublin, 1789), pp. 42–3.

43. Campbell, *Philosophical Survey*, pp. 61, 71–2.

44. Campbell, *Strictures*, p. 35; Spenser, *View*, p. 68.

45. Campbell, *Strictures*, p. 227.

46. Thomas Campbell, 'Sketch or Summary View of the Ecclesiastical and Literary History of Ireland', *Dublin Chronicle*, 8–11 Mar. 1788.

47. Campbell, *Strictures*, p. 203. O'Conor had claimed that agriculture was practised 'in the earlier Ages' (*Dissertations* (1766), pp. 102–3, 133).

48. William Blackstone, *Commentaries on the Laws of England*, 4 vols ([1765–9], London, 1826), I, p. 95; Campbell, *Strictures*, pp. 42–3, 40.

49. Ibid., pp. 51–2.

50. Quotation from O'Conor given by Campbell, ibid., p. 200. Campbell does not give a reference to O'Conor's work and I have been unable to find the quotation, but such a statement is implied in much of O'Conor's analysis of Henry II's policy in Ireland (e.g. see O'Conor, note 22, above).

51. Ibid., p. 201.

52. Ibid., pp. 328–9.

53. Ibid., p. 200.

54. It is now understood as a defensive measure to preserve the existing social and economic order within the colony (S.J. Connolly (ed.), *The Oxford Companion to Irish History* (Oxford, 1998), pp. 286–7).

55. Campbell, *Strictures*, pp. 251–2.

56. Ibid., pp. 336–8, 361–2, 371–3.

57. Ibid., pp. 200–201.

58. Ibid., pp. 360, 356.

59. Ibid., p. 360.

60. Ibid., p. 356.

61. See note 49 above.

62. Campbell, *Philosophical Survey*, p. 253.

63. *Idem, Strictures*, p. 356.

64. Ledwich to ?William Burton Conyngham, 13 Apr. 1779, N.L.I., ms. 1415, fols 125–7.

65. Lord Kames, *Sketches of the History of Man*, 2 vols (Edinburgh, 1774); Adam Ferguson, *Essay on the History of Civil Society* (Edinburgh, 1767). See R. Meek, *Social Science and the Ignoble Savage* (Cambridge, 1976), pp. 99–130.

66. Ferguson, *Essay on the History of Civil Society*, pp. 1–2.

67. M.M. Rubel, *Savage and barbarian: Historical Attitudes in the Criticism of Homer and Ossian in Britain, 1760–1800* (Amsterdam, Oxford and New York, 1978), pp. 33–7.

68. Ledwich, 'History of the Antiquities of Irishtown and Kilkenny', in *Collectanea*, II, no. ix [1781], pp. 366–7.

69. Ledwich, 'Essay on the Study of Irish Antiquities' in ibid., no. vi [1781], p. 96.

70. O'Conor to [Charles Vallancey], 12 Mar. 1779, in *O'Conor Letters*, II, p. 136.

71. Ledwich, 'Memoirs of Dunamase and Shean Castle' in *Collectanea*, II, no. vi [1781], p. 147.

72. Ledwich, 'A Dissertation on the Round Towers in Ireland' in ibid., p. 120–21.

73. Ledwich, 'Essay on the Study of Irish Antiquities', pp. 115–16. William Beauford also cited this as evidence of the persistence of the pastoral state (Beauford, 'Of the Origin and Language of the Irish, and of the Learning of the Druids' in ibid., no. viii [1781], pp. 227–8). In 1797 Vallancey also used this 1647 Confederacy order in support of his contention that the Irish were descendants of shepherds from the banks of the Indus river in India (Vallancey, 'On the Oriental Emigration of the Ancient Inhabitants of Britain and Ireland', *The Oriental Collections*, I, no. 4 (1797), pp. 312–3).

74. John Pinkerton, *Dissertation on the Origin of the Scythians or Goths* (London, 1787), in *An Enquiry into the History of Scotland*, 2 vols (London, 1789) II, pp. 68–9.

75. Ibid., pp. 68–9, iv–v.

76. Ledwich, *Antiquities of Ireland* (Dublin, 1790) pp. 135, 137.

77. Pinkerton, *An Essay on Medals*, 2 vols (London, 1789), I, pp. 118–28. Ledwich cited this section in *Antiquities of Ireland*, pp. 122–3.

78. Ibid., pp. 114, 116.

79. Ledwich, 'Essay on the Study of Irish Antiquities', pp. 87–9.

80. Ledwich to Joseph Cooper Walker, [23 Dec. 1788], T.C.D., ms. 1461(3), fol. 101.

81. For examples see Ledwich, *Antiquities of Ireland*, pp. 259, 261, 264.

82. Ibid., p. 270.

83. Ibid.

84. Ibid., pp. 260–61.

85. Ibid., p. 261.

86. Ibid., pp. 275–7.

87. Ibid., pp. 119, 351–2.

88. Ibid., p. 119.

89. Ibid.

90. Ibid., p. 214.

91. Ibid., p. 450.

92. Ibid., p. 197.

93. Ledwich to Walker, 17 Apr. 1787; Mar. 1787, T.C.D., Ms. 1461(2), fols. 225, 202.

94. Ledwich to Walker, 17 Apr. 1787, ibid., fol. 225.

95. Ledwich to Walker, 19 Jun. 1786, 13 Mar. 1787, ibid., fols. 120, 209.

96. Ledwich to Walker, 17 Apr. 1787, ibid., fol. 225.

97. Lord Charlemont to ?Malone, 18 Jul. 1795, *Historical Manuscripts Commission: 13th Report, Appendix, part viii*, pp. 263–4.

98. Lord Charlemont to Lord Moira, n.d., ibid., p. 380.

Seventeenth-Century Ghosts

1. David Hume, *The History of England from the Invasion of Julius Caesar to the Accession of Henry VII* (London, 1762), p. 299.

2. Hume, *The History of Great Britain. Vol. I. Containing the Reigns of James I and Charles I* (reprint of first edition [Edinburgh, 1754]: Harmondsworth, 1970), p. 119.

3. Ibid., pp. 459–61.

4. David Berman, 'David Hume on the 1641 Rebellion in Ireland', *Studies*, 65 (1976), pp. 101–12.

5. Nicholas Canny, 'What Really Happened in Ireland in 1641?' in Jane Ohlmeyer (ed.), *Ireland: from Independence to Occupation, 1641–1660* (Cambridge, 1995), pp. 31–2; *idem, Making Ireland British, 1580–1650* (Oxford, 2001), pp. 461–550.

6. W.E.H. Lecky quoted in P.J. Corish, 'The Rising of 1641 and the Catholic Confederacy, 1641–5' in T.W. Moody, F.X. Martin and F.J. Byrne (eds), *A New History of Ireland III* (Oxford, 1976, third impression, 1991), p. 291.

7. Ibid. For the work of recent scholars, see Brian Mac Cuarta (ed), *Ulster 1641: Aspects of the Rising* (Belfast, 1993), especially Hilary Simms, 'Violence in Co. Armagh, 1641', pp. 122–38.

8. Toby Barnard, '1641: a Bibliographical Essay' in Mac Cuarta (ed.), *Ulster 1641*, p. 175.

9. Corish, 'The Rising of 1641', p. 292.

10. John Temple, *The Irish Rebellion: or an History of the Beginnings and first Progresse of the Generall Rebellion raised within the Kingdom of Ireland, upon the three and twentieth day of October, in the year, 1641. Together with the barbarous Cruelties and Bloody Massacres which ensued thereupon* (London, 1646), pp. 1–2.

11. Canny, 'What Really Happened in Ireland in 1641?', pp. 25–6.

12. Barnard, '1641: a Bibliographical Essay', p. 175.

13. Thomas Bartlett, 'A New History of Ireland', *Past and Present*, 116 (Aug. 1987), pp. 214–15.

14. On the editions of Temple, see Barnard, '1641: a Bibliographical Essay', p. 179.

15. This was pointed out by Ann Laurence in her unpublished paper, 'English Images of the Irish: the Rising of 1641', Irish Historians in Britain Conference, York, April 1990.

16. Temple, *The Irish Rebellion* (London, 1746); ibid. (Cork, 1766).

17. Quoted in Jacqueline Hill, '1641 and the Quest for Catholic Emancipation in Ireland, 1691–1829' in Mac Cuarta (ed.), *Ulster 1641*, p. 160.

18. T.C. Barnard, 'The Uses of 23 October 1641 and Irish Protestant Celebrations', *English Historical Review*, cvi (1991), p. 914. See also James Kelly, '"The Glorious and Immortal Memory": Commemoration and Protestant Identity in Ireland 1660–1800', *Proceedings of the Royal Irish Academy*, 94c (1994), pp. 26–8.

19. Barnard, 'Uses of 23 October 1641', pp. 897, 894.

20. Quoted in ibid., p. 897.

21. From sermon quoted in ibid., pp. 900–901.

22. Ibid., p. 914. See also James Kelly, 'Conservative Protestant Political Thought in Late Eighteenth-Century Ireland', in S.J. Connolly (ed.), *Political Ideas in Eighteenth-Century Ireland* (Dublin, 2000), pp. 190–91.

23. Charles O'Conor to John Curry, 27 Nov. 1770, in *O'Conor Letters*, I, p. 279. See also O'Conor to Curry, 23 Oct. 1758, in ibid., p. 66.

224 Notes to pp. 144–6

24. Charles O'Conor, 'Account of the Author' in John Curry, *An Historical and Critical Review of the Civil Wars in Ireland from the Reign of Queen Elizabeth to the Settlement under King William*, 2 vols, ([1775] 2nd edn, Dublin, 1786), I, p. vi.

25. Hill, '1641 and the Quest', pp. 160–63.

26. Walter Harris, *Fiction Unmasked* (Dublin, 1752), pp. vi–vii. On this work, see Eoin Magennis, 'A "Beleagured Protestant"?: Walter Harris and the Writing of *Fiction Unmasked* in Mid-Eighteenth-Century Ireland', *Eighteenth-Century Ireland*, 13 (1998), pp. 86–111.

27. John Curry, *Historical Memoirs of the Irish Rebellion in the year 1641* (London, 1758), p. xxvi. It is very likely that this 'Advertisement' was written by O'Conor (see O'Conor to Curry, 17 Aug. 1757, in *O'Conor Letters*, I, pp. 34–5).

28. See Berman, 'David Hume on the 1641 Rebellion in Ireland', pp. 103–8.

29. On their pamphleteering, see C.D.A. Leighton, *Catholicism in a Protestant Kingdom* (London, 1994), pp. 90–111.

30. For the reported view of Anthony Dermot, Secretary to the Catholic Committee, see O'Conor to Curry, 29 Aug. 1757, in *O'Conor Letters*, I, p. 36. On attempts to introduce registration of clergy at this time, see Maureen Wall, 'Catholics in mid-century Ireland', *Catholic Ireland in the Eighteenth Century*, ed. Gerard O'Brien (Dublin, 1989), pp. 98–100.

31. Curry, *Historical Memoirs*, pp. 63–71.

32. *Idem, Historical and Critical Review*, I, pp. 195–205.

33. Barnard, '1641: a Bibliographical Essay', p. 183.

34. Vallancey to O'Conor, 20 Jan. 1771, R.I.A., Stowe ms. BI.2.

35. O'Conor to George Faulkner, 28 Oct. 1766, 13 Jun. 1767, in *O'Conor Letters*, I, pp. 205–06, 225–6; Thomas Leland to O'Conor, 8 Mar. 1771, R.I.A. Stowe ms. BI.2.

36. See Love, 'Charles O'Conor of Belanagare and Thomas Leland's "Philosophical" History of Ireland', *Irish Historical Studies*, 13 (1962), pp. 11–12.

37. Ferdinando Warner, *The History of the Rebellion and Civil War in Ireland*, 2 vols (Dublin, [1767] 1768), II, pp. 6–8. See also Barnard, '1641: a Bibliographical Essay', p. 182.

38. For a modern interpretation of these, see Raymond Gillespie, 'Destabilizing Ulster, 1641–2' in Mac Cuarta (ed.), *Ulster 1641*, pp. 118–19.

39. Curry, *Historical and Critical Review*, I, pp. 206–7.

40. O'Conor to Denis O'Conor, 11 Apr. 1775, in *O'Conor Letters*, II, p. 76.

41. [O'Conor], 'Advertisement' in Curry, *Historical Memoirs*, pp. xxvi.

42. Ibid., pp. ix.

43. Ibid., pp. xi–xii.

44. James Touchet, *The Earl of Castlehaven's Memoirs: or his Review of the Late Wars of Ireland* [ed. Charles O'Conor] (Waterford, 1753), editor's preface, pp. iv–vii. James Touchet, third earl of Castlehaven (1617?-1684) was a commander in the Confederate Catholic army from 1642 to 1651 (*Concise D.N.B.*, p. 1307).

45. It is likely that Curry was following the lead of Warner, who had used the term 'civil war' in the title of his study of 1641. Warner in turn was responding to Lord Clarendon, *The History of the Rebellion and Civil Wars in Ireland* (London, 1721), which was an appendix to his *History of the Rebellion and Civil Wars in England* (1702–4).

46. [O'Conor], editor's preface, Touchet, *Castlehaven's Memoirs*, pp. xiii, xv.

47. O'Conor to Curry, n.d., Clonalis, ms. 8.3.HS. 023. Incorrectly transcribed in *O'Conor Letters*, I, pp. 51–2. See also O'Conor to Curry, 23 Sept. 1758, in ibid., I, p. 64.

48. O'Conor to Curry, n.d., Clonalis, ms. 8.3.HS. 023.

49. O'Conor to Curry, 24 Nov. 1760, Clonalis, ms. 8.3. HS. 023. Incorrectly transcribed in *O'Conor Letters*, I, pp. 103–4.

50. O'Conor to Edmund Burke, 25 Apr. 1765, in ibid., p. 191.

51. O'Conor to Curry, 28 Sept. 1764, in ibid., p. 186.

52. O'Conor, manuscript draft of *Dissertations* (1766), Clonalis, ms. 8.4.HL.219.

53. O'Conor to Curry, 28 Sept. 1764, in *O'Conor Letters*, I, p.187.

54. O'Conor to Curry, 19 Aug. 1763, 13 Jul. 1764, 17 Jul. 1764, [23 Aug. 1764], in ibid., pp. 172–3, 181–3,. To judge from his extant correspondence, O'Conor did spend more time in Dublin, but on business rather than for reasons of scholarship.

55. O'Conor to Curry, 24 Jun. 1761, in ibid., pp. 113–14.

56. O'Conor to Curry, 1 Jun. 1766, in ibid., p. 198. Warner's first volume dealing with the pre-colonial period was published in 1763 (Ferdinando Warner, *History of Ireland* (London, 1763)). On Warner's *History* see also Leerssen, *Mere Irish*, pp. 387–9.

57. Warner, *History of the Rebellion and Civil War in Ireland*, II, pp. 6–10.

58. [John Curry] to O'Conor, 24 Nov. 1770, R.I.A., Stowe ms. B.I. 2.

59. Thomas Leland, 'On the Anniversary of the Irish Rebellion', *Sermons on Various Subjects*, 3 vols (Dublin, 1788), III, pp. 18–19.

60. Ibid.

61. Love, 'Charles O'Conor of Belanagare', pp. 2–4, 11–12.

62. Curry to O'Conor, 23 Dec. 1771, R.I.A., Stowe ms. BI.2. On Leland's self-characterisation, see O'Conor to Curry, 12 Feb. 1772, in *O'Conor Letters*, II, p. 9. For a good account, see Love, 'Charles O'Conor of Belanagare', pp. 10–15.

63. Thomas Leland, *The History of Ireland from the Invasion of Henry II*, 3 vols (London, 1773), I, pp. xli–xlii.

64. Ibid., III, pp. 88, 127.

65. Joseph Liechty, 'Testing the Depth of Catholic/Protestant Conflict: the Case of Thomas Leland's *History of Ireland*, 1773', *Archivium Hibernicum*, 42 (1987), pp. 20–21.

66. Leland, *History of Ireland*, III, pp. 128–9. Leland was correct – see Gillespie, 'Destabilizing Ulster, 1641–2', p. 113.

67. John Curry, *Occasional Remarks on certain Passages in Dr Leland's History of Ireland, relative to the Irish Rebellion of 1641* (London, 1773).

68. Love, 'Charles O'Conor of Belanagare', pp. 19–20.

69. O'Conor to Curry, 28 Jan. 1772, in *O'Conor Letters*, II, p. 7. See also, O'Conor to Archbishop Carpenter, 22 Nov. 1780, Clonalis, ms., 8.4. HS. 141.

70. O'Conor to Thomas O'Gorman, 14 Mar. 1781, in *O'Conor Letters*, II, pp. 161–2. The Huntingdon Library holds a series of twelve notebooks of traditional-style annals in Irish and English compiled by O'Conor, beginning in 35 BC and ending in the mid-seventeenth century (San Marino, Huntingdon Library, Sto 1405 (2 vols) and Sto 1415 (10 vols)).

71. O'Conor to O'Gorman, 6 Aug. 1783, in *O'Conor Letters*, II, p. 194.

72. O'Conor to O'Gorman, 17 Jan. 1781, in ibid., p. 158.

73. O'Conor to O'Gorman, 14 Mar. 1781, in ibid., pp. 161–2.

74. O'Conor to O'Gorman, 28 Jun. 1781, in ibid., p. 167.

75. O'Conor to O'Gorman, 15 Aug. 1784, in ibid., p. 217. On Campbell, see below.

76. O'Conor to O'Gorman, 2 Mar. 1784, in ibid., p. 202; O'Conor to O'Gorman, 14 Mar. 1781, in ibid., pp. 161–2. There is no trace of 'The Revolutions of Ireland' among the O'Conor papers at Clonalis. O'Conor said that he would burn it if he did not finish it (O'Conor to O'Gorman, 31 May 1783, in ibid., p. 189).

77. Leighton, *Catholicism in a Protestant Kingdom*, p. 37.

78. [O'Conor], 'Advertisement' in Curry, *Historical Memoirs*, pp. xvii–xviii.

79. O'Conor, 'An Account of the Author' in Curry, *An Historical and Critical Review*, I, pp. iv–v.

80. *The Complete Peerage of England, Scotland and Ireland, Great Britain and the United Kingdom*, 13 vols (London, 1910–40), V, p. 473. Gormanston to O'Conor, 5 May 1785, 23 May 1785, 26 Aug. 1785, San Marino, Huntingdon Library, Stowe Collection.

81. O'Conor to Lord Gormanston, 27 May 1785, 2 Jun. 1785, N.L.I., ms. 13,755 (29). These two letters to Gormanston and another to the Catholic Archbishop of Dublin, John Carpenter, are not in *O'Conor Letters*.

82. O'Conor to John Carpenter, 13 May 1785, N.L.I., ms.13,755(29).

83. Ibid.; O'Conor to Gormanston, 27 May 1785, ibid.

84. Quoted in James Kelly, 'The Genesis of "Protestant Ascendancy": the Rightboy Disturbances of the 1780s and their Impact upon Protestant Opinion' in Gerard O'Brien (ed.), *Parliament, Politics and People* (Dublin, 1989), p.102.

85. Details can be found in the following letters: O'Conor to Joseph Cooper Walker, 16 Feb. 1786, and 8 Mar. 1786; O'Conor to O'Gorman, 25 Feb. 1786, and 7 Mar. 1786 (in *O'Conor Letters*, II, pp. 237–42).

86. Thomas Campbell, *Diary of a Visit to England*, ed. J.L. Clifford (2nd edn, Cambridge, 1947), p. 97.

87. Walter Love, 'Edmund Burke and an Irish Historiographical Controversy', *History and Theory*, 2 (1962), p. 182.

88. Campbell to John Pinkerton, 6 Feb. 1788, Nichols, *Lit. Illus.*, VII, p. 773.

89. Campbell, *Strictures on the Ecclesiastical and Literary History of Ireland* (Dublin, 1789), p. 3.

90. Ibid., pp. 3, 42. Burke was not impressed by *Strictures* and instructed his son in 1792 to retrieve the manuscripts from Campbell: 'Let him not triffle [sic] with you. I have triffled in giving them to him' (quoted in Love, 'Edmund Burke', p. 194, fn. 28).

91. Campbell appears to have spent the best part of two years, from 1790 to 1792, on this project, apparently at the behest of Thomas Percy, who used Campbell's unfinished manuscript partly as the basis for his 'Life of Oliver Goldsmith', which was prefixed to *The Miscellaneous Works of Oliver Goldsmith, M.D.*, 4 vols (London, 1801) (Bertram H. Davis, *Thomas Percy: a Scholar-Cleric in the Age of Johnson* (Philadelphia, 1989), pp. 281, 295). Campbell's manuscript is in the British Library: Add. ms. 42517.

92. O'Conor called his 'the Revolutions of Ireland' (O'Conor to O'Gorman, 6 Aug. 1783, in *O'Conor Letters*, II, p. 194); Campbell had 'History of the Revolutions of Ireland' (Campbell to Bishop Percy, 25 Oct. 1787, in Nichols, *Lit. Illus.*, VII, pp. 771–2).

93. Love, 'Edmund Burke', p. 187.

94.   Ibid.
95.   O'Conor to O'Gorman, 14 Jul. 1784, in *O'Conor Letters*, II, p. 212.
96.   Ibid.
97.   Campbell, *Philosophical Survey*, p. 68; idem, *Strictures*, pp. 35–9.
98.   Campbell, *Philosophical Survey*, pp. 251–2.
99.   Samuel Johnson to Charles O'Conor, 9 Apr. 1757, quoted in James Boswell, *The Life of Samuel Johnson*, 2 vols (London, [1791] 1973), I, p. 195.
100. Campbell, *Strictures*, p. 3. In the letter Johnson urged O'Conor to write a history of early medieval Ireland 'when Ireland was the school of the West' (Johnson to O'Conor, 19 May 1777, quoted in Boswell, *Life of Samuel Johnson*, II, pp. 81–2).
101. O'Conor to O'Gorman, 28 Jul. 1784, in *O'Conor Letters*, II, p. 215.
102. O'Conor to Archbishop Carpenter, 29 Jul. 1784, Clonalis, ms. 8.4.HS. 141.
103. O'Conor to O'Gorman, 15 Aug. 1784, 27 Nov. 1784, in *O'Conor Letters*, II, pp. 217, 220.
104. O'Conor to O'Gorman, 15 Aug. 1784, in ibid., p. 217.
105. O'Conor to O'Gorman, 27 Nov. 1784, in ibid., II, pp. 220–21.
106. Campbell to Percy, 25 Oct. 1787, in Nichols, *Lit. Illus.*, VII, pp. 770–71.
107. Ibid., pp. 771–2.
108. William Camden, *Britannia*, ed. Richard Gough, 3 vols (London, 1789). Campbell's 'Historical Sketch' is in volume III, pp. 21–8.
109. On these letters and on Campbell's 'Sketch' in the *Dublin Chronicle*, see Love, 'Edmund Burke', pp. 187–90.
110. Campbell, *Strictures*, pp. 253–4.
111. Campbell to Richard Gough, 3 Mar. 1788, in Nichols, *Lit. Illus.*, VII, pp. 804–5.
112. Campbell to Percy, 15 Dec. 1788, in ibid., pp. 775–6.
113. Ibid.; Campbell, 'A View of the Revenues of Ireland', *Strictures*, pp. 404–18.
114. Campbell, *Strictures*, p. 322.
115. Ibid., pp. 351–3.
116. Ibid., pp. 353, 357.
117. Ibid., pp. 35–9.
118. *Dublin Chronicle*, 13–15 Mar. 1788; Campbell, *Strictures*, pp. 36–9.
119. Ibid.
120. Ibid., pp. 25, 27.
121. Ibid., pp. 25–6, 254. On Voltaire and Ireland, see Graham Gargett, 'Voltaire's View of the Irish' in Gargett and Geraldine Sheridan (eds), *Ireland and the French Enlightenment, 1700–1800* (Basingstoke, London and New York, 1999), pp. 152–70.
122. Campbell, *Strictures*, pp. 253–4.
123. Leighton, *Catholicism in a Protestant Kingdom*, pp. 89–127.
124. *Dublin Chronicle*, 13–15 Mar. 1788; Campbell, *Strictures*, p. 38.
125. Spenser had noted that the barbarous lifestyle of the Irish made them 'very valiant and hardy' (Edmund Spenser, *A View of the Present State of Ireland*, ed. W.L. Renwick (Oxford, 1970) p. 72).
126. Campbell, *Strictures*, p. 254.
127. Idem, *Philosophical Survey*, pp. 321–7.
128. Idem, *Strictures*, p. 253.
129. Edward Ledwich, 'History of the Antiquities of Irishtown and Kilkenny', *Collectanea*, II, no. ix [1781], p. 415.

130. Hill, '1641 and the Quest', p. 167.
131. James Laffan to John Curry, 1 Feb. 1776, R.I.A., Stowe ms. BI.2; Ledwich to Joseph Cooper Walker, 13 Mar. 1787, T.C.D., ms. 1461(2), fol. 209; Ledwich to Walker, 13 May 1786, ibid., fol. 107.
132. See James Kelly, '"We were all to have been massacred": Irish Protestants and the experience of rebellion' in Thomas Bartlett et al (eds), 1798: a Bicentenary Perspective (Dublin, 2003), pp. 312–30.
133. Hill, '1641 and the Quest', pp. 170–71, 165.
134. Jim Smyth, 'Anti-Catholicism, Conservatism and Conspiracy: Sir Richard Musgrave's Memoirs of the Different Rebellions in Ireland', Eighteenth-Century Life, 22, n.s., 3 (Nov. 1998), pp. 62–73.
135. David Dickson, 'Foreword' in Richard Musgrave, Memoirs of the Irish Rebellion of 1798 ([1801] 4th edn: Fort Wayne, Indiana, 1995), pp. vi–vii; Musgrave, ibid., p. 881n.
136. Ibid., pp. 851, 17.
137. Ibid., pp. 885, xxv. Musgrave's Memoirs had a considerable impact on conservative opinion in Britain as well as Ireland (see James J. Sack, From Jacobite to Conservative: Reaction and Orthodoxy in Britain, c. 1760–1832 (Cambridge, 1993), pp. 96–8, 240–42).
138. Musgrave, Memoirs, pp. 863–71.
139. Ibid., pp. 883, 853, 401. On Musgrave's use of the lexicon and tropes of barbarism, see Smyth, 'Anti-Catholicism, Conservatism and Conspiracy', pp. 66–7; Kevin Whelan, The Tree of Liberty: Radicalism, Catholicism and the Construction of Irish Identity, 1760–1830 (Cork, 1996), p. 138.
140. Musgrave, Memoirs, pp. 493, 823–4.
141. Ledwich lent Musgrave books while he was writing the Memoirs (Ledwich to Thomas Percy, 18 Jul. 1799, in Nichols, Lit. Illus., VII, pp. 817–18).
142. Affidavit by William Abraham, 27 Dec. 1784, Musgrave, Memoirs, pp. 604–5. On the Rightboys' 'carefully staged rituals of violence', see J.S. Donnelly, 'The Rightboy Movement, 1785–8', Studia Hibernica, 17–18 (1977–8), pp. 182–5.

Ascendancy, Rebellion and the Collapse of the Antiquarian Enterprise

1. For an early nineteenth-century novelist's use of this myth, see Tom Dunne, 'Fiction as "the best history of nations": Lady Morgan's Irish Novels' in Tom Dunne (ed.), The Writer as Witness (Cork, 1987), pp. 151–3.
2. Gerard O'Brien, 'The Grattan Mystique', Eighteenth-Century Ireland, 1 (1986), pp. 177–94; see also J.J. Lee, 'Grattan's Parliament' in Brian Farrell (ed.), The Irish Parliamentary Tradition (Dublin, 1973), pp. 149–59.
3. For a lively debate on the origins of 'Protestant Ascendancy' see: W.J. McCormack, Ascendancy and Tradition in Anglo-Irish Literary History from 1789 to 1939 (Oxford, 1985), pp. 61–96; idem, 'Vision and Revision in the Study of Eighteenth-Century Irish Parliamentary Rhetoric', Eighteenth-Century Ireland, 2 (1987), pp. 7–35; James Kelly, 'The Genesis of "Protestant Ascendancy": the Rightboy Disturbances of the 1780s and their Impact upon Protestant Opinion' in Gerard O'Brien (ed.), Parliament, Politics and People (Dublin, 1989), pp.

93–127; McCormack, 'Eighteenth-Century Ascendancy: Yeats and the Historians', *Eighteenth-Century Ireland*, 4 (1989), pp. 159–81; J.R. Hill, 'The Meaning and Significance of "Protestant Ascendancy", 1787–1840' in *Ireland after the Union: Proceedings of the Second Joint Meeting of the Royal Irish Academy and the British Academy* (Oxford, 1989), pp. 1–22; Thomas Bartlett, '"A People Made Rather for Copies than Originals": the Anglo-Irish, 1760–1800', *The International History Review*, 12 (1990), pp. 11–25; Kelly, 'Eighteenth-Century Ascendancy: a Commentary', *Eighteenth-Century Ireland*, 5 (1990), pp. 173–87; W.J. McCormack, *The Dublin Paper War of 1786–1788* (Dublin, 1993).

4. Peter Gibbon, *The Origins of Ulster Unionism* (Manchester, 1975), Chapter 2; L.M. Cullen, *The Emergence of Modern Ireland 1600–1900* (Dublin, 1983), pp. 25–38; Kevin Whelan, 'The Regional Impact of Irish Catholicism' in W.J. Smyth and Kevin Whelan (eds), *Common Ground: Essays on the Historical Geography of Ireland* (Cork, 1988), pp. 253–77.

5. J.S. Donnelly, 'The Rightboy Movement, 1785–8', *Studia Hibernica*, 17–18 (1977–8), pp. 120–202; James Kelly, 'Inter-Denominational Relations and Religious Toleration in Late Eighteenth-Century Ireland: the "Paper War" of 1786–88', *Eighteenth-Century Ireland*, 3 (1988), pp. 39–68.

6. Marianne Elliott, *Wolfe Tone: Prophet of Irish Independence* (New Haven, 1989), Chapter 15.

7. Thomas Bartlett, 'An End to Moral Economy: the Irish Militia Disturbances of 1793' in C.H.E. Philpin (ed.), *Nationalism and Popular Protest in Ireland* (Cambridge, 1987), pp. 191–218.

8. Jim Smyth, 'Popular Politicisation, Defenderism and the Catholic Question' in Hugh Gough and David Dickson (eds), *Ireland and the French Revolution* (Dublin, 1990), pp. 109–16; Elliott, 'The Origins and Transformation of Early Irish Republicanism', *International Review of Social History*, 23 (1978), pp. 405–28; Hereward Senior, *Orangeism in Ireland and Britain, 1795–1836* (London, 1966).

9. Cullen, 'The 1798 Rebellion in Wexford: United Irishmen Organisation, Membership, Leadership', in K. Whelan and W. Nolan (eds), *Wexford: History and Society* (Dublin, 1987), pp. 248–95; Whelan, 'Politicisation in County Wexford and the Origins of the 1798 Rebellion' in Gough and Dickson (eds), *Ireland and the French Revolution*, pp. 156–78.

10. Maureen Wall, 'The Making of Gardiner's Relief Act, 1781–2', *Catholic Ireland in the Eighteenth Century*, ed. Gerard O'Brien (Dublin, 1989), p. 145.

11. Kelly, 'Inter-Denominational Relations', pp. 42–3, 44.

12. Ibid., pp. 44–5; for the Whiteboys, see J.S. Donnelly, 'The Whiteboy Movement, 1761–5', *Irish Historical Studies*, 21 (1978–9), pp. 20–54.

13. Kelly, 'Inter-Denominational Relations', pp. 46, 52.

14. Kelly, 'The Genesis of "Protestant Ascendancy"', p. 115.

15. Ibid., pp. 125–7. For Kelly's latest thoughts on the 'Protestant Ascendancy' ethos and its evolution, see *idem*, 'Conservative Protestant Political Thought in Late Eighteenth-Century Ireland' in S.J. Connolly (ed.), *Political Ideas in Eighteenth-Century Ireland* (Dublin, 2000), pp. 185–220.

16. William Webb, *An Analysis of the History and Antiquities of Ireland, prior to the Fifth Century. To which is subjoined a General History of the Celtic Nations* (Dublin, 1791), p. iv. Webb is not listed in either Crone's or Webb's biographical dictionaries; according to his entry in the main catalogue of Cambridge University Library, he died in 1791.

17. Ibid., pp. 7, 177–8.
18. Ibid., p. 219.
19. Ibid., pp. 14, 67, 265–9. On Barnard, see Chapter 2 above.
20. Ibid., p. 270. On Leland, see Chapter 2 above.
21. Ibid., pp. 144, 160, 165.
22. Roderic O'Flaherty, *Ogygia*, translated by James Hely (Dublin, 1793), pp. lxxxiv–xci.
23. Hely, 'Translator's address', ibid., pp. v–vi.
24. Ibid., pp. vi, ix, viii.
25. J. Th. Leerssen, *Mere Irish and Fíor-Ghael* (Amsterdam and Philadelphia, 1986), pp. 420–21; Lawrence Parsons, *Observations on the Bequest of Henry Flood Esq. to Trinity College Dublin* (Dublin, 1795); E. Hayes, *Report of Cases argued and determined in the Court of Exchequer* (London, 1837), pp. 611–41. See Chapter 2 above.
26. Kelly, 'Inter-Denominational Relations', pp. 44, 47–9, 52–6, 58–60. See also McCormack, *The Dublin Paper War*, pp. 31–91.
27. O'Conor, Charles, 'Reflections on the History of Ireland during the Times of Heathenism; with Observations on some late Publications on that Subject. Addressed to Lieut. Col. Charles Vallancey', in *Collectanea*, III, no. x [1782], pp. 213–46; *idem*, 'Second Letter to Colonel Vallancey, on the Heathen State, and Antient Topography of Ireland', in ibid., no. xii [1783], pp. 649–77; *idem*, 'Third Letter from Charles O'Conor, Esq.; to Colonel Vallancey', in ibid., IV, no. xiii [1784], pp. 107–34.
28. Sylvester O'Halloran, 'A Martial Ode, sung at the Battle of Cnucha . . . with a literal Translation and Notes', *Transactions of the Royal Irish Academy*, 2 (1788), antiquities section, pp. 7–17. He continued to publish on medical subjects: O'Halloran, *A New Treatise on the Different Disorders arising from External Injuries of the Head* (Dublin, 1793).
29. Minutes of the Committee of Antiquities, R.I.A., 28 Feb. 1786 [no catalogue number]; Kelly, 'Inter-Denominational Relations', p. 46.
30. O'Conor to Thomas O'Gorman, 29 Oct. 1784, in *O'Conor Letters*, II, p. 219.
31. An account of the case can be found in ibid., Introduction, pp. x–xii.
32. Ibid.; O'Conor to O'Gorman, 28 Jun. 1781, in ibid., p. 167.
33. Vallancey passed on to Orde two letters from O'Conor in which he gave assurances of the loyalty of Catholics. One of the letters by O'Conor is undated but was written *c.* 25–30 Sept. 1784, and the other is from 13 Oct. 1784. They are not included in the Wards' edition of his letters. (Vallancey to Thomas Orde, 2 Oct. 1784, 16 Oct. 1784, N.L.I., ms. 16,350, fol. 40.)
34. Kelly, 'Inter-Denominational Relations', p. 50; see also James Kelly, '"A Wild Capuchin of Cork": Fr Arthur O'Leary' in Gerard Moran (ed.), *Radical Priests* (Dublin, 1998), pp. 74–92.
35. Vallancey to Orde, 2 Oct. 1784, N.L.I., ms. 16,350, fol. 40. O'Conor reported on the exchange to Charles Ryan, 22 Dec. 1784, in *O'Conor Letters*, II, pp. 221–2.
36. O'Conor to O'Gorman, 16 Oct. 1784, in ibid., p. 218.
37. O'Conor to Charles Ryan, 28 Mar. 1787, in ibid., p. 263.
38. See Chapter 6 above.
39. O'Conor, 'An Account of the Author' in John Curry, *An Historical and Critical Review of the Civil Wars in Ireland*, 2 vols (Dublin, 1786), I, pp. vii–viii, iv–v.

40. O'Conor to Charles Ryan, 28 Mar. 1787, in *O'Conor Letters*, II, p. 263. For the membership and workings of the Catholic Committee at this time, see 'The Minute Book of the Catholic Committee, 1773–92', ed. R. Dudley Edwards, *Archivium Hibernicum*, 9 (1942), pp. 92–111.

41. Ledwich to Walker, 17 Apr. 1787, T.C.D., ms. 1461(2), fol. 225.

42. O'Conor to Ryan, 28 Mar. 1787, in *O'Conor Letters*, II, p. 264.

43. Vallancey to O'Conor, 28 Feb. 1788, San Marino, Huntingdon Library, Stowe Collection; O'Conor to J.C. Walker, 13 May 1785, D.C.L.A., ms. 203, fols 5–6. See also Catherine Sheehan, 'The O'Conor Manuscripts in the Stowe Ashburnham Collection', *Studies*, 41 (1952), pp. 363–4.

44. Richard Woodward, *The Present State of the Church of Ireland* (Dublin, 1808), p. 53; Arthur O'Leary, *A Defence of the Conduct and Writings of the Rev. Arthur O'Leary during the late Disturbances in Munster* (London, 1788), pp. 123–4. See also McCormack, *The Dublin Paper War*, pp. 95–6.

45. R.B. McDowell, 'The Main Narrative' in T. Ó Raifeartaigh (ed.), *The Royal Irish Academy: a Bicentennial History, 1785–1985* (Dublin, 1985), p. 1.

46. Ibid., pp. 2–3; G.L.H. Davies, 'The Making of Irish Geography, Part IV: the Physico-Historical Society, 1744–52', *Irish Geography*, xii (1979), pp. 92–8; Charles O'Conor (S.J.), 'Origins of the Royal Irish Academy', *Studies*, 38 (1949), pp. 332–3.

47. Charles Smith, *The Antient and Present State of the County and City of Waterford* (Dublin, 1746); idem, *The Antient and Present State of the County and City of Cork*, 2 vols (Dublin, 1750); idem, *The Antient and Present State of the County of Kerry* (Dublin, 1756). For an excellent analysis of the surveys published under the auspices of the Physico-Historical Society, see Eoin Magennis, '"A land of milk and honey": the Physico-Historical Society, Improvement and the Surveys of Mid-Fighteenth-Century Ireland', *Proceedings of the Royal Irish Academy*, vol. 102C, no. 6 (2002), pp. 199–217.

48. Walter Love, 'The Hibernian Antiquarian Society', *Studies*, 51 (1962), pp. 422–8.

49. McDowell, 'The Main Narrative', pp. 10–12.

50. Ibid., p. 8.

51. Thomas Barnard, Bishop of Killaloe, who liaised with Sir Joseph Banks, President of the Royal Society, quoted in ibid., p. 9.

52. Barnard, quoted in ibid.

53. *The Charter of the Royal Irish Academy* (Dublin, 1997), p. 3.

54. Robert Burrowes, 'Preface', *Transactions of the Royal Irish Academy*, 1 (1787), p. xi.

55. Ibid., pp. ix–x.

56. Lord Charlemont, 'The Antiquity of the Woollen Manufacture in Ireland, proved from a Passage of an Antient Florentine Poet', ibid., antiquities section, pp. 22–3.

57. James Kelly, 'A "Genuine" Whig and Patriot: Lord Charlemont's Political Career' in Michael McCarthy (ed.), *Lord Charlemont and his Circle* (Dublin, 2001), p. 19; Charlemont, to Richard Sheridan, 10 Apr. 1790, *Historical Manuscripts Commission: 13th Report, Appendix, Part viii*, p. 123.

58. Chevalier Thomas O'Gorman, 'The Committee of Antiquarians of the Irish Academy', n.d., R.I.A., ms. 24/D/2, pp. 179–84. On O'Gorman, see Richard Hayes, 'A Forgotten Irish Antiquary: Chevalier Thomas O'Gorman, 1732–1809', *Studies*, 30 (1941), 587–96.

59.   McDowell, 'The Main Narrative', pp. 14–15.
60.   Quoted in ibid., no source given, p. 14.
61.   Ibid.
62.   Minutes of the Council of the R.I.A., 9 Jul. 1787, 3 Sept. 1787, 1 Oct. 1787, R.I.A., ms. 3/E/5.
63.   Thomas Barnard, 'An Enquiry concerning the Original of the Scots in Britain', *Transactions of the Royal Irish Academy*, 1 (1787), antiquities section, pp. 25–41.
64.   Minutes of Council of the R.I.A., 29 Nov. 1788, R.I.A., ms. 3/E/5; O'Halloran, 'A Martial Ode, sung at the Battle of Cnucha'. For an earlier draft of this paper, dated 29 Dec. 1787, see R.I.A., ms. 24/H/39.
65.   Theophilus O'Flanagan, 'Account of an ancient Inscription in Ogham Character on the Sepulchral Monument of an Irish Chief', *Transactions of the Royal Irish Academy*, 1 (1787), antiquities section, pp. 3–16.
66.   Charles O'Conor, 'Remarks on the "Essay on the Antiquity of the Irish Language" addressed to the printer of the *London Chronicle*, in the year 1772', *Collectanea*, II, no. viii (1781), pp. 340–41.
67.   Thomas Astle, *The Origin and Progress of Writing* (London, 1784), pp. 115–38.
68.   Charles Vallancey, 'Observations on the Alphabet of the Pagan Irish and of the Age in which Finn and Ossin Lived', *Archaeologia*, 7 (1785), pp. 277–9, 283.
69.   Ibid., pp. 279–83.
70.   R.I.A., Minute Book of the Committee of Antiquities, 9 Jun. 1785.
71.   Siobhán de h-Óir, 'The Mount Callan Ogham Stone and its Context', *North Munster Antiquarian Journal*, 25 (1983), pp. 47–9.
72.   Samuel Johnson, *Journey to the Western Islands of Scotland* (London, [1775] 1990), pp. 88–91.
73.   On the earliest of these, see Catherine Swift, *Ogam Stones and the earliest Irish Christians* (Maynooth, 1997).
74.   De h-Óir, 'The Mount Callan Ogham Stone', pp. 43–5. De h-Óir gives the following publishing details for Lloyd: Sean Lloyd, *A Short Tour or an Impartial Description of the County Clare* (Ennis, 1780), p. 9. I have consulted a manuscript copy of this book, entitled John Lloyd, 'Description of Co. Clare', Cork, University College Library, Special Collections; the reference to the Mount Callan ogham occurs on pp. 18–20.
75.   De h-Óir, 'The Mount Callan Ogham Stone', pp. 50–53, 54.
76.   O'Sullivan, 'The Irish Manuscripts in Case H in Trinity College Dublin', p. 229; on the fortunes of the Book of Ballymote before its donation to the R.I.A. by Thomas O'Gorman, see Alan Harrison, *The Dean's Friend: Anthony Raymond 1675–1726, Jonathan Swift and the Irish Language* (Dublin, 1999), pp. 96–9.
77.   Minutes of the Committee of Antiquities, R.I.A., Dec. 1786.
78.   Máire, Bean Í Sheanacháin, 'Theophilus Ó Flannagáin', *Galvia*, 3 (1956), pp. 19–29.
79.   O'Flanagan, 'Account of an ancient Inscription', pp. 3–4.
80.   Ibid., pp. 8–9, 14.
81.   O'Conor to O'Gorman, 1 Jun. 1784, 19 Jun. 1784, in *O'Conor Letters*, II, pp. 206, 210.
82.   In 1785, he wrote: 'If he [O'Flanagan] has deciphered it by a rule which must prove satisfactory to critics in that art, the discovery is a happy one' (O'Conor to O'Gorman, 22 Oct. 1785, in ibid., p. 228).

83. O'Conor to O'Gorman, 19 Jun. 1784, in ibid., p. 210.

84. O'Conor to O'Gorman, 1 Jun. 1784, in ibid., pp. 206–7. For his criticism of Macpherson, see O'Conor, *Dissertation on the First Migrations and Final Settlements of the Scots* (Dublin, 1766), pp. 24–9.

85. O'Conor to O'Gorman, 19 Jun. 1784, in *O'Conor Letters*, II, p. 210.

86. Ledwich, *Antiquities of Ireland* (Dublin, 1790), pp. 103, 88.

87. Ibid., pp. 103, 90–91.

88. On collectors, see Bernadette Cunningham and Raymond Gillespie, 'An Ulster Settler and his Irish Manuscripts', *Éigse*, 21 (1986), pp. 27–36; Alan Harrison, *Ag Cruinniú Meala: Anthony Raymond (1675–1726)* (Dublin, 1988); idem, *The Dean's Friend*; Diarmaid Ó Catháin, 'John Fergus MD, Eighteenth-Century Doctor, Book Collector and Irish Scholar', *J.R.S.A.I.*, 118 (1988), pp. 139–62; Catherine Sheehan, 'The Contribution of Charles O'Conor to Gaelic Scholarship in Eighteenth-Century Ireland', *Journal of Celtic Studies*, 2 (1958), pp. 222–31.

89. O'Sullivan, 'The Irish Manuscripts in Case H', pp. 233–8; Walter Love, 'Edmund Burke, Charles Vallancey, and the Sebright Manuscripts', *Hermathena*, 95 (July 1961), pp. 21–35. According to a letter by Vallancey to Charles O'Conor in 1785, Trinity were well advanced in plans to publish the Annals of Innisfallen in the original in a specially procured Irish typeface. The plan, which was the work of Thomas O'Gorman and the provost, Hely Hutchinson, was abandoned when Vallancey and O'Conor argued strongly that 'the annals of the 4 [sic] Masters were preferable – and those of Innisfallen but a puny work for the first publication' (Vallancey to O'Conor, 18 Sept. 1785, San Marino, Huntingdon Library, Stowe Collection).

90. Robin Flower, *Catalogue of Irish Manuscripts in the British Museum*, 3 vols (London, 1926–53), II, pp. 12–19.

91. William O'Sullivan, 'The Irish Manuscripts in Case H', pp. 229–30. The R.I.A. took responsibility for translating the Sebright collection of law tracts held in the library of T.C.D. (Minutes of the Antiquities Committee, 22 Feb. 1790, R.I.A.).

92. Revd Charles O'Conor to Joseph Cooper Walker, 6 Apr. 1788, T.C.D., ms. 1461(1), fol. 33. Eventually, on 31 May 1788, Council agreed that a letter should be written to the Cardinal Secretary of State, at Rome, requesting permission for O'Conor, as agent of the Academy, 'to see such manuscripts in the Vatican Library, as are likely to throw light on the Antient History of Ireland'. (Minutes of Council, 31 May 1788, R.I.A., ms. 3/E/5).

93. Minutes of Council, 4 Jul. 1785, R.I.A., ms. 3/E/5. On O'Gorman's scribal work, see Nessa Ní Shéaghdha, 'Irish Scholars and Scribes in Eighteenth-Century Dublin', *Eighteenth-Century Ireland*, 4 (1989), pp. 50–52.

94. Minutes of the Antiquities Committee, Dec. 1786, R.I.A.

95. Minutes of Council, 4 Jul. 1785, R.I.A., ms. 3/E/5; Minutes of Antiquities Committee, Dec. 1786, R.I.A.

96. Í Sheanacháin, 'Theophilus Ó Flannagáin', pp. 22–3. He was also employed by Trinity in 1786 to catalogue the newly acquired Sebright manuscripts (O'Sullivan, 'The Irish Manuscripts in Case H', p. 243).

97. Minutes of Council, 10 May 1788, R.I.A., ms. 3/E/5.

98. Ibid., 17 May 1788.

99. Minutes of the Antiquities Committee, 17 May 1788, R.I.A.

100. O'Conor to Thomas O'Gorman, 14 Jul. 1784, in *O'Conor Letters*, II, p. 212. See above, Chapter 5.

101. Thomas Campbell, *Strictures on the Ecclesiastical and Literary History of Ireland* (Dublin, 1789), p. 23; Ledwich to Richard Gough, 10 Dec. 1787, in Nichols, *Lit. Illus.*, VII, pp. 853–4.

102. Minutes of Council, 18 Apr. 1789, R.I.A., ms. 3/E/5.

103. Ibid., 8 May 1789; Minutes of the Antiquities Committee, 22 Feb. 1790, R.I.A. In January 1788, O'Conor's correspondent Clement Archer reported that O'Flanagan had confessed to him that he was having 'great difficulty in translating some fragments of the Brehon Laws' for the Academy (Clement Archer to O'Conor, 19 Jan. 1788, San Marino, Huntingdon Library, Stowe Collection).

104. Minutes of Council, 11 Feb. 1792, R.I.A., ms. 3/E/5; Minutes of the Antiquities Committee, 19 Dec. 1795, R.I.A.

105. Ibid., 20 Nov. 1790. In 1797 Thomas O'Gorman recommended O'Connell to the Antiquities Committee as 'the proper person to translate the Brehon Laws' (ibid., 18 Mar. 1797). On O'Connell, see Dermot F. Gleeson, 'Peter O'Connell, Scholar and Scribe', *Studies*, 33 (1944), pp. 342–8.

106. Í Sheanacháin, 'Theophilus Ó Flannagáin'.

107. Séamus Ua Casaide, 'Patrick Lynch, Secretary to the Gaelic Society of Dublin', *Journal of the Waterford and South-East of Ireland Archaeological Society*, xv (1912), pp. 46–50. See also P.J. Dowling, 'Patrick Lynch, Schoolmaster, 1754–1818', *Studies*, 20 (1931), pp. 461–72.

108. O'Sullivan, 'The Irish Manuscripts in Case H', p. 229. The manuscript was donated by O'Conor's friend Thomas O'Gorman, but appears in the Academy minutes as the gift of Vallancey (Minutes of the Royal Irish Academy, 6 June 1785, R.I.A., ms. 3/E/1).

109. McDowell, 'The Main Narrative', p. 21.

110. Minutes of Council, 14 Jan. 1797, R.I.A., ms. 3/E/5.

111. Ibid., 18 Feb. 1797, 4 Mar. 1797.

112. In 1786, Burke had written to Vallancey urging that translations of Irish manuscripts be published. The letter appeared in the *Dublin Chronicle* in April 1788. (Love, 'Edmund Burke and an Irish Historiographical Controversy', pp. 191–2).

113. Minutes of Council, 29 Apr. 1797, R.I.A., ms. 3/E/5.

114. Ibid., 16 Jun. 1792.

115. Minutes of the Antiquities Committee, 15 Jun. 1793, 19 Apr. 1794, R.I.A.

116. Ibid., 21 Jun. 1794, 20 Jan. 1798, 21 Apr. 1798. MacElligott's essay was borrowed from the Academy by Edward Ledwich in 1800 (ibid., 16 Jun. 1800).

117. Minutes of Council, 16 Jun. 1792, 5 Dec. 1705, 18 May 1799, R.I.A., ms. 3/E/5.

118. Thomas Campbell to Thomas Percy, 20 Feb. 1788, 15 Dec. 1788, in Nichols, *Lit. Illus.*, VII, pp. 774–5.

119. Bartlett, 'An End to Moral Economy', pp. 191–5.

120. Campbell to Thomas Percy, 5 Jan. 1792, in Nichols, *Lit. Illus.*, VII, pp. 786–7.

121. Campbell to Percy, 12 Jun. 1793, in ibid., pp. 789–90; Edward Ledwich to Percy, 23 Sept. 1803, in ibid., pp. 833–4.

122. See, for example, Walker to Pinkerton, 13 Mar. 1797, in ibid., p. 734.

123. Walker to Percy, 20 May 1797, 6 Jun. 1797, in ibid., pp. 740–42.

124. See above, Chapters 2 and 3.

125. R.B. McDowell, *Ireland in the Age of Imperialism and Revolution, 1760–1801* (Oxford, 1979), pp. 537–8.

126. For example, the novelist Charles Maturin, in *Melmoth the Wanderer* (1820), cited it in a footnote to an account of Catholic mob violence during the Spanish inquisition (Maturin, ibid. (London, 1989), pp. 256–7).

127. O'Flanagan, 'Translator's Preface' in John Lynch, *Cambrensis Refuted*, trans. Theophilus O'Flanagan (Dublin, 1795), p. ix.

128. See Chapter 5, above.

129. O'Flanagan, 'Translator's Preface', p. xiv.

130. Ibid., pp. ix, iv–v.

131. Ibid., pp. ix–x.

132. Ibid., p. 47.

133. Ibid., pp. xvi, 46–7.

134. Ibid., pp. xiv, 43.

135. Ibid., p. 47. Vallancey put him in touch with the publisher Luke White in May 1807 about bringing out the full version of *Cambrensis Refuted*, and found him rent-free lodgings in 1808 (O'Flanagan to John McNamara, 20 May 1807, 13 Jan. 1808, N.L.I., ms. 2981, pp. 2, 4).

136. O'Flanagan, 'Translator's Preface', p. xvi.

137. Ibid., pp. vi–vii.

138. Ibid., p. 42.

139. Giovanni Costigan, 'The Tragedy of Charles O'Conor: an Episode in Anglo-Irish Relations', *American Historical Review*, 49 (1943–4), pp. 33–5. In 1799, O'Conor was appointed librarian to the Marquis of Buckingham who had also arranged his grandfather's pension (ibid., pp. 35–7).

140. These form the basis of the O'Conor correspondence in the Royal Irish Academy and in the Gilbert Collection in the Dublin City Library and Archive.

141. Charles O'Conor (S.J.), 'The Early Life of Charles O'Conor (1710–91) of Belanagare and the Beginnings of the Catholic Revival in Ireland in the Eighteenth Century' (unpublished typescript dated 1930 lodged in the N.L.I., Dublin), pp. iv–v.

142. The Revd Charles O'Conor, *Advertisement* (1795), bound with a copy of *Memoirs of the Life and Work of Charles O'Conor of Belanagare* (Dublin, 1796) in N.L.I., catalogue no. J92 o.

143. Walker to the Revd Charles O'Conor, 24 Aug. 1795, Clonalis, ms. 8.4.HL.146.

144. Walker to Pinkerton, 25 Mar. 1800, in *The Literary Correspondence of John Pinkerton*, 2 vols (London, 1830), II, pp. 137–8. See above, Chapter 4.

145. Walker, 'On the Origin of Romantic Fabling in Ireland', *Transactions of the Royal Irish Academy*, 10 (1806), antiquities section, pp. 3–5, 21.

146. Ibid., p. 5.

147. Walker to Francis Douce, 7 Mar. 1809, Oxford, Bodleian Library, Douce d. 21, fols 214–15.

148. Walker to Douce, 27 Jun. 1809, ibid., fol. 234b.

149. Walker to Douce, 26 May 1809, ibid., Douce d. 23, fol. 128.

150. Walker to Pinkerton, 31 Oct. 1798, in *Literary Correspondence of John Pinkerton*, II, p. 37.

151. Monica Nevin, 'The Defence of the Southern Part of Ireland by General Vallancey, Chief Engineer', *J.R.S.A.I.*, 125 (1995), pp. 5–9. Vallancey believed that 'no invasion of consequence' could arise from the peasantry (quoted in ibid., p. 7).

152. Samuel Cooper to Joseph Cooper Walker, 20 Nov. 1792, N.L.I., ms. 798 [no fol.].
153. Minutes of the Antiquities Committee, R.I.A., *passim.*
154. Vallancey to Walker, 10 Jan. 1798, T.C.D., ms. 1461(4), fol. 74.
155. Minutes of the Antiquities Committee, R.I.A., 21 May 1810.

Epilogue

1. Vallancey to Walker, 14 Jan. 1799, T.C.D., ms. 1461(4), fol. 107.
2. Desmond Clarke, 'The Library' in James Meenan and Desmond Clarke (eds), *RDS: the Royal Dublin Society, 1731–1981* (Dublin, 1981), pp. 76–7; Terence de Vere White, *The Story of the Royal Dublin Society* (Tralee, n.d. [1955]), pp. 46–9. See also Vallancey to Walker, 21 Dec. 1802, 26 Dec. 1802 and 9 Jan. 1803, T.C.D., ms. 1461(5), fols 74, 76, 78.
3. Vallancey, 'On the Oriental Emigration of the ancient Inhabitants of Britain and Ireland', *The Oriental Collections*, I, no. 4 (1797), pp. 301–17; *idem*, 'The Oriental Emigration of the Hibernian Druids proved from their Knowledge in Astronomy, collated with that of the Indians and Chaldaeans – from Fragments of Irish Manuscripts', ibid., II, nos. 1–4 (1798), pp. 1–20, 101–21, 201–27, 321–48.
4. Vallancey, *Prospectus of a Dictionary of the Language of the Aire Coti, or, Ancient Irish* (Dublin, 1802), pp. 25–7.
5. Vallancey, 'A further Vindication of the Ancient History of Ireland' in *Collectanea*, VI, part 1 (Dublin, 1804); *idem*, 'An Essay on the primitive Inhabitants of Great Britain and Ireland' in ibid., [VII] (Dublin, 1807).
6. The notebooks of Charles Vallancey, vol. 1, R.I.A., ms. 12/K/33.
7. O'Conor died in 1791; Campbell in 1795; O'Halloran in 1807; Walker in 1810. William Beauford died in 1819; Ledwich lived on until 1823.
8. Leerssen, *Mere Irish*, pp. 435–9; *idem*, *Remembrance and Imagination* (Cork, 1996), pp. 75–6, 157–8. See also Damien Murray, *Romanticism, Nationalism and Irish Antiquarian Societies, 1840–80* (Maynooth, 2000).
9. The subscription was 24 shillings, compared to 5 guineas entrance and 2 guineas per annum for the Royal Irish Academy (J. Warburton, J. Whitelaw and R. Walsh, *History of the City of Dublin*, 2 vols (London, 1818), II, pp. 921, 930–31). Leerssen has described the scholars of the Gaelic Society as still having 'one foot in the hedge-school' (Leerssen, *Remembrance*, p. 158).
10. On McElligott see Séamus Ua Casaide, 'Richard McElligott, Honorary Member of the Gaelic Society', *Journal of the North Munster Archaeological Society*, 3 (1913–15), pp. 362–70.
11. 'Advertisement', *Transactions of the Gaelic Society*, I (1808), pp. iv–ix.
12. Clare O'Halloran, 'Irish Re-creations of the Gaelic Past: the Challenge of Macpherson's Ossian', *Past and Present*, 124 (Aug. 1989), pp. 93–4.
13. O'Flanagan, 'Preliminary discourse' to 'Deirdri, or, the Lamentable Fate of the Sons of Usnach, an Ancient Dramatic Irish Tale, one of three tragic stories of Eirin', *Transactions of the Gaelic Society*, 1 (1808), item 4, p. 1.
14. The Gaelic Society appears to have continued in low-key existence until it merged with the Iberno-Celtic Society in 1818 (Leerssen, *Remembrance*, pp. 76, 158, 246).

15. [Patrick Lynch], 'Life of the Author' in Geoffrey Keating, *A Complete History of Ireland, from the first Colonization of the Island by Partholan, to the Anglo-Norman Invasion*, [trans. and ed. William Haliday] vol. I (Dublin, 1811), pp. xxiii–xxiv. Haliday died the following year and no further volumes were published. Séamus Ua Casaide identified Patrick Lynch as the author of the introductory essay ('List of works projected or published by Patrick Lynch', *Journal of the Waterford and South-East of Ireland Archaeological Society*, 15 (1912), p. 112).

16. Ledwich to Thomas Percy, 14 Feb. 1807, in Nichols, *Lit. Illus.*, VII, pp. 842–3. Ledwich contemplated a third edition with further revisions (ibid.).

17. Minutes of the Antiquities Committee, 18 Feb. 1839, R.I.A. See also Joseph Leerssen, 'On the Edge of Europe: Ireland in Search of Oriental Roots, 1650–1850', *Comparative Criticism*, 8 (1986), pp. 103; idem, *Remembrance*, pp. 90–94. Another nineteenth-century follower of Vallancey was Henry O'Brien, whose *Round Towers of Ireland* (1834) pointed out the phallic shape of these monuments (ibid., pp. 117–20).

18. Joseph Raftery, 'George Petrie: a Reassessment', *Proceedings of the Royal Irish Academy*, 72c (1972), pp. 153–7; Leerssen, *Remembrance*, pp. 106–8, 112–17, 260.

19. Patricia Boyne, *John O'Donovan (1806–1861): a Biography* (Kilkenny, 1987), pp. 80–105. See also, Cathy Swift, 'John O'Donovan and the Framing of Medieval Ireland', *Bullán*, i (1994), pp. 91–103.

20. The nationalist publisher James Duffy brought out a new edition of Dermod O'Connor's translation of Keating's *Foras Feasa*, *The General History of Ireland* in 1841, and the first English translation of James MacGeoghegan's *Histoire de l'Irlande* in 1849 (Abbé Mac-Geoghegan, *The History of Ireland, Ancient and Modern*, trans. Patrick O'Kelly (Dublin, 1849)).

21. Thomas Davis, *Essays and Poems* (Dublin, [1846] 1945), pp. 113, 197, 198, 103, 98.

22. Samuel Ferguson, 'Hardiman's *Irish Minstrelsy*', *Dublin University Magazine*, 3 (Apr. 1834), pp. 456–78; ibid., 4 (Aug. 1834), pp. 152–67, 447–67, 514–42. See Leerssen, *Remembrance*, pp. 181–6.

23. Ibid., pp. 68–156.

24. Colin Kidd, *Subverting Scotland's Past* (Cambridge, 1993) pp. 219–80; idem, *British Identities before Nationalism* (Cambridge, 1999), pp. 123–45; idem, 'Teutonist Ethnology and Scottish Nationalist Inhibition, 1780–1880', *Scottish Historical Review*, lxxiv (1995), pp. 45–68.

25. E.g., Maria Edgeworth, *The Absentee* (1812); Lady Morgan, *The Wild Irish Girl* (1806); Charles Maturin, *The Wild Irish Boy* (1808); Gerald Griffin, *The Invasion* (1832).

26. Philip L. Marcus, *Standish O'Grady* (Cranbury, New Jersey, 1970), p. 14.

27. Standish O'Grady, *History of Ireland: the Heroic Period* (London, 1878); idem, *History of Ireland: Cuculain and his Contemporaries* (London, 1880). On O'Grady, see R.F. Foster, *The Irish Story* (London, 2001), pp. 10–17.

28. W.B. Yeats, *Prefaces and Introductions*, ed. W.H. O'Donnell (London, 1988), p. 67.

29. *Idem, Autobiographies* (London, 1955), pp. 220–21.

30. *Idem, Essays and Introductions* (London, 1961), p. 512.

31. E.g., *The Rose* (1893); *The Wanderings of Oisin* (1889); *The Old Age of Queen Maeve* (1903); *Baile and Aillinn* (1903); *The Two Kings* (1914).

32.   P.S. O'Hegarty (ed.), *A Bibliography of Books written by Standish O'Grady* (Dublin, 1930). O'Hegarty's major work was *A History of Ireland under the Union* (London, 1952).

BIBLIOGRAPHY

A. Manuscripts

Apart from Trinity College Dublin, none of the Irish archives consulted has consistently followed the standard convention of numbering manuscripts by a folio system. Thus, there are only occasional references in the notes to this study which incorporate folio (or sometimes page) references; where none occur, it should be taken that the items within manuscripts have not been numbered in any way.

Dublin, Royal Irish Academy:

4/A/27	Joseph Cooper Walker manuscripts: draft essays and letters.
3/D/8	Miscellaneous autograph letters: one from O'Halloran to O'Conor.
24/D/2	Thomas O'Gorman papers: 'The Committee of Antiquarians of the Irish Academy' (O'Gorman's answers to queries concerning the earliest form of Irish kingship).
24/D/4	O'Gorman papers: ms. prospectus of the Gaoilic [Gaelic] Society of Dublin.
24/D/18	Latin translation of part of the Annals of the Four Masters, by Francis Stoughton Sullivan; and miscellaneous correspondence of Thomas O'Gorman.
23/H/39	Letters to Charlotte Brooke from Charles Vallancey and William Beauford; O'Halloran, draft manuscript of the 'Martial Ode', 29 Dec. 1787.
12/K/33	Antiquarian notebooks of Charles Vallancey, including 'A Farewell to the Milesians'.
12/R/9–25	Correspondence of Lord Charlemont, Charles Vallancey.
24/E/7	Minute Book of the Select Committee on Antiquities of the Dublin Society.
3/E/5	Minutes of the Council of the R.I.A., commencing 1785.
No ref.	Minutes of the Committee of Antiquities, commencing 1785.
3/E/1	Minutes of the R.I.A., commencing 1785.
BI.1, BI.2, BI.1a, BI.2a	Stowe mss.: correspondence of Charles O'Conor, unfoliated, roughly in date order.
MR/16	Charles O'Conor's copy of James Macpherson, *Fingal* (Dublin, 1762) with annotations by O'Conor.

Dublin, National Library of Ireland:

G135	Ó Neachtain mss., Tadg Ó Neachtain's Gaelic rendition of the Punic speech from Plautus.
798	Ts. copies of correspondence of J.C. Walker with his brother, Samuel Cooper.
1,415	Records of the Hibernian Antiquarian Society, mainly in the form of letters from Ledwich, O'Conor, Beranger, Vallancey, Campbell and others.
3,899	Letters of Charles Vallancey to Thomas Burgess.
4,158	One letter from O'Halloran to Vallancey, 1772.
15,883(15)	Note (unsigned) on the education of Catholics by Charles Vallancey.
16,350	Letters from Vallancey to Thomas Orde, Chief Secretary, Dublin Castle.

Dublin, Trinity College:

1461 (1–7)	Letters to J.C. Walker from Edward Ledwich, Charles Vallancey, Daniel Beaufort, Revd Charles O'Conor.

Dublin, Dublin City Library and Archive, Gilbert Collection:

203	Letters of Charles O'Conor to J.C. Walker and John Curry.

Castlerea, Co. Roscommon, Clonalis House:

OCD 8.3.HS.023	106 letters of Charles O'Conor to John Curry.
OCD 8.3.HS.026	70 letters of O'Conor to John Curry.
OCD 8.4.HL.071	Letter from J.C. Walker to Charles O'Conor.
OCD 8.4.HL.072	Fragment of letter in Walker's hand, re: Carolan.
OCD 8.4.HL.146	Two letters from Walker to Revd Charles O'Conor.
OCD 8.4.HL.157	Fragments in Charles O'Conor's hand.
OCD 8.4.HL.219	Charles O'Conor, fragment of draft memoir; draft of 2nd edn of *Dissertations* (1766).

London, British Library:

Add 21,121	Letters of Charles O'Conor to Thomas O'Gorman.
Eg. 87	Charles Vallancey's copy of John O'Brien's *Focalóir Gaoidhilge-Sax-Bhéarla, or an Irish-English Dictionary* (Paris, 1768), with annotations by Vallancey and Charles O'Conor.
Eg. 201	Letters of Charles O'Conor to George Faulkner.
Eg. 212	Edward Ledwich, 'Observations on Irish Records', n.d. but after 1804.

Oxford, Bodleian Library:

Douce d. 21	Douce mss: letters from J.C.Walker to Francis Douce.
Eng.lett.b.23	Two letters by Sylvester O'Halloran to Lord Macartney, 1781–2.
Uncatalogued letter	Sylvester O'Halloran to ?, 2 Dec. 1779, tipped into O'Halloran's *A General History of Ireland* (1778), catalogue no. G.A. Ire 4⁰19.
Ms. Eng.lett.c.19	Letter of Charlotte Brooke to William Hayley, n.d. but written after 1789.
Ms. Eng.lett.c.361	Letter of Theophilus O'Flanagan to John Nichols, bookseller, 21 Jan. 1796.
Percy.c.2, fols 33–6, 39–40	Letter from Thomas Percy to Joseph Cooper Walker, and two replies from Walker to Percy.

Edinburgh, Edinburgh University Library:

La.II.509, 588, 598, 599	Laing mss.: correspondence between Joseph Cooper Walker and sundry Scottish minor literary figures.
La.III.379	Laing mss.: letters from Daniel Beaufort, Charlotte Brooke, Charles O'Conor to Grimar Thorkelin.

San Marino, California, Huntingdon Library:

Stowe Collection:	Papers of Charles O'Conor, 1747–1828 – read on microfilm, Special Collections, Boole Library, N.U.I. Cork.

B. Printed Primary Sources

Abercromby, Patrick, *The Martial Atchievements of the Scots Nation.* 2 vols. Edinburgh, 1711–15.

Archdall, Mervyn, *Monasticon Hibernicum.* Dublin, 1786.

Astle, Thomas, *The Origin and Progress of Writing.* London, 1784.

Barnard, Thomas, 'An Enquiry concerning the Original of the Scots in Britain', *Transactions of the Royal Irish Academy*, 1 (1787), antiquities section, 25–41.

Beauford, William, 'Of the Origin and Language of the Irish', in *Collectanea de Rebus Hibernicis*, ed. Charles Vallancey. Vol. II, no. vii [1781] Dublin, 1786, 218–49.

Beauford, William, 'Druidism Revived: or a Dissertation on the Characters and Modes of Writing used by the Irish in their Pagan State, and after their Conversion to Christianity', in *Collectanea de Rebus Hibernicis*, ed. Charles Vallancey. Vol. II, no. vii [1781] Dublin, 1786, 161–249.

Beauford, William, 'The Antient Topography of Ireland. With a Preliminary Discourse. Illustrated with a Map of Antient Ireland', in *Collectanea de Rebus Hibernicis*, ed. Charles Vallancey. Vol. III, no. xi [1783] Dublin, 1786, 249–426.

Beauford, William, 'Caoinan: or some Account of the Antient Irish Lamentation', *Transactions of the Royal Irish Academy*, 4 (n.d.), 41–54.

Blackstone, William, *Commentaries on the Laws of England* 4 vols [1765–9], London, 1826.

Boece, Hector, *Scotorum Historiae*. Paris, 1527.

Boswell, James, *The Life of Samuel Johnson*, 2 vols. [1791], London, 1973.

Brooke, Henry, *The Farmer's Letters to the Protestants of Ireland*. Dublin, 1745.

[Brooke, Henry], *An Essay on the Ancient and Modern State of Ireland*. Dublin and London, 1760.

Brooke, Henry, *The Tryal of the Roman Catholics of Ireland*. Dublin, 1761.

Brooke, Henry, *A Collection of the Pieces formerly published by Henry Brooke*. 4 vols. London, 1778.

Brooke, Charlotte, *Reliques of Irish Poetry*. Dublin, 1789.

Brooke, Charlotte, *Reliques of Irish Poetry. To which is prefixed, a memoir of her life and writings, by Aaron Crossly Seymour*. 2nd edn. Dublin, 1816.

Bryant, Jacob, *A New System, or, an Analysis of Ancient Mythology*. 3 vols. London, 1774–6.

Burgess, Thomas, *An Essay on the Study of Antiquities*. 2nd edn, Oxford, 1782.

Burrowes, Robert, 'Preface', *Transactions of the Royal Irish Academy*, 1 (1787), ix–xvii.

Caesar, Julius, *The Conquest of Gaul*, trans. S.A. Handford. Harmondsworth, 1951.

Campbell, Thomas, *A Philosophical Survey of the South of Ireland, in a series of letters to John Watkinson, M.D.* London, 1777.

Campbell, Thomas, 'Sketch or Summary View of the Ecclesiastical and Literary History of Ireland', *Dublin Chronicle* (Dec. 1787 – Apr. 1788).

Campbell, Thomas, *Strictures on the Ecclesiastical and Literary History of Ireland*. Dublin, 1789.

Campbell, Thomas, *Diary of a Visit to England in 1775*, ed. James L. Clifford. Cambridge, 1947.

Cartright, John, *Take your Choice!* London, 1776.

Charlemont, Lord, 'The Antiquity of the Woollen Manufacture in Ireland, proved from a passage of an antient Florentine Poet', *Transactions of the Royal Irish Academy*, 1 (1787), antiquities section, 17–24.

Charles-Edward, Thomas, and Fergus Kelly (eds), *Bechbretha*. Dublin, 1983.

Comerford, T., *The History of Ireland, from the Earliest Account of Time, to the Invasion of the English under King Henry II.* Dublin, 1752.

Cook, James, *The Explorations of Captain James Cook in the Pacific as told by Selections of his own Journals 1768–1779*, ed. A. Grenfell Price. New York, 1971.

Cox, Sir Richard, *Hibernia Anglicana: or, the History of Ireland from the Conquest thereof by the English, to the Present Time*. 2 vols. London, 1689–90.

[John Curry], *A Brief Account from the most authentic Protestant Writers of the Causes, Motives and Mischiefs of the Irish Rebellion on the 23rd day of October 1641*. London, 1747.

Curry, John, *Historical Memoirs of the Irish Rebellion in the year 1641*. London, 1758.

Curry, John, *Occasional Remarks on certain passages in Dr Leland's History of Ireland, relative to the Irish Rebellion of 1641*. London, 1773.

Curry, John, *An Historical and Critical Review of the Civil Wars in Ireland from the Reign of Queen Elizabeth to the settlement under King William*. 1st edn, Dublin 1775; 2nd edn, 2 vols. Dublin, 1786.

Davies, Sir John, *A Discovery of the True Causes why Ireland was never Entirely Subdued*. [1612] repr. Shannon, 1969.

Davies, Sir John, *A Discoverie of the True Causes why Ireland was never Entirely Subdued*. Dublin, 1761.

Davies, Sir John, *A Report of Cases and Matters in Law, resolved and judged in the King's courts in Ireland.* (Dublin, 1762).

Davies, Sir John, *Historical Tracts.* Dublin, 1787.

Davis, Thomas, *Essays and Poems.* Dublin, [1846] 1945.

Edwards, R. Dudley (ed.), 'The Minute Book of the Catholic Committee, 1773–92', *Archivium Hibernicum*, 9 (1942), 3–172.

Evans, Evan, *Some Specimens of the Poetry of the Ancient Welsh Bards.* London, 1764.

Ferguson, Adam, *An Essay on the History of Civil Society.* Edinburgh, 1767.

Ferguson, Samuel, 'Hardiman's *Irish Minstrelsy*', *Dublin University Magazine*, 3–4 (Apr. and Aug. 1834), 456–78; 152–67, 447–67, 514–42.

Forman, Charles, *A Defence of the Courage, Honour, and Loyalty of the Irish Nation.* London, 1731.

Gibbon, Edward, *The History of the Decline and Fall of the Roman Empire* [1776–88] ed. David Wormersley. 3 vols. London, 1995.

Giraldus Cambrensis [Gerald of Wales], *The History and Topography of Ireland [Topographia Hiberniae]*, trans. John J. O'Meara. Mountrath, Portlaoise, and Atlantic Highlands, N.J., 1982.

Giraldus Cambrensis, *Topographia Hibernica et Expugnatio Hibernica.* London, 1867.

Grose, Francis, *The Antiquities of Ireland.* 2 vols. London, 1791–5.

Hamilton, William, *Letters concerning the Northern Coast of the County of Antrim.* Dublin, 1786.

Harris, Walter (ed.), *The Whole Works of Sir James Ware.* 3 vols. London, 1739–45.

Harris, Walter (ed.), *Hibernica.* Dublin, 1747–50.

Harris, Walter, *Fiction Unmasked.* Dublin, 1752.

Historical Manuscripts Commission, 'The Manuscripts and Correspondence of James, first Earl of Charlemont', in *Twelfth Report, appendix, part x* and *Thirteenth Report, appendix, part viii.* 2 vols. London, 1891–4.

Hume, David, *The History of Great Britain, Vol. 1. Containing the Reigns of James I and Charles I.* [1st edn, 1754] repr. Harmondsworth, 1970.

Hume, David, *The History of England from the Invasion of Julius Caesar to the Accession of Henry VII.* 8 vols. London, 1762.

Hume, David, *The History of England from the Invasion of Julius Caesar to the Revolution in 1688.* 8 vols. London, 1788.

Innes, Thomas, *A Critical Essay on the Ancient Inhabitants of the Northern Parts of Britain, or Scotland.* 2 vols. London, 1729.

Jamieson, John, *An Etymological Dictionary of the Scottish Language.* 2 vols. Edinburgh, 1808.

Johnson, Samuel, *Journey to the Western Islands of Scotland.* London, [1775] 1990.

Jones, Edward, *Musical and Poetical Relicks of the Welsh Bards.* London, 1784.

Jones, Sir William, *The Works of Sir William Jones.* 13 vols.: London, 1807.

Jones, Sir William, *The Letters of Sir William Jones*, ed. Garland Cannon. 2 vols. Oxford, 1970.

Kames, Lord Henry Home, *Sketches of the History of Man.* 2 vols. Edinburgh, 1774.

Keating, Geoffrey, *Foras Feasa ar Éirinn: the History of Ireland*, eds and trans. David Comyn and P.S. Dinneen. 4 vols. Dublin, 1902–14.

Keating, Geoffrey, *The General History of Ireland*, translated by Dermod O'Connor. London, 1723.

Keating, Geoffrey, *A Complete History of Ireland, from the first Colonization of the Island by Partholan, to the Anglo-Norman Invasion*, ed. and trans. William Haliday. Dublin, 1811.

Keating, Geoffrey, *The General History of Ireland*, trans. D. O'Connor. Dublin, 1841.

Keating, Geoffrey, *Eochair-sgiath an Aifrinn . . . , an explanatory Defence of the Mass*, ed. Patrick O'Brien. Dublin, 1898.

Keating, Geoffrey, *Trí bíor-ghaoithe an bháis*, ed. Osborn Bergin. Dublin, 1931.

K'eogh, John, *Vindication of the Antiquities of Ireland, and a Defence thereof against all the Calumnies and Aspersions cast on it by Foreigners*. Dublin, 1748.

[Ledwich, Edward], *Antiquitates Sarisburienses*. Salisbury, 1771.

Ledwich, Edward, 'An Essay on the Study of Irish Antiquities', in *Collectanea de Rebus Hibernicis*, ed. Charles Vallancey. Vol. II, no. vi [1781] Dublin, 1786, 83–116.

Ledwich, Edward, 'A Dissertation on the Round Towers of Ireland', in *Collectanea de Rebus Hibernicis*, ed. Charles Vallancey. Vol. II, no. vi [1781] Dublin, 1786, 119–43.

Ledwich, Edward, 'Memoirs of Dunamase and Shean Castle in the Queen's Co.', in *Collectanea de Rebus Hibernicis*, ed. Charles Vallancey. Vol. II, no. vi [1781], 147–59.

Ledwich, Edward, 'The History and Antiquities of Irishtown and Kilkenny from Original Records and Authentic Documents', in *Collectanea de Rebus Hibernicis*, ed. Charles Vallancey. Vol. II, no. ix [1781] Dublin, 1786, 349–562.

Ledwich, Edward, 'On the Style of the ancient Irish Music', in Joseph Cooper Walker, *Historical Memoirs of the Irish Bards*, Vol. I of 2 vols. 2nd edn, Dublin, 1818, 240–57.

Ledwich, Edward, 'Observations on our Antient Churches', *Archaeologia*, 8 (1787), 165–94.

Ledwich, Edward, *Antiquities of Ireland*. Dublin, 1790.

Ledwich, Edward, *Antiquities of Ireland*. 2nd edn, Dublin, 1804.

Leland, John, *View of the Principal Deistical Writers*. 3 vols. London, 1754–7.

[Leland, Thomas], *An Examination of the Arguments contained in a late Introduction to the History of the Antient Irish, and Scots*. London, 1772.

Leland, Thomas, *The History of Ireland from the Invasion of Henry II with a Preliminary Discourse on the antient state of that Kingdom*. 3 vols. London, 1773.

Leland, Thomas, *Sermons on various Subjects*. 3 vols. Dublin, 1788.

Lynch, John, *Cambrensis Eversus*. n.p. [?St Omer], 1662.

Lynch, John, *Cambrensis Refuted*, trans. Theophilus O'Flanagan. Dublin, 1795.

Macalister, R.A.S. (ed. and trans.), *The Lebor Gabála Érenn*. 5 vols. Dublin, 1938–56.

Macalister R.A.S. (ed. and trans.), *The Lebor Gabála Érenn*, new Introduction by John Carey. 5 vols. Dublin, [1938–56] 1993.

MacGeoghegan, James, *Histoire de l'Irlande*. 3 vols. Paris, 1758–62.

MacGeoghegan, James, *The History of Ireland, Ancient and Modern*, trans. Patrick O'Kelly. Dublin, 1849.

Mac Giolla Eáin, Eoin, *Dánta, Amhráin is Caointe Sheathrúin Céitinn*. Dublin, 1900.

Macpherson, James, *Fragments of Ancient Poetry*. Edinburgh, 1760.

Macpherson, James, *Fingal, an Ancient Epic Poem, in six books*. London, [Dec. 1761] 1762.

Macpherson, James, *Temora, an Ancient Epic Poem, in eight books*. London, 1763.

Macpherson, James, *An Introduction to the History of Great Britain and Ireland*. London, 1771.

Macpherson, James, *The Poems of Ossian and related works*, ed. Howard Gaskill with an introduction by Fiona Stafford. Edinburgh, 1996.

Macpherson, John, *Critical Dissertations on the Origin, Antiquities, Language, Government, Manners, and Religion of the Ancient Caledonians, their Posterity the Picts, and the British and Irish Scots*. Dublin, 1768.

Madden, Daniel Owen (ed.), *The Speeches of the Right Hon. Henry Grattan*. 2nd edn, Dublin, 1854.

Malcolme, David, *An Essay on the Antiquities of Great Britain and Ireland*. Edinburgh, 1738.

Malcolme, David, *A Collection of Letters, in which the Imperfection of Learning, even among Christians, and Remedy for it, are hinted*. Edinburgh, 1739.

Maturin, Charles, *Melmoth the Wanderer*. [1820] London, 1989.

Maurice, Thomas, *Sanscreet Fragments, or interesting Extracts from the Sacred Books of the Brahmins, on subjects important to the British Isles*. London, 1798.

Maurice, Thomas, *A Dissertation on the Oriental Trinities*. London, 1801.

Molyneux, William, *The Case of Ireland's being Bound by Acts of Parliament In England, Stated*. [1698] reprint Dublin, 1977.

Morgan, Lady, Sidney Owenson, *The Wild Irish Girl*. 3 vols. London, 1807.

Moryson, Fynes, *An Itinerary*. London, 1617.

Moryson, Fynes, *An History of Ireland*. 2 vols. Dublin, 1735.

Musgrave, Richard, *Memoirs of the Different Rebellions in Ireland*. Dublin, 1801.

Musgrave, Richard, *Memoirs of the Irish Rebellion of 1798*, foreword by David Dickson. [1801] 4th edn, Fort Wayne, Indiana, 1995.

Nichols, John, *Illustrations of the Literary History of the Eighteenth Century*. 8 vols. London, 1817–58.

O'Brien Eileen (ed.), *The Convert Rolls*. Dublin, 1981.

O'Conor, Charles, *Dissertations on the Antient History of Ireland*. Dublin, 1753.

O'Conor, Charles, *Dissertations on the History of Ireland*. 2nd edn, Dublin, 1766.

O'Conor, Charles, *A Dissertation on the First Migrations and Final Settlements of the Scots in North-Britain: with occasional Observations on the Poems of 'Fingal' and 'Temora'*. Dublin, 1766. [Bound with *Dissertations on the History of Ireland* (1766), but paginated separately.]

[O'Conor, Charles], 'Remarks on the Essay on the Antiquity of the Irish Language. Addressed to the Printer of the *London Chronicle*, in the year 1772. Signed "Celticus"', in *Collectanea de Rebus Hibernicis*, ed. Charles Vallancey. Vol. II, no. 8 [1781] Dublin, 1786, 337–48.

O'Conor, Charles, 'Reflections on the History of Ireland during the Times of Heathenism; with Observations on some late Publications on that Subject. Addressed to Lieut. Col. Charles Vallancey', in *Collectanea de Rebus Hibernicis*, ed. Charles Vallancey. Vol. III, no. x [1782] Dublin, 1786, 213–46.

O'Conor, Charles, 'Second letter to Colonel Vallancey, on the Heathen State, and Antient Topography of Ireland', in *Collectanea de Rebus Hibernicis*, ed. Charles Vallancey. Vol. III, no xii [1783] Dublin, 1786, 649–77.

O'Conor, Charles, 'Third Letter from Charles O'Conor, Esq.; to Colonel Vallancey', in *Collectanea de Rebus Hibernicis*, ed. Charles Vallancey. Vol. IV, no. xiii [1784] Dublin, 1786, 107–34.

O'Conor, Charles, *Memoirs of the Life and Work of Charles O'Conor of Belanagare*. Dublin, 1796.

O'Donnell, W.H. (ed.), *Prefaces and Introductions by W.B. Yeats*. London, 1988.

O'Flaherty, Roderic, *Ogygia Vindicated*, ed. and trans. Charles O'Conor. Dublin, 1775.

O'Flaherty, Roderick, *Ogygia, or, a Chronological Account of Irish Events*, trans. James Hely. 2 vols. Dublin, 1793.

O'Flanagan, Theophilus, 'Account of an ancient Inscription in Ogham Character on the Sepulchral Monument of an Irish Chief', *Transactions of the Royal Irish Academy*, 1 (1787), antiquities section 3–16.

O'Flanagan, Theophilus, 'Translator's Preface' in John Lynch, *Cambrensis Refuted*, trans. Theophilus O'Flanagan. Dublin, 1795.

O'Flanagan, Theophilus (ed. and trans.), 'Deirdri, or, the Lamentable Fate of the Sons of Usnach, an Ancient Dramatic Irish Tale, one of three tragic stories of Eirin', *Transactions of the Gaelic Society*, 1 (1808), item 4.

O'Grady, Standish, *History of Ireland: the Heroic Period*. London, 1878.

O'Grady, Standish, *History of Ireland: Cuculain and his Contemporaries*. London, 1880.

O'Halloran, Sylvester, 'The Poems of Ossine, the Son of Fionne mac Comhal, Reclaimed. By a Milesian', *Dublin Magazine*, (Jan. 1763).

O'Halloran, Sylvester, 'A Letter to Mr Macpherson, occasioned by his Dissertation on the Poems of Temora. By a Milesian', *Dublin Magazine*, (Aug. 1763).

O'Halloran, Sylvester, *Insula Sacra*. Limerick, 1770.

O'Halloran, Sylvester, *An Introduction to the Study of the History and Antiquities of Ireland*. London, 1772.

O'Halloran, Sylvester, *Ierne Defended*. Dublin, 1774.

O'Halloran, Sylvester, *A General History of Ireland, from the Earliest Accounts to the Close of the Twelfth Century*. 2 vols. London, 1778.

O'Halloran, Sylvester, 'A Martial Ode, sung at the Battle of Cnucha' . . . with a literal translation and notes', *Transactions of the Royal Irish Academy*, 2 (1788), 7–17.

O'Halloran, Sylvester, *A New Treatise on the Different Disorders arising from External Injuries of the Head*. Dublin, 1793.

O'Halloran, Sylvester, 'The Letters of Sylvester O'Halloran', ed. J.B. Lyons, *North Munster Antiquarian Journal*, 8–9 (1961–3), 168–81, 25–50.

O'Hegarty, P.S. (ed.), *A Bibliography of Books written by Standish O'Grady*. Dublin, 1930.

O'Leary, Arthur, *A Defence of the Conduct and Writings of the Rev. Arthur O'Leary during the late Disturbances in Munster*. London, 1788.

Parsons, James, *Remains of Japhet*. London, 1767.

Parsons, Lawrence, *Observations on the Bequest of Henry Flood Esq. to Trinity College Dublin*. Dublin, 1795.

Percy, Thomas, *Reliques of English Poetry*. 3 vols. London, 1765.

Pinkerton, John, *Select Scottish Ballads*. 2 vols. London, 1783.

Pinkerton, John, *Ancient Scottish Poems*. 2 vols. London and Edinburgh, 1986.

Pinkerton, John, *A Dissertation on the Origin of the Scythians or Goths*. London, 1787.

Pinkerton, John, *An Enquiry into the History of Scotland preceding the Reign of Malcom [sic] III or the year 1056*. 2 vols. London, 1789.

Pinkerton, John, *Essay on Medals*. 2 vols. London, 1789.

Pinkerton, John, *The Literary Correspondence of John Pinkerton*. 2 vols. London, 1830.

Price, Liam (ed.), *An Eighteenth-Century Antiquary: the Sketches, Notes and Diaries of Austin Cooper (1759–1830)*. Dublin, 1942.

Richardson, John, *A Dissertation on the Languages, Literature and Manners of Eastern Nations*. Oxford, 1777.

Royal Irish Academy, *The Charter of the Royal Irish Academy*. Dublin, 1997.

Scott, Sir Walter, *The Antiquary*, in *Novels and Tales by the Author of Waverley*, 12 vols. Edinburgh, 1819, vols. 4–5.

Smith, Charles, *The Antient and Present State of the County and City of Waterford*. Dublin, 1746.

Smith, Charles, *The Antient and Present State of the County and City of Cork*. 2 vols. Dublin, 1750.

Smith, Charles, *The Antient and Present State of the County of Kerry*. Dublin, 1756.

Smith, John, *Galic Antiquities*. Edinburgh, 1780.

Smith, John, *The Life of St Columba*. Edinburgh, 1798.

Spenser, Edmund, *A View of the State of Ireland as it was in the Reign of Queen Elizabeth*. Dublin, 1763.

Spenser, Edmund, *A view of the Present State of Ireland*, ed. W.L. Renwick. Oxford, 1970.

Stewart, Alexander, *Elements of Gaelic Grammar*. 2nd edn, Edinburgh, 1812.

Temple, John, *The Irish Rebellion: or an History of the Beginnings and first Progresse of the Generall Rebellion raised within the Kingdom of Ireland, upon the three and twentieth day of October, in the year, 1641. Together with the barbarous Cruelties and Bloody Massacres which ensued thereupon*. London, 1646.

Toland, John, *Christianity not Mysterious*. London, 1696.

Toland, John, 'A Specimen of the Critical History of the Celtic Religion and Learning: containing an Account of the Druids', in *A Collection of Several Pieces of Mr John Toland*. 2 vols. London, 1726.

Ussher, James, *A Discourse of the Religion Anciently professed by the Irish and British*. 4th edn, London, 1687.

Vallancey, Charles, *An Essay on the Antiquity of the Irish Language. Being a Collation of Irish with the Punic Language*. Dublin, 1772.

Vallancey, Charles, *A Grammar of the Iberno-Celtic, or Irish Language*. Dublin, 1773.

Vallancey, Charles, 'Part of the Ancient Brehon Laws of Ireland', in *Collectanea de Rebus Hibernicis*, ed. Charles Vallancey. Vol. I, no iv [1780] Dublin, 1786, 657–72.

Vallancey, Charles, *A Grammar of the Iberno-Celtic, or Irish Language. The Second Edition with many Additions*. Dublin, 1781.

Vallancey, Charles, 'A Continuation of the Brehon Laws, in the original Irish, with a translation into English', in *Collectanea de Rebus Hibernicis*, ed. Charles Vallancey. Vol. III, no. x [1782] Dublin, 1786, i–lxx, 71–126.

Vallancey, Charles, 'Some Remarks on the Round Towers of Ireland', in *Collectanea de Rebus Hibernicis*, ed. Charles Vallancey. Vol. III, no. x [1782] Dublin, 1786, 193–6.

Vallancey, Charles, 'Preface', in *Collectanea de Rebus Hibernicis*, ed. Charles Vallancey. Vol. III, no xii [1783] Dublin, 1786, i–clxxv.

Vallancey, Charles, 'Observations on the Alphabet of the Pagan Irish and of the Age in which Finn and Ossin Lived', *Archaeologia*, 7 (1785), 276–85.

Vallancey, Charles, *A Vindication of the History of Ireland*. Dublin, 1786. Reprinted in *Collectanea de Rebus Hibernicis*, IV, no. xiv [1786].

Vallancey, Charles, 'On the Oriental Emigration of the Ancient Inhabitants of Britain and Ireland', *The Oriental Collections*, I, no. 4 (1797), 301–17.

Vallancey, Charles, 'The Oriental Emigration of the Hibernian Druids proved from their Knowledge in Astronomy, collated with that of the Indians and Chaldaeans – from Fragments of Irish manuscripts', *The Oriental Collections*, 2, nos. 1–4 (1798), 1–20, 101–21, 201–27, 321–48.

Vallancey, Charles, *Prospectus of a Dictionary of the Language of the Aire Coti, or Ancient Irish.* Dublin, 1802.

Vallancey, Charles, 'A further Vindication of the Ancient History of Ireland', in *Collectanea de Rebus Hibernicis*, ed. Charles Vallancey. Vol. VI, part 1 Dublin, 1804, 1–59.

Vallancey, Charles, 'An Essay on the Primitive Inhabitants of Great Britain and Ireland', in *Collectanea de Rebus Hibernicis*, ed. Charles Vallancey. Vol. [VII] Dublin, 1807.

Walker, Joseph Cooper, *Historical Memoirs of the Irish Bards.* Dublin, 1786.

Walker, Joseph Cooper, *An Historical Essay on the Dress of the Ancient and Modern Irish.* Dublin, 1788.

Walker, Joseph Cooper, 'On the Origin of Romantic Fabling in Ireland', *Transactions of the Royal Irish Academy*, 10 (1806), 3–21.

Walker, Joseph Cooper, *Historical Memoirs of the Irish Bards.* 2 vols. 2nd edn, Dublin, 1818.

Warburton, J., J. Whitelaw and R. Walsh, *History of the City of Dublin*, 2 vols. London, 1818.

Ward, Catherine Coogan, and Robert E. Ward (eds), *The Letters of Charles O'Conor of Belanagare.* 2 vols. Ann Arbor, 1980.

Ward, Robert E., John F. Wrynn, and Catherine Coogan Ward (eds), *The Letters of Charles O'Conor of Belanagare: a Catholic Voice in Eighteenth-Century Ireland.* Washington, D.C., 1988.

Ware, Sir James, *De Scriptoribus Hiberniae.* Dublin, 1639.

Ware, Sir James, *The Antiquities and History of Ireland*, trans. Robert Ware. Dublin, 1705.

Ware, Sir James, *The Whole Works of Sir James Ware concerning Ireland*, ed. Walter Harris. 3 vols. Dublin, 1739–45.

Warner, Ferdinando, *The History of Ireland.* London, 1763.

Warner, Ferdinando, *The History of the Rebellion and Civil War in Ireland.* 2 vols. Dublin, [1767] 1768.

Webb, William, *An Analysis of the History and Antiquities of Ireland, prior to the Fifth Century. To which is subjoined a General History of the Celtic Nations.* Dublin, 1791.

Whitaker, John, *History of Manchester.* 2 vols. London, 1771–5.

Whitaker, John, *The Genuine History of the Britons asserted, in a Full and Candid Refutation of Mr Macpherson's Introduction to the History of Great Britain and Ireland.* Dublin, 1773.

White, Gilbert, *The Natural History and Antiquities of Selbourne*, ed. William Jardine. [1789] London, 1853.

Wilford, Francis, 'An Essay on the Sacred Isles in the West, with other essays connected with that work', *Asiatick Researches*, 8 (1805), 245–367; 11 (1810), 11–152.

Wilford, Francis, 'Essay on the origin and decline of the Christian Religion in India', *Asiatick Researches*, 10, (1808), pp. 27–126.

[Wilson, Charles], *Select Irish Poems translated into English.* Dublin, n.d. [c. 1782].

Woodward, Richard, *The Present State of the Church of Ireland.* Dublin, 1808.

Yeats, W.B., *Autobiographies.* London, 1955.

Yeats, W.B., *Essays and Introductions.* London, 1961.

Young, Arthur, *The Autobiography of Arthur Young*, ed. M. Betham-Edwards. [1898], repr. New York, 1967.

Young, Mathew, 'Antient Gaelic Poems respecting the Race of Fians, collected in the Highlands of Scotland in the year 1784', *Transactions of the Royal Irish Academy*, 1 (1787), antiquities section 43–119.

C. Reference Works

Complete Peerage of England, Scotland and Ireland, Great Britain and the United Kingdom. 13 vols. London, 1910–40.

Concise Dictionary of National Biography. Oxford, 1925.

Connolly, S.J., (ed.), *The Oxford Companion to Irish History.* Oxford, 1998.

Crone, J.S., *A Concise Dictionary of Irish Biography.* Dublin, 1937.

Dictionary of National Biography, eds Leslie Stephens and Sidney Lee. 66 vols. London, 1885–1901.

Munter, Robert, *A Dictionary of the Print Trade in Ireland 1550–1775.* New York, 1988.

Strickland, W.G., *A Dictionary of Irish Artists.* 2 vols. [1913] repr. Shannon, 1984.

Webb, Alfred, *A Compendium of Irish Biography.* Dublin 1878.

D. Secondary Sources

Aarsleff, Hans, *The Study of Language in England, 1780–1860.* Minneapolis and London, [1967] 1983.

Andrews, J.H., 'Charles Vallancey and the Map of Ireland', *Geographical Journal,* 132 (1966), 48–61.

Bannerman, John, 'The Scots of Dalriada', in *Who are the Scots?,* ed. Gordon Menzies. London, 1972.

Barnard, T.C. [Toby], 'The Uses of 23 October 1641 and Irish Protestant Celebrations', *English Historical Review,* cvi (1991), 889–920.

Barnard, Toby, '1641: a Bibliographical Essay' in *Ulster 1641: Aspects of the Rising* ed. Brian Mac Cuarta. Belfast, 1993, 173–86.

Barnard, Toby, 'Protestantism, Ethnicity and Irish Identities, 1660–1760' in *Protestantism and National Identity: Britain and Ireland c.1650–c.1850.* eds Tony Claydon and Ian McBride. Cambridge, 1998, 206–35.

Barry, Kevin, 'James Usher (1720–72) and the Irish Enlightenment', *Eighteenth-Century Ireland,* 3 (1988), 115–22.

Bartlett, Thomas, 'An End to Moral Economy: the Irish Militia and Popular Protest in Ireland', in *Nationalism and Popular Protest in Ireland,* ed. C.H.E. Philpin. Cambridge, 1987, 191–218.

Bartlett, Thomas, 'A New History of Ireland', *Past and Present,* no. 116 (Aug. 1987), 206–19.

Bartlett, Thomas, '"A People Made Rather for Copies than Originals": the Anglo-Irish, 1760–1800', *The International History Review,* 12 (1990), 11–25.

Baumgarten, Rolf, 'The Geographical Orientation of Ireland in Isidore and Orosius', *Peritia,* 3 (1984), 189–203.

Bean Í Sheanacháin, Máire, 'Theophilus Ó Flannagáin', *Galvia,* 3 (1956), 19–29.

Beckett, J.C., 'Introduction: Eighteenth-Century Ireland', in *New History of Ireland IV: Eighteenth-Century Ireland 1691–1800,* eds T.W. Moody and W.E. Vaughan. Oxford, 1986, xxxix–lxiv.

Beckett, J.C., 'Literature in English, 1691–1800', in *New History of Ireland IV: Eighteenth-Century Ireland 1691–1800,* eds. T.W. Moody and W.E. Vaughan. Oxford, 1986, 424–70.

Bell, A.S., (ed.), *The Scottish Antiquarian Tradition.* Edinburgh, 1981.

Berman, David, 'David Hume on the 1641 Rebellion in Ireland', *Studies,* 65 (1976), 101–12.

Berman, David, 'Enlightenment and Counter-Enlightenment in Irish Philosophy', *Archiv für Geschichte der Philosophie*, no vol. (1982), 148–65.

Berman, David, 'The Culmination and Causation of Irish Philosophy', *Archiv für Geschichte der Philosophie*, no vol. (1982), 257–79.

Berman, David, and Alan Harrison, 'John Toland and Keating's History of Ireland (1723)', *Donegal Annual*, no. 36 (1984), 25–9.

Binchy, D.A., 'The Linguistic and Historical Value of the Irish Law Tracts', *Proceedings of the British Academy*, 29 (1943), 195–227.

Black, George F., *Macpherson's Ossian and the Ossianic Controversy. A Contribution towards a Bibliography*. New York, 1926.

Boyne, Patricia, *John O'Donovan (1806–1861): a Biography*. Kilkenny, 1987.

Bradshaw, Brendan, 'Geoffrey Keating: apologist of Irish Ireland' in *Representing Ireland: Literature and the Origins of Conflict, 1534–1660*, eds Brendan Bradshaw, Andrew Hadfield and Willy Maley. Cambridge, 1993, 166–90.

Breathnach, Pádraig, 'Metamorphoses 1603: dán le hEochaidh Ó hEoghusa', *Éigse*, 17 (1977/78), 169–80.

Burke, Peter, *The Renaissance Sense of the Past*. London, 1969.

Burke, Peter, *Popular Culture in Early Modern Europe*. London, 1978.

Burrow, J.W., *Gibbon*. Oxford, 1985.

Canny, Nicholas, 'What Really Happened in Ireland in 1641?' in *Ireland: from Independence to Occupation, 1641–1660*, ed. Jane Ohlmeyer. Cambridge, 1995, 24–42.

Canny, Nicholas, *Making Ireland British, 1580–1650*. Oxford, 2001.

Champion, J.A.I., '"Manuscripts of Mine Abroad": John Toland and the Circulation of Ideas, *c*.1700–1722', *Eighteenth-Century Ireland*, 14 (1999), 9–36.

Champion, J.A.I., 'John Toland, the druids and the politics of Celtic scholarship' *Irish Historical Studies*, 32 (2001), 321–42.

Clark, G., 'The Invasion Hypothesis in British Archaeology', *Antiquity*, 40 (1966), 172–89.

Clarke, Desmond, 'The Library' in *R.D.S.: the Royal Dublin Society, 1731–1981*, eds James Meenan and Desmond Clarke. Dublin, 1981, 75–87.

Connolly, S.J., *Religion, Law and Power: the Making of Protestant Ireland, 1660–1760* (Oxford, 1992).

Corish, P.J., 'The Rising of 1641 and the Catholic Confederacy, 1641–5' in *New History of Ireland III: Early Modern Ireland 1534–1691*, eds T.W. Moody, F.X. Martin and F.J. Byrne. Oxford, 1976, third impression, 1991, 289–316.

Costigan, Giovanni, 'The Tragedy of Charles O'Conor: an Episode in Anglo-Irish Relations', *American Historical Review*, 49 (1943–4), 32–54.

Cowan, E.J., 'Myth and Identity in Early Medieval Scotland', *Scottish Historical Review*, 53 (1984), 111–35.

Cristea, S.N., 'Ossian v. Homer: an Eighteenth-Century Controversy', *Italian Studies*, 24 (1969), 93–111.

Cronin, Anne, 'Sources of Keating's "Forus Feasa ar Éirinn"', *Éigse*, 4–5 (1943–7), 235–79, 122–35.

Cullen, L.M., *The Emergence of Modern Ireland 1600–1900*. Dublin, 1983.

Cullen, L.M., 'The 1798 Rebellion in Wexford: United Irishmen Organisation, Membership, Leadership', in *Wexford: History and Society*, eds W. Nolan and K. Whelan. Dublin, 1985, 248–95.

Cunningham, Bernadette, 'Seventeenth-Century Interpretation of the Past: the Case of Geoffrey Keating', *Irish Historical Studies*, 25 (1986), 116–28.

Cunningham, Bernadette and Gillespie, Raymond, 'An Ulster Settler and his Manuscripts', *Éigse*, 21 (1986), 27–36.

Cunningham, Bernadette, 'The Culture and Ideology of Irish Franciscan Historians at Louvain, 1607–1650' in *Ideology and the Historians*, ed. Ciaran Brady. Dublin, 1991, 11–30.

Cunningham, Bernadette, *The World of Geoffrey Keating*. Dublin, 2000.

Davies, G.L.H., 'The Making of Irish Geography, Part IV: the Physico-Historical Society, 1744–52', *Irish Geography*, xii (1979), 92–8.

Davis, Bertram H., *Thomas Percy: a Scholar-Cleric in the Age of Johnson*. Philadelphia, 1989.

Davis, Leith, 'Birth of the Nation: Gender and Writing in the Work of Henry and Charlotte Brooke', *Eighteenth-Century Life*, 18 (1994), 27–47.

Deane, Seamus, *Celtic Revivals*. London, 1985.

Deane, Seamus, *Strange Country: Modernity and Nationhood in Irish Writing since 1790*. Oxford, 1997.

de h-Óir, Siobhán, 'The Mount Callan Ogham Stone and its Context', *North Munster Antiquarian Journal*, 25 (1983), 43–57.

Delury, John P., '*Ex Conflictu et Collisione*: the Failure of Irish Historiography, 1745–90', *Eighteenth-Century Ireland*, 15 (2000), 9–37.

de Vere White, Terence, *The Story of the Royal Dublin Society*. Tralee, n.d. [1955].

Donaldson, William, *The Jacobite Song: Political Myth and National Identity*. Aberdeen, 1988.

Donnelly, J.S., 'The Rightboy Movement, 1785–8', *Studia Hibernica*, 17–18 (1977–8), 120–202.

Donnelly, J.S., 'The Whiteboy Movement, 1761–5', *Irish Historical Studies*, 21 (1978–9), 20–54.

Dowling, P.J., 'Patrick Lynch, Schoolmaster, 1754–1818', *Studies*, 20 (1931), 461–72.

Dukes, Paul, 'Ossian and Russia', *Scottish Literary News*, 3, no. 3 (Nov. 1973), 17–21.

Dumville, David, *et al*, *Saint Patrick, AD 493–1993*. Woodbridge, Suffolk, 1993.

Duncan, A.A.M., 'Hector Boece and the Medieval Tradition', in *Scots Antiquaries and Historians*, Abertay Historical Society. Publication no. 16. Dundee, 1972, 1–11.

Dunne, Tom, 'Haunted by History: Irish Romantic Writing 1800–50', in *Romanticism in National Context*, eds Roy Porter and Mikulas Teich. Cambridge, 1988, 68–91.

Dunne, Tom, 'Fiction as "the best history of nations": Lady Morgan's Irish novels', in *The Writer as Witness*, ed. Tom Dunne. Cork, 1987, 133–59.

Dunne, Tom, '"A gentleman's estate should be a moral school": Edgeworthstown in Fact and Fiction, 1760–1840', in *Longford: Essays in County History*, eds Raymond Gillespie and Gerard Moran. Dublin, 1991, 95–121.

Durkacz, V.E., *The Decline of the Celtic Languages*. Edinburgh, 1983.

Elliott, Marianne, 'The Origins and Transformation of Early Irish Republicanism', *International Review of Social History*, 23 (1978), 405–28.

Elliott, Marianne, *Wolfe Tone: Prophet of Irish Independence*. New Haven, 1989.

Esposito, M., 'The Patrician Problem and a Probable Solution', *Irish Historical Studies*, 19 (1956), 131–55.

Flower, Robin, *Catalogue of Irish Manuscripts in the British Museum*. 3 vols. London, 1926–53.

Ford, Alan, 'James Ussher and the Creation of an Irish Protestant Identity' in *British Consciousness and Identity: the Making of Britain, 1533–1707*, eds Brendan Bradshaw and Peter Roberts. Cambridge, 1998, 185–212.

Foster, R.F., *The Irish Story: Telling Tales and Making it up in Ireland*. London, 2001.

Gantz, Kenneth F., 'Charlotte Brooke's *Reliques of Irish Poetry* and the Ossianic Controversy', *Studies in English*. Austen, Texas, 1940, 137–56.

Gargett, Graham, 'Voltaire's View of the Irish' in *Ireland and the French Enlightenment, 1700–1800* eds Graham Gargett and Geraldine Sheridan. Basingstoke, London and New York, 1999, 152–70.

Gargett, Graham, 'French books connected with the French Enlightenment published in Ireland, 1700–1800' in *Ireland and the French Enlightenment, 1700–1800* eds Graham Gargett and Geraldine Sheridan. Basingstoke, London and New York, 1999, 243–84.

Gaskill, Howard, '"Ossian" Macpherson: towards a Rehabilitation', *Comparative Criticism*, 8 (1986), 113–46.

Gaskill, Howard, 'Herder, Ossian and the Celtic' in *Celticism*, ed. Terence Brown. Amsterdam and Atlanta, GA, 1996, 257–71.

Geoghegan, Vincent, 'A Jacobite History: the Abbé MacGeoghegan's *History of Ireland*', *Eighteenth-Century Ireland*, 6 (1991), 37–56.

Gibbon, Peter, *The Origins of Ulster Unionism*. Manchester, 1975.

Gibbons, Luke, 'From Ossian to O'Carolan: the Bard as Separatist Symbol' in *From Gaelic to Romantic: Ossianic Translations*, eds Fiona Stafford and Howard Gaskill. Amsterdam and Atlanta, GA, 226–51.

Gillespie, Raymond, 'Destabilizing Ulster, 1641–2' in *Ulster 1641: Aspects of the Rising* ed. Brian Mac Cuarta. Belfast, 1993, 107–22.

Gleeson, Dermot F., 'Peter O'Connell, Scholar and Scribe', *Studies*, 33 (1944), 342–48.

Goldie, Mark, 'The Scottish Catholic Enlightenment', *Journal of British Studies*, 30 (1991), 20–62.

Grafton, Anthony, *The Footnote*. London, 1997.

Green, E.R.R., 'Thomas Percy in Ireland', *Ulster Folklife*, 15/16 (1970), 224–32.

Greenway, John L., 'The Gateway to Innocence: Ossian and the Nordic Bard as Myth', *Studies in Eighteenth-Century Culture*, 4 (1975), 161–70.

Hadfield, Andrew, *Edmund Spenser's Irish Experience: Wilde Fruit and Salvage Soyl*. Oxford, 1997.

Harbison, Peter, *Beranger's Views of Ireland*. Dublin, 1991.

Harbison, Peter, *Beranger's Antique Buildings of Ireland*. Dublin, 1998.

Harbison, Peter, *Cooper's Ireland: Drawings and Notes from an Eighteenth-century Gentleman*. Dublin, 2000.

Harbison, Peter, *'Our Treasure of Antiquities': Beranger and Bigari's Antiquarian Sketching Tour of Connacht in 1779*. Bray, Co. Wicklow, 2002.

Harden, Donald, *The Phoenicians*. Harmondsworth, 1980.

Harrison, Alan, *Ag Cruinniú Meala: Anthony Raymond (1675–1726)*. Dublin, 1988.

Harrison, 'John Toland (1670–1722) and Celtic Studies' in *Celtic Languages and Celtic Peoples*, eds C.J. Byrne, Margaret Harry and Pádraig Ó Siadhail. Halifax, N.S., 1992, 555–76.

Harrison, Alan, 'John Toland's Celtic background' in *John Toland's 'Christianity not Mysterious': Texts, Associated Works and Critical Essays*, eds Philip McGuinness, Alan Harrison and Richard Kearney. Dublin, 1997, 243–60.

Harrison, Alan, *The Dean's Friend: Anthony Raymond 1675–1726, Jonathan Swift and the Irish Language*. Dublin, 1999.

Harvey, Anthony, 'Early Literacy in Ireland: the Evidence from Ogam', *Cambridge Medieval Celtic Studies*, 14 (Winter 1987), 1–15.

Hayes, E., *Report of Cases argued and determined in the Court of Exchequer*. London, 1837.

Hayes, Richard, 'A Forgotten Irish Antiquary: Chevalier Thomas O'Gorman, 1732–1809', *Studies*, 30 (1941), 587–96.

Hayton, David, 'Anglo-Irish Attitudes: Changing Perceptions of National Identity among the Protestant Ascendancy in Ireland, ca. 1690–1750', *Studies in Eighteenth-Century Culture*, 17 (1987), 145–57.

Hewson, Michael, 'Edward Ledwich's Gift', *The Long Room*, 30 (1985), 29–31.

Hill, J.R. [Jacqueline], 'National Festivals, the State and "Protestant Ascendancy" in Ireland, 1790–1829', *Irish Historical Studies*, 24 (1984), 30–51.

Hill, J.R., 'Popery and Protestantism, Civil and Religious Liberty: the Disputed Lessons of Irish History 1690–1812', *Past and Present*, 118 (1988), 96–129.

Hill, J.R., 'The Meaning and Significance of "Protestant Ascendancy", 1787–1840', in *Ireland after the Union: Proceedings of the Second Joint Meeting of the Royal Irish Academy and the British Academy*, Oxford, 1989, 1–22.

Hill, Jacqueline, '1641 and the Quest for Catholic Emancipation in Ireland, 1691–1829' in *Ulster 1641: Aspects of the Rising* ed. Brian Mac Cuarta. Belfast, 1993, 159–72.

Hill, Jacqueline, 'Corporate Values in Hanoverian Edinburgh and Dublin' in *Conflict, Identity and Economic Development in Ireland and Scotland, 1600–1939*, eds S.J. Connolly, R.A. Houston, and R.J. Morris. Preston, 1995, 114–24.

Hill, Jacqueline, 'Ireland without Union: Molyneux and his Legacy' in *A Union for Empire: Political Thought and the British Union of 1707*, ed. John Robertson. Cambridge, 1995, 277–81.

Hill, Jacqueline, *From Patriots to Unionists: Dublin Civic Politics and Irish Protestant Patriotism, 1660–1840*. Oxford, 1997.

Hill, Christopher, 'The Norman Yoke', in *Puritanism and Revolution*. [1st edn, 1958] Harmondsworth, 1990, 58–98.

James, F.G., 'Historiography and the Irish Constitutional Revolution of 1782', *Eire-Ireland*, 18 (1983), 6–16.

Jenkins, G.H., *The Foundations of Modern Wales, 1642–1780*. Oxford, 1987.

Jennings, Brendan, *Michael O Cleirigh: Chief of the Four Masters and his Associates*. Dublin and Cork, 1936.

Johnson, J.W., 'Chronological Writing: its Concept and Development', *History and Theory*, 2 (1962), 124–45.

Kavanaugh, Ann C., *John Fitzgibbon, Earl of Clare*. Dublin, 1997.

Kearney, Richard, 'John Toland: an Irish Philosopher?' in *John Toland's 'Christianity not Mysterious': Texts, Associated Works and Critical Essays*, eds Philip McGuinness, Alan Harrison and Richard Kearney. Dublin, 1997, 207–222.

Kelly, James, 'Inter-Denominational Relations and Religious Toleration in Late Eighteenth-Century Ireland: the "Paper War" of 1786–88', *Eighteenth-Century Ireland*, 3 (1988), 39–68.

Kelly, James, 'The Genesis of "Protestant Ascendancy": the Rightboy Disturbances of the 1780s and their Impact upon Protestant Opinion', in *Parliament, Politics and People*, ed. Gerard O'Brien. Dublin, 1989, 93–127.

Kelly, James, 'Eighteenth-Century Ascendancy: a Commentary', *Eighteenth-Century Ireland*, 5 (1990), 173–87.

Kelly, James, '"The Glorious and Immortal Memory": Commemoration and Protestant Identity in Ireland 1660–1800', *Proceedings of the Royal Irish Academy*, 94c (1994), 25–52.

Kelly, James, *Henry Flood: Patriots and Politics in Eighteenth-Century Ireland.* Dublin, 1998.

Kelly, James, '"A Wild Capuchin of Cork": Fr Arthur O'Leary', in *Radical Priests*, ed. Gerard Moran. Dublin, 1998, 74–92.

Kelly, James, 'Conservative Protestant Political Thought in Late Eighteenth-Century Ireland', in *Political Ideas in Eighteenth-Century Ireland*, ed. S.J. Connolly. Dublin, 2000, pp. 185–220.

Kelly, James, 'A "Genuine" Whig and Patriot: Lord Charlemont's Political Career' in *Lord Charlemont and his Circle*, ed. Michael McCarthy. Dublin, 2001, 7–38.

Kelly, James, '"We were all to have been massacred": Irish Protestants and the Experience of Rebellion' in *1798: a Bicentenary Perspective*, eds Thomas Bartlett *et al.* Dublin, 2003, 312–30.

Kidd, Colin, *Subverting Scotland's Past: Scottish Whig Historians and the Creation of an Anglo-British Identity, 1689–c.1830.* Cambridge, 1993.

Kidd, Colin, 'Gaelic Antiquity and National Identity in Enlightenment Ireland and Scotland', *English Historical Review*, cix (1994), 1197–1214.

Kidd, Colin, 'Teutonist Ethnology and Scottish Nationalist Inhibition, 1780–1880', *Scottish Historical Review*, lxxiv (1995), 45–68.

Kidd, Colin, *British Identities before Nationalism: Ethnicity and Nationhood in the Atlantic World, 1600–1800.* Cambridge, 1999.

King, E.H., *James Beattie.* Boston, 1977.

Kliger, Samuel, *The Goths in England. A Study in Seventeenth- and Eighteenth-Century Thought.* 2nd edn. New York, 1972.

Lamont, Claire, 'Dr Johnson, the Scottish Highlander, and the Scottish Enlightenment', *British Journal for Eighteenth-Century Studies*, 12 (1989), 47–56.

Lee, J.J., 'Grattan's Parliament', in *The Irish Parliamentary Tradition*, ed. Brian Farrell. Dublin, 1973, 149–59.

Leerssen, J.Th. [Joep], 'Antiquarian Research: pPatriotism to Nationalism', in *Talamh an Eisc: Canadian and Irish Essays*, eds Cyril Byrne and Margaret Harry. Halifax, Nova Scotia, 1986, 71–83.

Leerssen, Joseph. Th. [Joep], *Mere Irish and Fíor-Ghael: Studies in the Idea of Irish Nationality, its Development and Literary Expression prior to the Nineteenth Century.* Amsterdam and Philadelphia, 1986.

Leerssen, Joseph. Th. [Joep], 'On the Edge of Europe: Ireland in Search of Oriental Roots, 1650–1850', *Comparative Criticism*, 8 (1986), 91–112.

Leerssen, Joep, 'Anglo-Irish Patriotism and its European Context: Notes towards a Reassessment', *Eighteenth-Century Ireland*, 3 (1988), 7–24.

Leerssen, Joep, 'On the Treatment of Irishness in Romantic Anglo-Irish Fiction', *Irish University Review*, 20 (1990), 251–63.

Leerssen, Joep, *Remembrance and Imagination: Patterns in the Historical and Literary Representation of Ireland in the Nineteenth Century.* Cork, 1996.

Leighton, C.D.A., *Catholicism in a Protestant State: a Study of the Irish 'Ancien Régime'.* Dublin, 1994.

Leneman, Leah, 'A New Role for a Lost Cause: Lowland Romanticisation of the Jacobite Highlander', in *Perspectives in Scottish Social History*, ed. Leah Leneman. Aberdeen, 1988, 107–24.

Lennon, Colm, *Richard Stanihurst. The Dubliner, 1547–1618*. Dublin, 1981.

Levine, J.M., *Humanism and History: Origins of Modern English Historiography*. Ithaca and London, 1987.

Liechty, Joseph, 'Testing the Depth of Catholic/Protestant Conflict: the Case of Thomas Leland's "History of Ireland" 1773', *Archivium Hibernicum*, 42 (1987), 13–28.

Love, W.D., 'Edmund Burke, Charles Vallancey, and the Sebright Manuscripts', *Hermathena*, 95 (1961), 21–35.

Love, W.D., 'The Hibernian Antiquarian Society', *Studies*, 51 (1962), 419–31.

Love, W.D., 'Charles O'Conor of Belanagare and Thomas Leland's "Philosophical" History of Ireland', *Irish Historical Studies*, 13 (1962), 1–25.

Love, W.D., 'Edmund Burke and an Irish Historiographical Controversy', *History and Theory*, 2 (1962), 180–98.

Lyons, J.B., 'Sylvester O'Halloran, 1728–1807', *Eighteenth-Century Ireland*, 4 (1989), 65–74.

McCafferty, John, 'St Patrick for the Church of Ireland', *Bullán*, 3 (1997–9), 87–101.

Mac Cana, Proinsias, 'The rise of the later schools of "Filidheacht"', *Ériu*, 25 (1974), 126–46.

McCormack, Bridget, *Perceptions of St Patrick in Eighteenth-Century Ireland*. Dublin, 2000.

McCormack, W.J., *Ascendancy and Tradition in Anglo-Irish Literary History from 1789 to 1939*. Oxford, 1985.

McCormack, W.J., 'Vision and Revision in the Study of Eighteenth-Century Irish Parliamentary Rhetoric', *Eighteenth-Century Ireland*, 2 (1987), 7–35.

McCormack, W.J., 'Eighteenth-Century Ascendancy: Yeats and the Historians', *Eighteenth-Century Ireland*, 4 (1989), 159–81.

McCormack, W.J., *The Dublin Paper War of 1786–1788*. Dublin, 1993.

MacDonagh, Oliver, *States of Mind*. London, 1983.

MacDonald, Kenneth D., 'The Rev. William Shaw: Pioneer Gaelic Lexicographer', *Transactions of the Gaelic Society of Inverness*, 50 (1976–8), 1–19.

MacDougall, H.A., *Racial Myth in English History: Trojans, Teutons, and Anglo-Saxons*. Montreal and Hanover, New Hampshire, 1982.

McDowell, R.B., *Ireland in the Age of Imperialism and Revolution, 1760–1801*. Oxford, 1979.

McDowell, R.B., and D.A. Webb, *Trinity College Dublin, 1592–1952*. Cambridge, 1982.

McDowell, R.B., 'The Main Narrative', in *The Royal Irish Academy: a Bicentennial History, 1785–1985*, ed. T. O Raifeartaigh. Dublin, 1985, 1–92.

McGuinness, Arthur E., 'Lord Kames on the Ossian Poems: Anthropology and Criticism', *Texas Studies in Literature and Language*, 10 (1969), 65–75.

McLoughlin, T.O., *Contesting Ireland: Irish Voices against England in the Eighteenth Century*. Dublin, 1999.

MacQueen, John, 'Temora and Legendary History' in *From Gaelic to Romantic: Ossianic Translations*, eds Fiona Stafford and Howard Gaskill. Amsterdam and Atlanta, GA, 1998, 69–78.

Magennis, Eoin, 'A "Beleagured Protestant"?: Walter Harris and the Writing of *Fiction Unmasked* in Mid-Eighteenth-Century Ireland', *Eighteenth-Century Ireland*, 13 (1998), pp. 86–111.

Magennis, Eoin, '"A Land of Milk and Honey": the Physico-Historical Society, Improvement and the Surveys of Mid-Eighteenth-Century Ireland', *Proceedings of the Royal Irish Academy*, 102c (2002), 199–217.

Malcolmson, A.P.W., *John Foster: the Politics of the Anglo-Irish Ascendancy.* Oxford and Belfast, 1978.

Manuel, Frank, *Isaac Newton: Historian.* Cambridge, 1963.

Marcus, Philip L., *Standish O'Grady.* Cranbury, New Jersey, 1970.

Martin, F.X., 'Diarmait Mac Murchada and the Coming of the Anglo-Normans', in *New History of Ireland II: Medieval Ireland 1169–1534*, ed. Art Cosgrove. Oxford, 1987, 43–66.

Mason, R.A., 'Scotching the Brut: Politics, History and National Myth in Sixteenth-Century Britain', in *Scotland and England 1286–1815*, ed. R.A. Mason. Edinburgh, 1987, 60–84.

Matthews, William, 'The Egyptians in Scotland: the Political History of a Myth', *Viator. Medieval and Renaissance Studies*, 1 (1970), 289–306.

Meek, Donald E., 'The Gaelic ballads of Scotland: Creativity and Adaptation' in *Ossian Revisited*, ed. Howard Gaskill. Edinburgh, 1991, 19–48.

Meek, Ronald L., *Social Science and the Ignoble Savage.* Cambridge, 1976.

Millett, Benignus, 'Irish literature in Latin, 1550–1700', in *New History of Ireland III: Early Modern Ireland 1534–1691*, eds T.W. Moody, F.X. Martin and F.J. Byrne. Oxford, 1976, repr. with corrections,1978, 561–86.

Mitchell, Sebastian, 'James Macpherson's "Ossian" and the Empire of Sentiment', *British Journal for Eighteenth-Century Studies*, 22 (1999), pp. 155–71.

Momigliano, Arnaldo, 'Ancient History and the Antiquarian', *Contributo alla Storia degli Studi Classici.* Rome, [1955] 1979, 67–106.

Murphy, Gerard, *The Ossianic Lore and Romantic Tales of Medieval Ireland.* Dublin, 1961.

Murray, Damien, *Romanticism, Nationalism and Irish Antiquarian Societies, 1840–80.* Maynooth, 2000.

Nevin, Monica, 'General Charles Vallancey 1725–1812', *J.R.S.A.I.*, 123 (1993), 19–58.

Nevin, Monica, 'The Defence of the Southern Part of Ireland by General Vallancey, Chief Engineer', *J.R.S.A.I.*, 125 (1995), 5–9.

Nevin, Monica, 'Joseph Cooper Walker 1761–1810', *J.R.S.A.I.*, 126 (1996), 152–66.

Nevin, Monica, 'Joseph Cooper Walker 1761–1810, Part II', *J.R.S.A.I.*, 127 (1997), 34–51.

Ní Sheaghdha, Nessa, 'Irish Scholars and Scribes in Eighteenth-Century Dublin', *Eighteenth-Century Ireland*, 4 (1989), 41–54.

O'Brien, Gerard, 'The Grattan Mystique', *Eighteenth-Century Ireland*, 1 (1986), 177–94.

O'Brien, M.A., 'Irish Origin-Legends' in *Early Irish Society*, ed. Myles Dillon. Dublin, 1954, 36–51.

Ó Búachalla, Breandán., 'Na Stíobhartaigh agus an tAos Léinn: Cing Séamas', *Proceedings of the Royal Irish Academy*, 83c (1983), 81–134.

Ó Búachalla, Breandán., 'James our true King': the ideology of Irish royalism in the seventeenth century', in *Political Thought in Ireland Since the Seventeenth Century*, eds D.G. Boyce, Robert Eccleshall and Vincent Geoghegan. London and New York, 1993, 7–35..

Ó Catháin, Diarmaid, 'Dermot O'Connor, Translator of Keating', *Eighteenth-Century Ireland*, 2 (1987), 67–87.

Ó Catháin, Diarmaid, 'John Fergus MD, Eighteenth-Century Doctor, Book Collector and Irish Scholar', *J.R.S.A.I.*, 118 (1988), 139–62.

Ó Catháin, Diarmaid, 'Charles O'Conor of Belanagare: Antiquary and Irish Scholar', *J.R.S.A.I.*, 119 (1989), 136–63.

Ó Catháin, Diarmaid, 'An Irish Scholar Abroad: Bishop John O'Brien of Cloyne and the Macpherson Controversy' in *Cork: History and Society*, eds Patrick O'Flanagan and Cornelius G. Buttimer. Dublin, 1993, 499–533.

O'Conor, Charles Owen, *The O'Conors of Connaught*. Dublin, 1891.

O'Conor, Charles (S.J.), 'Origins of the Royal Irish Academy', *Studies*, 38 (1949), 325–37.

Ó Cuív, Brian, 'The Irish Language in the Early Modern Period', in *New History of Ireland III: Early Modern Ireland 1534–1691*, eds T.W. Moody, F.X. Martin and F.J. Byrne. Oxford, 1976, repr. with corrections,1978, 509–45.

Ó Cuív, Brian, 'Irish Language and Literature, 1691–1845', in *New History of Ireland IV: Eighteenth-Century Ireland 1691–1800*, eds T.W. Moody and W.E. Vaughan. Oxford, 1986, 374–422.

O'Donovan, Jim, 'The Militia in Munster, 1715–58', in *Parliament, Politics and People,* ed. Gerard O'Brien. Dublin, 1989, 31–47.

O'Dwyer, Peter, *Céli Dé. Spiritual Reform in Ireland 750–900.* 2nd edn, Dublin, 1981.

O'Flaherty, Patrick, 'John Pinkerton (1758–1826): champion of the Makars', in *Studies in Scottish Literature*, ed. G. Ross Roy. Vol. 13, University of South Carolina, 1978, 159–95.

Ó Háinle, Cathal, 'Towards the Revival: some Translations of Irish Poetry, 1789–1897', in *Literature and the Changing Ireland*, ed. Peter Connolly. Gerrard's Cross and Totowa, N.J., 1982, 37–57.

O'Halloran, Clare, 'Irish Re-creations of the Gaelic Past: the Challenge of Macpherson's Ossian', *Past and Present*, 124 (1989), 69–95.

O'Halloran, Clare, '"The Island of Saints and Scholars": Views of the Early Church and Sectarian Politics in Eighteenth-Century Ireland', *Eighteenth-Century Ireland*, 5 (1990), 7–20.

O'Halloran, Clare, 'An English Orientalist in Ireland: Charles Vallancey (1726–1812)', in *Forging in the Smithy: National Identity and Representation in Anglo-Irish Literary History*, eds Joep Leerssen, A.H. van der Weel and Bart Westerweel. Amsterdam and Atlanta, GA, 1995, 161–73.

O'Halloran, Clare, 'Ownership of the Past: Antiquarian Debate and Ethnic Identity in Scotland and Ireland', in *Conflict, Identity and Economic Development: Ireland and Scotland 1600–1839*, eds S.J. Connolly, R.A. Houston and R.J. Morris. Preston, 1995, 135–47.

Ó Muraíle, Nollaig, *The Celebrated Antiquary Dubhaltach Mac Fhirbhisigh (c. 1600–1671): his Lineage, Life and Learning.* Maynooth, 1996.

O'Rahilly, Cecile (ed.), *Five Seventeenth-Century Political Poems.* Dublin, 1952.

O'Rahilly, T.F., *Early Irish History and Mythology.* Dublin, 1946.

O'Sullivan, Donal, *Carolan: the Life, Times and Music of an Irish Harper.* 2 vols. London, 1958.

O'Sullivan, Anne, and O'Sullivan, William, 'Edward Lhuyd's Collection of Irish Manuscripts', *Transactions of the Honourable Society of Cymmrodorion*, (1962), 57–76.

O'Sullivan, William, 'The Irish Manuscripts in Case H in Trinity College Dublin catalogued by Matthew Young in 1781', *Celtica*, 11 (1976), 229–50.

Owen, A.L., *The Famous Druids.* Oxford, 1962.

Pawlisch, Hans, *Sir John Davies and the Conquest of Ireland.* Cambridge, 1985.

Piggott, Stuart, *The Druids.* London, 1968.

Piggott, Stuart, *William Stukeley. An Eighteenth-Century Antiquary.* 2nd edn, New York, 1985.

Piggott, Stuart, *Ancient Britons and the Antiquarian Imagination. Ideas from the Renaissance to the Regency.* [London], 1989.

Pocock, J.G.A., *The Ancient Constitution and the Feudal Law. A Study of English Historical Thought in the Seventeenth Century.* Cambridge, 1987.

Pocock, J.G.A., *Barbarism and Religion: vol. ii Narratives of Civil Government.* Cambridge, 1999.

Poppe, Erich, 'Leibniz and Eckhart on the Irish Language', *Eighteenth-Century Ireland,* 1 (1986), 65–84.

Rae, T.I., 'The Scottish Antiquarian Tradition', in *Scots Antiquaries and Historians,* Abertay Historical Society. Publication no. 16. Dundee, 1972, 12–25.

Rae, T.I., 'Historical Scepticism in Scotland before David Hume', in *Studies in the Eighteenth Century,* ed. R.F. Brissenden. Vol. 2, Canberra, 1973, 205–21.

Raftery, Joseph, 'George Petrie: a Reassessment', *Proceedings of the Royal Irish Academy,* 72c (1972), 153–7.

Reed, Eugene E., 'Herder, Primitivism and the Age of Poetry', *Modern Language Review,* 60 (1965), 553–67.

Reeves, William, *The Culdees of the British Islands.* Dublin, 1864.

Reynolds, Susan, 'Medieval "Origines Gentium" and the Community of the Realm', *History,* 68 (1983), 375–90.

Richter, Michael, *Medieval Ireland.* London, 1987.

Roberts, Brynley F., 'Edward Lhuyd and Celtic Linguistics', *Proceedings of the Seventh International Congress of Celtic Studies.* Oxford, 1986, 1–9.

Rubel, M.M., *Savage and Barbarian: Historical Attitudes in the Criticism of Homer and Ossian in Britain, 1760–1800.* Amsterdam, Oxford and New York, 1978.

Said, Edward, *Orientalism.* 2nd edn, Harmondsworth, 1985.

Schwab, Raymond, *The Oriental Renaissance. Europe's Rediscovery of India and the East 1680–1880.* New York, 1984.

Scowcroft, R.M., '"Leabhar Gabhála". Part 1: the Growth of the Text; part 2: the Growth of the Tradition', *Ériú,* 38–9 (1987–8), 81–140, 1–66.

Senior, Hereward, *Orangeism in Ireland and Britain, 1795–1836.* London, 1966.

Sheehan, Catherine, 'The O'Conor Manuscripts in the Stowe Ashburnham Collection', *Studies,* 41 (1952), 362–9.

Sheehan, Catherine, 'The Contribution of Charles O'Conor of Belanagare to Gaelic Scholarship in Eighteenth-Century Ireland', *Journal of Celtic Studies,* 2 (1958), 219–37.

Sher, R.B., *Church and University in the Scottish Enlightenment. The Moderate Literati of Edinburgh.* Princeton, New Jersey, 1985.

Simms, Hilary, 'Violence in Co. Armagh, 1641' in *Ulster 1641: Aspects of the Rising,* ed. Brian Mac Cuarta. Belfast, 1993, 122–38.

Simms, J.G., 'John Toland (1670–1722), a Donegal Heretic', in *War and Politics in Ireland, 1649–1730,* eds D.W. Hayton and Gerard O'Brien. London and Ronceverte, 1986, 31–47.

Smith, Anthony, *The Ethnic Origins of Nations.* Oxford, 1987.

Smith, Bernard, *European Vision and the South Pacific.* New Haven and London, 1985, second printing 1988.

Smith, R.J., *The Gothic Bequest. Medieval Institutions in British Thought, 1688–1863.* Cambridge, 1987.

Smout, T.C., *A History of the Scottish People 1560–1830.* London, 1989.

Smout, T.C., 'Problems of Nationalism, Identity and Improvement in Later Eighteenth-Century Scotland', in *Improvement and Enlightenment*, ed. T.M. Devine. Edinburgh, 1989, 1–21.

Smyth, Jim, 'Popular Politicisation, Defenderism and the Catholic Question', in *Ireland and the French Revolution*, eds Hugh Gough and David Dickson. Dublin, 1990, 109–16.

Smyth, Jim, '"Like Amphibious Animals": Irish Protestants, Ancient Britons, 1691–1707', *Historical Journal*, 36 (1993), 785–97.

Smyth, Jim, 'Anti-Catholicism, Conservatism and Conspiracy: Sir Richard Musgrave's *Memoirs of the Different Rebellions in Ireland*', *Eighteenth-Century Life*, 22, n.s., 3 (Nov. 1998), pp. 62–73.

Snyder, Edward D., *The Celtic Revival in English Literature, 1760–1800.* Repr. Gloucester, Mass., 1965.

Stafford, Fiona, *The Sublime Savage. A Study of James Macpherson and the Poems of Ossian.* Edinburgh, 1988.

Stafford, Fiona, 'Primitivism and the "Primitive" Poet: a Cultural Context for Macpherson's Ossian' in *Celticism*, ed. Terence Brown. Amsterdam and Atlanta, GA, 1996, 79–96.

Stern, Ludwig C., 'Ossianic Heroic Poetry', *Transactions of the Gaelic Society of Inverness*, 22 (1897–8), 257–325.

Sullivan, Robert, 'John Toland's Druids: a Mythopoeia of Celtic Identity', *Bullán*, 4 (1998), 19–42.

Swift, Cathy [Catherine], 'John O'Donovan and the Framing of Medieval Ireland', *Bullán*, 1 (1994), 91–103.

Swift, Catherine, *Ogam Stones and the Earliest Irish Christians.* Maynooth, 1997.

Sznycer, Maurice, *Les Passages Puniques et Transcription Latine dans le 'Poenulus' de Plaute.* Paris, 1967.

Thomson, D.S., *The Gaelic Sources of Macpherson's 'Ossian'.* Edinburgh and London, [1952].

Thomson, D.S., 'Bogus Gaelic Literature *c.*1750-*c.*1820', *Transactions of the Gaelic Society of Glasgow*, 5 (1958), 172–88.

Thuente, Mary Helen, *The Harp Re-strung: the United Irishmen and the Rise of Literary Nationalism.* Syracuse, 1994.

Trautmann, Thomas R., *Aryans and British India.* Berkeley, Los Angeles, London, 1997.

Trench, C.E.F., 'William Burton Conyngham (1733–96)', *J.R.S.A.I.*, 115 (1985), 40–63.

Trevor-Roper, Hugh, 'The Invention of Tradition: the Highland Tradition of Scotland', in *The Invention of Tradition*, eds Eric Hobsbawm and Terence Ranger. 2nd edn. Cambridge, 1985, 15–41.

Trumpener, Kate, *Bardic Nationalism.* Princeton, New Jersey, 1997.

Turner, Cheryl, *Living by the Pen: Women Writers in the Eighteenth Century.* London and New York, 1992.

Ua Casaide, Séamus, 'Patrick Lynch, Secretary to the Gaelic Society of Dublin', *Journal of the Waterford and South-East of Ireland Archaeological Society*, xv (1912), 47–61.

Ua Casaide, Séamus, 'List of Works Projected or Published by Patrick Lynch', *Journal of the Waterford and South-East of Ireland Archaeological Society*, xv (1912), 107–20.

Ua Casaide, Séamus, 'Richard McElligott, Honorary Member of the Gaelic Society', *Journal of the North Munster Archaeological Society*, 3 (1913–15), 362–70.

Vance, Norman, 'Celts, Carthaginians and Constitutions: Anglo-Irish Literary Relations, 1780–1820', *Irish Historical Studies*, 22 (1981), 216–38.

Vance, Norman, *Irish Literature: a Social History.* Oxford, 1990.

Vance, Norman, 'Volunteer Thought: William Crawford of Strabane' in *Political Discourse in Seventeenth- and Eighteenth-Century Ireland*, eds D. George Boyce, Robert Eccleshall and Vincent Geoghegan. Basingstoke and New York, 2001, 257–69.

Wall, Maureen, 'The Rise of the Catholic Middle Class in Eighteenth-Century Ireland', *Irish Historical Studies*, 11 (1958), 91–115.

Wall, Maureen, 'The Quest for Catholic Equality, 1745–78', in *Catholic Ireland in the Eighteenth Century: Collected Essays of Maureen Wall*, ed. Gerard O'Brien. Dublin, 1989, 115–33.

Wall, Maureen, 'The Making of Gardiner's Relief Act, 1781–2', in *Catholic Ireland in the Eighteenth Century: Collected Essays of Maureen Wall*, ed. Gerard O'Brien. Dublin, 1989, 135–48.

West, Shearer, 'Polemic and the Passions: Dr James Parsons' "Human Physiognomy Explained" and Hogarth's Aspirations for British History Painting', *British Journal for Eighteenth-Century Studies*, 13 (1990), 73–89.

Whelan, Kevin, 'The Regional Impact of Irish Catholicism', in *Common Ground: Essays on the Historical Geography of Ireland*, eds. W.J. Smyth and Kevin Whelan, Cork, 1988, 253–77.

Whelan, Kevin, 'Politicisation in County Wexford and the Origins of the 1798 Rebellion', in *Ireland and the French Revolution*, eds. Hugh Gough and David Dickson. Dublin, 1990, 156–78.

Whelan, Kevin, *The Tree of Liberty: Radicalism, Catholicism and the Construction of Irish Identity, 1760–1830.* Cork, 1996.

White, Harry, *The Keeper's Recital.* Cork, 1998.

Whitney, Lois, 'English Primitivistic Theories of Epic Origin', *Modern Philology*, 21 (1924), 337–78.

Wilde, William, *Memoir of Gabriel Beranger.* Dublin, 1880.

E. Unpublished Papers and Dissertations

Davis, Leith, 'Harping on the Past: Joseph Cooper Walker's *Historical Memoirs of the Irish Bards*' (paper delivered at American Society for Eighteenth-Century Studies Conference, Notre Dame, Indiana, 1998).

de Valera, Ann, 'Antiquarian and Historical Investigations in Ireland in the Eighteenth Century' (M.A. thesis, University College Dublin, 1978).

Harvey-Wood, E.H., 'Letters to an Antiquary: the Literary Correspondence of G.J. Thorkelin (1752–1829)' (Ph.D. thesis, Edinburgh University, 1972)

Laurence, Ann, 'English Images of the Irish: the Rising of 1641' (paper delivered at the Irish Historians in Britain Conference, Apr. 1990).

Le Roy Stewart, Larry, 'Ossian in the Polished Age: the Critical Reception of James Macpherson's Ossian' (Ph.D. thesis, Case Western Reserve University, 1971).

Magennis, Eoin, "'Vulgar errors and defects": Walter Harris (1686–1763) and the Task of Dealing with the Ancient Irish Past' (paper delivered at a conference in University College Cork, May 2002).

O'Conor (S.J.), Charles, 'The Early Life of Charles O'Conor (1710–91) of Belanagare and the Beginnings of the Catholic Revival in the Eighteenth Century' (typescript, dated 1930, lodged in the National Library of Ireland, Dublin).

O'Reilly, William, 'Charles Vallancey: Cartography and the Archaeology of Orientalism', paper delivered at a seminar at the Centre for Human Settlement and Historical Change, N.U.I. Galway, May 2003).

INDEX